Kila ndege huruka na mbawa zake

Every bird flies on its own wings

A Swahili proverb

Home Between Crossings

Sultan Somjee
author of Bead Bai

CreateSpace

7290 B. Investment Drive

Charleston, SC 29418

USA

To Gulshard Niju
Speaking to memories,
Put aside

Sultan Somjee
March, 2018

To Zera the keeper of kanga,
I have a story to tell

Every time I look at your wedding chest that you call kasha, I think of the hundred kangas it stores. There may even be more. I listen with wonder how your kangas tell stories of your kith and kin, and friends, all women. Some have passed away like your grandmother Bibi, and your mother and your aunts, each one a grand personality in the long line of your matrilineal descent who taught you to treasure the kanga as the cloth of remembrance of the Ocean's stories when you were little. You keep their memories in the fragrance of oudh and jasmine flowers, and care for them so their colours do not fade and they do not feel aged to the touch. These rectangular pieces of cloth of beauty that some call the 'Talking Cloth of the Ocean' are stacked in your wedding chest, the kasha, and you wrap them around you to feel the presence of your ancestral mothers in the hidden insides of an ancient language that fathoms the wisdom and colours of Asia and Africa. I know one has to be a Swahili to understand the msemo sayings written on the kanga that you say call for attention to listen. "But actually," you tell me, "it means calling the heart. In Swahili, 'Wasikia? – Do you hear?' also means, 'Do you feel?' " A native to the language has that gift of knowing the kanga's words as she knows its art. The two easily evade the non-native.

Not many admirers of the kangas in your kasha know that the wraps have sayings of joys, and torments in coded wisdoms set in bright colours and patterns of Africa. Not many know the kangas are about lives of women from the islands and shores of the Indian Ocean that washes eastern Africa to the inland cultures.

It was this coast that greeted my great grandfather when his dhow from India finally touched the old slave port of Mombasa in 1900 or thereabouts after losing the route in the storm. The family story has it that it was the crow that showed the captain how to reach the Swahili coast. Then at the market in Mombasa he spread his straw mat under the palm tree where the crows rested in the shades of the fronds, and sold his beads.

It was this coast that has been hosting travellers, workers and merchants from Asia earlier than the 10th Century AD. The archaeologists tell us that when the settlers built stone towns, a civilization of a race mixed Asian and African was born. They call them the Swahili or simply the People of the Coast.

I know you hold Swahili oral traditions in the kangas in your kasha like stories on shelves in the library. I know women like yourself are the keepers of feminine memories of the shore from Kismayo to Kilwa . But most of all, you are the patron of my writing. This much I know is true.

What I did not know was that with my Indian ancestors sailing in the dhows there also came stories and the cloth. These commodities from Gujarat and Kacch on the western coast of Hindustan, crossed over to ancient civilizations of Lamu and Kilwa, Zanzibar and Mombasa, and those of inland cultures where they settled.

One story is about beads of guru-pir. There came to the ancestral coast of India in the 14th century, an African who was not a soldier nor was he a craftsman. He was certainly not a slave. They said he was tall, and of dark complexion like the shine of a bead carved out of a natural stone of the tint of black pearl. His complexion had the appearance of the nobles who bathed in herbal waters and whose bodies were oiled by slaves. His name was Sidi Mubarak Nob and in his bag he carried beads of many colours, shades and sizes. He was especially known for his fine agate stone beads. They called him the bead merchant of Saurashtra. The legend has it that he told stories and sang songs about the colours of the rainbow, and about tones and shines of beads that won the hearts of the women of Saurashtra. With the passage of time he came to be called Bawa Gor. This was about the same time as when the Sufi bards came to Saurashtra from Persia, and laid the Satpanth faith among the Lohana Khoja who called them guru-pirs with deep reverence.

Sometimes, Guru-pir Bawa Gor lived alone in the mountains or the desert, and when he came to the towns he sang melodious songs about the beauty of beads and God. Like the veneration songs of the Satpanth Khoja, the black guru-pir's hymns would give the bead meanings that brought worship close to the worshiper. Years went by, and then one day when he came down from his wanderings, he sang about the Great Mystery. People gathered around him mystified by the revelation he brought. Some danced the goma, and some played the malunga, and so they vanquished the demon from their lives. Thus with the stories, music, dance and agate beads, veneration of Guru-pir Bawa Gor grew among the Sidis of Saurashtra.

The keepers of the shrines of Guru-pir Bawa Gor would tell you he was a bead merchant, that he was black, and that he came from eastern shores of Africa facing India on the Indian Ocean. They would tell you that the Sidis came in dhows from Africa to India. This much they would say they know from their ancestors. What we know is that Bawa Gor is the guru and pir of the Sidis of Saurashtra like Sadardin is the guru and pir of the Ismaili Khoja. That Bawa Gor, the guru and pir, is the Indians' African ancestor. That at his shrine they crack a coconut, dance the ngoma they call goma in Gujarati, and sing a hymn. The ancient town where Guru-pir Bawa Gor lived is called Ratanpur. Ratan in Gujarati is a bead carved out of precious stone and it's also a woman's name. Ratanpur is a town in Saurashtra.

Another story is about the cloth. Sikander, also known as Alexandra the Great, called Saurashtra the 'Land of the Loom'. For centuries Saurashtran textiles were fashioned into clothing and fabric art by cultures around the Indian Ocean and beyond. In Egypt the pharaohs used them as winding sheets for pyramidal burials. In eastern Africa Indian textile was used for clothing and trade, and researchers suggest that later it fashioned the kanga. The printed patterns on the kanga divulge influences of dyes, art and motifs of African heritages, and those from around the ocean, India and even Europe. Today, the repertoire of kanga designs, and wordings on them called mithali or msemo (Swahili for a proverb or saying), reveal artistic and literary exchanges between oceanic and inland migratory routes and settlements. Some designs and phrases are universal, and some are uniquely ethnic, but all have found beauty and meaning in the hearts of diverse societies that inhabit eastern Africa, where you find women wearing the kanga and telling stories.

For many generations, Swahili women have been the keepers of the kanga. The cloth keeps tender remembrances of their relatives and close friends, mostly women and among women. It adorns them, comforts them and has given the women a voice to speak to their ancestral feminine memories, to express and protest what may not always be spoken because of local etiquettes that befit the woman's family and bearing.

Contents

vii

Snap of the umbilical cord

The airplane stops and revs on the tarmac before take-off. As the engine's whirr intensifies, Moti Bai presses her palms over her ears and hums guru-pir's raga into the drone as she used to into the buzz of the bees on the veranda of her bead store in Nairowua. Her feelings are with the land and her nephew Anil. How he used to make burring engine noises playing safari rally with Diamond on the linoleum floor of her home when his mother, Monghi Bai, her dear little sister, visited Nairowua, and stayed a month or so with her. Anil would be there, one with the crowd watching the airplane depart from Jomo Kenyatta International Airport. It is one of the darkest last quarters of the night in Nairobi when clock alarms ring to wake the Satpanth Ismailis to come to meditation. Perhaps, like her, he would be nurturing memories of his aunt Moti Bai leaving for Canada.

At first, they hugged at the shoulders saying goodbye, he taking care not to press his burly chest onto his aunt. Then in an outburst of emotions, they embraced each other fully, both weeping, he more profusely than her. Unconsciously, in the thought of Anil, Moti Bai touches her neck to feel her nephew's tears on the warmth of the throbbing artery behind her earlobe. From the double pane window, framed in circular plastic, she looks down. "One final look at my birthland," she says. She imagines the tyres of the East African Airways plane lifting up from the land. The airplane's whirr continues over the pulsation of the raga's hum in her ears as it ascends over the diminishing runway. The wheels in double pairs come up at an angle towards the bracket groove below the wings and when they clank lock, tucking into the underside of the wings, she feels a jolt in her abdomen like it was her umbilical cord at the navel snapping. In the twilight, she sees the fence around the Nairobi National Park, a pencilled line on the savannah running parallel to the Mombasa road, forking towards Kilimanjaro in the clouds, and Nairowua. She was riding above the clouds for the first time in her life. It was a world in the middle, neither up nor down, the kati kati nowhere world. The airplane wobbles in this mid-world, and then it begins to soar, sliding up at a slant, roaring through the palpable void. Then it flies like an arrow shot at Enkai, the Infinite Blue of Beauty, the Maasai She Sky over Kenya. "Shu-khar," Moti Bai breathes out from the depth of her abdomen and holds her naval. Her hands are pressed in underneath the cold metal buckles. Finally, she lets go a sigh of extrication.

She watches the snows of Kilimanjaro to her right. How the snow glistens in the light of the pre-dawn moon. How it brings back feelings that live in thoughts. Then through the window across the seats, Mt. Kenya glistens too, glancing past in the penumbral moonlight that deepens the blue of the sky before the burst of colours. The Swahilis would call the blue of the sky in the impinging darkness, bulu saaji, meaning the dense blue of the opaque depth of ocean.

Like a sly smuggler, Moti Bai is slipping out between two snow peaks, reluctant birthing thighs of Africa at the equator where she was born. Her heart lives there, her fingers speaking to beads drawing art out of savannah country to make the emankeeki from the colours of Kenya

2

imitating Akyni the Dawn. Like her sister Njoki, the one who is born again, Akyni brings a new day that Moti Bai sees coming before anyone else on the land below.

But how did it happen that she was leaving her birthland? So suddenly, she thought, opening her eyes from an awaking dream. She must leave the dream behind like the passing song of Nairobi's night watchman waiting the day. When the sun rises, he would disappear together with the song.

Part One

The story between famine and floods

Seasons are like beadwork and patterns on the kanga. They are like patterns of clouds in savannah sky and gardens made in heaven. Picture patterns are like words of the storyteller, some bold and some in shades of grey in-between.

There are days when the heart feels so light that words fly out of the mouth like birds. Then there are days when the heart feels so heavy that words plummet to the ground. Seasons on the savannah are like that too. They are so much like emotions of joy and happiness, guilt and envy, hate and love. You cannot leave one out, without embarrassing the other when you tell a story.

If you were to paint a face to Moti Bai's story, it would be like that of Nairowua, the small town in Kenya colony, where she lives with her family close to the equator in Great Britain's East African Empire. Here on a clear day, you can see Kilimanjaro waiting like an elder sitting on his haunches under a white blanket, impatient to tell you his story too. If Moti Bai, the narrator, were to describe the face of her story to you, it would be the story of the people of many beliefs and traditions who work the earth differently here, and they speak diverse languages. They live separately, but side by side, and they see the same African sky. They also tell their stories in their own words and differently like Freda who is Moti Bai's house help and Ole Lekakeny, Moti Bai's companion who is her mentor too.

The warm river in Nairowua meets the cold river called Usa from the Snows of Kilimanjaro. Nairowua is not far from the confluence, below the mountain that the Maasai call The House of God. There, in the shadow of the mighty Kilimanjaro, below its glaciers, once lived a hunter from America who too made stories. They called him Seneeta, because the combinations of sounds in his name were strange to Maasai ears when he said his name was Ernest Miller Hemmingway. How could they say the name in their language when they could not even hear the way he said it? But Moti Bai must hurry now and tell her story and speak the words like how she hears them and knows them. So listen. First, she must remind you how to listen to her story:

Listen to my story like how you see an avatar
A god with many heads, hands, and even eyes
He's not prophet of Abraham
With just one or two of each
For he works in multiple ways
And plays a flute in one yoog
In another, he carries Zulfikar the sword
Warrior Naklank destroyer of demon kings
He may be a fish or half-human, half a beast
But a god avatar nonetheless
My story is like that one avatar in many

Famine of Ol-ameyu

It's the end of the decade. 1940 is turning into 1950 when I return to Nairowua after four long months in Nairobi. In a few days, the shanty street town where I was born twenty eight years ago will be proclaimed a city. I left the people in the bazaar erecting colourful oriental style wooden archways under which processions will pass. Archways display festivities the Indian way like when there are weddings of wealthy bazaar merchants' sons or when there are visits of the royal family. I saw some shopkeepers painting the fronts of their stores to make them look clean and new. The government was giving out loads of Union Jacks to fly on cords tied from a light pole to a light pole along the route of the parades.

Seated in the front seat of the Merali Bus, I see the land and the sky in two halves from the front and side windows. Over the khaki sweep of the savannah, there is not a tree in sight like the infinite blue sky above without a cloud. This is the land where the travellers breathe the sky wherever they go. At the back, passengers cough as if they are barking out in a chorus over the assiduous growl of Merali Bus spewing black clouds into the dust. I look at craggy euphorbia plants thumbing up to the sky, and remember this road that had taken me to Nairowua, a sixteen year old bride sitting in Ford's sofa seat with Haiderali. His hand weighing down on my shoulders. That was a little over eleven years ago. It was green everywhere and I thought this land of the Maasai was a paradise on earth.

Now, sitting on a wooden bench seat padded over with my blanket, I ride over the same road's rock strewn gullies into the desert land. Once in a while, a rock gets thrown from under the grind of tortured tyres up at my dust-fawn windowpane. Each time, my stomach lurches and my eyes fall on Diamond, my six-month-old boy, asleep in the fold of my cross-legged palothi. Vapour from the angry exhaust ascending from the sheet metal floor, and fine dust steaming in through the rubber window linings, assault my nostrils. The bus-body-rattle fills my ears. I fan away hot air over Diamond with my recipe notebook. He smiles to me thinking it's a game I play with him.

If I were an eagle, I would want to soar up like a spirit bird out of my head. I would see the bus, a speck of green painted tin box over khaki-brown savannah land. Spectral Ol-lerai acacias stare like colourless widows, de-adorned, shaven heads, rejected brides of the earth. The great drought of Ol-ameyu eats the flesh of the land like a disease that eats the body. She is thirsty, scorching and ruthless like Chapanyo Dukar the great famine in India that led my Dadabapa to come to Africa. Now images of the dry earth of his birth village of Haripur that he talked about when he was ill with malaria and I nursed him, merge into the African landscape I see through the bus window. I look at the white napped Nubian vultures whirl into the depth of the savannah sky still and sober without the movement of the clouds. Yet, another gang of these avian scavengers sit motionless on whittled Ol-debbei, their scrawny necks loop like ropes as they peer over sun-bleached zebra bones, speckled over the dry bed of the River Athi.

Seated on my hard wood seat, perched high above the riverbed, I see a woman's sweaty dark skin shine in the sun. She appears to be standing in a waist deep fissure in a rock at the base of the trestle that supports the bridge where once mighty waves broke. My silent stare comes to fix on her through the dust brushed window of the bus negotiating a curve to come to the bridge. I fall back, withdrawing into myself when I see the woman pouring muddy water from one calabash into another. I hold Diamond to my chest. Standing on the floor between my feet is a basket full of bottles of sparkling sweet Nairobi water. There is a thermos full of tea with lots of sugar, milk, and a pinch of ginger prepared by Ma Gor Bai with caring hands to take away the tiredness of travelling. I would like to give her my basket. Ah! If only I could reach her from out of my window. But, I don't even lift a finger. It's a thought that comes to me like a prayer without the deed.

The bus slows down almost to a standstill, droning over the shaky bridge whose sun split boards creak under our weight. I see her again there just below my window. The woman is so close to me now, I could slip the basket over to her out of the window. It would fall gently near her and topple over. I see her feet are pressed into a groove on the wall of the waterhole two times her height in depth. Then I see another woman with bare shoulders and like her, she is bent over at the bottom of the well. She is scraping up water, thick brown liquid, the colour of earth and handing her calabash over to her companion standing above her. Once again, the thought to give them my water comes to me. But I withdraw into the shell of the onlooker's guilt making myself feel sorry and helpless. Or is it the pity of the privileged? Numbness seizes me like depression of the mind. Let the bus move on to another

10

scene – pirshah is all I will say like a rich lady praying to alleviate the misery of the poor. Yet, a prayer is not what will quench their thirst. It will soon be over. I wish the bus would leave the bridge fast. It moves so slowly, moaning over the wooden planks like it was pained by the landscape of the drought.

I pray again, but for whom do I need to pray? For what? To console the thirsty women? Or to absolve me, the other woman seated and comfortable, bottles of water between my legs and fortunate? Forgive me, my Mowla. I have done no wrong. I keep praying. The prayer lets my guilt-ridden sadness pass as the bus finally crosses over the bridge to the other side. Neither of the two women even so much as raises the head to look at the pitying black Indian eyes from the window of the Merali Bus passing by over them. They do not wave, or smile to show welcome to the travellers passing through their land as they would at another time.

The bus crosses over into a blanched sea of earth and then it curves back along the dead riverbank, and again, I see the two women of the waterhole in the riverbed. I see another person on the ground now. She is a gaunt grandmother koko. She pours out chocolate slime into a trough from which a white calf drinks. Its lanky head droops between two shoulder blades stabbing the air out of her rib bones. Its tail hangs from the spine, scraggy and outsized. The tail does not switch with life to shove off flies clustered on its festering wounds like pecked marks from the vultures' stone beaks. Its skin, drained of fat and flesh, laps below the stomach. Pirshah, a prayer from viewing the horror of misery comes to my lips. Behind the white calf, I watch how gracefully the lappet faced vulture

11

spreads its wings taxiing down. How majestically it closes its wings and waits, covert like a thief. The white calf gulps down chocolate water, greedily, ceaselessly, unaware of the preying eyes of the scavenger awaiting its collapse. The earth's thirst sears my throat. I take a sip of water. Then gulp down more. Laboured growling of the Merali Bus fills the afternoon's silence on the barren land like a death wail moaning the loss of life. I see the old woman crouching down to sit, her chin falling to her chest and eyes cast down. The vulture hop-flies, folds its wings and stays behind her sitting in the shadow of the riparian acacia. Four slanted spectral fingers shade the miniature dust dune that one gust of wind would blow into a cloud. The vulture has the patience of the lioness before she leaps on the doe unaware of the killer's still stare.

Far into the belly of the drought, I spot gazelles in the simmering haze over the dry-hot land. Joy comes to my heart. There is life over there. See! The gazelles would have licked the burnt turf before the fierce sun evaporated the ash dew, and they are alive prancing with life. Then a doubt clouds over the passing cheer in my heartbeat. It could be a mirage or a picture from my mind eleven years ago returning. Like my gaze, my memory teases the story back into the present.

Father and son

In the jamat khana in Nairowua, we say the tasbih, standing up for half an hour. We pray pleading for mercy to end the famine of Ol-ameyu. For Mowla's baraka to shower his blessings and bring rain to the waterless country. Here, in the jamat khana, I come to let my eyes stay on Saheb's photograph on the wall so I may know peace in the hope that the thirst of the land will soon be satiated. His picture hangs above the pendulum clock in a varnished box donated by my husband's father Devji Momna. I know now I will always live in Nairowua, and she who lives in me will also live here with me. "You, married into Devji Momna family *nah*? That brings prestige to your father," Ma Gor Bhai began telling me as soon as I felt a little better, implying what every Khoja woman knows. That a girl once married suits better in her husband's home as if she was his ornament and her father's honour. But there was also another reason. Though of humble peasant descent from India, the Devji Momna family was now in business. That was thought worthy of Khoja Gujaratis for they did not serve anyone to fill their bellies. That I was married to Haiderali, the eldest son of a mukhi and that he had a shop, bought respectability to my father's name.

Here, I want to sing my heartfelt cries into the songs of the jamat khana to forget where I would want to be. I want to sing aloud into the loneliness, spoken out in the choral music of women chanting to let go of torments trapped in their hearts reluctant to open. My voice will be

13

one in the unison ginan. The song that takes me to my feelings, clings to its echo in the sanctum of the prayer hall like how the sinking sun clings to the radiance of its orange in the horizon. Smiles have evaded the family since my arrival from Nairobi. The dishonour of my leaving home for six months carries the not so noble a shame that goads around the house, hurting not just me, but the family. The mere over-the-shoulder looks in the jamat khana and the false half-sorrys, fake half-comforting, hesitant smiles inform on hints of previous private talks about the pious Devji Momna family that claims to be honourable. How those looks would meet my eyes, and then at once turn away on second thought. They hurt me because I did not honour the pledge of husband-duty that holds the marriage. That's the Khoja wife's revered calling.

Our house is on the main Nairowua-Nairobi road that runs to Tanganyika just 60 miles out of Nairowua. The house itself is quiet most of the day except for my husband's brother Kabir talking about some comical incidents, mostly about the women I know. The incidents that had happened at the jamat khana while I was away. How he comes to know about women's mishaps, I don't know. Mishaps like how on one chandraat new moon evening when the jamat khana was packed thaaso thas, Zera Bai put on Gulbanu Bai's sandals identical to hers but older than hers, both pairs from the African Boot Co in Nairobi's European bazaar, and walked away into the dark after the service. That happened while men were chatting and families were re-wrapping and organizing how they would carry their naandi dishes and dal bowls, and milk in bottles on their walk home. No one really laughs, just head nods or at the most, an effort to grunt over an unwilling smile. There is no eagerness to hear even when Kabir narrates the

14

latest encounter between an irate bai, whose name he did not know, and Mohamed Mendo. He elaborates the episode making it larger than it would be, gesturing like a dance girl, and the irate bai's narrowing eyes, and twisted lips showing her disgust. It is no secret that Mohamed Mendo's cockroach gaze crawls over women's backsides as they bend over to pick up their sandals at the shoe rack after the jamat khana service. People say he behaves so only in the evenings, for during the day, Mohamed Mendo would not so much as turn his neck to look at a pretty bai passing by his shop on the main street, three houses away from our bead store towards Temple Road. Kabir tries talking so Haiderali, Ma and Zarina may at least smile when we meet at the table to eat together. Instead, we let the moment pass, eat and go away leaving each other's company. Most of all, away from my face that has brought so much shame called sharam to the Devji Momna family. I cannot make the Devji Momna family like me, not even Zarina who is closest to me. Whenever I smile at her as I used to, she looks away showing she does so intentionally. Then she would turn her face gradually to the side so I would notice the frown on her that she would otherwise not have facing me. I feel so small that even child Zarina snubs me, and so fragile that a slight puff of wind bends me over like a blade of grass in the sea of savannah..

My joy of the day comes from listening to echoes of Haiderali playing with Diamond, making sounds of animals in a game he invents as he plays along wanting the son to know his father again. Like telling him about the lion that lives next door and how the hyenas play the laughing game, competing who laughs the longest through the night without breathing in – hee-hee-hee-thee-thee-thee. He is the father who makes Diamond laugh. The father who

15

makes funny animal sounds. The father who took him from my arms at the steps of the Merali Bus before I stepped down. Diamond screamed and protested, thrashing his small hands on Haiderali's chest. Haiderali is with Diamond most of the time between his sleeping and feeding hours. The boy practically lives in the shop, moving from sitting on the counters to the arms of his father, and Ma who sits in the morning on my chair and frequently dozes off in the sun. Then there is Diamond's Kabir kaka uncle who loves to throw him up in the air until the child throws up the morning's feed.

This year, the cold season is unusual. The earth has turned hard, crisp and broken during the drought. Under the feet, it feels like crackle wheat gum paak cut crisscross, and cooled to brittle dryness on the tin platter. Two itinerant Kucchi Khoja bead merchants have been sleeping in the jamat khana because they cannot go on with the journey due to the famine of Ol-ameyu. I have seen the younger one before. He came to see Dadabapa at his duka-shop in Jugu Bazaar, showed him samples of beads and discussed the quality, markets, taxes, prices, and such other talks that bead merchants speak about among themselves. Then he would disappear for a year or so, roaming the countryside by rail and road. He was just a boy then, about fifteen or sixteen years old. I know him because I served him tea and sometimes lunch. Dadabapa told me they called his grandmother Nanima on the dhow to Africa and that the boy's father was a travelling bead merchant for Alidina Visram, who was called the merchant king of East Africa. The two men come home for breakfast. I make parothas for them to eat with sweet spiced mango syrup, and offer half a basin of water between them to wash the dust off their faces. They would then wash their feet

16

sharing the water. Giving water to guests to clean themselves is a custom that I must follow. Nairowua spring is just a trickle and it costs 10 cents for two debe-tins that the carrier brings home once a day. I have not ever seen Nairowua River so stagnant, banks crowded with cattle and goats hurdling over each other in the mud pool. The health office at the DC's enclosure has issued a warning not to drink the river water. The sign reads: HATARI DANGER.

Khanu Bai cooks lunch for the two itinerant bead merchants and they go to Zera Bai's home for dinner after the evening prayers. We say arrival of unexpected guests is baraka, a blessing, and we break the chapatti together and share the morsel on the table during famine. Sharing roji, meaning our daily nourishment as written by destiny, is a Khoja custom. Dadabapa would tell us at meal times, if we have only a grain of rice in the house, we must split it and share with any fellow Khoja who arrives at our doorsteps. Or we would have offered the grain to the guest first as we offer drinking water during these drought stricken days, knowing in that gesture are memories of how by sharing our roji meals our forefathers walked the land across Africa and survived. From our meagre meals, we also offer a handful for the daily naandi with shu-khar on our lips, meaning thankfulness for the day's nourishment. We pay our daily tithe from our little earnings during Ol-ameyu, because the blessings we receive in return will multiply. Such is our belief. Such is the faith we put in Saheb to survive the season.

Drifting thoughts

I live with the Devji Momna family that feels the shame I bring to them. I am a part of the family because I am married to the eldest son. My children are expected to propagate the Devji Momna name. Yet, I feel an outsider. My mind lives partly in Nairobi with my past seeking comfort speaking to memories of creating new things. Like embroidering new designs on the velvet cloth, chanting old ginans with different inflections and learning new recipes. It's often while I am at peace sitting cross legged in palothi on the arm chair feeding Diamond in my lap, that I drift to the days when the sickness in my head separated my body from the mind.

During the first few weeks in Nairobi, pills from Dr Mustafa made me sleep as much during the day as during the night. I hardly saw my son Diamond. Sometimes, I did not know where he was, where my mind wondered and whose mind was in my body. "Sakina, I brought Diamond to you when his lips slurped the air searching for your breast. But you were asleep," said Stepmother Gor Bai to me.

What I remember is Ma Gor Bai holding me to sit at the table to eat. I also remember the spirit woman's fiery eye balls fixed on my face. When I turned my face, she clamped her hands on my jaws and shook my head like a rattle. Then with her palms still cupped on my face she made me look back deep into her eyes. The Kikuyu herbal man was kinder. The tea he gave me was like quinine tonic

18

but for the murky colour. I still have a bottle of his tea and sip one mouthful at night. Later, Dr Mustafa began reducing the pills. Gradually I was more awake than asleep during the day and time went by. Ma Gor Bai spoke often to me and she sang the songs of guru-pir into my ears when I began waking up and feeling the morning air. I watched the sky colours over Nairobi at sunrise as long as I could as I used to when I was little. I watched the stars at night and remembered Askari Bakari. How he sang the kasida while he embroidered the caps taking the needle in the pinch of his plump fingers.

I tell myself remembering the moments of excitement, how I learned to cook new dishes listening to the women's programme on the Kenya Hindustani Service. Dishes like carrot kheer and white barfi mee-thai made with recipes using English idlemilk that is recommended for all Indian sweets. From the absakan widow, Bhachi Bai, who makes chai in the jamat khana kitchen at dawn, I learned to make kadho chai with English idlemilk. I also learned how to steam yellow dhokra dough the new way, using English stomach powder called ENO. I learned how to knead dark tepla flour with jaggery syrup that would not soak in oil and keep floating when fried.

At dawn and dusk I sat in the jamat khana in thrall to the music of ginans. I was absorbing sounds of the chant of the Guru-Pir faith. When I was better I began teaching young girls at the religion school as I used to before my marriage. I would show them through repeated exercises how to form the tenor of the mantra in their maturing voices. I thought deeply about what Meethi Bai had told me about how we keep secrets of Sufi lexes sleeping over the codes of ancient Vedas. So must I live, my one side over the hidden other side. I embroidered velvet cloth to fill my heart and tell my eyes to flatter my recovering mind. All that helped me to keep away from her whose talk clouds over my true voice.

It was the first long rest I had after my marriage. But it was not the same home I had left - Monghi is married and lives in Kisumu on the lake, Shamshu has a job at the post office in Mombasa. My Dadabapa lies by his beloved Sohn Bai in the graveyard at Kariokor. There where frangipani flowers clustered on milk sopping branches, shade them both from the fierce afternoon sun. Meethi Bai closed the lodge because the English law no longer allows prostitution. Not that the law did not exist before. But when the Indian women in town were few, no one cared while Indian workers and military men were many.

Meethi Bai sold her house and now lives by herself on River Road behind the jamat khana by the Sufi mosque with the green dome so she can be close to her beloved Devdasi. Devdasi's children call her Grandmother Ama. She also lives close to Saheb's takht, this royal divan where she prays in the stone jamat khana's corridor at midday every day. Meethi Bai continues to come home to my stepmother's satsang once a month, and there in the courtyard among a gathering of women, she sings like a woman put aside by her man. Like an old pot, they say, no longer good for cooking but you could use it to store grain and keep it tucked away somewhere unseen. Noordin kaka uncle moved to the Congo with his family – Kaki Bai aunty, my dear cousin-sister Malek, and cousin-brother Bahdur. My father spends most of his time alone in the duka-store. In the afternoons, Stepmother Gor Bai comes in and works

20

on beads while he sleeps. On most mornings, my father would take Diamond along with him for a baby talk, sitting him on the glass counter where Dadabapa used to sit me.

Feeling Diamond nursing at my breast four times a day and then again at night when jeering hyenas dented the silence of Nairobi's Indian Bazaar, brought back family thoughts. The silence of the bazaar at night is such that you feel it swell the darkness like air pumped into a balloon. It's the type of silence that you imagine outside from inside the house. A void in the dark habited by spirits walking above the ground in white shrouds. The silence when you remember what you want to forget. My body wanted to be wanted by Haiderali, but my mind said I would have to be wanted by his mother to be wanted by him. Haiderali saw himself as she did, her son who was a husband to me.

My story in pictures speaks to memories that are unpredictable when they come. There is no way I can foresee when the mood to recall the peaceful or painful, beautiful or ugly, comes to me. Or for how long it will stay with me. Or what pictures it will show me inside. Will it come because I ask, or will it come not invited, and all of a sudden assail me? Yet, I know my feelings will always live with me, and because they live, my thoughts will also live, and make pictures whatever aura they come cloaked in. When they appear, they paint my story not hers, she who lives in me. She of the spirit world is the other in me.

21

Kunguni bedbugs

I spend most of the day cleaning the house more than I remember ever doing it before. Tracing paper like dust lay under the bed, cupboards, and my dressing table. The house, except for the kitchen and Ma's bedroom, had been neglected while I was away. Ma seems to have aged all of a sudden after her fall in the kitchen, face down when she lost some of her teeth. She is less active but more stubborn, though less noisy taak taak. Perhaps, it's the loss of her front teeth that pushes her lips inwards, curving down under a line of stiff white bristles that makes her look older and obstinate. No longer does she snap sharp looks of annoyance at me if I don't do whatever she wants me to do, the way she wants it or if I am late doing it. Anyway, we hardly talk to each other. My body is sore, covered with tender red patch-spots made by kunguni bedbug bites. So many bites are around the midriff that they have merged into one enlarged blotch on either side of my waist. The itching is annoying and embarrassing, especially in the jamat khana when I scratch unconsciously with both my hands locked in a cross embrace unable to control myself. Sometimes, even while I sing the ginan, I catch myself scratching before the Nairowua jamat. It would be a disgrace if someone suspects I have bedbug bites. People will not sit near me in the jamat khana. They will avoid me at the volunteers cleaning group meetings. Bedbugs are the lowest and meanest of all bugs that put shame on those who harbour them. Moreover, bedbugs are bloodsuckers. I have been taking all the beddings together with the bed into the courtyard and leaving them in the heat of the fierce midday Ol-ameyu sun. Twice a day, I pour boiling water through the joints and cracks in the wood frame of our double bed. I mop the floor of our bedroom with water mixed with enough DDT to turn it milky. I ignore Ma complaining about the smell of DDT, which makes her breathing difficult. Most of all, I make sure Johnson's baby powder accompanies Diamond wherever he goes with Haiderali as if it were his second milk bottle.

There is no doubt it's Haiderali who has brought the bedbugs, sleeping jem tem, meaning anyhow, here and there, in Majengo and in servants quarters while I was away in Nairobi. He hunts women like Seneeta hunts animals, the lion bearded American with the gun and a pen and notebook. One would have thought Ma Jena Bai, who had been previously kula-kichwa-yangu, meaning eating-my-head, with her persistent taak taak, complaining about hygiene and cleanliness in the home, would have said something and shared my distress if not anger. She is the one in the family most terrified of not only kunguni bedbugs, but of all bugs, But she says nothing. It was when I told her about her son's habit of visiting prostitutes that she got so annoyed with me that she began to shake, and spit-blurs for words slurped out of her rubbery lips. Anyway, nowadays she talks like she's chewing air, words without diction relapsing from the slack grind of her gums. It needs careful face-to-face listening to understand her.

"You want to expose family bhoparo, making shameful secrets known to the world? … All families are like that … There are scandals … there always will be … but we protect family honour for the sake of children … Who will give your son their daughter? Who will take your

23

daughter? … A daughter from a scandalous family? … Have some shame of sharam," says Ma breaking sentences, spluttering some words and slurping back unformed words, her body shaking with ire. Ma's words put resentment in me. Am I always looking for an argument to fight back, to affront her, to offend her wherever I can? Why does she think I will be pregnant with a girl child? Why does she talk like that about my unborn daughter? I think again while returning the beddings piled high over my head. No, it's not just her. Why do we talk about women as if they were things? How often we say, Kone chokari dithi? Whom did you give your daughter to? Koni chokari lithi? Whose daughter did you take? We talk of taking and giving a girl in marriage as if she was a thing. A thing. Just a thing to give and take in a marriage deal between families. We don't talk of a boy like he were a thing to give and take in marriage, do we? I burn inside unable to say what I want to, to a helpless Ma. From that day, I keep quiet about Haiderali's secret ways and everything else. In fact, I regret I complained about her son. Now I speak only when I have to, like I would ask, "Where do you keep cumin seeds? Or where is this or where is that spice bottle?" Spices in the kitchen have been misplaced or bottles not refilled. Bottles half-full or empty stand smudged with yellow, brown, mustard and red marks left by her fingers. There are no caring words between Ma and me though I am aware of her needs, like when and how she wants her chai, and her bathing water in a low bucket; how she would like her khichedi and rice masticated with ghee. I know she needs a glass of water, a hot water bottle and a cough syrup bottle and a teaspoon by her bedside every night. Ma does not come to the kitchen anymore, not because she does not like to watch over me, but because she finds it difficult to sit on

24

the floor stool. And she holds the fear of falling on the kitchen floor again. Now, I am who I have been waiting to be in my kitchen. When she comes back from school, on most days, Zarina comes to help to cook and clean. I tell her what to do.

All the time, during the day, I long to return to my chair on the shop's veranda. I want to be with my talking beads and Ole Lekakeny. "Now remember, you need to see the colours mix and spangle in your eyes like how you hear the ginans mix ragas in your ears. Keep art throbbing in you, and you will be happy," said Stepmother Gor Bai pressing her fingers into mine as if telling them to look after me when we said goodbye at the Merali Bus Stop on River Road in Nairobi. An artist's fingers are her eyes. They keep the art.

I am en-tomononi in Maasailand

When July came, and the fog, I found myself looking forward to the afternoon's chill in the static air of the veranda while sitting there with Ole Lekakeny. I could not wait one more week to begin working with the beads to save my mind from slipping into a pit of darkness. The work in the house does not cease. This house is such that, the more I work in it, the more I find work, here-there, everywhere. Work that is beyond the routine of cooking three meals a day, sweeping and washing that now includes diapers and baby clothes. Nevertheless, in the afternoon, Maasai colours nourish me and I don't need to take a nap like Ma, Haiderali and Kabir.

When three young Maasai men stop by the veranda, I feel a sudden surge of joy seeing the people of the land again. They watch the bead display from the murrum walkway for a while before they come up the uneven granite steps onto the veranda. They stand so close to me that I can smell the earth on their sweaty, oil-ochred bodies. The three men with red handsome earth-caked hairdos hold several bead strings in their open palms, shifting and tilting their heads to catch the glint of the sun and make a comment that I do not understand. The response is a smile, and I know it's an appreciation of loveliness that is the delight of e'sikar when the mind is free of thoughts to indulge in the beauty of the moment in art. They study the beads for a while, eyes inclined, arms on each other's shoulders, standing cross-ankle, knotted in a group, talking excitedly as if they were one voice in different tones like hues of red beads. As if they were the beads they hold. In their eyes, I see dawn's lustre that the sparkle of beads sparks, the beauty that comes from their history, their daily lives, their geography, a heritage held by the majesty of the land and poetry of their language. Their emotions too are said in the eye-sparkle. The brightness comes as if from their hearts like the hearth that flames light at their mothers' homesteads. It's like the light of the hearth inside their dark homes as in the pattern of narok on their ankles. A line of bright red, the fire, set in pitch dark blue beads that the Maasai call narok, meaning black. I watch their muscle toned bodies, oiled and ochred to a radiance at this time when the land has lost its own. Though I do not know what they say, their hearts speak to me of happiness through the eyes looking at the rainbow laid over their open palms. They are all wearing identical red sheets, unlike Ole Lekakeny who wears a red chequered blanket; they carry long bladed spears unlike Ole Lekakeny who carries the peace staff as becomes an elder.

"These young men will be graduating from warriors to junior left hand elders soon after the drought of Ol-ameyu," Ole Lekakeny explains to me in his usual spontaneous manner, speaking quietly in a tone that asks attention in its softness. "This is not yet the right time to buy beads. We have lost many cows. Wavering air shimmers far over the savannah. Crisp and monotonous, the drought dries the earth. It smells the same as it looks." Then standing up, he leans his peace staff on the inside of the doorframe and loosens his blanket over him, preparing to sit down again on his crate. He carries his peace staff wherever he goes. When their warrior days are over, men at

27

the homesteads carve such batons out of the wood of the African hardwood tree. That is the custom of the just graduated seniors. "The famine of Ol-ameyu has stolen our children. Calves stick out their tongues to their mothers' udders, lapping over limpid lumps that they remember full and robust. They imagine the milk from their mothers will fill their stomachs, is it not so, *si-ndio?*" Ole Lekakeny's words roil the insides of my stomach. In his words I see the image of the white calf and the three women at the waterhole under the bridge on my trip back to Nairowua. He talks with staid anguish in his eyes that are losing the shine of youth. His lopped ears weighted with copper are still too, like his eyes.

I look at Diamond, my chubby baby with a shine in his opaque grey eyes. The kind of baby eyes that when he looks at you, it is as if he understands mother's love talk. He fascinates the family endlessly with his odd way of crawling, sitting on his little bum. Diamond begins to doze in his cradle with his bottom up, his head buried in the pillow and grunting like a bull before falling into deep sleep. He sleeps under a mosquito net in the old Gujarati cradle that straddles on four red lacquered legs, rounded and connected by a horizontal pole, also red lacquered with yellow floral sketches. To the pole are attached two arched iron hinges at the two ends that sway the pouched baby bed. In it, Haiderali, Diamond's father, once slept more than a quarter of a century ago. I would imagine Ma rocking the cradle as I am sitting by the beads as she would have in the same chair. Diamond stirs a little and then unexpectedly lets out a wail as he tries to turn around on his stomach. I rock the cradle, pulling the cotton cord tied to the armrest of my chair and sing a lullaby while I continue to sort the saen beads, measuring them in teaspoonful heaps of five colours: five each of white, red and blue, to one each of orange and green. The colours repeat into patterns, and the patterns to the rhythm of the cradle's clacks as it swings back and forth. Diamond lays crouched and seems restless in his cot. I continue working with beads, pulling the rope that is tied to my foot, singing the lullaby I once sang to my sister, Monghi, while putting her to sleep:

હીરો મારો નાનો	*My little Diamond*
પાતલે બેસી નાયો	*Bathes sitting on the stool*
પાતલો પડી ખસી	*The stool slips*
હીરો મારો પડી હસી	*My Diamond bursts out laughing*
Lala, lala, lala	*Sleep, sleep, sleep*
mmm…mmm…mmm	*mmm…mmm…mmm*

Diamond calms down and slips into soft slumber and at once, everything around me is quiet. My mind takes me to Kini and Ntinti. Their babies. Ole Lekakeny told me they both had more children that year, and they do not come to the bead shop because they live on the other side of Kilimanjaro by the ash lake called Amboseli. Ole Lekakeny calls them in-tomonok or the women who prayed for children, and are granted their wish. "They are blessed," he would say to me. I wonder how this prolonged drought affects them. When I left, they were mothers of three children each in the homestead: milking the ding calves and kids, cleaning the kraal; fencing, building and repairing houses; fashioning skin clothes; repairing bead ornaments and more.

"How do Kini and Ntinti manage the work in the homestead with so many children?" I ask Ole Lekakeny.

"En-tomononi," says Ole Lekakeny addressing me. He calls me en-tomononi with respect. I am the woman who came to Nairowua as a bride, who prayed and now who has been granted her wish for a boy child. I am now en-tomononi all over Maasailand. Ole Lekakeny, like all the Maasai who come to the shop, address me as en-tomononi, giving me the dignity of motherhood, and making me know they know my contentment of becoming a mother. Had I been living in the homesteads, I would have adorned myself with beads and colours that celebrate motherhood. "Your age group sisters work with other women of the homestead. Grandmother Koko and co-wives help to cook and look after the babies."

"I want to see them," I say suddenly.

He nods. Whenever I asked again about seeing Kini and Ntinti, Ole Lekakeny nodded and days went by. Months went by. The drought of Ol-ameyu ended, seasons of short rains and long rains passed with the years. I don't remember when I stopped asking Ole Lekakeny about Kini and Ntinti. Their memories faded as I grew into a woman. Like how memories of my Rani Bagh friends paled into my childhood in the Indian shantytown of Nairobi where I was born and where Africans were a minority.

Evenings at the jamat khana close the day's frame each day with the Saurashtran chant. It's the song in folds pleated in resonances that connect my community of Ismaili Khoja of Nairowua to their ancestral place. That's the frame of origin that stays in the heart over border crossings.

Ma Jena Bai

Ma Jena Bai refuses to go to the Catholic Hospital when she has a fall again. This time she hits her hip on the ledge of the kitchen step. Now she lies in bed in shock and pain. Every day I make spinach or khadi khichedi or just black millet raab porridge and feed her with my own hands, though I have little time. I need to take care of my second child, a girl, who was born at the Mission Hospital two years after my return to Nairowua. On the sixth day after her fall, Ma asks Haiderali to bring my mother's red gold bangle with a leaf clasp from Zarina's wedding jewellery box that's in the wall safe in the duka-store. Here Haiderali keeps his gun for hunting, some documents and wads of bank notes for payments to the wholesalers on his next safari to Nairobi.

"Take this. Forgive me," Ma tells me turning her head slightly to the bangle on the bedside stool.

I pick up the bangle. My eyes trace the gold ring that sits over the three lifelines on my palm. What fate holds my life in the gilded circle now? My moist eyes question lines of my kismet in the gold cage. I feel Zarina sitting on Ma's bed, close to her head, watching me.

"No," I hack out a curt refusal placing the bangle on Ma's chest. Hearing my no, her wheezy breathing jumps to rapid chest heaves, short and audible. The bangle rolls over the sheets falling to the floor. I do not pick it up.

"Forgive me! Tobha!" begs Ma. Her trembling spread out fingers make a pyramid. Kabir leaves the room.

"But I forgive you," I reply. I mean it but I keep my vrt, meaning my self-pride in her house. My daughter-in-law self-pride. I begin straightening and brushing the bed sheets. Zarina stands up to leave the room. Haiderali picks up the bangle. I don't want to look at that bad luck kisirani gold. Things are like people. When a thing you love brings bad luck, that is kisirani, you don't want to see it again. When a friend you love does fitina, meaning back biting you, you hate her as much as you loved her before. That's how I see my bangle now. I know Ma had kept my bangle for her daughter's wedding. I do not hate Zarina because of that. My bangle would add honour to the Devji name - family honour is measured by the weight of gold in the bride's jewellery box.

Haiderali's eyes widen, looking at me, turning from severe to sad. Then, by a slight lift of his chin, he indicates I should take the bangle. I don't. He asks softly, "Su *chhe*?" meaning what's the matter, meaning why am I not talking the bangle? He waits.

"Thapo! Thapo!" Kabir's yelling from outside flow over thuds of the bouncing ball and fast padding feet skirting Ma's cheerless room. "Take it," Haiderali says finally. I hear his heart hurting in the two words heavy on his tongue. I feel his watery eyes pleading. They tell me he is at my mercy, begging me to accept the bangle. I long to see my grandmother's red gold bangle shine on my wrist again. I long to feel its gold weight at the bone of my wrist. I long to keep the heirloom of my family on me, not so much for the memory of my grandmother who I never knew, but to feel rooted, to belong and show where I come

32

from. That's what family gold means to an Indian woman. But, I also want Haidu to know my wound has not healed. My pride hurts. A hurting pride will not let the wound heal. My refusal is forged in hate of the humiliation I suffered. I was robbed of my dignity when I was a bride so young. He too must suffer now, because he chose his mother over me when I had given him everything he desired in the body of a woman.

"Tobha!" says Ma again, meek of voice and pain of insult of daughter-in-law. She wants to bring her hands closer together, but she cannot control her stick fingers held together by her outsized knucklebones. Her hands flop down on her chest. Her speech is a throaty gruff almost inaudible through short gasping breath. "Tobha! Tobha!" she repeats, beseeching me for forgiveness. At that moment the children's tennis ball from the outside hits the loose window pane and shakes it like a rattle.

"Yes, I forgive you," I say, deliberately showing no emotions as I walk to the window. I see Kabir, Diamond and Zaibun playing around the mango tree. My heart stifles between anger that comes from the old insult, and hard pity without compassion as if it were something evil outside me, helping me now, finally, to heal through revenge. Revenge yes: not accepting the bangle back, yet forgiving Ma. I feel my dignity return. A victory. The moment when I feel like the queen. I am in control.

I keep quiet looking at Ma's open jaw, half-open, exposing her tobacco stained few front teeth. My silence suppresses the seething rage in me sharpened by pity. I suppress the guilt. I will not let it control me. Ma looks helpless, a fallen queen, the second time. The first time was when the white police officer in khaki pants came to arrest

Kabir. That was when he worked for a short time with the East African Power and Lighting Company as a meter inspector. He became greedy and fiddled with the light meters for chini chini under the table money from wealthy Indian merchants. Ma rolled in the dust, hitting her head with the heels of her palms, clutching the boots of the white policeman, begging him not to throw her son into jail. She pleaded that her son was a good man, and swore on her life, he would never steal their electricity again. But the officer handcuffed Kabir and led him away. Ma and I remained in a hurdled embrace both weeping on the dirt. Kabir spent nine months in prison.

I hear Haiderali's heavy breathing. He stares at me, eye-begging me to take back the red gold bangle. He sits leaning forward on the edge on the metal frame of Ma's bed and wipes tears with fisted palms. But I will not be blackmailed by his tears. Looking down, I continue preparing fresh sheets for changing Ma's soiled bedding. Haiderali cannot make me do things as he wishes just because I am bound by my sacred husband-sewa duty vows. I took the vows myself silently and alone when we married. My sullen bitterness is stubborn and silent, and over the years, has grown into a rock. I feel sweetness soothing over the long anguished humiliation of a slave daughter-in-law and abused wife. Now I feel bold inside, brazened by defiance surging in me. My refusal to accept the bangle was insolence that hurt them both and they cannot do anything to me. The obstinacy steels me, and gives me control over myself, more control than ever before since I stepped over the su-astik stencilled in rice, a young bride into a new life with the Devji Momna family.

Nevertheless, I will fulfil my duty as a daughter-in-law. That is custom. Every day, I will clean and replace the turmeric paste on Ma's swollen hip that is so painful that she cannot turn by herself. I will feed her, comb her hair and massage her limbs till she falls asleep. I will make fresh chapattis soft as wool with a teaspoon of ghee on each one for Ma to chew with her gums. But I do not cook for her or feed her with love in my hand. There was not a bat of eyelid or even a concealed shift of guilt in my eyes to the feelings of my unkindness. That surprised me.

Ma Jena Bai talks a lot to herself during the day. At night she mutters in sleep. Sometimes, she is a little girl talking to her mother and making rangoli patterns with powder colours. Sometimes, she even throat laughs in her sleep showing her bare gums. We hear Bapa-ji's name in her sleep talk and awake talk. There is not much difference between day or night for her as she lies motionless on her bed living in two worlds.

Looking at Ma I try to read the life she had had so I can see the woman in her and understand us both. So I may learn to love her like how two women companions do. But when I try, it takes me to the other woman in me who probes into bitterness of my thoughts. I look at Ma again. I see a helpless dying old woman with whom I live. I feel regret not love.

In my story the two storytellers in me come together, and sometimes, they annoy each other. She has not left me. Or is it that I put the blame of hating Ma on Mama Khelele to console myself? To say I am not like that?

Bead in his tasbih

It was a Tuesday on a hot afternoon in February, when the men folk buried Ma beside Bapa-ji at the Nairowua Ismaili cemetery beyond the Black Moslem township of Majengo. Like the Asian prayer houses, the cemeteries of Shia and Sunni, and the Hindu crematorium stand side by side with a stone wall dividing them. That night, while putting Diamond to sleep, he asks where Ma has gone.

"To Mowla Bapa," I say.

"When will she come back?"

"I don't know. She likes Mowla Bapa, so I think she will stay a long time with him."

"Does Mowla Bapa like her?"

"Yes, Mowla Bapa likes everyone."

"Will she be alone with Mowla Bapa?"

"No, there are many who live with Mowla Bapa. She is now one bead among many in his tasbih."

"Are they all old beads?"

"Yes," I say after a thought.

"Do you think Ma will tell stories to Mowla Bapa and play chanace with him?"

How shall I respond to the innocence of the child? It breaks my heart to see his grey eyes asking with earnest expectation of a happy answer from me.

"Maybe, if he has the time."

"Ma knows so many stories about Krishna and Rama. Only Ma plays chanace with me, and I win. You never have time to play chanace with me and you don't tell me stories. You don't sleep with me. You love Zaibun more than me."

"I love you as much as I love Zaibun."

"Then why you don't play with me?"

"I will play with you tomorrow, I promise. Now go to sleep. Close your eyes and start pirshah, pirshah. I am listening."

Diamond begins his night prayers in rhythmic repetitions:

Pirshah, pirshah, pirshah. Mowla Bapa, please send Ma back. Pirshah, pirshah, pirshah Mowla Bapa, please send Ma back. Pirshah, pirshah, pirshah, Mowla Bapa please ...

Thoughts assail me. How I pressed the chaikop to Ma's lips, draining the tea into her mouth as she gulped down draughts of air. I should have been more patient. I cried for the beauty of care for the elderly that evaded me because the grudge of humiliation would not leave me. Like a thief, I slip away from my son's pain missing Ma. I slip away from mother's aching heart, and daughter-in-law's guilt for not loving her mother-in-law. It was a difficult night to pass.

Haiderali sleeps on the sofa. No one speaks. It's quiet and dark. After midnight, when he comes to bed with me. I burst into tears. I want to say I am sorry, but I cannot utter the words. Instead, I bury my head in my pillow and sob. When I try to sleep, I am awakened by dream thoughts, and dream pictures. The mother in me feels the pang of pain of loss in Diamond, and the lie I told him. I try to keep my eyes open, holding them back from slipping into sleep that pick on my taunts and rebuffs levelled at the helpless old woman in the armchair in the courtyard. Then she appears. No, not Ma, the other one who eats my head. She begins to taunt me to run away into the acacia grove at the river where she would meet me, but alone.

She says, "You killed Ma. You must run."

I press closer to Haiderali, into his man sweat and smell in the tender warmth of mid-sleep. His eyes are closed, but I can tell by the broken drift in his breathing, he keeps waking up. He is thinking of Ma. Perhaps, his childhood with her, waiting on the kitchen paatlo stool for Ma to give him the first chapatti from the clay-hot plate with ghee melting into golden veins over russet jaggery paste. Or, is it arguments over me behind closed door churning over in his head that make him toss and turn? I draw closer and put my arm over him, on his bare stomach between the vest and pyjama cord over the navel. He does not move. I hear his breath aspirating muttering. Have I annoyed him so much that he would not even put his hand over my arm as he always did when I put my arm over him, even when he was exhausted after a hunting trip or safari let alone rolling over to the side to face me? How I wish he would say my name, and funnel air over his grooved tongue through the flesh of his lips to part the slip of hair over my eye. The way he would when he desired me. I feel the wanting of a wife at this hour of his loss. But Haiderali lies still like a forest log. I feel his coldness towards me even in his sleep.

My husband's rejection bites into the guilt in me, and sometimes, comforting self-pity when my vrt, meaning my self-worth that I must show to hold my dignity, freezes my tongue to beg for forgiveness. Because I cannot let them go, emotions thus stay entombed in me. Sometimes, these feelings heave resentment that pass on to rage. I blame Haiderali for not speaking out to his mother when I could not. Is it my fault that I begrudged Ma Jena Bai when he favoured her over me? All these years of my youth were wasted without joy between Ma and me, for us both living under one roof. Two women who should have been friends and supporting each other. Helpless and alone in bed, I slip into despair, and then anguish while mourning Ma's death and my lost youth.

I put my thoughts to beads. The beadwork begins with the oval shaped red and black beads gathering like magical warriors to protect me. The pattern they form around me is that which Ole Lekakeny calls boma. A boma is a thick fence of acacia and thorny bushes circling the Maasai homestead to keep women and children safe inside from the night's predators. As the circle stabilizes, the beads roll in easily to their places, but I have to make them stand, each one held separately in the pinch of my fingertips.

"E'sikar!" I shout jumping up to join them in the circle of beads that the Maasai call tuntai. Rass, meaning ecstasy, fills me. Watch now, for there is a sign that the boma wishes to be coloured with tuntai beads, to mature, to become full like a girl at puberty.

I am one bead among many in the boma of beads. We are all bead-sisters joined by colours into combinations as unique as we are.

I work word into word like how I work bead into bead. I put them so close together that there is no space for the meddlesome one who lives in my head to push her way in. She is not beautiful. How can she be? She has no colour nor a verse to sing. No shine and no rhythm. She is not wanted by the beauty of my art. She is the one I call Mama Khelele, the noisy one who made me hate Ma.

Bench with lion feet

It's several months after Ma's death. Haiderali is a changed man. He continues to go to the jamat khana every evening long after the forty days of mourning are over, and he has also started to attend the dawn meditation, waking up every day at 3 am. Even on Sundays, he rushes back from the card game on the lawn at the DC's office so he would not miss the evening prayers. And every day he would want me to prepare a dua-prayer dish of food for the jamat khana. I cook the offering with great care to make it not only delicious but also eye-catching in its presentation so people would ask: Whose home did this dish come from? I would go to the vegetable market myself to pick the freshest leaves and tenderest tubers. Sometimes, tears well my eyes while I pray for Ma's soul to rest in peace when I am cooking for her. The care I give to preparing the food offerings for Ma helps to ebb my guilt. "But," I ask myself, "does it lessen Haiderali's anger?" I see in his eyes what he does not say in words. When he lies on me his touch has no love for me. No more does he whisper into my ears, "Walls have eyes." I want to hear his words gushing through gasps of short breaths as he ejaculates into me, and then he turns around and sleeps while I lay on my back with eyes wide open to the darkness dense with the smell of alcohol.

One day, almost six months after Ma's death, Haiderali vowed to install a bench with wrought iron lion feet at the naandi table in the jamat khana, in Ma's memory, and told the mukhi about his intention. He did not ask my opinion. It would be at the spot where Ma enjoyed doing her volunteer-sewa work in the evenings on the veranda, and it would have Ma's name on it on a brass plate in English. That's where the polio-crippled girl used to come to sit on a makeshift bench. After the girl's mysterious death, the place has been taken over by the woman from Moshi, whose mind, people say, has shifted. They say the woman became demented after her eighth delivery, five years ago. They said it was because her faith in Saheb had weakened and the spirit entered her. Now she sits there smiling to the air and to her kaarki, meaning her she-black maid, Jennifer. I would want to talk to her and show her Saheb's picture and tell the spirit to leave her, but I am afraid it may leave her and settle in me. The maid lives with the woman with shifted mind and her son. Jennifer and Freda, our house help, are good friends and of the same build and glowing brown complexion so different from matt Indian skin-brown. In fact, they look so alike that one would think they were sisters. Haiderali agreed to employ Freda after Zaibun was born, to help me with the housework and take care of our two children and Ma. Her name is Freda, but Ma called her Farida.

Zaibun was born at Saint Mary's Catholic Hospital two years after Diamond and like him she was delivered by Naaras Nasira. The voice in my head came and went but I knew her better now. How empty were her threats! I remembered what Dr Mustafa had told me in Nairobi, "She is like a barking dog that does not bite."

Some stories come from memories probed, embellished, stunted and twisted, whether imagined or real. How can I know what is real, when there come times when

42

my mind is not my own as it was before Diamond was born?

"But how can stories be real anyway?" she asks. I have given her the name of Mama Khelele for she is noisy, and asks questions about things to which I have no answers. She asks me to have power over me, and call me stupid, like how grown-ups ask children questions they cannot answer to show they are adults and know better.

Yes, stories enter the deep territory of the brain that mixes and digests all stories, and then they live in pictures of wits, fear, lies and half-truths. That leaves the mind to wonder whether it's me who possesses the stories or someone else. It does not matter who is the owner of the mind full of tales because it's the imagination that matters not memories.

Nevertheless, to quieten her, for her voices are haughty and demanding at times, I must embroider a tapestry in bright zari threads into my mind, and start putting beads in colours of the emankeeki over her voice. Colours too have voices of their own.

Mr and Mrs Show

On Thursday mornings, I have time to do my community service or sewa and that opens up my heart. There, in the jamat khana, I would meet Zera Bai and Khanu Bai, both members of the volunteers cleaning committee. Everyone in the Nairowua jamat is in one or the other volunteer-sewa group, a tradition that's in every Guru-Pir faith. "Sharing a spiritual thought or a kind deed for the welfare of another is a prayer," Ma Gor Bai used to tell me. "The greatest sewa is when you humble yourself, going down on your knees in the jamat khana, as low as the servant mopping the floor in your house. You too are a servant in God's house. Humility is close to prayer." Sewa washes away sins. Sewa is the doorstep to dharma - repaying for the comforts of life that one enjoys. Sewa means to give. On Thursdays, the volunteer-sewa women and non-volunteer-sewa women as well, bring broken or loosened up tasbihs to me. I would repair the beaded strings later during the week sitting in the bead store. That is also community-sewa for the Satpanth jamat, and besides that, I am liked by the women I would otherwise not come to know. They would say, "Her name Moti Bai fits her well, for she is our Bead Bai."

Girls in the jamat khana, who have accompanied their mothers on Thursday sewa work, take turns to look after four year old Diamond. I leave Zaibun in Freda's care while she cleans the kitchen and irons the clothes. Zaibun has got so accustomed to being in a kanga tied to Freda's back that she cries when put in the swing cot to sleep. I remember the skin warmth and the sweaty feel of Hawa's body when she carried me around, cradled up in a kanga tied to her back. The girls look into Diamond's bright grey eyes and baby talk, lisping words into hisses. Outside, passers-by sometimes stop and gather around Macho Paka, the Cat Eyed Boy. That's what they call Diamond in town, Macho Paka. Diamond enjoys the attention but wails when hungry. Like his father, he gets angry when hungry. Until then, I have time to be with my friends, and do some cleaning in the jamat khana. Sometimes, Rhemu Bhai, my friend Zera Bai's husband, carries Diamond sitting on his forearm, unaware that his pot belly gaps out through his buttoned up one-size-too-small shirt. The exposure of an isolated patch of sparse hair and male nakedness is half funny and half embarrassing to the girls who giggle with their palms over their teeth, and eyes laughing. In his bicycle duka-store, which is between Merali Bus Station at the BP Petrol Station and the jamat khana, Rhemu Bhai sweet talks with Diamond, who relishes chewing the white figurine of tyre-man Dunlop with his baby teeth. The tyre-man is attached to a bunch of Rhemu Bhai's store keys that jingle to Diamond's great amusement. The boy also enjoys sitting on the glass counter and sharing the penda with Rhemu Bhai's son. Mehboob is older than Diamond and like his father, loves to play talking games with my son.

In fact, Rhemu Bhai is loved by all the children of the jamat because of the penda sweet that he always seems to have with him. When Rhemu Bhai has a good business month, he has the children line up before him seated on the LATE MUKHIANI MRS DOLATKHANU KARMALI JADAVJI MEGHJI memorial bench, outside the prayer hall of the jamat khana. People say he dotes on the performance of his own

45

generosity played before the jamat, and that is another reason why they call him Rhemu Show. At such performances, displaying generosity and his love for the children, Rhemu Show would tap his left cheek with his finger while holding out a penda sweet saying, "Puppy for bapa here." Accordingly, the children would plant a puppy kiss on his cheek. Parents smile from afar, amused by Rhemu Bhai's antics and his love for their children. This public act was also to let the jamat know that he had had a good business month and that he was sharing his happiness. Making children happy, they say, helps to ward off misfortune of kisirani that comes from envy. And that's belief.

When Rhemu Bhai's scrap metal business or the bicycle business is not doing well, Zera Bai cooks su-kreet for the jamat khana, and prepares a meal of samosa and chai to break the morning fast of the women at the prayer gathering of the Fast of Sati Ma. That is her manta, meaning her heart's desire put before Saheb so their businesses may prosper. Zera Bai actually prefers to be called Mrs Rhemu, and the Khoja jamat would call her Mrs Rhemu to please her. However, in the jamat, Zera Bai is better known as Mrs Show, while the Maasai call her En-turuai, which as Ole Lekakeny explained to me, means, She Who Likes Ornamenting Herself. But in town among the house helps, both men and women working in Khoja homes and shops, Zera Bai is called Mama Maradadi, which means The Decorated One in Swahili. True Zera Bai pampers her face with paint and powder.

A paraphernalia of trinkets on her fingers and arms, around her neck and in her hair, nose and ears flashes with the movements of her hands, and her head nods up-down and to the sides. She carries herself like a mobile decoration on her straight-back walk, attesting that the names that the different communities of Nairowua have given her are well earned.

Sometimes, in the afternoons, sitting on my chair by the bead panels, when the sun blazes outside, and Ole Lekakeny is dozing with his chin pressed to his chest, my mind wanders. Sometimes, I think about the three communities of Nairowua living side by side, each day interacting with each other, who have given names to Zera Bai in their languages. Yet, no one community would know her name given by the other, so separated we live in multi-apartheid Kenya. Come to think of it, they would have names for many of us, I am sure. I tried to coax Freda to tell me what I am called, but she would not tell me. She said there was no name for me, just Mama Diamond meaning Diamond's Mother, but when her face lit up as she spoke, I knew she was lying. She must have given me a name that would relate to my habit or my looks, if not something I like to carry or like to wear. Who knows me better than Freda? Who knows us better than the servant who lives with us outside the normal boundaries of civility and discretion that we draw around friends and relatives?

Making samosa is not all the cooking-sewa that Zera Bai does; there is more. Khanu Bai and I go to Zera Bai's house to help in the kitchen when she cooks a rich meal for the Repast of Seven Little Virgins. Her samosas, both vegetable and meat, always turn out crispy kaarak and you munch them kaarak kaarak. And about her sweet and sour tamarind chili chutney to go with the samosas, people would say, vat nah karo, meaning, don't even say it. It's so flavoursome that the tongue click clacks at the singe of the

47

lick. Sweetened ghee glistens over orange rice spangled with nuts. All this with Tree Tops orange juice. What child would not like such a treat? Finally, Lalaprashad's famed gritty semolina sweets, the pendas from Nairobi, peak the fare.

After feeding the girls, Zera Bai gives each little one a vial of perfume and a handkerchief with colourful flowers embroidered at the tips of the four corners. Moreover, the handkerchiefs have a crocheted coloured border all around the muslin. "These are imported handkerchiefs from China," she would say while handing them over. She and Rhemu Bhai earnestly believe such an elaborate ceremonial meal embellished with gifts for the Seven Little Virgins would remove any evil in the way of their business and prosperity.

The ritual feeding of Seven Little Virgins continues among us, the Guru-Pir Khoja of Africa, meaning the Khoja of the Satpanth faith that binds the wisdoms of the gurus and pirs in the sacred song called the ginan. I was one of the Seven Little Virgins at Naaras Dai Bai's feast for girls from the Indian Bazaar of Nairobi. She called me Saki not Sakina that was my name before I was married.

How stories go back and forth carried in memories of ritual foods that are many. Like when we have guests and we call it blessings of baraka. Like when the lone Ismaili traveller passing by our town has a meal with us, and we say it's the blessing of roji, meaning the meal on the table was intended to nourish the traveller as if that was written in his destiny. Or the daily offering of prayer foods that have various names for they mean different things like victuals for daily dua-prayer for one's salvation, or for peace of the ancestors or seeking blessings of the pir or even Saheb, and more. Then there are the communal meals that remind us of the common origin, and that partaking collectively is itself blessings of togetherness.

I feel my stories are like the ritual foods of the Khojas of Africa of the guru-pir and pir-shah traditions becoming one in the embrace of the Satpanth. First, the food is prepared with great joy and care in expectation of blessings to come from the offerings. Then, it is decked and laid out by nurturing hands full of mother-love as gifts honouring the dead or Mowla, the guests or the family. Finally, the meals are savoured, eaten and digested like a good story. The Maasai around my little town of Nairowua on the savannah say to tell a story is to eat a story relishing the taste that stays on the tongue.

Safari ants

When short drizzles begin in Nairowua, they settle the dust, and one can finally sniff the humidity bracing the crisp air, and smell the red earth. Diamond is playing in the courtyard when I hear his screams, sounding very much like the other evening when he saw a green snake nestled for the night in his baby shoe. My body tightens. My breath halts. Rushing out of the kitchen, I find Freda had already removed Diamond's pants and plucked out a safari ant from his groin. No sooner do I pick my son up, pressing him to my chest, than I hear Zarina's frantic calls. She is standing at the shop's veranda alarmed, her frozen finger pointing to a belt of ants so thick that you cannot see the ground underneath. The ants are marching in chunks, scrambling over each other with military determination. A thick tide of shiny, deep transparent, hundreds of brown-black glossy particles moving like a rippling millipede of infinite feet. I see Ole Lekakeny hurrying. I hear him muttering, "Good omen when ants come to your doorstep at the first drizzle of the season, *si-ndio*, is that not so?" He is clutching a kerosene bottle in each hand. "It's a sign of life reviving the land, *si-ndio* - yes? There will be rain this season." He bounces with joy.

Looking closely, the old man diverts the ants' path, pouring a few drops of kerosene at a time. He starts at the steps, moves to the veranda, and then to the corners of the store. He watches closely after each drip, how the ants disband and regroup when their march is interrupted by the deadly smell. He studies their collective strength, their defiance, their persistence and continues a dribble here, a dribble there, each time scrutinizing how the ants scatter and reorder, taking care not to drop the kerosene over them. "God's creatures go in peace. Go home in peace to your mother," he speaks to them. This goes on for little over an hour until Ole Lekakeny is satisfied that the ants have changed their course. At last, the safari ants circumvent the veranda, and move towards the acacia grove. "One does not kill God's creatures of the savannah," he tells me when he returns to the store. "They keep away from oil-water." Taking the half-empty bottle of kerosene from him with one hand and supporting Diamond sitting on my hip with the other, I begin trickling kerosene into all the stone and wood cracks that I can find. I see there are still some ants scurrying around in panic, looking for the lost trail to rally along with the main stream.

At the jamat khana, while talking about the invasion of safari ants in Nairowua, I realize that they have passed through only our side of the town and no one else is even aware of them. We chat about the safari ants, each one adding her personal encounter with the ants at some point in her life. Then the conversation slips into encounters with honeybees, wasps, those stinging hairy caterpillars, jiggers and scorpions. We sweep the straw prayer mats and dust the windowsills of the prayer hall. There has been much dust accumulating inside the building during the dry months. The dust is an ideal habitat for dudus, meaning bugs. Every lady volunteer has a story to tell about a sting she or someone in her family experienced at the first drizzle of the season.

Haiderali calls us the Fagia or Broom Committee, the way our men jest about women's groups. But officially, we are the jamat khana's Cleaning Committee that keeps the prayer hall spotless and tidy like our own home. "The jamat khana is Saheb's house and it has to be even cleaner than our homes," Zera Bai would tell us as if we did not know. As a trio, Zera Bai, Khanu Bai and I make a good work team, and that brings us closer as friends.

As days go by in our little town on the savannah , we feel more comfortable sharing the secrets of the heart that torment women coming to the middle age. In between, we talk about our children and anything new that we have recently purchased or planted in our kitchen gardens, or learned to cook, knit, or whatever else women do in our small town.

"I started to make a photo album when I was in Nairobi, you know," I am talking while sweeping the red and green straw carpet stitched together into one wall-to-wall prayer mat. The new straw mat was a donation from the mukhi when he was nominated to the office.

"All my photographs are in heaps pressed into English chocolate tins. But the precious ones are in envelopes between folds of my saris wrapped in merikani cloth packages in my bedroom cupboard," says Zera Bai, picking up brooms lying on the floor. Then with the three feathery river grass brushes at the hip, Zera Bai walks towards us, moving like a peacock. The trembling tail trailing her.

"I too want to make a photo album. But I do not have many photographs, you know," says Khanu Bai. Like me, all Khoja women want to make a photo album after their marriage like it were to reclaim lost maiden memories,

52

and exhibit new ones in the making out of their girl dreams. Or even to put their torments into pictures recalling happier times. Khanu Bai is the captain of the Saafai Cleaning Committee and there is talk that she will soon be appointed the major of all the jamat khana volunteers. Zera Bai is her vice-captain. The army-style designation of volunteers lingers on in our Saheb's house of prayers long after the World Wars are over. My Noordin kaka uncle, in his moment of despising the Ismailis, used to make fun of the military titles we use in the jamat khana, the house of peace and prayers.

All three of us have now removed our pachedi-shawls, folded them neatly, and placed them underneath the low jamat khana table. On the table sits the white porcelain bowl called khum, containing water made holy by dissolving a pinch of the grey loam rolled into a pill from the battlefield of the first of holy wars between Shias and Sunnis. The soil was made sacred, my Dadabapa would tell me, when it soaked in the blood of the martyred in the mythical fields of Karbala, somewhere in Arabland. Beside the porcelain bowl gleaming on the impeccable white cloth over the low floor table at which the reciter of the dua-prayer sits cross-legged, is a half burnt candle, its wick erect like a black needle, and a grey powder patch made by last evening's ash from the burning loban gum. At the moment, without a thought, I see these articles of communion appear to me through Maasai eyes of Ole Lekakeny. How in jamat khana ceremonies, we configure water, soil, light and smoke, mother earth's primordial elements, to include them in Satpanth devotions celebrating nourishment for the soul.

On the white cloth there is also a heap of entangled tasbihs of varied colours and bead sizes that I have repaired, or made new ones mixing and matching beads from the abandoned and broken ones.

My words are like beads in the knotted heap of multiple tones of coloured tasbihs on the low jamat khana table. Words that take different meanings in shades of responses to the mix of stories in stories entangled in my life. They are like the lost tasbihs mingling in a clutch-pile on the low jamat khana table. Sometimes I wonder, if the tasbihs could speak, what stories they would tell about the owners who abandoned them like orphans at the jamat khana door?

Part Two

The Keeper of Stories

Whatever it grants to vision and whatever its manner, a photograph is always invisible: it is not it that we see.

Roland Barthes (1915 –1980)

In 1972 when they were expelled from their homeland, the Uganda Asians packed their photo albums in their suitcases. What invisible memories would they be carrying leaving home? They knew the new land where they were going was called Canada, and no more. This was at their second crossing.

The singers among the refugees carried their handwritten hymn books, and most had their tasbihs on them, slipped into quickly accessible places like in their pockets and handbags. Some had them wrapped around their wrists like a talisman for a safe journey into the unknown. The Imam's photograph was tucked in somewhere safe, often into the hand luggage.

These were small things of comfort for the heart, similar to those their forefathers had at the first crossing from India that they called Des. That was more than a century ago from around 1850 when wars of independence, colonial taxation and famines ravaged Saurashtra. They knew the new land where they were going was called Africa, and no more. This was at their first crossing.

My photo album

Two weeks after the incident of the safari ants, Zera Bai and Khanu Bai visit me at home. They are sitting by my side on the sofa, on either side, sipping chai. I open my photo album. Khanu Bai half cradles the album in the fold of her legs as she removes her eyeglasses holding them by the rim over the photographs. The other half of the opened album falls on my lap in the middle of my dress stretched over the swell of my belly. Khanu Bai's pastel blue frock, taut across her knees pinnacled over her thighs, is plain, meaning it has no prints.

"Your dress is plain like a bed sheet," remarks Zera Bai, bending her leg over the other to bring her one foot up on the sofa; the other foot dangles below not touching the marble glaze of linoleum. On her suspended bare, fair and arched foot, runs a blue vein from a sparse patch of hair over the ankle ball. She has her big toe nail long and filed to perfection of a polished ruby and like her other toenails, painted blood red.

"My family story lives between these two covers," I say, embracing the photo album closer to me with both my hands as if it were my baby. The album rises and falls with my breathing, the abdomen bulging under a scattering of green paisley whorls on my white cotton dress. We are all wearing ankle length dresses as is the Khoja habit.

"The family photo album is the keeper of stories," says Khanu Bai putting on her glasses now and adjusting the white pad of cotton wool behind her ear. I see her eyes fixed in admiration of the album's red hardboard cover on which are glued seashells from the Indian Ocean.

"It's a present from my brother, Shamshu," I say, caressing the seashells with one finger. "He gave it to me when he started work at the Post Office in Mombasa. A gift from his first pay money." I talk with pretend humility veiling over my mixed pride and delight. "And this is the best photograph I have of Saheb in colour. It's from my friend Noori, daughter of Bwana Picha, our neighbour in Jugu Bazaar."

"The photograph is a blessing. Such a picture is always a prayer on the first page in the family book of pictures," says Khanu Bai. "But it's so small like a playing card."

It is, indeed, a fine photo of Saheb wearing a black fez hat without the usual tassel, and a paisley patterned red robe on which are gold medallions and bright silver stars – accolades of service to the English feudaldom, as my Noordin kaka uncle would have said. My kaka uncle's words were full of cynicism when talking about Saheb or even Saheb's wives, as if he resented Saheb marrying English women. But the glittering array of jug mug stars on Saheb's chest makes me proud of him, like he were a victorious prince avatar stepped out of the battle in the Mahabharata. Before turning over the page, I trail my finger along the top edge feeling its line in the groove of my finger. I feel the same sensation as of zari thread slipping through my fingers, and so for a while, I continue running my finger back and forth. How my fingers keep memories of embroidery I did in my childhood! The baby in my belly kicks as if sharing the sensations with me and letting me know he is feeling the touch too. My friends notice the smile of gratification on my face and they smile too, without saying they know the feeling of fulfilment that pregnancy brings to a woman. Shu-khar, I say within. Thank you Mowla for the contentment of mother feeling. Shu-khar is the breath of the heart. I say shu-khar many times.

"ખરાબર છે - barabar *chhe*," says Khanu Bai, meaning it's fine, ending the sentence with the છે *chhe* verb or part verb, the way we Gujaratis speak. She means it's a proper way to open the photo album with Saheb and his family first before coming to our own images. "I am collecting Saheb's family pictures to begin my album," she says stroking Saheb's picture with her finger, the one that has fading henna in a semi moon on the cuticle from the last Khush-ali.

I lift the folds of my frock at the knees to shift my legs to one side. My right leg numbs so quickly. I have difficulty sitting cross-legged in the jamat khana and backaches kill me.

"Saheb's picture will keep the evil eye away from your family images, *nah*?" adds Zera Bai, resting her pearl ringed finger on the assemblage of Saheb's family photographs. Like her toes, her fingernails are painted ruby red. I nod. "Kisirani of jealousy is the worst type, *nah*?" continues Zera Bai, fading her sentence into a soft *nah* question inviting consent not a query. It is her manner of talk alluring a nod, if not a spoken yes. The smell of perfumed coconut hair oil clouds over my face as she leans forward closer to the photo album like she wants to be in the picture with Saheb. Who would not want to be with Saheb in this photograph by Bwana Picha?

"Bwana Picha is the marriage photographer of Nairobi. He is the best known of all the family photographers, you know. His father's store was in the same line as my grandfather's bead and blanket store in Jugu Bazaar," I reminisce, suddenly wanting to tell my friends about the street where I lived as a girl.

I turn over to the next page. Two portrait pictures of Haiderali and me held by corner hinges stare at me. At once, both Zera Bai and Khanu Bai recognize these as proposal photographs exchanged by our two families during marriage negotiations. "Your offer photo is so plain, Moti Bai. Joh toh! Just look! How could such a photo attract a modern boy like Haiderali?" asks Zera Bai. I look at myself on the shiny rectangular piece of black and white paper. The picture of me at fifteen restores me to myself, meaning who I want to be. I keep quiet. How do I answer such a question? My photograph was sent to Haiderali's family after our marriage was agreed by our two families. Lost in my feelings, I do not explain. Sometimes, my feelings take away my words. Sometimes, my feelings bring out words from my heart.

"When my relatives saw this photograph of Haiderali in an English sports jacket and a dotted scarf muffled around his neck," I say pointing to Haiderali's picture in sepia, "everyone agreed he was, undoubtedly, a desirable match for the family. My parents said I would suit in such a family. A right match for the English speaking man, they said." But Haiderali spoke little English. He speaks more now, but less than my brother Shamshu and Razak, his milk-brother. The two can speak the language like parrots mixed with some words from Gujarati and Swahili - the way our men speak nowadays. That English, I understand half-half. At least, I get an idea about their conversation, unlike the talk of white men in newsreel at the cinema or the BBC news on the radio that Kabir listens to.

"My Kaki auntie, and even Meethi Bai, thought Haiderali and I made a set. "Tik *chhe*," they agreed in unison. Now, I really don't know about our set. It's your kismet, no matter how careful the parents are when choosing the right boy for you from a worthy family. But then, my parents had no choice because I was promised to the Devji Momna family by my Dadabapa," I say looking aside for a while, mulling over what I had just said. Should I have said it? Did I want to say it or did it just slip out? The thought has been recurring in my mind more than ever before now that this year I will be thirty. Whenever Haiderali touches me at night without love or words, I am not sure. My body stiffens, tells him no. "Su *chhe*? – What is it?" he demands in anger, intimidating me with su *chhe*? question, and throws himself on me as if to punish me because I dared. I want him to listen to my heart, not see me the way he does, like a man in need of satisfaction. My pride is hurt. My body insulted. Is my heart telling me to show my photo album to my friends so they will listen to me because my husband does not? Perhaps, but one thing I am certain of, I know in our group, we know how to keep secrets. But I cannot speak what is in my heart today. Here my family's honour is stronger than our friendship.

I feel strange looking at my proposal photograph today. It's the first time that such thoughts of my relationship with Haiderali come when in company of friends. After Ma's death, I have noticed changes in Haiderali's behaviour. The photograph brings self-talk in me as if the past is speaking to the present. I used to dream about my future looking at the photo, now I worry about the present. After his evening bath on Saturdays, Haiderali pads himself with Johnson's Baby Powder, little oudh dabbing behind the ears, and after the jamat khana prayers, he disappears. He tells me he is going to play cards with friends. Last Saturday, I kept my eyes on him after the jamat khana service. I saw him walking into darkness towards Majengo. What friends of his live in the black township? He returns late. I have not eaten waiting for him.

"Where have you been?" I ask.

"Card game," he replies.

"Dhaap *chhe!*" I tell him it's a made-up story. He knows now I know he lies. My aspirated *chhe* is terse almost a throaty yell implying it is unquestionably a lie.

"Have you eaten? I will sit with you. Come let's eat," he says. He is genuine. But coming from him at that moment, I am irritated that he should even show concern for me, a wife who does not eat before the husband comes home.

"Tell that to your black whore!" I yell at him.

I burn on those dusky veiled women of Majengo. I see them at the vegetable market. Their skins are the colour of roasted almond, their eyes kohl smeared, shiny and snaring. I wonder if they are as full of love and life as those eyes of Riziki, my sister-in-law, Shamshu's other wife. I wonder if they are younger than I am. If their breasts are firmer? Thighs softer, tighter? Haiderali likes dusk skinned women in bed. Is it because he was nurtured by a native ayah like I was by Hawa? However, Indian men's mothers prefer filmy skinned girls to be their daughters-in-law.

62

White skins would adorn homes and festive evenings in the jamat khana in frocks and saris that glitter jug mug. I burn on those dark women. Haiderali slips in under the quilt. I burn on black. I hate black. I am what she, the one who inhabits me, tells me who I am, rancorous black Kali at this hour of the night when I need a man. She says, "My sister, my avatar, Haidu is getting tired of one marriage." Mama Khelele puts doubts in my mind.

"But Moti Bai's proposal photograph is so plain. So dull like a passport photo *chhe nah*?" says Zera Bai throwing a frank nah question that expects a yes look from Khanu Bai not me.

I respond fatafat, meaning quickly, "But here, look at my wedding photo. Not so dull, is it? There was some touching up here and there by Studio One." My wedding photograph follows the two proposal photographs in my album. "My Stepmother used to say it was Bwana Picha's imagination that created beautiful marriage photographs to grace our living room wall. I had two more copies made, smaller prints, one for the photo album and one for my parents' living room. It stands on the lacquered box of their new PYE radio gramophone," I say.

Zera Bai and Khanu Bai admire my wedding picture for a rather long time looking at the details. I study it again because of their stares though I have seen it a thousand times before. In the photograph, I am the sixteen-year-old bride in adult clothing holding a basket overflowing with plastic flowers under an arch over which trails a mock streak of leaves, every branch in full bloom of miniature jasmine. I stand beside Haiderali, my eighteen year old groom in an English woollen suit holding a fat hard cover book, a rolled up diploma tied with ample ribbon, and a stern look of success on his photo white face. He is slim and looks learned with colonial authority dressed up in white's man's clothes. A graduate standing upright over me with a tie on his neck. I run my forefinger over his image like how sometimes when loneliness overwhelms me, I go to the photo album to be the girl in me to meet Haiderali, the husband of my heart. A husband who gives me security.

I let my look stay on the photo in a frozen moment as though I was there, years back, and I admire myself in my previous life, and he, like someone with whom I lived a long time ago. Suddenly, I feel Khanu Bai shift by my side. She feels uneasy. Our hips touch though not our upper bodies. I feel the comforting warmth of an elder sister by my side.

Hee-hee-hee-thee-thee-thee

We meet again, this time at Zera Bai's house. At first, I thought one afternoon would be enough, but the photographs have kindled some sort of unsaid, unexplainable joy in us. They have opened glimpses into our lives we normally don't talk about. There is the mother's pride and the girl's prime in the photographs not said about oneself for that would be boastful, and therefore not modest. My family photo album is a secret delight that lights a lamp inside like a glow in my heart. So, when we thought of meeting again to see the photographs, if only just one more time, it was to return to those moments that open the way to reach the chamber of our inner selves.

I carry my Black Magic chocolate box with me, packed with jumbo size black and white, some sepia, photos. That's where they would be until I buy a second photo album from Nairobi. Zera Bai's house is an old wooden building with a courtyard behind Rhemu Bhai's bicycle shop. Rabia Godoro, the new mukhi's daughter-in-law, rents a part of the courtyard where she spreads cotton in the sun for making mattresses. Rhemu Bhai keeps the other part of the yard, a corner where he stores scrap metal he has been collecting piece by piece over the years. Once a month or so, he heaps a pile of broken, tangled and twisted bits and pieces of iron, tied together with tyre tube straps, and has his man carry it to Merali Bus bound for Nairobi.

With exaggerated care as if she were showcasing, Zera Bai lifts the cardboard top of her Bata shoebox brimming with photos. She has painted flowers in red and yellow pencilcolours on the brown shoebox like it were a kanga. Crowned with bellowed shoulder sleeves, her dress sports cloud prints - blotches in colours riot over her. Tongolo ten cents size plastic buttons in matching mixed colours run down her neck to the waist. Zera Bai is often talked about, if not admired, if not envied, for keeping on top of the fashion chart from Nairobi's textile bazaars.

"Wait till you see my wedding photo," says Khanu Bai looking for the photo in her English biscuit tin. "Look at me. Even in my wedding picture I am not smiling."

"My marriage photograph is the same. There is no smile on my face. Laughing hee-hee-hee-thee-thee-thee like an alley hyena does not suit a good-family girl, my mother would tell us girls," says Zera Bai. We laugh now, puffing out hah hahs, remembering how we were not even allowed to smile outside our homes and how we would be admonished if we smiled broadly in the presence of guests.

"See we don't smile in the photographs, but we put on a robust smile later when we look at the photographs," says Khanu Bai. She is the one in our group who is the quietest, yet she makes us chuckle with unanticipated comments. Yes, to show we were pleased with ourselves would be arrogance, not the Indian humility considered proper for marriageable girls. We understood women's teeth were certainly not for display.

"It was Bwana Picha who took my proposal photo in his studio on Government Road," continues Khanu Bai. "He made me look down, my face slightly at an angle. A distant filmi dream look away from the camera, away from the world." Her voice sounds apologetic as if to imply she was not the one who asked to be photographed like a filmi

66

star. "In my youthful hair, he attached a rosebud, you see here, hanging loosely. He then ruffled my hair a little at the side. 'For silver light,' he said." Khanu Bai takes her hand to her hair. "He told me to support my chin on the back of my hand, half opening my fingers to the air as if they had no life." She lifts her hand to her chin. "You know, like how English memsahebs in Woman's Own make their fingers look so scrawny drinking coffee in tiny cups tipping over their fingers. Then he told me to smile and when I did, he jumped up, 'No! No! Not like that. Not completely.' Then he showed me how to half smile," says Khanu Bai. We smile remembering our own proposal photo taking day. After a pause, she says more, "He made me into another me and I made Mamdu see who I was that I was not. I am not she in the photograph. My picture lied to Mamdu's eyes." Zera Bai and I break into gurgles, spontaneous private pleasure. Khanu Bai frowns slightly. Sucking in my cheeks, I hold my shaking belly with both my hands. It was a sudden passing twinge of pregnancy, not the laughter.

"We were poor Khoja teenage girls from tin roofed shanty homes, looking for filmland - marbled palaces and rose gardens on the wall posters at the studio. We wanted to look filmi beautiful waiting for our Dilip Kumar, *nah*?" cackles Zera Bai sensing Khanu Bai was not pleased with our mischief put to her. "Movies kindled our desires to be screen beauties in Indian clothes jug mug. Was that us? Who we were?" asks Zera Bai, her outwardly innocent question cloaked in a snide look at Khanu Bai. She shows obvious playfulness, as is her character, whereby she makes her point and not anger anyone. Plucking at her long cotton dress at the waist to slacken the elastic underneath, she continues, "We were all marriageable girls with dreams in our eyes, *nah*? How we went to the photo studio in borrowed dresses, masquerading as stars of triple A movies Awara, Aan, Anarkali!" How we kindle lost happiness from photographs like post views of our lives when we were young and aspiring to be brides. How I hold on to those days. How actors inspired us and lighted our imagination. But we were not expected to reach there. That was the Indian puzzle planted in our upbringing. The proposal photograph was that fleeting happy moment as illusory as our desires.

"Do our husbands expect us to carry that dream face eternally?" asks Khanu Bai. Then to my surprise, she replies herself, "Yes, I think they do. Mamdu married my studio photo. But women's bodies wane. They change after childbirths unlike the photographs." Her words are burdened with regret. "Now we read love stories from the jamat khana library to complete our girl dreams."

"That's why the English gave us make-up compacts *nah?*" says Zera Bai with a broad smile as if to take away the pain from Khanu Bai's voice. I smile with her. "I make myself look like a screen actress to keep my husband in my control."

I find the picture I was looking for.

It is Shamshu's engagement photo taken in the City Park in Nairobi. "That's Khati Bai, still a teenage girl, betrothed to my brother, Shamshu. Set *chhe*. We thought," my voice splits in excitement. "See the bougainvillea shower over her shoulder, and Shamshu, a school boy in silk tie. See how he stands like a true filmi hero. Pukka Dilip Kumar *chhe* in a love-song scene among flowers under cotton clouds. The ugly bumblebee nipping into a fair bloom, *chhe nah?*"

"Very fine set *chhe*," concurs Khanu Bai.

"They match. Totia *chhe*?" Zera Bai asks if they have children.

"No children. Four years married," I say showing deliberate regret on my lips pressed in and down, and a headshake.   It hurts that my Dadabapa's name will be erased in the community. "They have adopted Khati Bai's sister's daughter."

"An evil eye has scanned over Khati Bai's abdomen that's brought kisirani of bad luck. Coastal people and their witchcraft," Zera Bai's remark hints at Shamshu's second wife who is from the coast. Her name is Riziki, but they call her Shamshu's rakheli bai, meaning his kept woman. She lives somewhere in the Swahili town concealed from the watch of the Khoja jamat. However, when her story sneaks out, as such stories tend to, it is told in chup chap hush hush words, whispered behind fingers over lips showing reluctance to gossip. My family just pretends their marriage does not exist. That includes Shamshu himself. Neither does he talk about his two children by Riziki. There is no photograph of Riziki in any of our family albums in Nairobi or Mombasa, or in my Black Magic chocolate tin. She is a private relative we say cutting short further queries.

"Has Khati Bai been to Ambe Ma's temple?" enquires Khanu Bai. I nod.

"How can you even think of that?   That's in the past. It's a desi thought. Such Hindu customs should be buried with our ancestors in India! We must change our Indian thinking, modernize and be pukka Moslems," interjects Zera Bai. Khanu Bai and I keep quiet. Zera Bai is quick to notice our silence and makes a suggestion,

"Instead, Khati Bai should offer prayers to fill the gap between wanting and receiving. I would tell her to feed the poor with her own hands at the shrine of the railway coolie saint. You know Sayed Bhagha Ali's tomb at Mackinnon Road?"

"You know my stepmother comes from a family of shrine keepers in India. She knows," I reply.

We look at Shamshu's stance and pose. His one hand is stretched out holding a bougainvillea blossom to the girl's heart, the other slaps over his own. He stands askance, as if he were singing the most romantic filmi hit song. His head is tilted a little up to the drifting clouds in the sky as in desi movie.

"This is a proper engagement pose. Nice scenery *chhe*," says Zera Bai to my delight. I am proud of my brother Shamshu's cinema looks in the photograph, and his gesture of commitment to love his bride-to-be.

What love? What India?

In between our meetings to see photographs, we exchange recipes and have a proper cup of chai together. A cup of tea that takes away the day's tiredness. You feel each gulp going down the gullet and the warmth settling in the abdomen on a warm African afternoon. Zera Bai, Khanu Bai, and I are like children of one stomach – watoto wa tumbo moja, as we say in Swahili, meaning siblings. Sometimes intentionally, sometimes because the moment of being in the photograph, calls for thoughts otherwise not said. And sometimes, because feelings transcend without a word spoken like an aura that a photograph carries. No wonder Ma Gor Bai did not want to be photographed. "Your spirit lives in photographs when you die," she used to say. We live the moments sharing our images and private thoughts.

Looking at Khanu Bai's wedding picture, Zera Bai and I wait for her to say something about her husband, Mamdu Bhai. Like after marriage when did Mamdu Bhai fall in love with her. But she is quiet and we do not ask. We wait. She unties her hair, holding the hairpins in her mouth while she rolls, tightens, and turns the tail back into a firm spiral bun above the nape. She jabs hairpins back into her hair, one into the middle of the bun, one under the bun and one each at the sides where her hair in arches looks like it was plastered with black varnish. We watch her throwing her pachedi-shawl over her head, patting it down at the crown. I think of last week when Mamdu Bhai slapped

Khanu Bai in the jamat khana because of an argument over naandi food. Did she buy too much? Did she not buy what he wanted to eat that night? Did she pay too much? Nobody knows. We just heard a sharp spank that hushed everyone around. Khanu Bai said nothing; she did not even cry or wince. She just turned around and walked towards her home all alone in the dark, something women do not do, especially during this time when whispers are rife about native uprising against the English. I notice Khanu Bai is pressing the corner end of her pachedi-shawl balled in her fist.

"When marriages fade in midlife, they get picked up again when old age creeps in. Heart love glows when body love dies," says Zera Bai looking at Khanu Bai.

We keep quiet searching ourselves. I nod, but there is no expression on Khanu Bai's face. Meanwhile, Zera Bai had slipped out some photographs from an envelope from her handbag. I get a whiff of stale oudh scent from the envelope that was possibly wrenched out from under her folded saris in merikani cloth wraps stacked like panes in her airtight bedroom cupboard. There is a photograph of old Saheb's grandsons, two princes leading the prayers on the Day of Sacrifice of the Lamb in the stone jamat khana of Nairobi. And another of the Nairobi jamat khana, blazing a thousand electric bulbs into the African night. The two photos steal my heart. What Ismaili woman would not want these pictures in her family album?

There are more photos in her shoebox, some of picnics. Women sitting in palothi with folded legs in a circle and men folk sitting similarly at a distance absorbed in a game of cards. Some have their legs stretched out on the spongy Kikuyu grass. Around them is a spread of picnic nasto, meaning snacks. I remember how we used to pack several round Luo baskets with chevdo, sliced lemon pieces, red chilli-packed potatoes, watery chickpea potato curry, sweet and sour tamarind chilli chutney, and thick kadho chai in thermoses. In the background, thunders the spectacular Thika Falls.

"Fine scenery *chhe*," comments Zera Bai. Silence.

Drawing attention to myself, I heave out a sigh, running my finger along the serrated edge of the photo of Diamond at the community Baby Show. He is a plump boy, sitting naked but for a white strap, a mop of black hair on his head. He is holding a silver cup, a trophy as tall as he is. I smile to my two friends' sighs of admiration. Diamond's photo prompts Zera Bai to dig through a pile of photographs in her shoebox, and she comes out with a picture of two bare chested Punjabi wrestlers. "You see, Diamond looks like them, *chhe nah?*" says Zera Bai giggling, and nudging me with her elbow, her *chhe* nah queries nods from us.

"Hai hai, Joh tho! Just look at them!" Khanu Bai and I exclaim together looking away from the photograph like it were a shame to see.

"Will you have these naked men in your album?" asks Khanu Bai in a hardly audible voice. "They look bhoonda. Obscene *chhe*." Her quiet *chhe* is firm. Silence again.

"You know, Rhemu is a fan of these two champions. And these photographs, I found them in Nooran Mubin with Saheb's holy family. Imagine that!"

"What a place to keep them!" interrupts Khanu Bai exclaiming.

73

"Rhemu wants to frame and hang them on the wall. I say, never in my house," continues Zera Bai.

"Hai hai! They wear just a strip like Diamond Devji at the Baby Show!" Khanu Bai blushes. We laugh again. Groggy halted sounds from the throat cover up for our lascivious eyes. Zera Bai puts the two pictures in a separate envelope from the rest of the photographs and slips them to the bottom of the box. She has arranged the photographs in a stack in the box, beginning with Saheb's family pictures at the top, then her proposal and marriage ones, followed by the family and picnic photos, as she would have them arranged when she starts her photo album. The wrestlers go to the bottom in the box. They are outsiders, Punjabis and naked.

But how do I tell them I suspect I may have other children? They would be my step children, olive skinned boys and girls with tight wire curls, half-Asian half-African, playing in Majengo's dusty warren of lanes. Children fathered by Haiderali when he wanted more in a woman than me. Children of his rakhel bai, meaning his kept woman. When he kept glossy English magazines under the mattress and ran his fingers over the flesh of women in high heels, and red painted toes. There are no photos of my half-caste stepchildren in my photo album or even in the house anywhere. These children would not be at the Community Baby Show or seen at the jamat khana though they are fathered by an Ismaili. A Khoja's children by his rakhel, meaning his kept woman, are not Khoja enough we say. They cannot be part of the jamat; they will not inherit from the father what belongs to my children. I want to say this to my friends, and open my heart to them. But my mother-in law's rebuke taunts me: "You want to expose

74

family bhoparo advertising shameful secrets? … Who will take your daughter if you have one? A daughter from a scandalous family?" The tender warmth in my belly may be a girl again. Zaibun, my daughter, needs a sister. Every girl needs a sister. I must protect their honour.

"I want to show you a photograph with a proper background. It's a dream photo for my new album.," Khanu Bai shows us a glossy black and white photo that's larger than the rest covering her full palm. "That's me and Mamdu on the marble bench before the Taj Mahal," says Khanu Bai. She says nothing about the Taj Mahal. That's what I wanted to hear. The photo itself appears to suggest Khanu Bai and Mamdu had come to the Taj Mahal not to see the shrine, but to have this picture taken as if this splendid marbled wonder of the world were a studio. As if the shrine would repair and confirm their broken love.

"Your love is witnessed by this monument to love forever. The scenery is suitable for romance, barabar *chhe*," says Zera Bai. "I mean, posing for such a photograph is like taking the marriage vows again. This one would look fit in your photo album, in the centre page. A true love picture *chhe*. You are so lucky you made it to the Taj Mahal," says Zera Bai. "I wish my Rhemu would take me to the Taj Mahal for a picture. I want to see India. Kacch and Gujarat"

What Kacch? What Gujarat? What India? These are some distant pictures in my head. Pictures that are not even mine. Vicarious pictures that stir my heart yet I have not been there. Pictures like some witch's crafted tales imagined from an ancient land. Nor are they tales in my father's head. Hazy, frightful tales in Dadabapa's malaria nightmares. Dark pictures in memory's pulses of the orphaned child in

75

him. They live in pain of yearning, sighs of loss, and far away words of the immigrant. Words like dhow, Bombay, Saurashtra, Haripur, raj, Kala Pani, des, avatar and Taj Mahal. They come from the motherland of Indian Khoja recalled in dying memories two generations gone by. Yet the emotions live in the mist-like nostalgia. Now the ancient is resurrected, made new and modern. Beauty portrayed in love photos before the Taj Mahal, and in the cinema, the hideout of Indians of Africa to bond with the origins in half-hearted thoughts.

The new screen explodes before my eyes, chaotic East meets West in make-believe filmi India. Dazzling colourscapes. Hindi actors energized, dancing workouts and spirited teenage jives. What India? India of the magic screen wailing painful melodies, grotesquely unsuited arranged marriages and depressing poverty. A poverty amidst the thick glitter of gold. Amidst the hopelessness of women's destinies? Noisy India. Impossible India. Glossy India. India of prying English values into her caste purity and the inextricable grind of human misery. Hindi filmi images of starving children in Boot Polish run through my mind. Images of violence play in my head - religious massacres, crimes, rape and corruption. India of Gandhi's book is the India I know. India of dark toiling men and women. India of my Dadabapa's stories in my memories of him. But do I want to be there?

Yet my heart leaps to the name of the new weekend release Indian movie in Nairobi. I want to hear everything about it - first who are the actors, then about the songs. The story need not be told when the songs say it all. I need to know everything about the movies at once like the new and innovative recipes of cooking curries.

Part Three

Adornments

Three artefacts of beauty in narrator Moti Bai's suitcase adorn her imagination and bring her comfort when saddened by life. She calls the artefacts her three secret sisters.

One of them is called the bandhani. The bandhani is the eldest and brightest of the sisters, austere in her looks. She reminds Moti Bai of Khanu Bai, her friend who is older in years than she is and carries herself with self-respect. No Khoja lady would have the bandhani on her shoulders and not feel dignified, and keep her head high even if it were just once a year on Khush-ali day. Their grandmothers, they would remember, were shrouded in white when they died but on top of the shroud was laid the brilliant bandhani for it was said, they were leaving home to wed Saheb.

The Maasai emankeeki was made for Moti Bai by her friends, Kini and Ntinti. The emankeeki is the openhearted extrovert middle sister of the three. "The emankeeki is so much like my friend Zera Bai," Moti Bai would say when admiring the beaded necklace. Since their walk down the Nile, the Maasai had learned about the colours from the eye harvesting beauty from the land and the sky.

If you must speak about Moti Bai's kanga that came to her as a gift from Riziki, her brother Shamsu's second wife, let it be after you have heard a kasida. A kasida, if you do not know, is a hymn for the heart to sing. It's then when the heart beats rhyme with the kanga's colours, that you begin to grow into its art. The art and colours may appear badly matched to the outside eye. But not so to the Swahili eye. In the native gaze, the colours and patterns live in one

78

home, each one is mke mwenza, meaning the co-wife or rather wife-friend as the Swahilis would say.

Moti Bai's kanga has a picture of a red cashew nut tree. She received the kanga from Riziki, her sister-in-law. The script on the kanga reads NAPENDA LAKINI NASHINDWA – I LIKE TO BUT I NOT ABLE TO. Yes, it sounds mysterious because the saying is coded, that is to say it has another meaning, perhaps even a double meaning like how Swahili sayings are. In all, kanga designs are meant to keep the onlooker trapped in thoughts impelled by the proverb while enthralled by the cloth's good looks. "The kanga is more like me who lives in her own self-talk," Moti Bai would say reflecting on herself.

Thus, Moti Bai must dream and tell her story stirred by the three art artefacts in her suitcase. Each one invites her to intuit beauty and sense the pleasure in it. They are, in fact, like three sisters who carry different personalities but come from one mother art. They help her to dream, and, being an artist, Moti Bai knows she must continue to dream to tell her story. To her, in fact, both come from the same place in the heart.

If you were to ask her, why she tells her story, she would say, "It's my dream not my will to tell the story. The will resides in the mind and is stubborn. The will is not as large and as free as a dream."

Mitti attar, the fragrance of earth in raindrops

I hear rain approaching and the evening squall. I feel nauseated. The sickness that comes from the abdomen carries a feeling of balmy sweetness. I have had that before. Looking over through the windowpane, I see the shower's spraying shafts shift in the glow of the young moon. Such an evening as this calls for quietness of thoughts. Silence to remember what is not said.

How quickly have the years passed by. Ma has receded into the memory of a mother-in-law forgiven and forgotten but for her photograph hanging like a lonesome, kind old lady with her pachedi-shawl over parted grey hair. There are days when Haiderali would take down the picture, dust the frame, and speak to it in rasping whispers, and sometimes, he looks at me. He has not forgotten my cruelty to his mother during her final days. He rebuffs me in the jamat khana. He makes it obvious that something unpleasant happened between us before Ma's asal ma vassal, meaning return to the origin.

My thoughts mingle with music of Kalidas' rain poem flooding over me like raindrops drumming the corrugated sheet iron roof. We had just recently had the roof painted red once again over the blistered pleats formed during the heat of the drought. Listening to water, soaking in rain verses, my skin breaks into pinheads. Falling water heightens my yearning for Haiderali loving me. The sound of rain releases that feeling in smells of the touch of man on woman. Humid and warm. The touch of his flesh and our wet skins.

Maasai pastoralists around Nairowua call land the Skin of God. They say land, God's skin, lives absorbing the heat and the cold, perspiring and healing the wounds we make on her, always rejuvenating and releasing sweet perfumes. Dadabapa used to sing rain love poems to stay in the lure of earth smell freed by the first droplets from the sky. He would sing to the lazy fragrance he called mitti attar or earth's perfume in the drizzle. He would sing how season after season, the attar remained faithful to the earth of Africa. The first fall of rain discharges the perfume like the touch of oudh on the pulse of the wrist. Like mitti attar, writes Narendra in *Africa Samachar*, oudh resides in nature – the agar tree that grows in deep woods of Asia.

When the rains abate, mitti attar's fragrance changes to a different notch like how the warmth of human skin changes oudh's scent. The earth is refreshed and young as if it were an aging body cherished in perfumed bath. When the scent mellows in air, it rises to yet another note altogether, the way the rub of oudh on one wrist against another elevates its aroma to another shade.

Dadabapa brought with him water poems and cloud poems with his childhood memories and sang them into the seasons of Africa. He sang each poem in its resonance of rain, soft padding the earth or crushing over footpaths, or dancing tiptoe over pools in Nairobi's bazaar street like hopping dragonflies. That's how I memorized the rain in sounds of water of Indian monsoons sweeping over Kenya, my birth country.

81

The storm wind continues to groan around the corrugated iron sheet house like a drove of buffaloes charging the dark. Raindrops pelt with such fury that I cannot hear the children playing in the next room. Awe fills me with beauty of this stormy East African evening. There is solitude that darkness of thunder, lightning and storm bring to the heart. In the chaotic moment when the skies whirl, I feel my senses numb into tranquillity of the earth's womb.

I am crouching in my mother's womb waters again. I want to remove my clothes and fall on Haiderali on my pregnant stomach. Let him know how it is to hold the sweetness in the swell of the belly. Mother beauty, mother love, mother tolerance, mother compassion come to me in one feeling from my stomach carrying his third child.

It's father's baby. Listen to his heart over my heart and over the veteran monsoon rain echoing the woman in mother nature's abdomen. My head on his chest, my body bare and fleshy middle aged, losing muscle hardness. Our warmth locked in one clasp around the unborn baby. I wrap my arms tight over me imagining Haiderali's embrace, and stare at the rain through the windowpane. Women imagine what we do not do, must not do, and must never show in such rash filmi behaviour. Our feelings are our weaknesses that we put to dreams to get over them and let pass to another such moment.

From Zaibun to Almas

We were unable to go to the jamat khana last evening because of the rainstorm. It was one of the heaviest downpours I have ever seen in Nairowua. First, there were several blasts of wind that came screaming down Mt Nairowua, and then, the rain thundered down on the rooftop. I gave Freda a mat and a blanket to sleep in the children's room and not in the servant's quarters across the courtyard. It poured continually throughout the night. In the morning I see pools of water all around the house. It looks like we are living in a boathouse. There is not a single cloud in the sky.

"I was afraid of the storm," says my four-year Diamond at breakfast. "Then Kabir kaka uncle cuddled me to sleep."

"Kabir kaka uncle has bad dreams like me," says my two years old daughter pointing to her chest. A bead of yellow pollen moves on her upper lip when she talks. My first thought was to pick the yellow pollen from her lip, I but decide to leave it there as I look at my little fairy for a moment longer and fill my mother's eyes with the charm of innocence on her child face.

My daughter has not forgotten how she used to scream at night when she was called Zaibun. Nightmares assailed her sleep after she was weaned off breast milk. Some spirit would not let her be at peace. Ole Lekakeny advised me to consult the spirit woman of the mountain who advised me to change her name. "Your child has been misnamed. It is a kisirani name that brings bad luck dreams," said the spirit woman who lives on Mt Nairowua. We call her Almas now.

Almas sticks out her tongue at Diamond in mischief. I see a red rose petal on her tongue move with the teasing words she is learning to shape.

"You are chewing rose petals again and so early in the morning? Go, spit it out! One day the little dudu bug hiding in the petal will bite your tongue." I try to discourage the habit, but Almas loves the taste of rose flower on her tongue and I know my threat will not work. About her age, was I not like her? Hawa and I used to keep rose petals on our tongues until they disintegrated into spit. Then we swallowed them and put fresh ones on the tongue.

I feel guilty that Kabir, whose room is not even next to the children's room as my bedroom is, could hear their cries during the storm and he, not me, went to calm them. I was lost listening to the passion that the turbulent music of a rainstorm summons in me - the passion of a woman wanting to be loved.

Waves like flocks of feather

When strong winds blow through Nairowua heading towards Mt Nairowua, and when dark clouds soar over the summit of the mountain, the same winds slide down the slopes with rain. It's time to close the windows before the gales come roaring in and push the frames off the hinges.

It continues to rain for the next three days, starting mostly in the evenings around dua-prayer time. That's saa moja, the first hour of dark in Swahili. Rain pours into the night turning to light drizzle in the morning. It's difficult to walk to the jamat khana through muddy pools and showers. We leave home as soon as there is a break in the rains. Zarina and I return home in the dark soaking wet on some nights with our sandals drooping down from one hand and, in the other, we hold naandi in plastic bags.

"You will not believe it!" whispers Khanu Bai when she sees me in the jamat khana library. She had arrived the previous day from Nairobi. "The savannah is under water, flat like the kitchen senio tray," she says showing me her palms joined and facing up. Damji Bhai Jetha, the librarian, hisses from his desk loud enough for the three women browsing at the shelves to turn around. They each give us glances one after the other making it obvious we are intruding into their quiet time. We go out to talk more.

The next day in the shop Ole Lekakeny says the same, "The plains are Ol-pun-yata, a lake from horizon to horizon.," he teaches me to say 'Ol-pun-yata', that means Flood Plains in Maasai.

I remember what Khanu Bai said to me last evening "Merali Bus," she said, "stood wedged in the mud for two days and two nights in the middle of the water. Mowla only knows how I survived! Thank Mowla I had a full thermos of tea and some chapattis and kebabs. We could not leave the bus. Children urinated in the bus. Men stepped down into the water. We women ..." She did not complete the sentence.

"Zebras, giraffes, gazelles, and all God's creatures on the grassland have climbed up higher onto the hills, all the way from the Maasai Plains of Kajiado to the Mara," says Ole Lekakeny.

"Fathers and boys from all the homesteads follow the paths made by the savannah's feral animals. They go with their donkeys, goats and cows up the hills. The women go separately with children to the homes on high pastures," says Ole Lekakeny.

Every evening in the jamat khana, we say tasbihs standing up for the end of the famine caused by the flood. These are followed by prayers for the end of the uprising against the English rule in Kenya. We pray for peace to return to the land.

"This year brings floods to Kilimanjaro with the rain winds, *si-ndio* - is that not so?" says Ole Lekakeny. "Elders have left their hearths and gone into solitude. They gather on Ol Donyo Lengai, the most aged and wisest of all the mountains of the Great Valley. Its wrinkles have

86

furrowed deeper in this season's rainwater. When the elders left to pray, they took with them sacrificial animals of all colours pure and unblemished of birth marks and fight marks. Then those on the other side of Ol Donyo Keri's patterned head are raising machetes to soak the earth red. That will anger her. We pray for beauty of peace to return to the land."

For the next three days, I listen to the winds that come gushing through the Ol-debbei tree at the front veranda and then to the sound of hailstones thrashing the sheet iron roof. Fear grips me at times. As a child, I remember how the floods of Nairobi terrified me. I remember the sudden change in our walking paths, the pauses in our daily routines, the silence in the bazaar, and the emptiness in the jamat khana. We sat longer hours by the red glow of the kitchen stove because the light bulbs died. That was when the bridge over the swamp river was washed away by the roaring waters. It was an old wooden bridge that the workers of Nairobi called Daraja ya Nyanjiru. Mary Muthoni Nyanjiru was the anti-pass protest leader who demanded the release of Harry Thuku. It was Harry Thuku who had called on the workers of Nairobi to burn the kipande-pass like Gandhi had previously done in South Africa. Then, like Gandhi, he too was arrested. There was a massacre, and Mary Muthoni Nyanjiru was killed. How could I forget her story? I was born that day in March 1922 in the Indian Bazaar. The day that would change the story of Kenya.

Far at the back of the open courtyard, intermittent currents of humid air flap the loose tin roof over the pit latrine booth under the lone Ol-tepesi acacia. Here the aged giraffe with a slit ear, browses at sunrise before the people leave their houses. For now, Haiderali will temporarily need to nail down the roof over the pit latrine before the next downpour. But will he have time? Does he ever have time nowadays to fix things in the house? Like to fix the broken handle of the pressing iron or replace the missing screw on the shelf bracket, or repair the kitchen window that's hanging on hinges? Meanwhile, I will tell Kamau to put some rocks on the roof of the pit latrine so it does not fly away with the blundering winds. We recently employed Kamau to assist Freda with house work.

Other animals - jackals, wild dogs and hyenas, prowl the streets at night like they own the town looking into garbage dumps. We keep the chickens secured with iron mesh netting over their houses like how the white missionaries keep their chickens in the yard. Deep dark cumulus clouds hang in the weighed down sky.

I see the clouds in the eyes of poet Kalidas - full pregnant Indian women, their kohl dappled eyes and blackened elongated nipples tender on burdened breasts. I gaze at gold zari streaks edged by silhouettes when the sun glimpses past the laden black. Not a leaf moves, not an animal babbles. The savannah in the moment of calm before the thunderstorm stirs Krishna Bhagti, that is Saheb Bhagti, that is the path to God Bhagti, the meditation. The meditation that keeps Mama Khelele to the distant portal of my mind. I want to play the divine flute, dance the garba, put my eyes into Saheb's own and absorb his darshan-deedar. Or else embroider zari, make bead necklaces in my imagination and sing the welcome rain songs of Kalidas, the poet of Gujarat, to the African sky about to open up and drench the earth.

Meditating into beauty of rain, my mind finds quietness away from the noises in my head. All my thoughts converge into the sights and sounds of Africa in a rainstorm, and then when Om hums in my head, I ponder on its drone. How Om has many languages, many colours, many feelings of beauty like tones of dawn. Ali-Om is even bigger. It's vast like the savannah's landscape and rains on the plains together. Like Satpanth, my universe.

I often hear Ole Lekakeny speak about the land and rains. He too has been meditating on the beauty of the two. They call him the storyteller of the savannah. The elder who spends the night alone in the Forest of the Lost Child.

"It's now the season of ol-opir le nkare. That is the season of flocks of water-feathers like courting ostrich pairs running on flapping wings over the savannah. It's also the season of great beauty of rivers and making dreams," he says.

Land is the ornament of God

At night, I keep awake wondering what the new designs of Muain Sidain would look like. They would be fashioned by women's fingers at the homesteads when their exhaustive wanderings of the eyes over the land searching for art finally bring them to deliberations. It would be then when the deliberations are concluded and consultations across the savannah are done, that a pattern is agreed upon. The new pattern will be called Ol-nyankusi, so named after the upcoming age set of young warriors. Their name suggests 'those-who-capture-for-themselves', meaning they are independent and self-providers.

Every night as I stare in the dark, I imagine how the artists in the homesteads would be working out the new designs in lines of beads balancing the colours of nature. Would they lay them on the ground as I did? Would it come from the geography of mountains and hills over the savannah, or would it emerge from patterns of the mighty River Mara in torrents, or the languorous River Athi at the far borderland of Maasai and the Kamba? It would be even from studies of coats of some feral and some homestead animals, looking at them now with different eyes. Or it would be from the silence of the yellow crispy grasses and the cloudless sky. Anything tranquil is beautiful and can inspire art. Beauty is peace too, they say, do they not? Or perhaps, this time, art will emerge from the first raindrops becoming waves of feather. Whatever the inspiration, colour codes matter. These colour codes are not easily deciphered by the eye alone for they have to be put to the mind and read in the language of trees, mountains and rivers. The language of nature that tells you about the legends and mysteries of the Maasai universe. Like a seeker, I put my eyes to Maasailand art for a moment of contentment. The contentment of the native in embrace of her birthland.

One thing is certain. This season will see rejoicings like never seen before and for that, many bodies, males and females, will be adorned in such a manner as to show eloquence in abundance that beauty of the land celebrates. That is custom. That is indigenous. Many beads will be needed for display on the store's veranda where I sit in the afternoon. There will be much work for me when the new stock arrives. I will need help.

~ ~ ~

Ole Lekakeny

My name is Ole Lekakeny. My name means Dawn for I was born when the colours in the sky were pure. Dawn is the most auspicious time to pray for blessings because at that quiet moment we are surrounded by peace and beauty. It's also the most auspicious time to meditate, reconcile and to forgive and love. Such is the power of the moment of the rising sun.

I was born when the Germans ruled Tanganyika and the British ruled Kenya. They fought heavy battles over the land that belonged to neither of them and they hurt the earth with metal shells that exploded into clouds of poison dust and rock. Indian and African soldiers walked the land like swarms of safari ants. The Europeans divided my homeland without asking our elders, and so Maasailand remains divided to this day into two countries.

The beauty of water in the first rains of the season is revealed to us by children herding goats. They sing the song of the coming rain, describing shapes of clouds and how the black clouds play games with the white ones in the shadow of blue. Their voices are sometimes drowned by thunder but they do not stop singing. Their chorus is relayed from one homestead to another, and it rings across the savannah like an echo.

Ash from savannah fires of the drought months churns in rain pools, soaking the earth and nourishing the grass that would fatten the cows and goats. Once again the zebra, impala, wildebeest, and above all, the tall mosaic giraffe will frolic in the crispy mist blanketing over the rays of the morning sun. Giraffes are the first to walk the blackened earth. Nimbly, they browse through pale green shoots on Ol-tepesi acacias, inviting the grazers to follow them to the grass below. In no time then, green under the blackened earth, tenderer than the first growth will sprout. The second growth will be young, healthy and fresh in colours of the wild olive. These colours will change the smell of air and the art of beads from the last age group.

That's when hard stemmed plants will shoot up and send their roots deep down to the warmth of Ol Donyo Lengai. There, where the elders meet to pray. There, where I would like a ritual performed for me over a sacrifice - an unblemished white goat, so I may live in peace with my ancestors. There, where the roots of the plants release the healing juices of tubers made in the volcanic earth.

"Drink the root water once a day, first thing in the morning when the body has rested and is calm, accepting healing," I tell Moti Bai when I bring the healing tubers from the volcanic earth. She listens well and trusts the roots of the earth.

The twice deferred coming of age ceremony will commence soon after the flood waters have receded. Elders right across the Maasailand will let each other know they have seen footsteps in red mud dry up and crack around the homesteads. We will soon see the herders roaming about the town once again, and know the Maasai have descended from the hills. It's the time of joy when creativity in bead art will flourish.

This season Diamond's mother and I will need help in the shop to collect, sort, and arrange beads that bring new designs. These will be creations of women's art celebrating men and themselves as mothers od new warriors. The coming age of Ol-nyankusi warriors will be the most celebrated in memory. Young green of the wild olive has returned to the savannah after a long season of murky colours and drowned grasses.

Kini and Ntinti will bring some samples of the new bead patterns for me and Moti Bai to see as before. We will learn how to see the art of this new age of men through women's minds. We will narrow our eyes and look deep into the tones, shines and shades. It will be a new way to see art of the new age, and know the ornament of God, our land, the way we did not know.

Safari to buy beads

It's chilly in the room where I am sitting at my dressing table removing hairpins, one by one and scratching my scalp. The sweet fragrance of Ayurveda oils rises from my hair as I undo my braid. A thick lustrous darkness like a black aura hangs around me. I listen to torrents of water running from roof gutters down to the side of the wall into the overflowing water tanks. Diamond's song, laughter, and yelps of 'Chal! Chal! - Let's go! Let's go!' riding on Kabir's back are only just audible. The horse trots on all fours to Mombasa, to his grandmother, Ma Gor Bai:

ડાગ માગ ચાલે મારો ધોળી	*Trot trot walks my horse*
ચાલ ધોળી ચાલ મોંમબાસા	*Let's go horse let's go to Mombasa*

"Why this sudden safari to Nairobi, Haidu?" I ask impulsively. At such moments words do not come easily to my tongue, and when they do, they jump out of my mouth in anger. Haiderali is lounging on the bed reading *Chakram*, his monthly magazine of jokes that arrived just that evening with the delayed Merali Bus from Nairobi. Every evening for the last three days, he grumbled about the overdue delivery of *Chakram*. If it was my *Africa Samachar* that was delayed, he would not even know it. Now I hear him laughing to himself, his eyes glued on the comic double page in the middle.

"The roads will be wet and slippery for some days until the sun gains strength," I tell him. He does not hear me.

My voice quakes. "In the jamat khana, people talk about the Mau Mau in Nairobi." To clear my throat, I fake a sharp khokharo cough like that of my grandfather Dadabapa. "Khanu Bai's parents live in Nyeri, you know, near Mt Kenya. They speak Kikuyu, you know. She tells me it is not safe to travel to Nairobi. Mt Kenya has not been at peace since the riots of the women against the ban on girls' circumcision. Then came Hitler's war and thousands of Kikuyu men were taken into the English army. And now the Mau Mau." I remember Gangandeep kaka uncle coming to Dadabapa's shop to collect funds for Kikuyu Independent Schools and at the same time pass on news from the night paper. Now, some say those schools were classrooms of the Mau Mau rebels and curse those who supported them in name of education..

"Don't listen to your Khanu Bai, and bring her panic home. I am not a missionary opposing women's circumcision or a colonial land grabber. I am a bead merchant," responds Haiderali. I watch him through my own reflected movements of hands, while also listening to the rain pattering the roof. My hair flows like ebony waves through the comb. Scooping up a creamy blob of firmed coconut oil, I rub it back and forth into my scalp feeling the comforting pressure of my fingertips. I want Haiderali's covetous eyes to follow my massaging fingers, gliding over my hair, running to my neck. My heart thuds, my hands slacken. He ignores me. His eyes are on *Chakram*, he smiles to the women in the cartoons.

"Are you listening to what I am saying?" I ask.

95

"Kabir and I decided about the safari some nights ago. All arrangements have been made. The bus will be arriving tomorrow night. We are short of beads in all the colours of Muain Sidain of the new patterns. It's time of graduation ceremonies this year."

"But Haidu, must you travel in two days?" I ask to disguise the fear creeping into me. "Khanu Bai told me the Mau Mau burnt the Tree Tops Lodge in the Aberdares." While seated facing the mirror, I look at my eyes in the reflection, hoping they would meet his. But he is not searching my eyes today to make a hint. He does not want me today. I adjust my dress, lifting it up from the shoulders and dropping it at my feet so the blue flowers fall spreading around me as in a bride's sari.

"The king's daughter, Elizabeth, entered the forest in the evening, a princess. In the morning she emerged a queen. God Save the Queen!" Haiderali responds singing mockingly. "God save Queen Elizabeth Alexandra Mary! The new anthem reverberated in the jungles of Kenya before the BBC played it. Mau Mau detests this safari lodge on their land transformed into an English monument overnight." I am aware of the talk in the jamat khana about the burning of the Tree Tops Lodge, but *Africa Samachar* has been silent apart from a three line news item.

"The Mau Mau count us with the English. We must be careful. Not show sides."

"I am no English royalty or the DC. What have the Mau Mau to do with me? I am a bead merchant not a bloody settler on their homelands. I am loyal only to my customers," says Haiderali. "Maasai eunoto rituals are due. Our customers are expecting us to have enough beads in their right colours, sizes, shapes, lustres and prizes to adorn

96

their families. New retailers at Kilimanjaro and Ol Donyo Lengai are already asking for more beads. We have only a little stock left. Three boxes? It takes months for Maasai mothers to prepare all the sets of ornaments that they will be wearing this year. Emergency or no emergency, I have to go to Nairobi." All of a sudden, for a second, a streak of lightning sparks on the windowpane like a flashlight, brightening the red rose and green liana prints on the curtains. I wait to hear the crack of thunder, and then, wait again for the ensuing distant rolling rumbles to subside before continuing to speak again.

"Can you not delay your trip until the rains are over, Haidu? Next week, when the Merali Bus returns?" He knows I am more concerned about the Mau Mau than the rains. He knows next week, I will find another excuse to dissuade him and delay him again.

"No!" he whacks the magazine down at his side. "You will not let me read in peace! No safari? Until when? Until the rains are over? Until the emergency is over? Churchill says the problems of East Africa are the problems of the world. I heard it on the radio. Shall I wait until all the problems of the world are solved only to go to Nairobi? We will declare bankruptcy while waiting for troubles of Africa to be solved!"

"What does Churchill mean?"

"I don't know," says Haiderali in a calmer tone now having had his outburst. "Listen, Moti Bai, all arrangements have been made. I have told you this before. Listen one more time. I have given my word to Rajan Lalji bapa. We had agreed he would give me the beads on credit before chandraat and I would settle the accounts by the next new moon. I need to clear the account with him to get more

97

beads. We can sell the beads in the coming month before the eunoto season begins." He is reading again and I hear his laughter rumbling over the pattering rain on the tin roof.

"Must you go in two days, Haidu? Before the roads are little dry? The new moon of chandraat is two weeks away. Why not travel next week."

"I do not want to be late. My word is my honour," says Haiderali heaving a sigh. "Your wasi wasi wavering anxiety will bring bad luck of kisirani to journey!"

"God be with you then! Have you given thought to the insurgency, Haiderali Devji?" My voice cracks. I am annoyed and resign from talking more.

"Trust the English. How can a primitive band of rebels calling themselves Mau Mau, wielding machetes, stand against the Empire? Only ten years ago, the English defeated German army equipped to the teeth with machine guns, bombers and tanks." Haiderali talks with disdainful confidence. "We need a watchdog. That's what we need now. Mamdu and Rhemu have brought dogs home. Did you know? People say dogs are good for security. Keep strangers away from the courtyard. "

"I don't like dogs."

"A dog is like a guard. You will feel safer."

"But I don't like dogs."

"He will be kept leashed in the courtyard. At night he can be set loose. Khanu Bai and Zera Bai don't seem to mind dogs even if they don't like them. They know the animals are there for their safety."

"Who will feed the dog?"

98

"Kamau will make maize meal with meaty bones for the dog."

"Your dog will mess my courtyard. You know I spread lentils and pickle mangoes in the sun. I take beddings into the courtyard, the children play in there."

"Kamau will keep the courtyard clean."

I see Haiderali is determined to bring a dog. How can he do that? He knows I don't like dogs in my courtyard. Besides that, I want to raise chickens, not dogs. I keep quiet. He changes the subject, "Do some of my shop work when I am gone. Count the cash in the evening after closing the duka-store, and Kabir will enter it in the accounts book. Keep Saheb's tithe money aside. Take the stock of things if I am delayed for more than a month, and make space for the new stock of beads from Nairobi. I have told Kabir to order six dozen brown paper bags, medium and small sizes, and a large size ball of sisal twine. Check what other items - Vicks, Aspero, match boxes - we get a special discount on Three Stars from the wholesaler Magan Bhai. Also check if Ten Cents cigarettes need replacement on the front shelves. Tell Kabir what we need. Don't forget to take the tithe money to the jamat khana every day. I want my safari to be safe and successful."

"Tik *chhe*," I reply, "but I need Zarina to help Ole Lekakeny with the beads when she comes back from school. She is fifteen and should do some work in the shop. She does not have to go to play badminton every day. We are coming closer to the eunoto ceremony as you say." Haiderali listens, keeping quiet. "Ole Lekakeny is getting old. He sleeps in his chair in the afternoons until Ole Kitungat comes to fetch him."

"Who is Ole Kitungat?"

"Don't you remember? He is Kini's, son. He was born soon after I came to Nairowua. She is the one you sent the sampu calf to. We visited them. Don't you remember? They say Ole Kitungat has lazy legs. He would not make a good herder. He keeps losing goats, so they sent him to the mission school. He lives with Ole Lekakeny in Majengo."

"Help from a teenage boy is a blessing for an old man living alone," says Haiderali.

The stress of worrying about Haiderali awakens her. She sleeps in my head so furtively that her voice is not apparent outside, even as it causes a storm in my head so much so that she drives sleep away. The next evening going to the jamat khana, I daub kohl under my eyes to brighten the dimness of their light and mask the shadows below. I put on a pachedi-shawl with a stiff zari border, and pull it forward, just a little more than usual over the edge of my forehead so the sparkle would deflect peering looks into my face that would prompt them to ask, "Kem Moti Bai, tik chhe? - Why Moti Bai, are you not well?" One short question that sounds superfluous and innocent yet probes deep.

My nose adornment

The next evening, sitting before the mirror of the dressing table as I do every night before going to bed, I see Haiderali stretched out on the bed in his white perforated vest and pyjama pants. The look on his face tells me he is uneasy. He is not reading *Chakram*, perhaps, he is done with the cartoons. His eyes dart from my back to the wall and rests on my hair. I am combing my hair to the side to relax the day's stress on the roots at the parting in the middle. I make a new parting at the side and then two loose uneven braids that fall in front over my chest. Haiderali's look tells me, he is thinking of something else not me. Something he wants to say. Like how to word a concern or is he going to finally make me feel guilty for being unkind to his mother? Will he blame me for her death? I can hear what he will say calculating his tone so it hurts, "You killed my mother and I could not tell you to stop." I have seen such a look on him before. It's not a love look. But it's not a hate look either. It's a look of regret like blaming himself. Perhaps, he is puzzling over postponing his safari tomorrow. Perhaps, he will say he will wait for more news about the Mau Mau from Nairobi. Perhaps, he will use an agent like Magan Bhai, to do business for him in Nairobi.

Then, when he starts to speak, it's in deliberate sentences, "Business is picking up but not that well. We need more money for stocking beads for the eunoto rites. If we have sufficient amount of beads in the store, we can sell them quickly and make a profit big enough to pay our debt and even invest in more stock." I narrow my eyes. Why is he telling me about business, something he does not usually talk about to me? I become suspicious and keep still, saying nothing. The rain has been sporadic this evening. But when it falls, it's sudden, in gusts lashing at the tin roof, the side walls, and then it subsides as quickly as it comes.

"I need money," says Haiderali tapping his nose. Silence. Uneasiness devours me like a sensation of fright running through my body. "Why do you not respond?" he asks after a while trying to probe into my petulant silence. I take my time combing my hair before turning around facing the soles of his bare feet. Outside in the lull between the downpours, I hear the water tanks gurgling and tossing the overflow into muddy rivulets rushing towards the stream at the rocks in the acacia copse. Haiderali pulls up the quilt and covers himself to the waist. How can I respond? My thoughts make me numb, my tongue is constricted. Is he suggesting that I give him my diamond nose siri-button to raise money for the beads and pay off his debt? That's the only ornament of value left on my body. How can I do that? How can he do that to me? My nose siri-button is the adornment of my marriage, like the ginan is the ornament of Satpanth.

"Take the two yellow gold bangles in the safe, your mother's bangles," I say.

"No!" he snaps. "They are sacred. Ma gave them to you. Always have them with you. Besides that, we need more money than the value of the bangles."

We remain quiet for a while, and I let the past feelings of these kisirani, meaning ill-fated bangles run through my body, letting them go. I don't want to think

102

about Ma at this time of the evening. The rain has cooled the heat of the tin roof. A chill sets in.

"When times are better, we can stock up for many years to come," he dares to say, oblivious to the expression on my face that changes from confusion to anger. I feel the wife's muted distress such as the one that comes from resignation to the will of the husband. In it is a hurting resentment that I can do nothing about. A resentment of hopelessness. I stop questioning his intention. I stop myself from breaking into tears because I want no sympathy from Haiderali. I do not want him to put his hand on me and say, "Everything will be alright, trust me, my heart, my Nargis."

"After the floods the pastures are lush, and green like new leaves of wild olive. Maasai's cattle will double in number. There is plenty of milk already in the market. The acacias are teeming with honey bees," says Haiderali feeling light hearted and clear in mind, "the pastoralists are prospering and so shall we." I do not reply, not even with m…m… that I would hum in politeness when unsure of whether to say yes or no. My lips seal my first response. Haiderali's talk is vanki chuki vaat, that is not straight talk, and that sickens me. I lift my dress to the ankles in readiness to walk away to the courtyard and into the rain. The water and the wind will absorb what's stifling me.

"We can furnish the house with the furniture you always wanted from Ahmed Brothers, and even buy some land to build a house, you know, near the Greek plantation. We will build a bungalow," Haiderali coaxes me. He sweet talks to accommodate his lie. Like last year when he sold my gold chain to buy beads from the merchant across the border in Tanganyika who had gone bankrupt. "You can plant roses and jasmine, even have a fruit garden that you

103

always wanted." I do not say a word. I am sulking within, without any outward expression on my face. "What shall I bring you from Nairobi?" I don't reply. "This time, I will not forget the picture of the sugar faced English boy with tears on his chubby pink cheeks. So meetho sweet, snow white yet melancholy. Rhemu told me where he got the picture you saw in their house."

I say nothing. Haiderali is asking me to give him my nose siri-button, not my opinion. As he continues talking, I feel like being pounded in my own kitchen mortar.

"I need the money now to buy more beads. Buy a water tank and I think we should join a higher mandali prayer group in the jamat khana. What do you say?" He coaxes me. It will bring prestige to me when Haiderali is admitted into a prayer group of a higher order. How can I say no? It would be an exclusive group in the hierarchy of a reticent structure to which Zera Bai and Rhemu Bhai belong. Perhaps, Haiderali will be able to buy more stock from wealthy Khoja wholesalers in Nairobi who are members of the trusted order. The magazine by his side slips down from the bed. It sits on the polished cement open at the middle double page. I see a cartoon of a large sari clad woman sitting in the middle of a room. Pointing at the cartoon, Haiderali tells me, "See it says Partition," and he laughs aloud. He does not pick the magazine up.

Some things need to be done when the time comes. Women make sacrifices in business families. That is tradition. But what will people say? Haiderali unstraps his Roamer wristwatch and begins to wind it between his tobacco stained fingers before laying it on the side table for the night. He is ready to sleep which annoys me. Does he think what he just said is nothing to upset me about? Does he just want to leave me to sleep with the feelings he has left me with? Anger-sadness-disgust-irritation-distress-resignation take turns in my mind.

To save face, I sold my marriage gold set - earrings, bracelets and the necklace, piece by piece. That helped to continue running the bead business when there were no customers like during the recent floods and the drought before the floods. I feel the weight of my duty to my husband in his time of need, but submitting to it would be painful. To remove my seven diamonds nose siri-button from my body would be humiliating. It is not honourable for a woman of my status and age to be de-adorned. The bandhani and the nose siri-button were entrusted to me and I must bequeath them to my daughter-in-law, Diamond's wife, so she may be adorned with honour as she steps over the threshold into my house and takes over the responsibility from me of running the family home. I have a ruby ring too, but I do not think of it as my own because it belongs to my sister, Monghi Bai, who lives in Kisumu with her husband. She too has a son.

"When we grow richer, I will bring back your diamond nose siri-button, even a bigger one," promises Haiderali. "The business is doing well, but with a little more capital we can do better." There is silence in the room, but for the sound of the storm rain strumming over the tin roof into the quiet of darkness. He sees the bead business like a tree. It must keep growing bigger and bigger, and bear more and more fruit. Otherwise, it dies.

I rest my head on the pillow and wish I could run away with the receding storm. I cannot go to Ma Gor Bai who loves me like her own stomach child, but at marriage she disowned me like every Khoja mother who disowns her daughter yet continues to love her. That is custom. A mother's happiness is to see her daughter live at a distance, not with her. I think of the weaverbirds on the Ol-lerai tree chirping free and joyful around their swinging drooping nests in the afternoon heat. I listen to the rains return and then pottering to a stop, and then the dogs start barking as they begin night games. Their barking does not disturb me the way it disturbs Haiderali. I imagine the dogs of Nairowua sprinting and running in the moonlight, free of the demands of their masters. They would be ransacking bins, making and breaking relationships in the dark, and I yearn to be where they are. Their barks deepen the night's space. Then comes the hungry hyenas' ha ha hacking from the river forest, wrapping over the woofs and yaps of town dogs. I want to dissolve into their world and let the sounds of feral animals absorb the thoughts of shame speaking in my constricted body.

As if in protest to my silence, Haiderali puts on his pyjama shirt and leaves the room. Now on the veranda he sits at the dining table. He does not light the lantern or candle. The familiar crusty sharp smell of raw tobacco of Ten Cents cigarette comes into the bedroom through the slit open door and it irritates me. I remember the time when my father's business was not doing well at Jugu Bazaar in Nairobi, and he asked Ma Gor Bai to forfeit her ornaments. There was tension in the home for many weeks when Ma Gor Bai, unlike me, protested loudly so Dadabapa, the family head, could hear the shame called sharam befalling her, before finally parting with her dowry that she came with from India.

How Haiderali's mother, Ma Jena Bai used to instruct me! "We are Momnas of Saurashtra. When

106

Aurangzeb came, he looted Satpanth villages, imprisoned the pir and killed the men. The women crushed, stamped and made plaster of hay, dung and mud, and built the homes again. He burnt the harvest. The women ploughed the fields and harvested. . The woman's dowry puts rice on the eating mat when there is none in the house. Was it not my dowry I gave to Haiderali, my son, to buy beads when we arrived in Nairowua?"

Never to fall into the pit of dependency of mothaj was what I had learned early in life. Thoughts churn in mind like a whirling storm. That was how we understood freedom. That was how we understood dignity. That was how we understood honour. In fact, to a Khoja there is no difference between freedom, dignity and honour. To be free of mothaj is the ethic we carried from the villages of our Satpanth forefathers. It was better for a wife to give up her sacred gold, than for the husband to beg a handful of rice for his children from the community. That would make him a mothaj, a slave who does not own his own livelihood. It was better for the wife to be unadorned than for the husband to be shackled to a chain of obligations. Mothaj would keep the family in a cage of shame called sharam. Is this not the reason why we, the Satpanth Ismailis, pray each day in the jamat khana for Mowla to keep us free of mothaj?

My story weaves feelings that shape my words. Without feelings, there would be no words that come from my heart. Once again I sing Wasikia to remember how I must tell my tale. I had learned the song from my maid and child care taker, Hawa who was also my companion when I was little. Hawa sang Wasikia like a lullaby while rocking me to sleep in the cradle of her arms with my ear pressed to her heart and my body in the warmth of hers both covered in one kanga. We were two girls, children in embrace listening to the hyenas' mirth breaking through Hawa's heartbeat over the melody of Wasikia.

To listen to my story you must listen to my heart
Like how you listen to the smell in Swahili
Wasikia harufu? Do you hear the smell?
Or listening to how the cold enters your body
Wasikia baridi? Do you hear the cold?
Or even listening to joy in your heart you say
Wasikia raha? Do you hear happiness?
To feel the pain in Swahili is to listen to the pain
Wasikia uchungu? Do you hear pain?
When you listen to my story listen to your body
When I ask Wasikia? Are you listening?
I also mean, are you feeling?

Freda and Kamau

While preparing the breakfast table, as is her morning routine after feeding and dressing up the children for school, Freda talks with Jennifer, who is sitting on the grass in the courtyard in bright morning sun with her legs stretched out in front. Jennifer, a recently employed caregiver ayah of the demented woman who lives down the street, has come to borrow sugar for her mama. I hear Kabir's whispered voice from the washroom teasing Freda, calling her Farida, lovingly mimicking Ma who could not remember the name of our house help even after constant right name lessons from him. During the day, I see how sixteen year old Freda, the Kamba girl from the Catholic Mission of Nairowua, plays with my children. How happy they are when she sings to them while gives them a bath. Sometimes, she would take them to the vegetable market, Almas snuggled on her back in a kanga sling and Diamond walking by her side, complaining, protesting, wanting to be carried too. Looking at Freda padding barefoot on the powdery red earth, I would often think of Hawa, our maidservant in Nairobi when I was little. How she used to take me around Jugu Bazaar, sometimes on her back in a kanga wrap, sometimes, I walked by her side with her little finger hooked into my big finger. We walked barefoot along the shaded shop verandas and the cracked red murrum roads of Nairobi. But my children wear Bata tennis shoes and clothes that are washed and ironed daily.

Freda has spread a green cloth over the old teak table, covering its patina created out of constant swabbing of ghee and curries with damp kitchen cloth. Haiderali calls this blotched shredded rag, stained brown and well passed its time, but always around offering itself to be used, Ma's masoto rag. It's a piece of cloth from my worn out cotton dress that was handed down to me from Ma because it was too tight for her on the stomach. I remember the patterns still visible in faded colours on the masoto cloth.

As I pass the dining table, a stale smell of curry from the green tablecloth just spread out hits me. The tablecloth has large hand size darkened spots, each looped with a ring of ghee that has absorbed into the fabric, leaving a pungent spicy oil film on top.

"Freda!" I call out and in no time she is standing before me. "You have not changed this table cloth for months, have you? Change it today after breakfast. Make sure you replace the table cloth once a week. I have told you this before. I don't have to repeat it every week. And soak the masoto rag tonight in hot water. Add a teaspoon full of bicarbonate to the water. Give it to Kamau to wash it tomorrow. Now hurry up. Do you hear me?" Sometimes, I wonder if she understands me when I see her face blank as clay slate before me. "Do you hear me - nasikia?" I repeat. The same face again. Freda's Swahili is limited. She speaks like the local politician, and like Kamau who was brought up in Kikuyuland.

Few in Nairowua speak the Swahili I grew up with in companionship with Hawa and her father, Askari Bakari, both native speakers of the language and with my stepmother, Ma Gor Bai, a Zanzibari herself. It was the coastal Swahili of poets and storytellers, and of singers of

110

taraab and sailors that I spoke with the three of them. It would be the Swahili of the Indian Ocean. It would be the Swahili of the Quran and navigation over the infinite waters guided by stars and the wind, and songs of the trade caravans of the Swahili over the land. It would be the Swahili prose of the palaces of Zanj kingdoms; the Swahili of slave masters and of rebellions. That's the Swahili born of a civilization forged over a millennium of meeting of the ocean languages and a myriad of vernaculars rich in the grammar and metaphors of the land of this verdant continent. The fact that as an Asian, I speak better Swahili than Freda and Kamau baffles them.

Sometimes, I catch myself becoming breathless admonishing Freda and Kamau in my seamless harangue, always speaking down to them. When I look at myself through Hawa's eyes, I know I am commanding, reminding and correcting, never listening. I know somewhere in the distant part of my head where I do not go anymore, how I speak to Freda and Kamau comes from our difference. My tone makes that known. The kind of tone that says I am above you. I employ you. Even my words when spoken with measured politeness cannot veneer over our difference. How we dress our prejudices in questions and taunts thought of in Indian minds and said in Swahili that befuddles the African. My heart was with Hawa, my maid in Nairobi when we were both girls, she four years older, my companion until I got married. How she would be hurt by hissing grimaces of someone or other in the house. She told me because she was black, we did not care about her feelings.

I know Freda knows I belong to my race and to its manner of talking to servants. In fact, we talk like that to all blacks as if it were expected of Asians like we were born with it. That's how Haiderali's mother, Ma Jena Bai, spoke to Freda, the schoolgirl from the Catholic mission. Speaking to Freda, her sentences more often than not started with wewe, she pronounced veve, like an accusation, not a gentle u before a verb that softens commands in Swahili. She knew she miscalled Freda and so avoided her name. Never saying asante thankyou or tafadali please to the servant. Moreover, Ma's Swahili words sounded like they were dunked in Gujarati like biscuit in chai. But when I told Stepmother Gor Bai what Hawa said to me, she replied, "And such arrogance grows with wealth and school education. We develop heads of Khoja slave masters. They were many of us among the wealthy Indian slavers of Zanzibar when the Sultans ruled. But there were also amongst us those who were servants and poor peasant folks who fled from the famines in India. It was like that. Now when the English rule, Indian workers are spoken to by rich Indians of the bazaar like the English to them. It is like that."

I try to change my tone. Calm and controlled now, I ask Freda again, "Freda, tell me, do you understand what I am saying?" But even as I speak, I know my voice has no conviction. How could it? It's my class voice speaking. The voice of authority in the house. Voice of the master. The voice of a superior race. The voice of the privileged. The voice of an Asian.

Or is it because I think she is tempting Haiderali with her body in the bloom of puberty? My questioning myself does not calm me and I try not to ask myself so many more questions that in the end, have no answers, just irritations from my imaginings.

112

"I will be going to the vegetable market later, after bwana has left for Nairobi," I continue to say. Intentionally, I put my eyes to the money plant to show she needs to water it. The plant has climbed up the wall of the inside veranda where the old teak table stands and where we dine. From the pot that stands on a stool by the washbasin, I have trained it to go upwards, to pass behind Saheb's Diamond Jubilee poster and then bending to the side towards Saheb's new photograph. It's the picture that Haiderali had cut out from Africa Ismaili and had it framed. Saheb is wearing a pin-lined striped three-piece suit and walking with a stride, smiling broadly, holding a tall black cylinder hat in one hand, and a walking stick in the other. His broad smile of happiness - because his horse wins the Derby, brings blessings of happiness to the home, never mind why he smiles.

Every morning I give routine instructions to Freda and Kamau like reciting my memorized prayers, and just as hastily. "I will pass by Mama Maridadi - we will go to the market together - I will be late - meanwhile, dust the furniture and sweep the rooms before mopping the floor sawa sawa - don't forget to dust under the beds and corners sawa sawa - use the new broom. Keep the washed clothes together to iron in the afternoon. Wash the tablecloth separately - don't stand at the karo talking to each other the whole day - do the breakfast dishes carefully - I don't want to see chipped edges again - cut two onions, thin slices - peel some ginger and garlic. Today Kamau can go to collect Diamond and Almas from school - and don't pass by your friends for a chat on your way back. Give warm milk with Ovaltine to the children when you return - little sugar - there are some Marie biscuits in the tin on the kitchen shelf - prepare chapatti dough - I will cook when I return. It

113

depends on what vegetables I get at the market. Don't waste time talking with each other the whole day."

Freda's dress is oversize, chequered blue and white. It has several stitches that burst open on the ball of her shoulder revealing her roast coffee skin. It's my old dress from Ma that I had shortened for Freda. I will give her a needle and thread when I come back from the market. I try to remember where I have kept my sewing things. On top of the clothes cupboard? Or in the drawer of the bedside table? One of the two places. I know they are in the Cadbury tin.

Stories in my head are like pictures in elegant frames on walls of the jamat khana library remembering men and women who built the community. They made our schools, clubs, clinics, social and prayer halls. Each memory picture in my head lives silently like the wall picture in the library separated from the other until its particular thought is awakened by a smell or sight, touch or sound, or even taste of something that would stir up an incident or an image. Framed stories are like framed pictures on the wall for each one tells its tale yet stays within its borders. Together they make many frames that makes one story.

~ ~ ~

Freda

My name is Freda. Fatha Dakitari at the Catholic Mission arranged for me to work for the Devji Momna family. I was fifteen years old and I had just completed my

114

primary school. My mother, who works at the mission, could not afford to send me to Nairobi to continue studying. That's what she told me but I think there were other reasons. I think she did not want me to go to the city without her because of what she had heard about other girls from our village. Some of them became prostitutes because they were poor and jobless in the big city full of men.

My mother herself belongs to the maweto group of women in Ukambani. That's how Kambaland is called in Swahili. We are Kamba people and among us there is an ancient custom that allows women to marry women. Such a marriage, of course, happens only in the traditional way because the priests at our church do not want to hear about such marriages because they do not understand them. And the law does not recognize maweto marriage.

There is a reason why women marry women in Kambaland and it has nothing to do with loving or even sleeping together the way a husband and wife do. The way Christians think of maweto marriage is not what it is. It's like this. When a rich woman cannot conceive naturally or when she becomes a widow and does not wish to marry again because she wants to keep the land, the field and the house of her deceased husband under her control, she takes a wife companion who is usually from a poor family. She pays the bride price of several head of cattle to the father of the girl. She supports her wife companion with all her requirements. Her wife companion is allowed to have man friends but not a husband. When the wife companion has children, they belong to the woman husband. The children inherit the woman husband's property and her name. In all respects, she is a father to them except that she is a woman.

My mother, who is called Nduta, ran away from her marriage because she fell in love with a man called Joseph who worked as a cook for the white missionaries at the Catholic Mission in Nairowua. Joseph had come home to our village called Ngelani on leave, when he started seeing my mother who was his childhood sweetheart. He wanted to marry my mother but could not afford the bride price to buy her back from her rich woman husband, and thus free her from the bondage of a maweto woman. My legal mother, the rich widow, asked for far too many cows from Joseph because she did not want my mother to leave her. She said, "I want Nduta to give me more children for I have fed and clothed her, and paid more cows to her father than any man in the village could afford." That's our custom.

The rich woman was getting old, and Joseph could not wait for her to die, so he persuaded my mother to run away with him carrying me with them. I was two years old and still breast feeding. My mother was reluctant for she feared breaking the customary law. She said to Joseph, "I will be cursed by the elders and made an outcast. My poor father will have to return the bride price. He has already sold the cattle to pay school fees for my brothers. He will be jeered for raising a bad daughter, and even made an outcast by his own peers. That will kill him."

"I will arrange for you to be baptised in the Catholic church in Nairowua. Neither the custom nor the curse will affect you then when you become a Christian," Joseph persuaded my mother. "I will send money to your father in small parts to buy cows to pay back your bride price."

So my mother agreed and they eloped one day when she was sent to Machakos town to buy groceries for her woman husband carrying me tied to her back. That's how I came to Nairowua deep in Maasailand near the big mountain and the river with warm water.

We stayed with Joseph in the quarters that the mission provided him, and both my mother and I were baptised in the church. It was not long before my mother was employed to do the laundry for the priests. When I was seven years old, I started school that was also run by the mission.

However, I was not happy in school because the students came to know I was a daughter of a maweto, and would not be my friends. There were students from different tribes of Kenya and many among them knew about maweto because they have such marriages too, but they keep them hidden to the outside people, the church and the law. However, within the communities they know the maweto children. The new society calls them outcasts.

I was happy to leave the mission and live with the Indian family at the Bead Shop in Nairowua. The Indians don't care and don't want to know who I am. They see all Africans as the same and do not understand our different ways. They only want a servant who works hard, is honest and looks after their children. I sleep in the servant quarters behind the shop. I work every day of the week all day without a break until Sunday. On Sundays, they allow me to go to the church. After the service I meet my friends and visit my aging mother. But the Indians don't know about my mother, or my step-father Joseph, and how I spend my Sundays. They just want to know about themselves, their business and their jamat khana.

The Indians think Kambas are gentle and reliable people who make good servants for them. That's how they speak about Africans among themselves. I understand their language but do not speak it. They call us good or bad, hard-working or lazy according to our tribes as if we are born with tribal characters. They say the Kambas are not Kikuyus who are deceitful and may even kill them. Recently, they have been talking about incidents in Nairobi and some other areas where the Special Branch, that is the secret police, found some Kikuyus at a strange oath taking ceremony at night. The Indians think it was some kind of witchcraft that the Africans do to do evil on others. But rumours of such night ceremonies are spreading in a way that brings fear to the heart. Some Kikuyus were brought to court and imprisoned because it's against the law to practise witchcraft. The prisoners insisted it was their traditional religion that they were practising not witchcraft, and so they were released after a short time in prison.

When Kamau sings Christian hymns, I like to sing with him but sometimes, his words change from praising Our Lord, Christ the Saviour, to praising Kimathi, whom he calls a patriot. They say he is the leader of Mau Mau. Kamau encourages young men with brave hearts to go to the forest, and condemns those who sell themselves into slavery working for the white men. Sometimes, instead of praying to Our Lord in Heaven, he prays to the God on Mt Kenya. I do not know the new words he puts in the old hymns, so I stop singing with him, but I listen. The tunes are the same as the church songs. The Indians think Kamau is a God fearing man. I am afraid of him though he has never touched me nor has he ever spoken to me with harsh words.

One day, Moti Bai asked me if Kamau practises witchcraft. She is suspicious. On some days, when he comes to work, he is so tired that he dozes. Of course, I do not tell her anything bad about Kamau though once I did tell her that Kamau sings his age group songs. His age group songs are warrior songs, actually, they are Mau Mau songs but she would not know that.

I know Moti Bai has doubts like all Indians have nowadays about Africans working in their homes. She cannot just fire Kamau because he has been working for her since he was just a boy, and he can wash and iron clothes to make them look like new. The family is dependent on him like they are on me for all the household work, care of the children and often for their little personal needs like taking the bathing water to the washroom, and running errands around the Indian homes in Nairowua. That's when I see my friends Jennifer and Grace. We have quick talks on small matters. Both Jennifer and Grace work for other Khoja families in town who are friends of my employers, the Devji Momnas of the Bead Shop in Nairowua.

Grace was born and brought up in Nairobi. We call her the smart city girl. She works for Mama Maradadi, the other Khoja lady who adorns herself like a guinea fowl and makes samosas. She is Moti Bai's friend. They call her Zera Bai.

Jennifer is a Kamba like I am but she comes from Kambaland that is far from my home village. My village is near Machakos town surrounded by lush hills and closer to Nairobi. Jennifer's village is in a dry and arid area that borders the Somaili homeland. There are many snakes there like pythons and puff aiders. It's also called the Shifta country where Somali bandits control the roads. Jennifer looks after an old woman whose mind is lost or kichwa potea as we say. Her eyes shift aimlessly like she's searching for her memory.

On Sundays when the three of us meet after the church service, we have long talks, and we cook together at my mother's home in the parish compound. We often joke about our Khoja employers citing what happened in the households during the week.

"When the Khoja go to khane in the evening, I get time to do what I like. I sing Kamba songs, listen to Kamba music on the radio and read Kabir's newspapers. I wish you could join me, but Moti Bai will not allow servants entertaining servants in her home, will she?" I joke about Moti Bai with my friends and they know that.

"Even if we can meet in your Moti Bai's house, I have no free time because I look after the woman with lost head and her eyes shift," says Jennifer. "I take her to khane every evening, and we sit there on the bench outside listening to the breeze, and the hymns they sing inside. The old woman knows the hymns, and sings with others who are inside."

"So she has not completely lost her memory, has she?" I ask.

"She knows the hymns and sings with the chorus but she has to be reminded that she is called Sakar Bai," says Jennifer. "It amazes me that khane songs do not go away from my kichwa-potea, lost-head, mama. Singing into the voices of the chorus is when she feels one with her people. The old woman forgets her own name but not the khane songs. Actually, it's a beautiful moment to see her sing and her eyes are closed."

"My mama, Moti Bai, sings khane songs when she is at home working," I add. "That's the time she is happy and feeling herself. There is something in those songs that the Khoja find magical."

"Anyway, I am planning to move in with Grace next month. We will share the room in the shantytown of Majengo. I will have more time to myself after work, listen to Kamba music and cook our own Kamba food. Will you join us?" I ask Jennifer.

"I wish I could. But it's impossible for me unless I find another job. The lady needs me twenty four hours. Will they allow you to leave their children without a maid at night?"

"I need to move out of the Devji Momna home. The children are big now. They can go to the washroom on their own. I have a feeling Moti Bai wants me to move out of the servants' quarters in her courtyard. I don't like the way she looks at me sometimes. I am looking for another job."

"She suspects you of sleeping with her husband?"

I keep quiet. I am offended by her question though she means no harm. Jennifer changes the conversation quickly.

"How do you manage the children? Do they listen to you? I have no experience looking after Indians' children."

"When they are naughty, I tell them to be good because Mowla Bapa is watching. I point at the photo on the wall. It impels awe and obedience in the children as it does in everyone else in the house. I learnt to say that from their mother."

"You know much about their beliefs and customs?" asks Grace.

"I know how to prepare the dua-prayer food dish for the souls of their ancestors. They have special remembrance days for the dead at khane when they prepare meals for them."

"How did you learn about their beliefs yet they are so secretive about khane?" asks Grace.

"From their daily routines and khane words. They kula-kitchwa-yangu, eat-my-head, ordering me around - Freda, do this, and Freda do that. 'Freda, iron my khane dress - Freda, bring my khane socks.' And the perpetual, 'Freda, hurry up, we will be late for khane!'

They both smile. Grace smiles because my rant reminds her of her own week at Zera Bai's. Jennifer because she finds it funny.

Merali Bus

"Freda!" I call out from the kitchen with my head turned towards the courtyard karo, "when you have washed the breakfast dishes, carry the luggage to Merali Bus."

Having kissed and hugged the children goodbye before they left for school, Haiderali is ready to leave the house. I hand him the Luo reed basket with a curved cane handle top. Then I place a pink tracing paper sachet into his palm. For a second, Haiderali looks at the packet, the size of a coat button tightly wrapped in pink creased paper. Quickly, he pushes it into the top inside pocket of his coat and taps it twice to make sure it is there securely seated in the corner of the inside pocket. The next two taps are light almost bouncy with fluted fingers like he is happy, congratulating himself. Our eyes meet for a fleeting second, but they have no radiance. He does not see my nose is bared of shine.

There is no concealed look in his eyes to suggest guilt, or a hint of apology as in the gesture of shaking the head as polite Indians would do to say, "It's regrettable." Or even a curl of the lip down to show reluctance in accepting my marriage diamonds. He acts as if he was doing no wrong to me. Perhaps, he will forgive me now for making his mother feel a mothaj for I have forfeited my dignity to his possession.

Haiderali begins to complain about Mochi Bhai as if to divert my look to his new pair of shoes, "Saalo Mochi!

123

These shoes are too tight and too many holes for the lace." Smell of raw leather floats up from his shoes.

I had put the tiffin with three compartments and an inverted bowl on top of the Luo basket. In the tifin's bottom compartment is heaped rice, still warm. In the middle, dry kebab curry prepared just so for the safari and in the top compartment, four chapattis and two pieces of mango pickle, a peeled onion and a fresh green chili from the garden. In the inverted bowl at the top of the tiffin, I have placed a saffron stained, orange ladoo. There is buttermilk chaas in one thermos and mixed masala chai in the other, the larger one. Lastly, wedged in at the sides, is a bunch of fat finger bananas each one ripened and yellow yet firm, a bottle of water and an empty cup and glass wrapped over in a hand towel. On top of the towel, there is a place for the brown paper bag. Haiderali has sent Kamau to fetch his regular bottle of Tusker beer.

Finally, when Haiderali's bh-toh, meaning travel food is ready, I slide a khaki envelope into the side of the basket, first conspicuously holding it up so he would notice it. There is a note I have written in Gujarati glued on the khaki envelope:

> Our marriage photograph. Have it painted by the Punjabi Sikh girl at Studio One, opposite Capitol Cinema on Harding Street at the Kenya Bus Terminal Station.

I don't tell Haiderali, I want it done just like the one of Zera Bai and Rhemu Bhai. He would know that.

Between the khaki envelope and the thermos, Zarina pushes in a misty plastic bag of white mint sweets, the size of soda bottle tops. It's her way of saying goodbye

124

to a brother she looks up to like a father. Then she rushes out to school.

Kabir and I follow Haiderali walking closely behind him as he hobbles along with a slight tilt of his shoe inwards. The morning sun glimmering through the clouds is weak. It's pleasant to walk in the morning air. Jennifer, who is on her way to the market, sees us and comes to help her friend Freda walking behind us all, carrying Haiderali's luggage balanced on her head. Jennifer walks beside Freda now with the Luo basket in her hand. Their talk and laughter flow into the growl of the distant road construction work. The morning sun glints brighter now that the clouds have disappeared.

Only when he had heaved himself up by the bar handle and stood half way up the steps does Haiderali look back at us. Caught by surprise, I turn around to look at his bag now lifted and passed on to the man standing on the bus roof. Haiderali takes his seat beside the driver. Behind him, everyone else is a Maasai, men with short simi blades and staffs, women with children. Two goats stand in the middle of the passage. The Maasai would be visiting kindred homesteads along the way, perhaps, going to settle disputes, or perhaps, to sell milk and honey at market centres along the way. It's Tuesday, market day in the district and the bus is crowded. Some may be going to the King George Hospital all the way to Nairobi to visit sick relatives. Haiderali takes a deep breath in and exhales a copious sigh bending down, he would be removing his new shoes not yet broken in. I remember how he dislikes the smell of the cow manure and sheep oil on ochred bodies, skin attires and goats. A smile spreads over me.

"Where did they put the bag?" I ask Kabir.

"Under the tarpaulin," replies the young man instead with a broad smile. He seems to understand Gujarati. Or is it that he knows the customary first question from Indians travelling by Merali Bus? He replies in Swahili, "I banded tight with sisal ropes and tube straps."

"Tik *chhe*," says Kabir. I see him giving coins to the young man. I don't know how much, but the man looks pleased.

"There will be a storm and much rain on the journey," I murmur to Kabir. He says nothing.

Haiderali waves as the bus snarls forwards. Only then, at that moment, our eyes search for each other coming together in a cuddle as when making love first by stealing looks before even touching.

On the way back I hear the distant rumble of thunder.

Unadorned

Rains fall again after an afternoon of bright sunshine, but there are no more storms, thunder and lightning. I look at myself in the mirror above an array of empty and half-full perfume bottles on my dressing table. The reflection of me wants to console my conflicted self, and come to bed with me giving me mother love and comfort. But I must leave her behind in the mirror. Now, it's young Kamau at the karo who enters my mind. His lustful body and the smiling face that breaks into laughter most unexpectedly. Sometimes, I don't know what to make of Kamau. In some ways, he is so benevolent to my children making uji maize meal porridge for them when they wouldn't eat the eggplant or karela curries I cook. They love Kamau and the uji he makes. Sometimes, he is amused by their child talk between Diamond and Almas, and joins them in their world. But in some ways, Kamau gives me an uneasy feeling like he is hiding something from me.

Having washed off the paste of yellow dal and milk, I soft pad my face. It's Zera Bai's recipe. "Dal bhajia paste with milk opens the pores and cleans the skin of Nairowua's dust," Zera Bai would advise me and Khanu Bai. I am determined to keep shadows and wrinkles away from my face as I age. All of a sudden, I am stunned to see my face without the nose siri-button for the first time since the day I was married. There is a pale spot on the left side of my nose where the skin has not tanned. The pinhole is visible like an ink mark. I put my finger to my naked nose and think of my disgraced face. It will be most noticeable and talked about chup chap, meaning in whispers in the jamat khana this Friday. I, who should maintain family honour, am now without the nose siri-button. I, the wife of the only son of Devji Momna, with two servants in the house and a son, am now standing before the mirror unadorned. I am my shamed face. I am left bare, stripped like a widow in humiliation, unworthy of adornment.

Does Haiderali understand an unadorned woman's pain? Would he understand the pain of a tree that loses its leaves? How will I wear my bandhani without my nose siri-button at Zarina's wedding? The words ache my head. Looking at my reflection in the mirror again, I feel the pang like a door slammed shut on my face. The reflection does not want to leave the mirror. The voice in my head whispers I am unadorned, old and ugly. A widow. The loudest scream in my head is a murmur of Mama Khelele. I press my finger on my cheek, and run it below my chin to feel the wrinkles. My tongue hops to feel the cavities in my teeth. Two fillings. Dentist Gulam in Nairobi may see more. One other I know is there in the back molar from where a sharp pain sparks at the touch of cold water. My hands cup under my breasts lifting them up to feel the loss of weight of youth. I stare at myself narrowing my eyes.

The thought of Meethi Bai comes to me. How she would show the locket of Sati-ma Draupadi that she wore close to her heart. She would hold it in her fist when she narrated the story of the polyandrous queen in the epic verse of Mahabharata. That was at the satsang meeting of the Khoja absakan widows wearing white and sitting desolate and unadorned. They wore no shine, adornment or colours of marriage.

The debt of my shopkeeper husband has de-adorned me today. Haiderali has made me Draupadi stripped of woman's dignity. I implore Saheb avatar to safeguard my honour from the wicked tongues. My stepmother Gor Bai used to tell me how ever since our forefathers landed on the shores of Africa, women have sacrificed to keep family dignity. And they fasted in the name of Sati-ma breathing in hope to keep poverty away, remembering the miracle of the Kacchi woodcutter's wife. The ballad of the woodcutter's wife who fasted and prayed reminds me how a wife's sacrifice assuages the family honour for she is a mother too. She fasts and prays not for herself but for her husband and her children abandoning what's hers. Such are the expectations of her destiny. Such is my culture. It's my turn now to pay the dues of family honour. But should I submit to sacrifice, prayers and fasting? The question torments me for my mind is divided.

I lay awake watching the high ceiling of my bedroom. Alone in the dreamy penumbra of my bedroom, I am glad to be myself, a relief that I feel in aloneness. I watch the light from the misty moon diffusing through the red rose and green liana cotton curtains filling the room dimly. I sense the solitude of the savannah around me, comforting, embracing and I imagine myself a little girl hidden in tall grass, feeling its crispy dry night warmth, and grassy smell. Soon, I will breathe the pure colours of the Maasai sky at dawn. Ole Lekakeny says the dawn colours make art that's perfect to the knowledge of the eye.

I pray into the Perfect of the Sky, Enkai the God, pausing at each pirshah to let my heart know the beauty that comes to my eye is from the faultless, the Naklank. I seek an answer to the way out from husband rule yet I pray for the safety of Haiderali in Nairobi and the strength of his wife's honour. I pray into my anxiety and slip into the picture of Muain Sidain on the painted Maasai horizon in my mind's eye. Then I touch Saheb's picture under my pillow and leave my hand to rest on it while I sleep. His radiance will flow to me in the touch and that's prayer enough. It will calm me to sleep like when I was little and upset with Ma Gor Bai because she had been harsh to me.

It's coming to midnight and no sleep comes to me. I remember I did not recite the dua-prayer today. Frustrations overwhelmed me and I rebelled against everything. Even religion. Dua not said on time may yet be said but frustrations return to awaken the rebel in me. I want to feel the stillness of the night alone in my thoughts yet I feel Haiderali's absence in the bed annoying. I am awake. O my wasi wasi in-between head not here, not there! I have a noisy head full of irritations. Is it Mama Khelele calling? Is it you? What now? I ask. But I do not allow her to answer me. It was a mistake to ask her. I try to draw pictures out of memories of my eye - the magnificence of the blue sky, the shadow of the patterned zebra in gallop, the rise and fall of the beads in the dance of the emankeeki, Saheb's face smiling. But her calls eat into my memory pictures before they are formed deepening the madness rolling into my mind.

Leaping out of the bed, I pull out the suitcase underneath and remove my three artefacts. I talk to them like how I used to talk to my Indian dhingly doll when I was little. They are my three secret sisters. We giggle together. We belong to the circle of secret sisterhood.

130

Tonight, we shall sleep together under my quilt, and they will adorn me in my dreams with the magnificence of the blue sky, the shadow of the patterned zebra in gallop on the savannah and the rise and fall of the beads in the dance of emankeeki.

That is how my story is told. Sometimes this way, sometimes that way, meaning hivi hivi, ruled by the imagination in my two minds. But it's to the patterned splendour of my artefacts that the artist in me finds the arbour to lay down my haunted head. I am at rest then when I put my heart over my distraught mind.

Part Four

Land is a broken string of beads

In the 1950s graphic descriptions of Kenya's Freedom for Land Movement, also known as the Mau Mau, shocked the world.

It was to the equatorial highland meadows and plains of Africa that disgruntled European aristocracy, displaced war veterans, economic and war migrants from Europe, and run away white plantation farmers from South Africa, came to settle and work. They built new communities but preserved the old cultures rooted in segregation of races, their diverse Christian creeds and Europe's nationalist patriotism. They drew secure boundaries around the Indian and African inhabitants of the land. So well established did the Europeans become that Kenya claimed to be Whiteman's Country after the declaration that the most fertile lands be reserved exclusively for European ownership.

What was narrated at dinner tables and at the Europeans only social clubs, in myths, fictions, films and tales of conquests and Tarzan's adventures, materialized in gruesome news and equally gruesome pictures of the Mau Mau in newspapers and newsreels that astounded the colonial imagination.

So intense was the anti-Mau Mau propaganda that it put terror in the hearts of Asian Africans. Some joined the Home Guard units and kept guns at home that they never had the occasion to use.

When Hussein Kanji Dossa Madhany, a Satpanth Ismaili man, was killed in a remote rural store on a white settler's plantation, the whole community felt like it was attacked. Quickly, a wave of fear permeated conversations in defence of the Empire and self-preservation. They said what the English said about the Africans was true. Now they had evidence. Their Imam whom they call Saheb, known as Aga Khan III to the world, responded to the panic in the community with a plain message to the family and the community:

I ASK MY SPIRITUAL CHILDREN NOT TO LOSE COURAGE OR GET EXCITED OR HAVE FEELINGS OF HOSTILITY TOWARD THE INDIGENOUS PEOPLE

The widow, gentle Shiri Bai, framed the message and hung it in her home as was the custom when Saheb sent a letter to the family with his own signature on it. To the Africans, Shiri Bai was known as Mama Mawele because each day she made forty rotlo millet bread as her prayer offering to the jamat khana. Such was the practice of devout widows in the community.

A few pious followers, whose habit it was to memorize and connect words and actions of the Imam like they were miracles, if not visionary forebodings, talked about an incident in Dar-es-salaam at the time of the Imam's Diamond Jubilee in 1937. They said how Saheb joined hands of a couple from South Africa in front of the jamat sitting before him in reverence, silence and shock. Neither the Khoja caste customs nor the council allowed such a marriage between a man who was a 'pure Khoja', as they put it, and a woman who was a half-caste whom they called 'coloured' in South Africa. The story of Habib and Miriam became a legend of the Khoja of Africa.

The Imam also advised the Ismailis to adopt African children. Perhaps, he thought it would help his followers to ease their cultural and racial differences. Some families followed his wish, and did bring abandoned black

135

children into their homes, but the panic and fear stayed in the community. The anti-Mau Mau propaganda was unremitting, not unlike the propaganda against the Germans during World War II still fresh in the minds of the subjects of the British Empire. Every day, the radio blasted fresh news of savagery, and newspapers brought home horrific pictures of machete hacked people, goats, cows, donkeys, and even white men's dogs hanging from roof eaves.

Haiderali's return

Haiderali arrives from Nairobi unexpectedly. It's November when the winds funnelling between Kilimanjaro and Mt Nairowua change directions flowing through the riverine acacia grove and cool the house. Haiderali's journey was planned to be three weeks long if not longer. He is back in less than two. He does not have the usual cheer on his face and the characteristic bustle he carries with him coming home after a long safari. The children's elated clamour dies down quickly when they realize they cannot jump onto their father's lap, and search his pockets for English toffees.

Usually, he would be happy when the safari is over because for six months to a year, he would not have to travel again. He would be happy also because he would have settled the shop debt, some of it if not all, and renewed his contacts with the suppliers. But most important, he would have invested in the trust of the bead wholesalers and that's honour in the eyes of other Khoja bead merchants. In fact, Haiderali's good reputation would be passed on to all the wealthy Khoja businessmen. They would be the members of the secret prayer assemblies of the most pious, revered as the most devoted to Saheb, and therefore, the most likely to be the community leaders. Knowing them would surely promote Haiderali's standing in the fellowship of the rich.

As before, after Haiderali's return, my feelings are mixed joy and anxiety. I am expecting a new stock of beads to arrive. Will the packages arrive safely? Would they be intact? Last time some of the containers were ripped opened by thieves, and once, the load fell off the rack from the top of the bus and we could not recover it.

I observe Haiderali from the corner of my eyes, unsure of how I should approach him. It's so unlike him, coming home after a long safari to slump at the table like he had just been relieved of carrying a heavy weight. It's so unlike him not to go from room to room calling out the children's names. Neither does he ask about their health. He sits inert in the manner of someone who does not want to be talked to. He does not ask about the month's sales. I want to hear about my family in Nairobi. How are Shamshu and Khati Bai getting along now that they have adopted a child? How are they coping with the Emergency?

"Everyone in Nairobi tik *chhe*?" I ask if they are ok.

Haiderali nods. Stories about the Mau Masu repeat going around Nairowua. They are said differently, though, in various African and Asian African ways and languages. They are told according to how the Emergency touches their fears. When I hear Mau Mau news on the radio, I know they will feed Nairowua town talk over the previous day's news. I know the horrors of Mau Mau come in multiple versions. Each version carries its own genus of anxiety intoned by fright in the voice of the storyteller.

Inside me, I feel relieved. Haiderali has arrived safely from troubled Nairobi. Mau Mau Nairobi. Colonial Nairobi. English Nairobi. I feel a load has been removed from my head. Stories about the atrocities committed by the rebels such as the devilish oath rituals using menstrual blood and burying the white settlers alive. These stories are picked up from the radio and lapped over other such stories

138

that come from beyond the official government media. Perhaps, they come from letters and visits of friends, and relatives from Nairobi and towns around Mt Kenya, and the White Highlands. Perhaps, they are conjured by night fears and Mau Mau spirit runners. But, to my relief, there is no story about the guerrillas raping women. Shu-khar I say, Africans don't do that. How does a family recover from such disgrace? I feel my prayers for Haiderali's safe return were listened to. I thank Saheb and make a promise to him, "For the next seven days, every day, I will take prayer offering of one black millet rotlo bread, and a jug of milk to the jamat khana."

Haiderali is wearing a new bushart, short sleeved with front buttons, each one the size of my thumb nail, three of which from the top left open, exposing his gold chain glinting in greying chest hair. Sweat sits on his brow. He has removed his shoes and socks. It's late afternoon.

"Tell Freda to bring my bag and the gunia-gunny sack from the ticket office," he calls out. That he has just walked from the Merali Bus station leaving his luggage behind shocks me.

"Was the journey good, Haidu?" I dare to ask finally. But he knows I usually ask him about his journey in this partly casual way when he returns from a long safari. However, this time I pretend I have not noticed his face that tells me his mind is wrapped up in worrying thoughts. I am eager to start a conversation, hoping I will know more – did something bad happen to him in Nairobi? Or did Merali Bus have an accident? Does he have a headache? Was the rattling in the bus too much? Or what?

"Good what? Ghand faatigai!" Haiderali replies with curt sarcasm. "My arse got ripped! That's how good

139

the safari was." I look at Freda from the corner of my eye. Her eyes are pressed in; her lips stretched and curled tight inward, suppressing an outburst of impetuous laughter. Haiderali embarrasses me before the servant with such bhoonda, meaning obscene, words. After a pause, he says more, likewise indicating he does not want to be disturbed, "I just need a strong cup of ginger chai, a hot bucket bath and sleep. That's all. I am very tired." He mumbles a few more times to himself in mixed anger and despair, "Saala tari tho ghand faatigai! - Silly fellow your arse got ripped!" I do not rebuke him for the language he uses in the house because his face tells me his anger comes from anguish. The anxiety of a family man that I had seen on Dadabapa's face when I was little, and the threat of bankruptcy loomed over his shop. There is also a measure of sadness in Haiderali's lightless eyes. Is it disappointment troubling him? Perhaps, the business talk did not go well. Perhaps, he did not get more beads on hire purchase having paid the debt on the previous stock. I am afraid he will let it out on me if I ask about the beads – how much stock was he able to purchase with the money cashed from my nose siri-button? How much did he manage to get on trust with an understanding that he would pay back with interest after the eunoto ceremonies are over? Are we not in the same prayer fellowship, the top-secret grouping of the dedicated murids as the whole-sellers of Nairobi? Surely, the wholesaler of beads must trust Haiderali, his mandali prayer group member. What could have gone wrong? We need a huge stock of beads when the pastures are green and cows wobble walking with hefty udders. That's when the next generation of youth is ready to be circumcised. Thereafter, the graduation ceremony of the older warriors to elderhood will follow. It could even be in three months.

Freda brings in Haiderali's luggage and then drags the gunia-gunny sack into the kitchen.

"What would you like to eat for dinner?" I ask. My voice is withdrawn, coaxing him like he were a stubborn boy refusing to eat. I call from the kitchen keeping a distance between us, while also keeping an eye on the chai on the charcoal stove.

"Make it simple," comes his softened voice, "don't start your matata nuisance about food." He pauses, and sighs as if he was going to say more, but he does not. He is brusque talking to me and I have been waiting for this moment that would relieve me of my worrying about him.

"Tonight we are not celebrating homecoming. No big meal. No stories from the city this time," I whisper to Freda. She knows. She understands everything that happens in the family though she does not speak Gujarati. I give her my usual instructions, "When you lay the table for supper tonight, use the washed table cloth, the blue one. And don't forget to iron the children's school clothes. Make the collars stiff with starch, no creases. Keep uniforms ready for school. Polish the shoes. Use Nugget not the other one. As for now, I will make pilau anyway. What will the family eat?"

Haiderali did not eat the pilau with the family and went to bed on an empty stomach. I too went to bed on an empty stomach like Ma Gor Bai when my father was upset with her and protested quietly by not eating the dinner she had cooked for him.

In the bed I inch closer to Haiderali. But he does not talk to me as he usually did after his travel, talking himself to sleep. Talking safari thoughts, concerns, joys,

141

observations blurring into sweetness that comes from contentment of two bodies in warmth of knotted legs, watched over by geckos on the ceiling. They wait still as stones for the moment to flick lick mosquitoes in the silence of the night. Perhaps, there is a wall between Haiderali and me because I was unkind to his mother.

The silence that falls over the room is not even from contentment said in the prayer of a thousand shu-khars. It would have been a coming home shu-khar slipping into holy names of 48 Ismaili Shahs or the Imams, and 48 pirs. Sometimes we say Pir Shah, and sometimes, Shah Pir. It does not matter for the Pir and Shah are one. I offer prayers chanting the three testimonies - the names of the Imams, the pirs and the ancient gods reincarnated now to perfection of Ali the unblemished Naklank. In him halted the evolutionary cycle of four Vedic yoogs akin to man the worshipper's own evolution. All the nine avatars carried a little stain except the tenth who is Ali the immaculate Naklank, the ultimate avatar of the last cycle in the era of Kaal Yoog or the Black Age. The Perfect One would rid the world of demons forever. That is my belief.

I turn my face to the dark spot on the wall where his picture is. Ever since I was little, my gaze into Saheb's picture was my meditation. The gaze carried me into the solitude of the night and dreams. But tonight, the disquiet of my thoughts about what happened to Haiderali in Nairobi is so profound that it blocks my meditative gaze towards the picture, gagging sleep.

Supaman America

When he wakes up in the morning, Haiderali's face is as tense as when he went to bed. During the night, he had woken up and walked about the veranda. Thoughts about what worries him bother me while I arrange the groceries from the gunia-gunny sack. Groceries like milled rice, milled millet, milled sorghum and milled wheat flour in brown bags from Ngara Flour Mill. Four types of lentils and seven spices from Babu Bhai's ration shop on Nairobi's River Road where Ma Gor Bai used to shop. The spice mill is still there run by Babu Bhai's son. On the kitchen shelves sits an array of sparkling English jam bottles, and a cupful of mung seeds for blessings of baraka beside Saheb's photograph that compels me to reverence. I tip over the brown paper bags and dispense various masala powders – coriander, red chili, turmeric, cumin and black pepper into the bottles. Aroma of freshly ground spices fills the warm air over the two charcoal stoves in my kitchen. There are also Gujarati confectioneries in the gunia-gunny sack, gifts from Ma Gor Bai - hard sev, crispy chevdo and soft gathiya chips. These I pour out separately into the English biscuit tins with colourful paintings and airtight lids. One has a country cottage covered in snow and the other red jacketed white men in tight black breeches and tall black hats, riding horses. Slender spotted dogs run beside the horses, and the whole men-horse-dog group with guns and bugles is chasing a fox, just one fox over the vast green meadows. Sometimes, I wonder if this red-jacketed tribe in England eats foxes. How would one cook a fox? Like other meats, I would think. I hear the English also eat other furry animals like rabbits.

And there are mee-thai sweets from Nairobi's famed Ngara Sweet Mart. I have seen how this sweet shop grow bigger and bigger with increasing railway and road traffic, and with expansion of Indian worker quarters and bazaars. Then there was a fire and the shop burnt down. After the fire, Lala Prashad's family built a stone building replacing the wooden one, as was the trend in the new elegantly planned capital of British East African Empire. Like a Flower Queen of the colonial kingdom, Nairobi attires herself the year round in paisley flower bunches of bougainvillea and feathery acacia foliage tops. I think Nairobi, my city, would be the most beautiful, a narcissist amongst all the most adorned cities of the tropical empires of imperial Europe. Nairobi's youth is everlastingly green and lavish. Her street parks burst with flaming shrubs and rock garden highways. I have preserved an article in *Africa Samachar*, a translation from an English magazine, describing what the writer called Nairobi's classic Victorian and Edwardian architecture, brought to perfection by fine Indian masonry in sand and grey granite stone. Law courts, railway headquarters, financial houses, the city hall, cathedrals, the European market and the post office stand on garden avenues. There are cinemas, play houses and international hotels plainly marked EUROPEANS ONLY at the entrances. Oriental temples, mosques with tall minarets. Churches with bell towers stand in assigned denominational spaces for Roman Catholics and Anglicans in their designated racial areas. The Europeans only live on high ridges, the browns in-between like at the malarious swampland of Ngara and not-to-be-seen blacks in the new stone built kiosk type housing estates on the dry barren plains at outskirts of Shauri Moyo, Kariobangi and Mbotela. That's towards the East of the city, towards the airport on the back cotton soil road. The three Kenyan races live in tripartheid areas demarcated by river valleys and forest groves. If not by nature then by manmade gardens like the City Park. And then there is the imposing Khoja Mosque, the jamat khana, the heart of Satpanth Khoja life where Government Road, Victoria Street and the Indian Bazaar come together in an avenue of palm trees, the hub of Indian commerce and fashion.

Finally, from the bottom of the sack, I remove a bunch of comic books tied in a round bundle with a sisal thread. These are for Diamond and Almas - Beano, Dandy, Dennis the Menace and Supaman. A receipt from Patwa Bookshop on Government Road shows Haiderali has paid in advance for a supply of more comics: Donald Duck and Tarzan, all to be delivered once a month to our bead store for the next twelve months.

Picking up the comic book Superman, Kabir, who has just come in from the shop for his afternoon cup of tea, looks at the flying man with closed fists slicing like a knife through the air. "Mr Supaman America," he mutters, flipping the pages and walking on to join his brother at the table. "Supaman America will come flying down from the sky to rescue Kenya. Mark my words," he says. What does he mean? Could it be that he means America will end colonial rule? Or that America will finish racism? Or even that America will fight the Mau Mau and defeat them completely, forever? I look at the magic man in red and blue clothes, flying like God's own horse angel Buraq who carried the Prophet to paradise in his sleep. The Supaman looks like a miracle maker. An unblemished American naklank avatar who would come flying from the sky and save Kenya from the demons of colonialism and the Mau Mau.

"These books are enjoyed more by the father and uncle than the children," I smile, and Freda smiles back on impulse as I anticipated. I know she also reads the comics when I take my afternoon nap. Sometimes, I am filled with envy, because Freda learned to read English at the Catholic mission. Ole Kitungat will also be visiting us just so that he can read the comics. After that, when everyone has read the comics, I will donate them to the jamat khana library for the avid young readers of English and viewers of fancy picture drawings from America.

Warm air blows in from the courtyard. The mango tree stirs bright green leaves quaking in the sedate sunlight of the afternoon in rural Africa. I select some fresh colourful pieces of mee-thai sweets carefully, fresh soft and moist, wrapped in edible silver paper. As I arrange them in Ma Gor Bai's coronation tin, I inhale the aroma of pure ghee and sugared milk rising like an invisible vapour. On the tin is a coloured portrait of King George V in full royal regalia and a heavy fur lined crown with a diamond cross at the centre. On the other side of the tin is a horse parade. I take this container, my prized English trophy and the red enamel pot of tea to the table. The bliss I feel in my heart puts a sprint in my feet. Haiderali does not move from the table to make room for me to lay the afternoon tea. I go around him.

What Nairobi?

While I pour the chai, I am expecting Haiderali to talk to Kabir about the films he must have seen at Film India and Green Cinema. I imagine myself sitting at the edge of the spongy plastic seat in the crowded cinema hall on a Sunday afternoon. I am little leaning back on my father's abdomen. Shamshu sits on my left, and Monghi is on my right on the same seat. She is pushing her weight on cousin-sister Malek sitting on Ma Gor Bai's left lap in the adjoining seat. Ma Gor Bai has her arms around cousin-sister Malek and cousin-brother Bahdur asleep with his head on her chest. The air is still, thick, warm and stuffy. It holds a stale tang of mixed cigarette smoke and men's sweet paan breath. Flashes of sandalwood and hair oil fragrances waft in-between odours of curried body sweat - the way Nairobi's Indian cinema halls smell. I am anxious to hear about the modern architecture of Shan Cinema that I have heard Zera Bai say looks like a castle in the shape of an egg. What would such a building look like?

"How is Nairobi?" asks Kabir. I know, like me, he wants to hear more about what we have been hearing on the radio that everyone is talking about, the night rituals of the Mau Mau. And like me he is cautious. Haiderali keeps quiet. Kabir begins to rotate the coronation tin inch by inch, studying the panoramic print of the regimented procession led by a golden carriage, drawn by elegant horses, trotting ceremoniously towards the grey face of Buckingham Palace behind the black iron grille.

"Nairobi? What Nairobi? Nairobi lives in terror as if it had plague. Fear infects all homes like a germ." Haiderali's words echo anger such as that which comes from anxiety. "Natives are burning their kipande ID cards and joining guerrillas in the forest." Haiderali continues with the same tone. He shifts frequently and does not conceal his uneasiness. With a sudden move of his arm, he then reaches out and opens the glossy chequered pack of White House Bakery bread. Clean, soft white, evenly cut slices lean forward like iron pressed sari folds laid on bed ready to be picked up and wrapped around the body. He butters the bread but his hand moves in jerks. "Changes are happening so rapidly that the English can no longer have control over law and order."

The two brothers sit at the old Indian teak table facing each other. They blow over hot chai to push back the cream and sup with audible alternative in-out lip movements. I am puzzled, I see Haiderali wants to talk, yet he stops me from asking, and now he stops even Kabir from talking with him. He shields himself with one rude word, What? Su *chhe*? Then in the gap between his spoken and mind-talk, he looks down pressing his shoulders inwards, slumping in his own nervousness like he were a shadow of his real self.

At night I hear his whispers. He talks and listens to himself and moves closer to me pressing his head into my bosom. Sometimes, he calls me by my name and sometimes, he calls me Ma. He says nothing. He just wants to hear me say hmm to know I am there. That calms him for a while. Mau Mau has broken the man. The fright has submerged his grief of Ma's death, and anger towards me.

Safari Rally

The next day, Haiderali does not go to the shop. Instead, he spends his time pacing unshaven from bedroom to the veranda, and round the parameter of the courtyard as if he was measuring the area with step lengths the way Sikh house builders do. He seems to be thinking – something to do about his trip to Nairobi, I imagine. Something business. I watch him. He picks up a green mango from the heap stacked against the veranda wall below the framed poster pictures of Saheb's Golden and Diamond Jubilees, and holds it in his hand. Throws it up in the air and catches it in the rhythm of his steps as he walks away. During the coming week, Freda will be picking out smaller sized mangoes, slicing them, and spreading them over merikani cloth on the wooden bench in the courtyard. While the sun dries the cut pieces, I will prepare the spices for marinating them in the blue lined ceramic jar that Kabir brought for me from the yard sale at the departing white farmer's house. If the pickled mangoes absorb the juices of the spices well enough, I will send some to my family in Nairobi and Mombasa in smaller English baby food bottles that Freda has cleaned, and kept to dry in the sun on the tin roof.

The veranda smells of freshness of mango sap. I pick some for prayer offering, and put aside six each for Khanu Bai and Zera Bai. But all the time, I worry about Haiderali's strange behaviour. I pretend to ignore him though I did try to talk to him earlier about what I had

149

heard about the Mau Mau from Khanu Bai and Freda. But he just stared at me like he had not seen me before. If that's what he wants, isolation, I will leave him alone.

I will bury some mangoes in Basmati rice that I store in the kerosene tin with a lid that I had ordered from Saifudin Bhai, the Bohra tinsmith on River Road in Nairobi. That was on Haiderali's earlier trip. The mangoes will ripen gradually in rice-warmth so their taste is retained, and no one will be able to tell the difference between them and those that have matured to rose redness on the tree.

At the wall on the opposite side of the heap of mangoes, Diamond and Almas munch on pilau as they play Coronation Safari Rally. Match boxes lined up in a trail. They are rally cars with Vic Preston in the lead, flying over the Rift Valley - a prominent crack in the shiny red cement veranda floor. After several stunts, Vic Preston is still in the lead, in fact, he is always in the lead. Almas is Mrs Chada who should not drive ahead of Vic Preston and win the race. Whenever Mrs Chada tries to overtake Vic Preston, Diamond reprimands her, "Stay back! You are not Vic Preston! I always win the safari rally!" Potatoes denoting checkpoints at Nairobi, Nakuru, Eldoret, and Kisumu, are mapped on the floor with considerable thought. I sit on the red cement with the children, my right hand in the bowl plate full of hot pilau, coaxing Diamond to eat a little more. Every few minutes I knead the pilau in my palm and roll it into a ball. "Eat if you want to be strong like Vic Preston," I entice Diamond, lisping words.

Diamond comes crawling to me with his hurt knee lifted, his tongue out, and I slide the pilau ball into his mouth. "Now say shu-khar to Mowla Bapa." Then he goes back to the adventure on the perilous safari track.

150

Diamond's knee is bandaged in yellow turmeric spotted piece of merikani cloth ripped at the seamed edge from Ma's threadbare bedsheet. It's from the box where there are more old sheets, tablecloths, long dresses, shirts and napkins that I now find useful as dusters, kitchen rags, mops and bandages. Kabir persistently calls the box 'Ma's legacy' and jokes about her thrifty ways even now when she is long gone. Almas comes forward to me with her mouth open. I take a teaspoon from the table and give it to her to feed herself. She is a quiet, ladylike girl, and has no stubbornness of a boy. A girl must not be spoilt, we say. No one will serve her food in her married home, her real home.

When Haiderali emerges from the bedroom looking like a confused man wearing freshly washed and pressed blue pyjamas, his eyes at once fall on Diamond like he noticed the yellow smudged bandage on his leg for the first time after coming from Nairobi. He tightens the white cord dangling at his waist while shifting his eyes from Diamond to me, questioning. Diamond looks at his father and hesitates, wondering if he should hobble up to him as he usually does for a mid-air spin. He decides not to, turns around, and continues playing.

"Diamond beta! Come here. What happened to your knee?" finally he asks. My heart misses a beat.

"I fell from the guava tree at school, bapa."

"How beta?"

"I slipped."

"I have told him so many times not to climb up that tree," I intercept in self-defence. As if it was my fault that Diamond fell off the tree. As if I had not told him not to

151

climb up the tree. In my heart, I know the boy cannot help climbing up trees.

"Were you alone?" Haiderali asks.

"His two friends were with him. The Hindu bank clerk's son and that boy from Halal Butchery in his class." I speak quickly to tell Haiderali I know the details before Diamond replies. Sometimes, Haiderali gets upset with me because I keep so busy in the house and the shop that I don't know where the children go to play and with whom.

"How bad is his knee?" he asks now looking at me with eyes that I don't want to look back into.

"It's just sprained a little. I massage it with warm mustard oil, apply turmeric paste and re-bandage it every day."

"It's healing. One week from today and he will walk to school," Kabir puts in his word. I feel relieved.

"Come, let me kiss your knee." Haiderali bends down and kisses the knee. "It will heal quickly now," he says. "How many days of school have you missed?"

"Three."

"And your homework? How will you catch up?" asks Haiderali.

"His friends come with the homework every day after school. They study together here. They are like brothers," I tell Haiderali.

"What are their names?" he asks.

"Raju Pandya, Inderjit Singh and Aslam Mohamed Khan. Mummy makes hot jaggery parathas for us when we finish our homework," says Diamond.

"Tik *chhe*," says Haiderali to himself.

I remember the days of my childhood when my friends came home to play thapo and hop-skip and jump in our courtyard in Nairobi. Ma Gor Bhai made tea and jaggery parathas for them like it was a family visiting from another town yet they were just neighbours.

I tell my story picking up words like fallen beads, one by one. Then I match the words like colours into a string of beads to make a necklace, a line. But when the string snaps, colours scatter, and my story falls apart. I pick the words again, one by one.

"But it's never the same necklace when you thread the beads again, *si-ndio*?" Ole Lekakeny would ask, "Is that not so?" He would ask though it's not a question expecting an answer. It's a question that is the answer the way he speaks.

Who are they, the Mau Mau?

A few days later, a knock on the back door at the courtyard strikes into the aura around the house made by Haiderali after his return from Nairobi. I have not even had the time to change my clothes that I wore to the jamat khana that evening when I hear Rhemu Bhai entering. "Hodi! Hodi! A visitor comes to hear news from Nairobi," he says.

Every day we listen to the radio and want to know more about the Mau Mau, the barbaric gang that is terrorizing the country. It is not because we just want to understand that we ask each other about the terrorists, but because the tone of the newsman on the radio puts so much alarm in us that we seek comfort speaking out our nervousness to each other. *The Standard* newspaper seldom arrives in Nairowua and now, even *Africa Samachar* is rare.

"Come in, come in, partner!" Kabir greets Rhemu Bhai extending his hand. "Have you had dinner? We are about to eat." He talks quickly.

"Yali," Rhemu Bhai greets me, "I have eaten but I would not mind a cup of Moti Bai's masala chai."

Haiderali says nothing as he sits down at the table. Rhemu Bhai and Kabir sit opposite him expecting him to talk right away about his safari. But Haiderali says nothing. Uneasiness grips me like fear of an impending epidemic.

154

Instead of saying something, Haiderali unfolds a newspaper page that looks like it had stayed pressed in his coat pocket for many days. Stale su-kreet ghee marks on it show up in patches over the matt print. "I have brought cuttings from newspapers in Nairobi to show you what's happening there. See for yourself what I cannot say." Haiderali spreads the newspaper page on the table between the plates and curry bowl. I gasp, Freda stares at the photographs while standing silent and transfixed. In her hand a salver of purring bhajia hot from the kitchen. In the pictures, there are black bodies, maimed and charred, strewn around the grass at a banana grove. Some eyes on the corpses are open, their teeth gleaming in the sunlight. One photograph shows a calf, its legs mutilated – machete cuts, still alive and tethered. A young woman is walking with her lacerated arm held in the palm of her other arm cupped over the elbow. The photographer had snapped the woman from behind so we cannot see her face. "Lari massacre at the lip of the Rift Valley," says Haiderali. "The Mau Mau wiped out an entire village of Kikuyu loyalists, their own people - men and women, with torch and machete."

Rhemu Bhai stares at the pictures. His outsized eye balls freeze under scruffy black eyebrows. Zarina drops the glass of milk in her hands. "Aar...r...r, kisirani. Misfortune coming," I hold back a cry biting over my lower lip. Some milk streams into the cracks on the floor. The rest meanders on the cement that Freda polishes every afternoon with the new Maxwell Floor Wax skating from wall to wall with her one foot on the green coconut husk.

"Children! There is glass here, do not come near the table," I call out intentionally, breaking the uneasy silence, and partly to keep my curious children away from the pictures on the table. "Ole Lekakeny says when the land is in pain, it's a bad omen. He says the land has been angered by the blood of her children on her skin. The earth is the mother," I say. Rhemu Bhai looks at me and then his eyes loop around the room, puzzled. The rest move their eyes down to the floor or away to the wall shifting from Saheb's smiling picture to the framed posters of his Golden and Diamond Jubilees, or to the clock in an ornate black gloss-painted wood box edged in gold. And then to the trailing money plant over the clock box. Only Freda nods. I ask quickly as if I do not want them to ask me to repeat or explain, "But I do not understand how is it that the Mau Mau are gaining in popularity? Who are they anyway?" No one replies. No one knows. We only listen to the radio.

"It was only a day after I had arrived in Nairobi that it happened. I woke up, startled, at three in the morning to the battering at my door," says Haiderali moving his feet to make room for Freda's hands mopping the floor underneath his chair. "I thought the Walji Hirji Guest House was on fire. No sooner than I had unlocked the door than white army boys burst into my room pushing me aside."

"Where are you hiding your wogs?" shouted the English boy. I could not speak. What wogs? I could not ask and did not know what he wanted. I began to shake. He pushed me again. I fell to the floor. He kicked open the cupboards." Haiderali's voice softened by his own words, quivers. He lights the cigarette he has been holding pressed between his middle and index fingers, and inhales deeply. Exhaling, he croaks out a whisper through a funnel of smoke, "He kicked me."

"Pirshah!" I exclaim under my breath.

Haiderali continues to smoke tapping the ash to the ground and lights the next cigarette off the butt of the last one smoked to the gold band at the filter.

"Then the madderchod ponga pulled me to a corner and overturned the bed, thrust bayonets through the ceiling. Cardboard slices rained down, large and small. White chalk dust." Haiderali continues staring into the darkness in the courtyard and then his eyes roam along the wall finding empty spaces, skipping Saheb's picture, the clock and the money plant. The mango tree lit by a shaft of moonlight, and with the night wind trapped in its leafy body, heaves and surges like a ghost. "They were carrying heavy machine guns, heavy boots crackled on the floor. Talked like the English gone mad. I could stop coughing."

"Pirshah, pirshah, pirshah ..." I begin to pray audibly.

"Pirshah ... pirshah ... pirshah," says Zarina entering from the kitchen, bringing a bowl of steaming rice. And then she stands by me, listening and lisping pirshah ... pirshah ... pirshah into the chorus.

"Such violence in Nairobi?" asks Kabir in bewilderment as he leans forward to pick a chapatti. The chapatti jerks, exaggerating his hand shaking as he dips it into the curry.

Rhemu Bhai picks up the cream over the chai on his little finger tip and pastes the brown streak over the cup's rim. Then sipping the chai between words, he sighs inside as if to say he knew it. "I have heard such stories from my wife's family. Now these pictures confirm they are true. The radio speaks the truth." His slurping sentences melt into Haiderali's drone.

157

"Yes. During the night, I heard these English teenagers rounding up the natives, shouting and kicking, and calling them wogs. I realized this is the English name for the Mau Mau. We did not sleep the next few nights, thought the raging white boys would break in again and arrest us."

"What did you do then?" asks Rhemu Bhai, perturbed as I pour chai into his cup, spilling some into the saucer. Haiderali hated being asked since he came back from Nairobi but now he describes what happened.

"We sat at the table in the back room in darkness, only a kerosene tin lamp with a squint wick that lit a patch on the floor below the table. Curtains fully drawn. This is what we did every evening. There was curfew so we could not go to the jamat khana. We said the dua under the table."

"Not even to the jamat khana!" I exclaim and at once feel relieved for I had been holding my breath.

"In the mornings, for the next three days, I saw natives squatting with hands on their heads. They sat inside barbed wire enclosures on Park Road and at Sir Ali Moslem Club on the opposite side of the street from the guest house. At the old English Race Course, a hundred more prisoners squatted on the turf where once fine Arabian stallions competed. It reminded me of the magazine photograph of the detention camp for Jews in Europe. It was like that if you want to know."

"That was only about a decade ago," says Kabir.

"The world forgets so soon," Zarina comments. She is growing up.

"At the guest house, we could not take it any longer so we began to leave one after another. Shamshu came in a jeep to take me to his new house. I was surprised to see him looking so smart, unusual for him, dressed in a khaki uniform, brass buttons with a crown on every one. He had a gun on his leather belt slapped to his waist," says Haiderali exhaling cigarette smoke through his nostrils with a sigh.

Nervousness grips me. "What? Shamshu with a gun?" I ask getting up. I could not imagine Shamshu dressed like an askari guard. How can he carry a gun? A Satpanth Khoja? My brother? I begin to clean a green splatter of chutney from the table's surface and dab a spill of chai near Rhemu Bhai. Then, I scoop up a blob of yogurt with a spoon. The cleaning up is normally not done until the dinner is over and then, that would be Freda's work, not mine any more.

"Yes, Shamshu, your brother. He told me he goes to the shooting range for training. Said he was a home guard on duty twenty four hours. I would be safe with him, he told me many times over." Haiderali pauses to light a cigarette standing straight from his lips like it were a pencil. And then he takes in a long swig like he was quenching his lungs thirsty for tobacco smoke. "He said after Operation Anvil there will be no Mau Mau left in the country. Thousands were arrested during this Operation Anvil. We saw city workers crammed in lorries barricaded with spirals of barb wire, jam-packed like cattle going to slaughter sheds. Even the Kikuyu wives of Asians were not spared."

"Where did they take them?" asks Kabir.

"To detention camps. Once I saw convoys emerging from the jacarandas of Delamere Avenue, moving towards Embakasi and Mombasa."

"Where is Shamshu's house?" I am impatient to hear about my brother.

"Behind St Teresa's Church in Eastleigh. Shamshu and Khati Bai were kind to me."

Zarina, Freda and I leave the men as the second quarter of the night lengthens. While sitting at the dressing table, dressing my hair for the night, I listen to men's talk. Haidu's drone is monotonous interrupted sporadically by Rhemu Bhai's slurp-in sentences and Kabir's quick talk over them. Haiderali sings. The song has no connection to their talk and then, as if drawn by the melody, Rhemu Bai and Kabir join in. In between they talk about filmi stars as if to allure the fear of emergency into the glamour of movies.

I was in bed but not asleep when I heard the back door shut after two Yali goodbye exchanges. Then came clangs of three stoppers before a block of wood was lifted with an audible exhale, and clamped against the door with a thud.

Newspaper photographs

"After two peaceful nights at Shamshu's house, we were attacked," says Haiderali looking at me. Silence. He waited a day to continue last evening's talk at the table.

My heart throbs. I see he wants to speak and wants us, especially me to listen. I pull out a chair. Zarina joins me, sharing the seat, both sitting touching shoulders. Rhemu Bhai puts his chin into the cup of his hand, his elbow pressed down to the table, head bowed forward, shoulders humped. Kabir's fingers are knitted in a ball resting on his lap. Freda leaves to take the dishes to the karo and comes back.

"It was around two in the dead of night when I heard the door break like there was an explosion. A rock jumped twice on the floor and landed near my bed. Splinters weighed down on my mosquito net. The revolutionaries entered immediately like it all happened at once: the bang, the rock, wood flying, and then faces, their phantom eyes, black wiry dreadlocks over me. They spread around the room with machetes. A smell like that of jungle animals filled the room. At that moment of horror, all I saw was their bloody eyes roving around the room like a flock of trapped birds. When one of them looked at me, I felt stabbed in the chest."

I run my toe on the concrete floor below tracing the thread-fine crack invisible to the eye from where I sit. I feel its groove in the rub of the soft middle of my toe. I begin

161

sketching the pattern of emankeeki as if by instinct. As if my toe knows from the fingers working on beads. As if my fingers are telling the foot what to feel, where to move and where to pause like how a thought tells the tongue what to speak, how quickly or slowly and when to break a sentence. It's a wonder how the body speaks within itself. The foot slides along the sliver line like it were a fine wire to bead. My eyes follow the colours in my mind: white red blue - white red blue - white red blue, 1 2 3 - 1 2 3 - 123. Sounds descend like raindrops to my ears: da thi nah - da thi na - da thi na - da thi na.

My skin swells, my heart beats with excitement, I walk the rhythm of e'sikar in the homestead where Kini and Ntinti live. The song-dance of emankeeki fills me. Through years of habit from childhood, my body has grown accustomed to make art in response to the disquiet in my mind. Without a thought, I slip into solace that the moment of creativity offers like falling into the grip of trance. Now my feet want to walk me away from the table talk, over to the patterned land under the blue sky where art is born. At this moment, there is nothing as comforting as sheltering under my Stepmother's pachedi-shawl. The song, the dance and the beads are one in the rhythm of e'sikar which is rass in Gujarati, meaning ecstasy. That is the moment when art births in you.

Haiderali continues to speak, his face flinching in the quiet moments between words. My mind awakens the body as if out of early morning dream, half inside, half outside. My eyes begin to adjust to the faces at the table. Coming to myself, I stand up and offer to pour more chai, holding the pot slightly titled towards Haiderali's cup. He does not respond. I pour the tea anyway, giving him a look

162

in a manner of a mother telling her child to drink the milk she puts before him. Words clutch my throat. I swallow saliva once and then again three more times. I show the pot tilted, spout forward towards Kabir and then Rhemu Bhai. Both raise their hands to say no.

"I heard them asking Shamshu for his gun, and then one of them hit Shamshu with the blunt side of the machete demanding bullets. Shamshu was dragged across the room and tied to a chair. They locked me and Khati Bai in the bathroom, tied us together back to back, and gagged us with dirty socks left for washing in the bucket. We sat there on the cold wet cement. Terrified. Our backs wet, absorbing each other's sweat. They kept the bathroom door ajar, thankfully because we could at least see Yasmin. I felt as if their eyeballs were fixed on me all the time. I continued looking down, pressing my chin to my chest and calling on Mowla."

"And Yasmin?" I ask. Yasmin was actually Khati Bai's sister's daughter. When her sister Gulshan Bai, was pregnant again for the sixth time, she promised to give her baby to Khati Bai even if it were a boy. It was expected of you to promise your unborn child to a close relative if she had no children of her own and you already had several. That was custom, and the child would remain in the family and that was what mattered. Moreover, it was Saheb's wish to limit children to five.

"Oh Yasmin! She is quite a girl!" Haiderali's face brightens. "She woke up bright eyed, smiling and talking excitedly as four year olds do, chattering to herself walking round her cot. Then she stopped and watched, wide eyed, inquisitively, puzzled at what was happening."

"Take everything you can carry. Quick! " called out the leader. "I heard his men calling him General Tembo. Immediately, the revolutionaries began ransacking; searching, emptying drawers, making bundles with bed sheets, shawls, saris, pachedi-shawls and ripped off curtains, and carrying them out.

From the cupboard, the freedom fighters started emptying Yasmin's clothes. Her dhingly doll cried musically, which fascinated one of them. He stood there momentarily turning the pink English dhingly doll over, and listening to the melodic note from its perforated back."

"My dhingly doll!" Yasmin cried out in Swahili. "I want my dhingly doll." She began crying and looking around for her mother.

"General Tembo turned around and looked at Yasmin. His bloodshot eyes stilled on the child. I froze. He was over six feet tall. He stood there like a giant by the cot. He had his palms on his hips, arms akimbo. His red eyes softened like a father's eyes put to his child appealing a favour.

"Don't take the little girl's ka-rendi doll, and anything else that belongs to this child," he instructed his men.

We listen in astonishment as Haiderali narrates the story of Yasmin.

"In the morning when the housemaid came to work, she untied us." Haiderali puts his hands on his head, his palms at the temples. In a way I am happy he had the courage to speak out the shock he kept in him for so long. He shakes his head holding it between his raised hands.

164

"These Mau Mau, how many are they? What do they look like? Where do they … ?" Zarina has many questions.

"How is Shamshu?" I ask before Zarina finishes her questions.

"He drove to Dr Haq's clinic by himself, and came back driving with one hand. The other was in a sling."

I watch Haiderali. He understands I want to hear more about my brother. What happened to him?

"Shamshu and Khati Bai moved downtown opposite the stone jamat khana. Rented one room near Ismailia Hotel," says Haiderali. "I saw the Mau Mau for the first time face to face. Their eyes were fiery and blood stained. Some wore dreadlocks. Some had animal skins; others wore coats and jackets, belts, pants, hats and other things like metal badges from the British army uniforms. They stank of wet earth and animals." Haiderali repeats.

We sit looking down, avoiding each other's eyes. Haiderali unfolds another newspaper page. His hand with a smoking cigarette between fingers, shakes again as he tries to straighten the wrinkled paper torn in the middle at the crease.

"See Zarina, this is what the Mau Mau look like." His voice turns tender inflating the grey silence in the room like whispers of lovers in the night. He begins putting the pieces of newspaper together pressing them to the table with his flattened palms. Then he slides them towards Zarina with hands kept pressed on the cuttings. "Day after the massacre at Lari, the English whipped back. Revenge with such vengeance! Africans in the neighbourhood were hunted down. Innocent villagers shot I am sure. Then, later, bodies of known Mau Mau were exhibited in public. See for yourself what the Mau Mau look like!"

Zarina's black eyes widen. Startled, her lips part. She pales. I turn my face away holding my breath, my hand on my heart. Kabir skims the two portions of the newsprint over the table towards him, and gazes into the pictures motionless without even a blink.

The photographs are of corpses. Some lie side-by-side, and some individually by the roadside like carcasses of drought famished cattle. They appear to be positioned for display at the Lari market square. All the cadavers lay on their backs, stiff like logs left to dry at the Punjabi's sawmill, facing up. Some have long kabuti army coats and long forest guerrilla dreadlocks. They are barefoot, their mouths open, emaciated bodies. I see black spots on their parted lips, and corners of their eyes on lean faces, parched and shiny in corpse-oils released by the scorching sunlight. The black spots are flies gathered on them like on rotten fruit. Some photographs are repeated as close ups. The dead must have been left there for two or three days for the villagers to come from near and far. View and spread the message: the serekali government means business. And for Nairobi and London photographers to make sufficient prints from all levels and angles to show the savagery of the black race. The gruesome ghosts would be printed on the middle pages of *Africa Samachar* and the fear of black terror would descend on every Asian household. The fear would transcend from our stealthy eyes holding the pictures to the faces of our African house helps, customers and passers-by. Foreboding images bring the most grotesque home.

The fear would caution us to keep our voices low as we walk home with quick steps after the jamat khana service before the curfew sirens howl through the streets.

"To me this looks like a government forewarning to those who support the Mau Mau. It's all propaganda!" says Kabir. Then he leaves the table. I hear him gulping water in the courtyard. Has he changed his heart? What are the young men thinking? Have they turned against the English so quickly. They would ask, "Is this true?" hoping to hear someone say, "No! This is not true. How can the black people we know behave like this?" That would push the encroaching fear away for a moment only to make room for doubt. Or that the young men are afraid they would be called to do national service in the army or forced to join the home guards?

Rhemu Bhai stands up to leave. "Yali," he says.

"Yali," come several mumbled responses.

Kabir returns to the table after locking the outside door and stands over the photographs, looking at them again, his bent finger to his lips.

"Tomorrow we must take a prayer food dish to say shu-khar for blessings of life," I say to Zarina who answers immediately with a nod. Inside, I say shu-khar for Haiderali's safe return from the horror of Nairobi. Zarina seeks agreement from Kabir with her eyes fixed on him as he walks out to the courtyard just catching her look. He does not turn around to say yes or at least give a nod. I would like him to come to the jamat khana so we may pray together like a family, something he has been avoiding except on Fridays.

Man called Kenyatta,
Father of the Nation

"Everywhere in Nairobi, I saw seventeen, eighteen, perhaps, nineteen year old English teenagers in khaki clothes, carrying machine guns. Shamshu said they had an evil name, something like Black Watch. They watched us in the dark. I avoided their shaitani cat eye looks. Whenever I saw them, I changed streets, entered shops." Haiderali's words muffle between munching the chapatti dipped in sweet mango breakfast pickle. "But I also saw demonstrations led by a Gujarati man called Ambu Bhai Patel. His wife, Lila Ben, marched with him wearing a Gujarati sari. She had a picture of the Mau Mau leader hanging from her neck and was carrying a poster: RELEASE MZEE BABA KENYATTA BABA TAIFA FATHER OF KENYA."

"Why do they support him? This Mau Mau leader, calls himself Kenyatta, true?" asks Rhemu Bhai. "You know this Kenya-taa, Light of Kenya, says in exchange for their land, the English gave them the Bible. But the Bible does not fill their stomachs." He pauses to reflect on his own words as if he had never really listened to them before.

"Kenyatta communist *chhe*? Terrorist *chhe*?" Haiderali breathes out each question with a puff. Anxious, double doubt questions quizzing himself. He thinks men like Rhemu Bhai and Kabir know more than he does because not that they read, but they listen to the BBC in English.

"I heard of another communist in Nairobi. They say he also fights for Kenyatta's release from prison. He is a Luo called Odinga. He also calls Kenyatta, the Father of the Nation. Says Kenyatta unites all, Kikuyu and Luo, Kalenjin and Maasai, one leader for all," says Rhemu Bhai.

"Now I hear the Indians in Nairobi have started a RELEASE KENYATTA COMMITTEE. More matata. A thousand Indian women signed a petition. Just think of that when no African has done such a thing! Dapandaya *chhe*! Signing a petition against the very English who protect them!" says Haiderali.

"Sounds like this man called Ambu Bhai Patel pukka Gandhi *chhe*," says Kabir.

"He walks about the streets of Nairobi in Gandhian clothes, hand-woven knee long coarse cotton shirt and Gujarati pants of course," responds Rhemu Bhai. Kabir's mocking laughter gets cut midway. Without the usual tapering into ha! ha! it changes into a tight grin as if forcefully contrived, lips stretched and curved down at corners. His face looks distorted in a saddened look by his contempt of Indians in Kenya, his own race.

"How can anyone not admire the English? The most technological, most educated, the richest, born to be rulers. England brings the rule of law and progress to her colonies." Silence follows Kabir's remark. I wonder if what he says can be true. If he himself believes in what he says when his mind changes like a chameleon on the acacia tree. Sometimes, he condemns the English, and sometimes, he says they are right. At times, he is so sure of himself that it's annoying to listen to his self-rightness. Yet, at other times, he seems not sure of himself, and becomes sad when humbled by doubt and his own view of himself.

169

"Who is sure of himself nowadays anyway?" I say to cheer him up.

"It will be peaceful now that they have arrested the leader of the Mau Mau, the communist terrorist," Haiderali breaks the silence. He has picked up new words listening to the European setters' recent speeches against Kenyatta.

"When the English put Gandhi in detention, he became more popular than he was before. That was a mistake. Detention of Gandhi created a bigger freedom movement than they could handle," says Kabir. I have noticed how he talks differently about Gandhi now that India helped by this naked fakir is freed of colonial rule.

"Ole Lekakeny told me Kenyatta is educated in England, and he has a Kikuyu wife who has an English co-wife," I nudge in.

"A native with an English second wife!" Rhemu Bhai hisses.

"I like him. He will remove colour bar from Kenya." I say this because I must say something about Kenyatta that the men do not see in him. But I do not continue because the men do not care to listen to what I have to say. It bothers me that Kenyatta's wife, is English. Will his wives be able to live together, share the farm work, share a husband? Will she till the land like Mama Wahu? Why did Kenyatta marry a thorki white woman when he is fighting the Whites? Now they are related, the Kikuyus and English. They are a family.

I hear stories about the atrocities of Mau Mau all the time. See what they did to Shamshu's family. They make me wasi wasi vacillating from one side to the other. Where

170

do I belong? Whose side am I on? A brown person not white, not black. Not a man.

Something is changing in Kenya that I cannot explain. I feel like I am losing a dream. The ground is shifting under my feet. My story is now fed by anxiety, hate and anger all at once. But mostly it's the doubts that fill my head. Doubts that storm over me like a whirlwind.

When suspicion changes to fear and fear to hate

For the next few evenings, Rhemu Bhai comes home about the same time, after jamat khana prayers and dinner. He says he enjoys the after dinner chai made by me but the fact is, he is worried like we are about the rebellion and how it would shape Kenya's future, more importantly Asian businesses and our lives. Exactly at 9 p.m., the three men gather around the radio to listen to the BBC. The massacre in Lari is mentioned again followed by a commentary on subsequent other killings of white families in their homes on the plantations. Once again, grotesque descriptions of the witchdoctor like rituals deep in the dark forests of Kenya put fear in our hearts.

The next day, a few people talk about the news – truths and half-truths, and even some self-made news that come from their anxiety. How the Mau Mau drink blood. How they bury people alive. How they walk unseen through the night. How fast they run and disappear into the air like spirits. How they mutilate before killing. How they maim animals. Kenya Hindustani Radio appeals to Asians to join the special police force, the CID and the local home guards units. It warns housewives to be cautious, and keep alert at all times, day and night. "Indirectly," says Kabir, "the government is calling on Asian men to join the forces to protect their womenfolk." He does not sound like he is in favour of the government. I pray Haiderali does not heed to the call.

There is emergency in the air. Emergency means trust no strangers, which means trust no Africans, even those quartered in your backhouse and those who have worked for you for many years, perhaps, even from their early youth. The governor appeals to us to be loyal to the crown and help the government defeat the terrorists. Asian families are prompted to keep guns, and quietly report any suspicious talk anywhere even at places of worship. Report even on Asians. Suspicion grows like an infestation of some insidious worm silently burrowing inside you. There is suspicion of all Africans, even those only passing by the house as they have always done as long as I remember. You can read fear in the look of suspicion in Asian eyes. How instinctively we change conversations and glance over the shoulder at the African house help. Is he listening? A kind of a self-questioning glance. How we stalk passers-by with our eyes. I notice how Haiderali has developed a habit of impulsively looking at the door every few minutes while working in the duka-store. How uneasy he becomes when an African enters the shop. Ole Lekakeny must have noted Haiderali's doubting gestures, wringing hands as if he were washing them in air; shifting eyes, so noticeable to anyone who knows him.

We speak like thieves afraid of being discovered as if by instinct responding to the atmosphere that wraps over the land like a blanket. From home to home and from mouth to mouth, facts-rumours-broadcasts trek around Nairowua like secret journeys. Chup chap talks, forewarning whispers and scanning glances, so the servants, the neighbours, the children would not hear conversations between two. Nowadays, it's difficult to know what's true and what's made in the chambers of the mind. It's said that fear is that sort of a carrier that mingles truth with

173

imagination. Emergency, the word itself is dreaded. It conveys some kind of a portent, a tragedy in waiting. In the jamat khana, listening to others rubs further terror into me in a kind of collective way – mass terror, terror of Blacks.

But the blacks are everywhere. Gradually the distance between me and Freda, Kamau, Jennifer and all their friends – African workers from Asian homes and stores, in fact, anyone who is not brown or white, grows larger. From the women's talk in the jamat khana, I feel there is an invisible wall of suspicion growing between Asians and Africans. Uneasiness pervades at home where we have no choice but be together. I cannot do without their housework – mopping the floor, scrubbing off yesterday's curry oil in pot bottoms, washing and ironing clothes, polishing shoes. How suddenly our house helps have become suspects? Our behaviour is changing so insidiously that we do not even realize it. They would know they are watched. That our attitudes have changed

"Do you suspect any of your servants?" asks Zera Bai. I look at her. She makes me feel unsure of myself when she asks such a question. I know she refers to Kamau, whose people, the Kikuyu, are the ones hunted down as the Mau Mau by the government. "Kikuyus are all Mau Mau. In fact, they are the Mau Mau. Savagery in their blood *chhe*. Do you not know?" Such questioning puts doubt in my head where there was none before.

"Would the innocent ones, those who have not taken the oath, also not be watched by those who have taken the oath?" I ask Haiderali looking over my shoulder first left, then right, like I were crossing the road.

"Yes," he replies, "they are caught between the two. The Mau Mau and the English. Like Najmu Chotara
174

between Asians and Africans. We like his nusu nusu - half half, Asian African blood," Haiderali smiles. "He is the new member of our card circle though he has not settled in Nairowua yet."

"Yes, I know."

Sometimes, I see Najmu Chotara at the jamat khana not always. People say he is half Khoja and half Maasai. Khanu Bai and Zera Bai both think that the men's card group accepted this outsider not because they like half castes but because they need him for his connections with his mother's Maasai clan, and the upcoming black politicians. I think so too.

I have known Freda and Kamau since they were in their teens, but I have never had such ugly feelings in me before the Emergency. Nowadays, it's not unusual to hear breaking news interrupt prime time Hindustani radio talk or Musa Ayub's Aap ki Farmaish, the popular song request programme. An authoritative voice like that of the white District Commissioner known by all as the DC, chills the blood:

Do not leave your house after dark - women should not walk alone - carry a gun - accompany children from schools - report any suspicious native in your area - check on your servants' visitors - keep your home locked during day and always at night - report at once any night visits to your servants' quarters – join the home guards and protect your family.

Each time such messages from the government are followed by the anthem: God Save our Queen. In the morning, someone or other brings *The Standard* to show us ghastly photographs as if to back up the previous evening's

175

frightful radio warnings. More savage attacks, hacking by machetes and equally savage oath rituals, and always more blood. These shape my feelings of the day reminding how I must not be trusting of Freda and Kamau. How can we not believe the government? How can we not trust the English who have ruled over us for centuries? Distrust and fear of Africans cram the air we breathe. They suffocate me with fear. Africans are everywhere. It's no longer the free air of Kenya we inhale. In the house, the shop and at the market, I begin to speak politely to Africans more out of fear than a change of my habitual manner of acting superior. They must have noticed the sudden change in my voice and wondered. I tell myself what I had never thought of before: It's their country after all.

Rhemu Bhai built a fence around his home to keep Zera Bai and his two children, a boy and a girl, safe and the puppy contained within the courtyard. The butcher Kasai had a stone wall made enclosing his backyard and he too keeps a dog now. Chunga, that's what he calls the dog, attracts many a curious look from his customers and is the talk of the town for it is the fierce type. A lion-like dog. Not infrequently, butcher Kasai would be heard boasting about his dog as he chops bones and slices steak. That his dog is the brother to the dog that Kaburu Boer had trained to keep the trespassing natives out of his coffee farm and orchards on the slopes of Mt Nairowua. We know that Boer Kaburu's daughter, known as Mama Bisekeli in town, began breeding Alsatian dogs to sell to Indians like the peaches she used to bring from her farm. That Chunga is ferocious like his parents and grandparents. That the dog's breed is called Alsatian. That Chunga is a German dog. Under his words, he says the dog is ruthless like Hitler, and of the cruel race that ruled this part of East Africa. The

Indian army fought to free Tanganyika from the Germans for the British to rule. This is how Germans come to the minds of the Asians of Nairowua close to Tanganyika border when they listen to butcher Kasai talk about his dog. Diamond says that in school Aslam, butcher Kasai's son, brags like his father does about the dog. Like how smart Chunga is. How it fetches a ball thrown into the bush. How he plays hide and seek games with it and how the dog keeps the Mau Mau away from their home. What a clever dog Chunga is. Now Diamond is pestering me. He wants a dog too. The butcher's shop is in fact, attached to his family home not far from Nairowua's market square and if the customers step aside out of the veranda, they would see the restless, slavering German dog chained behind the panelled gate made of wood. There is a sign nailed to a tree outside the gate written in bold letters: MBWA KALI. It is just like the signs seen in the European section of the town and at the entrances of their farms. Seeing how fierce, how hairy like the lion, how wild a beast it is, more Asians enquire about Alsatian dogs. Will the German dog eat Indian food? Where will it sleep? Will it bite children? They question in that order. Then they query, "My wife wants to know if it will come into the house or worse, into her kitchen." They had many questions, but their most important question that they put to each other is this: Would the Alsatian dog keep us safe from Mau Mau?

Every Asian family in Nairowua has a radio by now and every night on the Voice of Hindustani at nine precisely, it brings to us horrifying activities of the Mau Mau followed by the tune of God Save the Queen, and then the monotonous vibrations of the sitar strings playing Rag Karun, meaning Raga Melancholy. It's the same music before a funeral announcement. That halts talk. That

177

demands attention. That brings solemnity in the home. That brings reflective thoughts and anxiety. Accordingly, in time, the number of Alsatian dogs in the Asian areas rises to a level never seen before. In fact, Alsatian became a household name and MBWA KALI signs a common sight. At night it's not uncommon to hear the dogs of Nairowua regaling. In place of the old hyenas' hacking mirth, now you would hear howls and scattering snaps amid strained barks and stretched whimpers of Alsatians through the night.

I am afraid to enter Khanu Bai's home. Her Alsatian dog jumps on me and stains my dress in a welcome hold that sends shivers up my spine. I hate dogs. "My Alsatian smells family on you," says Khanu Bai smiling, exposing her pink gums, "and you wear a long dress like me. Hatari would bare his teeth should an African come to the gate."

How attitudes of their masters rub on dogs, suddenly, the thought comes to me. How these Alsatian dogs widen the distance between Indians and Africans as it has been between the white people and us. Ever since Kenya was declared a colony, work, residential areas, schools, hospitals and even public toilets fitted the three races into three classes like awkward pieces of a jigsaw puzzle. Dogs patrol the boundaries now.

Today if you walk around Nairowua's Asian areas, you will see MBWA KALI signs on the gates that put fear of a savage beast marauding. I hasten to get away from the MBWA KALI house though the sign is meant to keep blacks away not Indians. Now finally, the MBWA KALI sign makes the boundary between the two races secure, and more visible to each other than ever before.

Part Five

When elephants fight

Tembo wavili wapiganapo hurusha fumbi

When two elephants fight they raise dust

Swahili proverb

જયારે બે હાથી લટે તયારે કીડી કચરાય

When two elephants fight ants get trampled

Gujarati proverb

Africa is Black and White
Brown is invisible

"The country is changing. What next?" asks Haiderali. At the back of his mind like everybody's mind nowadays is one question, "How will Mau Mau change Kenya?" Actually, what Haiderali wants to know is, how will the change affect his business. "If the bead shop survives Mau Mau, we will. I am a bead merchant not a politician," he says.

"Things will not be the same for us Asians," says Kabir speaking louder than others into the silence of the moonless night. After Haiderali's return from Nairobi, Rhemu Bhai comes home on Saturdays for after dinner chai, smoke and chat at the table. It's men's group talk, so his wife, my friend Zera Bai, stays home. Moreover, he comes walking alone in the dark. "We are Asians, where do we belong? The raj sees Africa Black and White. Whatever side we join in, we shall never be counted as equal to Whites or Blacks. What does it matter who rules the country? The in-between Brown will always be a second class colour. A subject of white or black government, what does it matter?"

"The whole world sees Africa Black and White!" Rhemu Bhai interjects. "Brown is invisible but to itself. It's war now, we have to be either with the English or with the Africans." He says again, "English or Africans," waving his hand this time.

"In a war one is not invisible. If you stay in the middle, you will be counted one with the government and against the Kikuyus," says Kabir but then he quickly adds, "We don't see how the Kikuyus are themselves divided, loyalists and freedom fighters. Whom shall we support? Both sides are Kikuyus, natives, people of the soil." Kabir speaks with such confidence that you would think he had thought over this question for some time. He surprises me.

"True, it's a civil war," says Haiderali. His unlit cigarette hops between his lips. He strikes a match, and watches it purr into a flare. Then he holds the stick till the flame ebbs into a curl of smoke. He strikes another match to light the cigarette, and takes in a deep breath. Speaking through a cloud of smoke now, he says, "Every yoog fights the Battle of Mahabharata. Brothers fight brothers."

"On what side of the two brothers shall we stand? One is a loyalist and the other a rebel. Yet both are sons of one mother Mumbi," says Kabir irritated. I like his question.

"Asians will also fight one against the other over the Mau Mau. Look at Ambu Bhai and Makhan Singh! Are they not dividing us standing up against the English? How do we know if they are not hiding guerrillas in their water tanks? How do we know if they have supporters from those hidden anti-English groups, Hindus and Moslems? In Nairobi, I heard three Asians were arrested recently and taken to Lamu. I had not heard before of Pinto or Davinder Singh or Babu Bhai Patel. They must have been involved with the Kikuyus against the government to be detained in Lamu," says Haiderali, "but there are also CID spies in every Asian community." Now having overcome his silence after returning from Nairobi, Haiderali likes to

182

talk like a wise old man, and sometimes, he talks over Kabir's statements. But then everyone speaks more than they normally do. Is it anxiety pervading the homes or is it annoyance that their shops will be closed that put their worries to many words? Or that their moneymaking plans will be ruined? Their investments fail? Their shops looted? Their debts unpaid, they would declare bankruptcy and live in shame.

"From the way people talk in Nairobi, there must be more Mau Mau sympathizers among Asians around Mt Kenya than we know," says Rhemu Bhai. As is his habit, he sits on the chair with one leg resting over the other at the knee. While thinking between talking and listening, he moves his suspended foot up and down like a pendulum in harmony with his words. "I went to order two more water tanks from the Kala Singha on River Road. My father had bought our tanks there, but they told me the blacksmith was arrested for helping the Mau Mau make guns. What's the Punjabi's name? I forget."

"Jaswant Singh Bharaj?" asks Haiderali. "He is in detention with the rest of them. Probably he belongs to the Ghadar Party like the other two who shot Isher Dass on Victoria Street. Were they not paraded through the Bazaar and hanged? The lawyer worked hard for Indians in the Legislative Council. Look at his reward!"

"Was he not the one collecting funds from the bazaar Indians for Kenyatta's safari to England?" asks Rhemu.

"I think that's him who also accompanied Kenyatta to England to complain to the English about the settlers," says Haiderali. "But later, he changed and agreed with the English. He wanted Indian workers to wear the kipande pass on them. Imagine! Must be his English wife who changed him. He was shot. The workers said they would rather be hanged than wear the kipande ID around their necks."

"Look at the printer scholar Vidyarthi, and that grunting journalist Ahmed. They spend their days in and out of prison these days. What do they gain fighting the mighty raj? What did Hitler gain? What did Mussolini gain? What did Japan gain? Hopeless dreamers!" says Kabir, speaking as though he were reprimanding his brother. Everyone keeps quiet.

"Some of us Asians carry the freedom movement from India to Africa. But Africa is not ready for independence," Rhemu Bhai breaks the silence.

"Why not?" I ask. The question fell off my mouth. "Gandhi carried freedom from Africa to India. Now it's time to ask for the return of freedom to Africa. It's all in Gandhi's book." The men have not read the book. How can they know? "Do you not hear Kamau singing Funga Safari? He is saying something but our ears have turned deaf. It's a freedom song that says to prepare for a journey. Do you not understand Swahili?" Before I can say more, Haiderali rumbles out a cynical laughter like spasm from his throat tortured by a wedged fish bone. He cuts my nose - maru naak kaape *chhe*, makes me feel small. But I will say more. Husband's humiliation will not defeat me. I do not have to agree with him or any of the men. "Gandhi became a mahatma the great soul in Africa not India. Africa formed him. He arrived in South Africa wearing a three-piece English suit. Two decades later, he changed into peasant's dhoti, slippers carrying a walking stick like an African elder."

184

My husband ignores me; he is noncommittal, loyal only to his business. I hear him slurp in the last mouthful of a spongy bit of parotha sitting at the bottom of his cup together with the remaining chai. His cheeks swell. A calmness comes over his face from the sensation of the lump slipping down his gullet.

After Rhemu Bhai leaves, I sit down at the table where the men were sitting. To get away from their talk and how I was belittled, I must read. I must take my mind away from ruminating. They hurt me, yet I must keep my vrt, meaning my woman pride to show self-dignity. This month's *Africa Samachar* carries topics like Wind of Change, Mayhems of Mau Mau and Birth of New Africa. I put it aside. The articles will take me to the blood stained eyes of the Mau Mau that jump out of the pages like phantom stares. I need to read something different tonight that will take me to sleep. Perhaps, I will read the book from Kabir. That will help erase the evening's disquiet at the table, and take my thoughts away into the story of my people, the Khoja of India. *Kacch no Kajio – Fighting in Kacch* is about dissent among the Khoja resulting from quarrels over property, and the resulting assassinations in the cities and then, the burning of houses and the Naklank orphanage. I did not have the intention to read this book today. But, I need to read something that's not about Africa at present. *Kacch no Kajio* is set in faraway India in a faraway time. It's not quite a meditation story but it will hold my interest until I fall asleep.

Cousin-sister Malek

Rhemu Bhai does not visit again at night after the jamat khana service and dinner. It's as though the fear of war that envelopes the central parts of Kenya around Mt Kenya and Nairobi, blows over the country like a phantom and now it sits over Nairowua. Haiderali installed extra locks on all the doors and heavy wooden cross block panels across the two doors at the shop. All windows, even the kitchen window that would barely pass a child through it, have round iron bars.

Every night Haiderali and Kabir sit at the table on the veranda. Today they speak softly into the pale darkness with the new moon not yet half its full sphere. Zarina in her room, Freda and the children in the same room, are asleep. The house is soundless but for the brothers' talk-talk like muffled echoes serrated with silence. Although there is no curfew in Nairowua, the two brothers sit under the night light in an orange shade. I hear them. Their conversations begin slipping through the slit in the bedroom door not pulled in to shut. In between their talk-talk, there are long silences and sighs coming from Haiderali. They are discussing business and I hear Congo and Goma, and then my name is mentioned.

"Moti Bai's Noordin kaka uncle is in the Congo in a town called Goma by the volcano. Her cousin-sister, Malek, writes to her. She is a suitable girl, two or three years younger than Moti Bai, maybe a year or two older than you are, never married before and will make a mature wife. She is a tone darker than Moti Bai but as pious and understanding. I have met her. Knows housework. A good cook, in fact, a very good cook, and she learned to do business in small town at an early age," says Haiderali.

"Then why not married?"

"It's because of the father. Moti Bai's Noordin kaka uncle disavowed Saheb and started going to the Ithna Asheri mosque. A short man they used to call Noordin Dhururu in Nairobi. The family has fallen out of favour of our jamat because of him. But Malek, her mother and her brother, come to the jamat khana. Her mother, who is the last born child of mukhi Dharamshi of Nairobi, insists Malek marries a Satpanthi Khoja. Moreover, Malek's brother, Bhadur, has a child by a Tutsi woman. Another reason why Malek does not receive marriage offers from Khoja families. They converted the Rwandese to our faith so the family can be one."

Kabir does not reply. There is a short silence.

"This marriage will be a good choice. Through Malek's father, we can invest in the Congo and move west. Think about it," says Haiderali between puffs of Sigara Kali. He has no more Clippers or 555 cigarettes left in the house. "If only the Jews had accepted Uganda as their homeland."

"What if they had?"

"The English would never have given up on East Africa. We would have been one with Europe and America like Israel."

One discussion follows another. The brothers' voices get softer and their sentences disjointed. Why do they not involve me in decisions that affect me and my family? They sound like they are conspiring within the

187

family. They talk family affairs and politics. Talking politics means thinking like politicians, deceptively open, secretly selfish. Then I hear my name again.

"Moti Bai has Malek's photograph. You can look at it tomorrow or later in the week. I will talk to her."

After a while Haiderali says, "Moreover, now there is a new jamat khana in Goma. You will never be alone; there is a good size jamat and a club for young people."

"I must catch up with some sleep," Kabir yawns aloud as he stands up and stretches, ignoring or pretending not to be interested in what Haiderali had just said to him. But he did not say, "No" or "Not yet" or "I am not ready to marry."

"Tomorrow is a long day. I need to go to the bank in the morning. I hope Ole Lekakeny is not late again. He is getting on with age."

"You have the whole day then after the bank visit. Think about what I said. A Momna like you has little chance of finding a Satpanthi girl. Most are Khojas."

"In the afternoon, Rhemu and I plan to drive across the border to Tanganyika to see Jhansi ki Rani. We have been planning to go for a month but something or other comes up and we postpone the trip."

"Why don't you wait until the film is shown here? Anyway, it does not have songs worth listening to. Does it? Not worth the petrol."

"Did you not hear in Nairobi? Jhansi ki Rani is banned in Kenya."

"No! Why?"

"It's about a woman, an Indian warrior queen who fights the English raj. True story, they say."

"Why does the government ban Hindi movies? We will miss the songs if they make Indian films illegal. Indians are not Mau Mau. They like songs not politics."

"Shaheed the Martyr is also banned. Rhemu thinks it will not even be shown in Tanganyika."

"Why? That film at least has some good songs."

"It's the story of the freedom fight in India not the songs that the English object to. They are panicking. They think it will influence Asians to sympathize with the Mau Mau," explains Kabir.

"They want to keep us divided, Hindus and Moslems in India, Asians and Africans here. But even if we sympathize with the Africans, will they accept us as their compatriots?" asks Haiderali mincing words.

"It's us who are wasi wasi not here not there. It's not 'they' who divide us. The ants chose to divide themselves when they come to an obstacle. The English are as unsure of Asians as the Africans are of us." His reply carries a sudden flash of anger like of a caged animal unable to escape and be free. Kabir himself sounds wasi wasi unsure of whether to support the English or native Africans.

"Let the elephants fight and the ants look for new routes out through the battling Black and White feet," says Haiderali advising his younger brother like an elder if not reminding Kabir of his own words.

When Kabir leaves, Haiderali remains at the table alone on the veranda under the night light in orange shade.

I hear him singing scattered stanzas from guru-pir's sacred song. They are Satpanth verses recited in Razmnama by charioteer Krishna to the greatest of all marksmen princes, called Arjuna, in the battlefield:

Listen, O man of clay!
You came naked, so you will go naked
Why then hoard ye earthy treasures?
What will you lose that you cry for?
You came with nothing
You will go with nothing
Why then moan ye?
Whatever happens, will happen
It happens for good

In-between, Haiderali hums to fill in for the words he does not know. I hear his dispair, and the pain in the lament that consoles the bereaved. I imagine him sitting with his head drooping; his fingers pinnacled on his forehead, hissing the cigarette smoke out through his nostrils. There is a long silence, and then a long burp, a pop fart.

I lay awake listening to Haiderali's mood. I hear his Bata slippers walking paaht paaht to the bathroom. Then, he will come to bed. I turn around facing the wall, and breathe into the wet warmth of my pillow imagining Ma Gor Bai's palm padding over my tears.

When two elephants fight they raise dust

TEMBO WAVILI WAPIGANAPO HURUSHA FUMBI

"When two elephants fight, they raise dust," remarks Haiderali. We all know the African proverb. It's Saturday night again. I hear Rhemu Bhai's knock on the back door. The two brothers are at the table. Their talk today sounds like more of the same from last week.

"Yali," says Rhemu Bhai.

"Yali, Yali. Sit down," replies Kabir running his palm over the back of the chair near him.

Haiderali takes time before he would continue waiting for Rhemu Bhai to settle down, "When Blacks and Whites fight they raise dust. That brown dust will get into their eyes. When the battle ends you will see Whites and Blacks shaking hands, and kicking our brown arses." Haiderali speaks with sceptic flair that hums under his contempt like lesser sitar strings vibrating beneath the key cords. It's the tone that carries a suppressed suspicion of the white man, and the rising fear of the black man. He is the Indian, confused but possibly a coward caught between the two. All these years I have lived with Haiderali, I have come to know how he eats and sleeps, and how his thinking shaped by his anxiety, is cyclic. It finds no solutions. His fears, his inside anger and his suspicions are complemented by Rhemu Bhai nodding his head. Scorn and hate in Haiderali's voice throw my mind into disarray, my feelings run into his and I can no longer compose my thoughts.

I pour tea in Rhemu Bhai's cup the second time. Before the cup is half-full, he raises his palm suddenly on the heel resting on the table like it were the head of a startled cobra, indicating enough.

"We are a nuisance, the in-betweens of Black-White," says Kabir avoiding Haiderali's eyes. I read from the wince on his face, he does not like Haiderali's cynicism. Or does he want to disagree with his elder brother for the sake of it? That he does sometimes. He is still young.

"There is also a Gujarati proverb, WHEN ELEPHANTS FIGHT, ANTS GET TRAMPLED," says Kabir. Then bending down to the stool, he lifts the crochet cover and switches on All India Radio seemingly to get away from the argument and calm the irritation niggling him. The radio blares out Bande Ma Dharam, new India's national anthem. He changes the station quickly to Radio Pakistan. We listen to the end of a verse from the Quran with reverence, and then immediately a raucous voice bawls out Pakistan Zindabad, Hindustan Murdabad – Long Live Pakistan, Death to Hindustan. Kabir switches off the radio.

I ask Kabir, "So where do we belong, India or Pakistan, Kenya or England? Where will be the home of the Satpanthis who profess to be not Hindus, not Moslems, not English not Africans?"

"You talk of Hindus and Moslems, English and Africans as if they are countries," replies Kabir. "Both Africans and the English see us as Asians not as Hindus and Moslems. We belong with them."

192

I find it hard to believe the menfolk. Their country is where business is. I put my faith in Saheb who tells us to be loyal to the country of our birth. I will listen to what he says and put my trust in him. Let the men put theirs in their shops.

"On whose side shall we be? White or Black to escape the fate of ants?" Haiderali replies raising his hands above his head, palms facing in, directing his look towards Kabir not me. "Can Asians be all united as one people, be it on this or that side?" He flicks his hands from right to left. "Even the Luo are not joining the Kikuyu. If you feel white in your heart, Kabir, you will be used by the English. If you feel black, you will never be included among the blacks when the war is over." Haiderali pauses again, this time to light another cigarette wedged between his fingers at the knuckles. I can tell Kabir's talkback exasperates him. He is the elder brother in place of the father. The brothers seem to annoy each other with words. I think the root of their frustration is that they are not sure where to take the business to. Even if they sell the building with all the stock, where would they go to invest their money? I am glad when they both keep quiet not because they want to but because they feel lost.

"We stand between white racism and black uprising," says Rhemu Bhai soothing the tension that silence sometimes creates during meetings. It's a thought spoken aloud. "The situation has divided the Kikuyus into three. Mau Mau, the loyalists to the crown, the mission schooled nationalists in ties and suits, and the in-betweens who cannot decide where they want to be. Yet, they are all indigenous natives. The loyalists with the nationalists want to negotiate with the English, make deals under the table to

193

receive lifelong guarantees for protection against the revenge of the Mau Mau who call them Tie-ties. The Tie-ties want the departing English to promise them the settlers' plantations for themselves. There is no escape for the ants like us in the fight of elephants. "

"The ants will always find new routes under the grass, and over the rocks while the elephants fight," says Kabir through a smile.

Silence again. Rhemu Bhai begins shaking his suspended foot in quick motions. It irritates me. Haiderali lights another cigarette and holds it between his fingers at the knuckles.

"You will burn your hair on your fingers, Haidu," Rhemu Bhai jokes obviously to divert the tensed feelings around the table. When he looks at me, I smile not because of his joke but to be polite to the guest in my house. The way a wife should be – smiling at a distance to the male guest.

I hear the familiar clanking of aluminium pots, clinking glass and then water gushing with force from the tap at the karo in the courtyard. Freda has started to wash the dinner utensils. She is singing a church hymn in Swahili. Something about being saved from the evil. It is getting late, the children are asleep.

Kabir sees Rhemu Bhai out through the back door. "You have your whistle?" he asks.

"Yes I always carry it. Much to think about tonight, partner. Anyway, I will fill up the car and pick you up around two tomorrow," says Rhemu Bhai before he leaves. Kabir bolts shut the door and sits the horizontal iron bar across with a clank. I hear Rhemu Bhai's shoes scraping the silence of Nairowua's night as he passes by the kitchen window to come to the front of the house. He greets the night watchman employed jointly by three adjacent shopkeepers before he steps on the Nairobi-Nairowua road.

Haiderali stands up leaning on the back of the chair, lost in thoughts, the lit cigarette hanging from his inner lips. A dense haze of smoke covers his face. Before his safari to Nairobi, Haiderali had just one cigarette after dinner. Now he does not stop smoking until he falls asleep. He even smokes in bed.

The fear of Mau Mau builds in me. There are moments when it seizes me so much that my eyes carve out figures in the dark. I click-pull the cord on the double light bulb hanging from the veranda ceiling, to switch to the night light. I leave it on, dismal as it is in the opaque orange shade. We had it fitted after Diamond was born.

Forbidden readings and the cinema

"Why don't the English ban Naastik the Atheist?" asks Haiderali looking puzzled when the brothers talk again after dinner. I know the film that we had watched together bothered him. He wanted to walk out of the new cinema hall converted from Manu Bhai's warehouse but he stayed on because of the songs. It was sultry inside the hall with no windows, and lacking air but so shocked was the audience that no one moved.

Partition scenes were a horror. I wouldn't watch this film again even for the songs. Hindus and Moslems incinerating trains crammed with refugees. I cried with the anguished mothers both Hindu and Moslem. I wanted to go out for a breath of fresh air if not a glass of water. But how could I? Diamond's head was on my lap. Moreover, in Indian films, the best songs spring out at you at the saddest of moments.

"Is this what independence means? Lawlessness when the British leave. The film puts hatred into the eyes of Nairowua. Moti Bai tells me Hindu and Moslem women at the vegetable market see each other with daggers in their looks nowadays," says Haiderali to Kabir.

"That's exactly why Naastik the Atheist is not banned in Kenya," replies Kabir with a you-should-know-that tone in his voice. I imagine a side smile on his just shaven face smelling of Old Spice over Sloane's shaving stick lather. He shaves at night so he does not have to in the morning. He gets up when he hears the clanks of the chain as Haiderali opens the doors. Then he comes straight to the table for breakfast.

"Anyway, songs of Naastik are classic. It's worth seeing Naastik because of the lyrics," Haiderali hums *Dekh tere sansaar ki halat kya hogayi Bhagawaan* – Have a look at what's happened to your creation, God.

There is that stillness that creates the ambience of late night, few words and long silences amid cigarette smoke curling white spirals in the penumbral light. It's like a scene from a movie. Like two gamblers drinking under a lamp in a cloud of cigarette smoke. A hyena cracks three eerie thee-thee-heeing laughs in the far-off darkness, and then an animal, I don't know what, howls like a ghost. The midnight stillness is trenchant, far from peaceful, like tension biting into ears.

"The government does not ban Naastik the Atheist so Asians see the horrors that independence brings. If it happened in India, it would happen in Kenya," says Kabir. "Independence means Mau Mau-like massacres among the tribes."

It is past midnight when Haiderali comes to bed. He sees me asleep on my back, one hand on my stomach and the other at the side on the old wooden tasbih with the two faced silver medallion, and three silver gunguru bells. Only recently Ma Gor Bai sent the tasbih with a notebook of her hand written ginan songs. The tasbih was wrapped in a page unevenly torn from a school exercise book. Ma Gor Bai had written just one line below the ruled line:

I am getting old. Mowla may call me any day.

197

I am not asleep, though I have my eyes closed. I am thinking. This tasbih that Ma Gor Bai wore around her wrist actually belonged to my mother, Rai Bai. Ma Gor Bai wore it as a reminder of the promise she made to herself when marrying my father that she would care for and nurture Rai Bai's three children *as* her own not *like* her own, she used to say. My two fingers hold one chipped bead firmly in the ninety nine bead tasbih.

Abruptly, Haiderali calls, startling me.

"Moti!" he says my name like I am waiting on him. Why is he calling my name at this time of the night? I open my eyes reciting the tasbih audibly, pirshah, pirshah, pirshah…shanti … pirshah. I hope he just wants water to drink. I pray he would not touch me tonight.

"Have you spoken to Zarina about the marriage offer and what we think of the match?"

"I have not spoken about the offer yet. I think there is time. She should go to college to learn typing first," my voice cracks. I expect Haiderali to talk back; he does not. Instead, he continues on a different subject.

"Tomorrow, show your cousin-sister Malek's photograph to Kabir."

"Is he responsible enough to make a family? I found a copy of *Blitz* under his bed today. You know, the government has banned this magazine from India." I do not tell him about the book by Subhas Chandra Bose that I took to read also from under Kabir's bed. The book is in Gujarati, and it's not banned but it's a communist book.

"How do you know this?"

198

"I read in *Africa Samachar*. And also about a ban on an English film called Bhowani Junction. It's about an Englishman who wants to marry a half Indian half English chotara girl, you know. I think the English film story is like of Kenyatta and his English wife. Love story between two races *chhe*."

"I know Jhansi ki Rani is banned, but not about the English film."

"That is old news. Let's go across the border to Tanganyika to see Jhansi ki Rani. It's still showing, Saturdays only." My heart calls me to see this film about the Indian queen who fought the English often going to the battle herself wearing armour.

"I will think about it."

"Let's go next Saturday. I want to see this film," I plead. "Kabir and Rhemu Bhai are going to Tanganyika tomorrow to see Jhansi ki Rani. You know it's not proper for me to go with them. And I cannot go on my own."

"For now, my mind is on business here not on films," Haiderali gives a firm reply.

"Business will always be here. Not this film."

"We have all the more reason to have Kabir married out of Kenya," Haiderali changes the subject. "He always wants to do what is forbidden, though he does not understand why. He would be the same if it were a black government. He understands neither the English nor the Africans. Yet, he likes everything modern. It's his age. I am sure he will also drive to Tanganyika to see Bhowani Junction if he hears about the ban here in Kenya. Marriage and family responsibility will keep him out of mischief.

Imagine moving here and there across the border just to see pictures! Burning petrol just to go to the cinema, heh?"

"What else is there to do in Nairowua? Young men need a change from the club. Jamat khana does not interest them at this age."

"Kabir likes to speed on rough country roads. He thinks he is a safari rally driver. Anyway, show him your cousin-sister's photograph. I think he will like her instead of eyeing Freda and masturbating. Why don't you give the maid some decent clothes that would cover her body?"

At this hour of night as I look to rest, Haiderali's words bring jealousy mingled with hate in me. I see Freda tempting him with her youth.

Some pictures of the mind stay there in the back alley of my head until provoked. If the feelings persist, they latch on reluctant to let go and halt sleep. So, I must tell my story to let my feelings flow out of me with my words.

Where there is no beauty, there is no peace

The next day, in the afternoon, while I wait to hear my children playing in the courtyard, and know they are back from school, I work with beads on the store's veranda. Ole Lekakeny, sitting opposite me on his crate, is watching over my fingers. I do not feel his gaze preying on me ready to find a fault. His eyes are like Step Mother Gor Bai's eyes on me when I embroidered with her. I tell the old man about Haiderali's safari to Nairobi.

He listens to my narration, says nothing for a while. His eyes make quick shifts. And then he replies, after two more shifts of eyes like he needed to bring his words from a place deep inside his thoughts, "The land is a broken string of beads," he says, "and a broken string of beads is not the same when you mend it, *si-ndio* - yes? That is how the Elders of the Tall Grass speak nowadays."

I hear Diamond and Almas. Their voices come first from a distance, and then I hear padding feet running around the courtyard. They are back from school, and soon they will run in and out of the shop veranda. They pass by me followed by Freda. Diamond is teasing Freda, "Kabir kaka uncle." He is amused when Freda, with a finger to her lips hisses, "Sh...sh..." trying to stop him. The more she hisses sh...sh..., and blushes, the more he taunts her, testing his new found male aptitude of putting a girl to embarrassment. He is so much like my brother Shamshu,

201

who played boy Krishna with Ma Gor Bai stealing mee-thai sweets from her pantry, and how he loved imitating the suggestive naakhra, meaning coquettish gestures, at Meethi Bai's lodge. Little boys do that, and they learn about the nature of women, and courtship. Then when becoming men, they cautiously test the limits of their alluding wit. Almas follows running behind them.

On my table by the armchair, I make clusters of tall tuntai oval beads in three bright colours - red, white and yellow, and one colour dark, which is dusky blue. I see these as colours of the four yoogs in Satguru-pir's devotional song. I will make a tasbih of the patterns of the land's splendour. Caplets of Muain Sidain will be the ornament of God – his mountains, rivers and forests. His beauty in his ninety nine names told in the Satpanth tasbih beads that hold the land and his Light in a circle. It will be a tasbih of osotua which means peace in Maasai which is also beauty in Maasai. That's the correct design for the tasbih I have in mind.

"When there is no beauty in the land, there is no peace because God is away," says Ole Lekakeny. "Across the Mara at Lake Victoria thousands of our neighbours, fishermen in villages, are stricken by o'nyong-nyong. The disease accompanies Mau Mau, both ugly. It eats the joints and spreads like grass fire. Maasai elders are at the sacrificial prayer meeting on Ol Donyo Lengai to plead the Supreme One to be always present with them, and keep the ugly faces of o'nyong-nyong and Mau Mau out of Maasailand. God is beauty. Without it, there is ugliness of disease, famine and violence."

"I also wish to make a sacrifice at Ol Donyo Lengai when the engoiteeko runs the blue sky again," I tell Ole Lekakeny.

"It will be better to sacrifice a he-goat, *si-ndio* - yes? Mature goat of pure white coat without blemish. That will be when the mountain thunders and He speaks. It is most potent when God speaks, and engoiteeko runs the blue sky showing beauty, *si-ndio*, is that not so? Beauty is peace, which is God's face," says Ole Lekakeny. Then he repeats like he was talking to himself the way old men do, "The right time to invite peace is when the zebra runs the sky or at dawn when the colours are pure, and it's beautiful everywhere, *si-ndio* - yes? The second sacrifice this time will be at the pure waters of Kilimanjaro across the border."

"But how will the elders cross the border from Kenya into Tanganyika to reach the pure waters of Kilimanjaro? Emergency laws do not allow border crossing for the natives. All natives. I have read that include the Maasai."

"The Maasai do not cross the border," says Ole Lekakeny, "the border crosses them."

Ole Lekakeny does not explain further and if he did, it would be a proverb and he would leave it there with a question *si-ndio* - yes? But what he said does not leave me, though I cannot ask him to say more.

After a while seeing a puzzled look on my face, he says, "The English made the border across Maasailand. They divided our land but we are one people. Their border crosses us, we don't."

"Can you then also arrange a sacrificial goat for me at the pure waters of Kilimanjaro? I will give you the money," I say after a pause.

"I will send a message to Ole Lenana's homestead tomorrow. The elders will also need three fat gourds of honey beer with the goat. I will be late in the morning."

"Do not tell anyone in this house about the sacrifice."

"I hear you. Sacrifice is a prayer and a prayer is a secret of the heart. But I need to know to tell the elders your heart's prayer. Just for them, what is the sacrifice for, mother of Diamond?" he asks without looking up.

"For peace in my home," I reply, "and beauty to return to the land."

Simba Amajansi

It's afternoon of the mid-dry season that comes between the short and long rains. The nomads of the plains visiting Nairowua walk along the pathway by the red earth road selecting areas in the shades cast by the Indian duka-stores. Below the Nairobi-Nairowua road, the coppice of Ol-debbei bead tree is clad in a crusty mat of fallen leaves and crumpling nests of weaver birds. On some days, burnt flecks of foliage from fires on the savannah scale up with the breeze and float in the air, drifting to the shop's veranda. Finally, some come to rest on my armchair.

"The earth swelters in the searing sun of this month of drought sky, *si-ndio?*" says Ole Lekakeny. There is a restless movement in his eyes, looking here and there as if they have lost the path where to look, where to glance, where to search for the beauty he knew. Now, everywhere he looks the grass is dry, brown and dead. He is standing on the veranda raised on granite stilts as he gazes far into the land over the depression of the acacia copse where the spring called Chemi Chemi turns into a stream. I dust the pillow on my chair. Ole Lekakeny speaks in rhythmic sentences as is the manner of his speaking to nature or the earth. "The Maasai landscape is parched, a patched black sod smelling of dead fire and smoke. Ostrich and gazelle seek the coolness of the green glades along the riverbanks where the grass is tall and succulent, soft in the shades where insects prosper under the fig trees sacred to us. Young boys take their fathers' cattle to the river dells and to the mountain where God rests, and they wait there in His lap until the rains come home."

Diamond comes running into the shop veranda laughing noisily, mischievously and gasping for breath at the same time. Simba, still a puppy, follows hot at his heels, panting and barking, wagging his tail rapidly, clearly enjoying the game. Almas breathing heavily and excited, enters after the two.

"What's this hoh-ha clamouring? You will wake up your father. Why did you let the dog loose?" I am enraged. "Take him back and tie him up right now! Keep him away from the shop!" I yell out at Diamond and then call out angrily, "Freda! Kamau!" Just at that moment, Simba lets out a fierce stream of hot urine right there at my feet. "Ar...r...r," I shriek, pulling my dress to the knees and jumping up, spilling the beads on the table that come crashing down to the cemented floor. The beads roll in every direction and into the pool of urine that's widening and reaching below my chair. I hear Freda screaming frantically at the back of the shop on her way in, not knowing what the chaos is all about. At once, Diamond standing now by Ole Lekakeny, urinates feverishly, wailing at the top of his voice and holding his crotch. Ole Lekakeny leaps up with a shout, "Chafu! Dirty!" He too shrieks. Almas confused at the sudden commotion, sobs soor soor. Haiderali, Kabir and Kamau make their presence in no time, each armed variously with a pestle, a broomstick, and a hammer. Their wide opened eyes shift and scan inside-outside the veranda with What? What? looks. What? What? ... Mau Mau?

"I told you I did not want a dog in the house!" I yell at Haiderali on my way to the bathroom, my dress lifted up embarrassingly high. Kamau and Freda laugh heartily, releasing the tension as they prepare to clean the mess on the veranda floor.

For several following days, Kamau and Freda would talk and joke about the incident. They give a new name to Simba the Alsatian puppy. They call him Amajansi, and each time they call him Amajansi, they both impulsively burst out laughing. Freda has yet one more story to share with Jennifer about the panicky Asians, and how the dog urinated on me, and how I reacted.

Khane socks

There are sporadic drizzles, and as if overnight, spot shoots of emerald grass sprout from under the black burnt loam of the savannah. I enjoy such a day sitting on the veranda, there where the breeze flows through the drizzle and is cool. I notice Ole Lekakeny is full of joy.

"Our herd boys will descend from the mountain and sit by their mothers' hearths, watching the broth bubble and listen to family stories, what happened in and around while they were away. Birds will flutter on Ol-lerai trees, bees will make honey, *si-ndio*, yes?" he asks.

While he talks, I watch makeshift roadside trenches gurgling red rain waters down the gradient to the brook at the grove. I wait for Ole Lekakeny to stop talking before I give him money for the sacrificial goat. The money is out of my savings from the kitchen and khane spending cash that I receive from Haiderali every Friday. Sometimes, I buy less milk when there is some left over from the previous day, and sometimes, I skip contributing the daily prayer money, though never the tithe for that averts misfortune. He doesn't know about my savings. If he does come to know, he will reduce my allowance that he has calculated with precision to the cent. I have learned to bargain well in the market and made friends with the vegetable women we call mama mboga.

Finally, the rain abates in the afternoon. That makes it easier now for Freda to fetch hot water from the samavat for the family's evening bath before the Friday prayers. In between, she dresses Almas and runs errands for Kabir. Diamond can put on his own clothes now. Each evening, we try to be at the prayer house in time for the special litanies for the end of the Mau Mau, and that takes twice the normal prayer time. We return home, walking with children sleeping on our shoulders. Our steps are quick, our hearts thumping, as if to escape from an ambush set by the insurgents.

"Freda! Khane soksi?" Kabir yells for his jamat khana socks. Freda rushes to him with a black pair of stretchable nylon socks rolled into a ball.

Kabir's khane socks are without holes and blurry transparent, which allow his well-shaped toes to be vaguely visible. His ash white feet have not seen sunlight since his childhood when he played barefoot with Maasai herd boys along the main street of Nairowua.

"You can tell a Khoja's class by the look of his socks in the jamat khana," he says looking at his own feet in nylon socks. I smile, and pass by Kabir carrying Haiderali's khane socks to him.

I smile again thinking of what Khanu Bai once said to me as we were sweeping the jamat khana mats, "Khoja wives look even after their husbands' socks. They would be lost without this service. Mamdu would wear dirty socks over and over again if I did not give him clean ones."

Meanwhile, Haiderali is humming a filmi song and dappling himself with Johnson's Baby Powder, twice over the joints. On Fridays, we dress up in our best khane clothes and use scents like oudh that we don't otherwise wear. I hurry to the kitchen and start organizing the day's

209

naandi, a plate of lamb pilau, while also keeping an ear on the commotion of dressing up in the house that tells me everyone is getting ready to go.

On his way out, Kabir tugs his sleeves cuffs, adjust the cuff links and wriggles his shoulders like he was fitting into his coat all over again. The next instant, and he is teasing Simba: Sa! Sa! ... Sa! Sa! Simba leaps up as if he was touched by a spark, barking ferociously and snapping the air imagining a thief. He startles me out of the gaze stilled in silent prayers I like to say looking into Saheb's photograph before I leave the house. I ask Saheb to keep his presence in the home while we are gone. In the evening, spirits visit empty homes. I also keep the loban gum burning over the diminishing heat of coal in the stove. The smoke will deter the spirits and mosquitoes alike.

The dead inhabit empty homes as they do Saheb's house, the jamat khana. The shrine is where poetic rituals entreat for our ancestral spirits to celebrate heavenly darshan-deedar, and thus be one with the Light of Origin. Today is Friday and I must say a separate dua-prayer for my Dadabapa with my palms pressed together over the sacrament of food - a portion from my family's roji, meaning, the day's nourishment assigned by destiny.

My story is told like counting beads on my tasbih. Each bead a word. Each bead made sacred by the holy word. When the ninety nine beads are counted it becomes one dua-prayer. They say God has ninety nine names. His virtues, his aspects, his power, his strengths. They are like the many arms of an avatar that too testify to his many names.

210

Zarina

As I open the bedroom door, I feel the air rolling in from the courtyard, picking up dust sweeping the ground. The Sunday morning air touches my face, it's cool and I feel lifted. Its flow infringes over the night's air, stagnant and stuffed with body odours, breath, cigarette smoke. Haiderali is asleep, perhaps, half asleep in morning dreams. I look at the sky and watch how the sun leers through the clouds falling into orderly lines in the engoiteeko formation from the absolute blue. It's one feathery zebra stripe over another. The blue is all over. This is sky country at the equator where you breathe the blue and the sun. If I do not see the infinity of the blue, and the colours of the dawn becoming a bright day, I feel sad like sadness of missing something you love, a sadness of loss of day's charm. I wonder if Ole Lekakeny is watching the sky beauty above him at this moment. Why do I ask when I know he would be watching like all the Maasai elders at this time that they know they are sharing with their peers across the land? But I ask the obvious out of habit to ascertain my thoughts. I know to look up to the sky in the morning comes naturally to Ole Lekakeny, as naturally as to his age mates wherever they are across the land this morning. That's how they remain connected by the sky patterns over the vastness of savannah. They know sky beauty is not pointed out, its presence is sensed as simply as breathing air for they are Maasai, the nomads of the grasslands. Blue, the Supreme Being, is the Omnipresence and its arms open in embrace over all beings - animals, plants, insects, birds and humans.

211

My skin yearns to be touched by the sensation of the sight of the sky on a clear day; my body infolds into an ecstasy of the early morning bliss in Nairowua.

As I pass by the veranda on my way to the kitchen, I throw a quick look around the courtyard to see where the chickens are. My eyes fall on Zarina standing behind the mango tree. What is she doing at this time sneaking behind the tree when she should be helping Freda with breakfast? The children will be up soon asking for their chai-toast-butter-jam. I follow her eyes and am stunned to see her watching Kamau at the karo washing clothes. His tyre sandals are leaning against the outer ledge of the karo. I have heard Freda call them Kamba Bata, affectionately joking, eliciting a roar of laughter from Kamau. He is wearing ragged khaki shorts today and a sleeveless netted vest with a tear at the naval, and as he lifts the round club above his head, his chest heaves under the skin-tight vest, his posterior muscles bulge and twitch, veins stand out on his arm in the sunlight. For a second, he holds the club high above the wrinkled ball of armpit hair before trashing it down on the clothes in a splash. He is singing what Freda had explained to me was a momboko dance song. "It is a Kikuyu song of his 1940 age group called Anake wa Forti," she said. Then she whispered "It's a warrior love song. Young men make their own warrior love songs."

Freda is Kamba, but she understands Kikuyu, who neighbour the Kamba. Kamau was born in Nyeri, the town surrounded by rolling hills between the gentle plains and meadows below the glaciers of Mt Kenya at the equator. Less than half a century ago, this land was coveted and transformed by the white settlers into Kenya's dairy and granary. Nyeri was where the elusive, mysterious and

212

defiant guerrilla leader of the Mau Mau, called Dedan Kimathi was born and where my friend Khanu Bai, the bead merchant's daughter, was also born. Kamau's body moves in the rhythm of jive of momboko as he beats the clothes. I stand transfixed shifting my eyes from Zarina to Kamau. My desire for man awakens through Zarina's youthful eyes, and I cannot turn my gaze away from them both. Freda on her way to the children's room, catches my look as a woman would at such moments lusting men, but she keeps a straight face as if she does not see me. She puts shame in me. I feel guilty. Freda has become the eyes and ears in this house. I have no secrets.

"Zarina! Come and help me in the kitchen at once," I call out shaking myself from her lurid gaze that had held me for a moment like a seizure. On entering the kitchen, I hear Haiderali humming at the basin. I smile inside and listen to a filmi song melody. It's the theme song from Awara the Vagabond. So catchy is the melody that I begin singing, my head moving dole dole Awara hun … hu hu hu … awara hun. I open the White House bread pack and lay four slices on the new grille on the charcoal brazier. It's a square piece cut from a cast iron window grid that Kabir picked up from a construction site on his way back from the bank. I wish Haiderali would sing more, and continue singing the rest of the day. It's six weeks after his return from Nairobi that Haiderali finally shaves. When he finishes, he calls Diamond to give him his used razor blade.

"And give this to your mother," he says, and continues humming.

"Put the blade in your compass box," I call out to Diamond loud enough for Haiderali to hear over his humming. "Only use it to sharpen your pencils. Don't play with it."

Suddenly, a shrill whistle blow in the house startles me. I stand up. Freda enters the room, puzzled, querying the look in my eyes. Diamond follows walking behind Freda, chuckling and grinning. He hands me a finger size police whistle made of solid steel, and is amused at our reaction. In an instant, without a thought, I slap Diamond across his face. Freda is startled. She begins scraping the burnt toast with the butter knife looking down, her face about to burst into tears.

The rest of the weekend passes by with Haiderali and Kabir talking like they were having small impromptu meetings. Often they spoke in low voices while I did my usual chores between the house and shop. Ole Lekakeny does not come to work as regularly as he used to. I begin to teach Zarina how to work with beads so she may know how to seek beauty scanning her eyes above her and around her as the Maasai do, as I learned. Then she would know the savannah animals and sky and the art they bear. After all, she lives here. "It is a start," I tell her when I show her the pattern keri. She does not show much enthusiasm; in fact, she does not like to work with beads at all and complains to Haiderali not me. Her mind is on badminton or maybe she is seeing a boy at the club. Freda too takes breaks in the evening. I suspect she is seeing a man too. It's their age.

"When Ole Lekakeny comes, he will tell you stories about the beads. You will learn quickly. For now, I have something important to tell you," I say to Zarina with a smile that tells her I have secret something that she would

214

want to hear. I speak to Zarina in soft persuasive words, nevertheless, seriously chup chap woman to woman talk.

That evening after the prayer routine at the jamat khana, and after warming, serving and eating our naandi dinner, I sit down at the dressing table and slowly begin undoing my hair – I remove a pin, stretch the hair and scratch the scalp, one action at a time. It's the time I can finally relax in the privacy of my bedroom. Children are in their room playing snakes and ladders with Zarina. I hear Freda singing a Christian hymn, something about 'Soldiers of God' as she splashes water over grimy ash smeared over the pots at the karo. I look at Haiderali resting on the bed through the reflection in the mirror. He is still, half naked to the waist, looking at my back, waiting.

"We talked today, Zarina and me," I start the conversation before Haiderali asks the question I am expecting from him.

"Does she like him? The offer from Kisii, I mean? What does she say?"

"Yes. She agrees."

"Is she completely agreeable?" Haiderali sits up.

"Yes."

"Has she seen his photograph?"

"Yes. She was surprised. She thought he is not bad looking. But I told her you agreed to accept the photograph because it is the best proposal offer that she has had in the last two years. And I told her the offer was negotiated through my sister Monghi Bai. The boy is Mulji Bhai's cousin's son. He calls Mulji Bhai his kaka uncle. The families were also neighbours once, and had joint family business in Kisumu before the war."

"Then we must arrange her marriage soon," Haiderali's sentences eat into each other. "Things are changing rapidly. It is better she goes to her own home. I will send a message to Mulji Bhai tomorrow and confirm our acceptance. Then we can send Zarina's photograph. Are you sure you don't want to send it for a touch up to Nairobi first? The artist can lighten her skin. Just a little."

"Let it be the way it is. Monghi Bai had seen Zarina when she was little. "

"Do as you like but hurry up," replies Haiderali. "We have some money kept for her marriage, and Ma has left some gold for her."

Haiderali takes a deep breath in and then sighs shu-khar several times falling back on his pillow. Taking his tasbih from under the pillow, he counts the beads: pirshah, pirshah, pirshah…santosh, santosh, shu-khar…shanti, shanti, shanti… It is the tasbih I had made for him of amber beads that I had bought from a Somali woman who traded in gold and amber. I made a zari knot in gold thread, the figure of double four that closed the loop of ninety nine beads in a tight tassel. I made the tasbih after his return from Nairobi because he cried in his sleep like a baby. In the shadows of trees on the bedroom wall, he pointed to soldiers carrying machine guns, and warriors with machetes.

I say my tasbih feeling each bead between my fingers. "These caplets are God's garland," Ma Gor Bai would say to bring me to respect the rosary, "it belongs to Him. Look after it with love in your heart." Before me, these beads were rolled by my mother, Rai Bai and then by Ma Gor Bai. Sometimes, my stepmother let me use her tasbih in the jamat khana when I was little sitting by her side. My hand knows the sharp edges of each of the chipped beads and the full round ones. My hand knows to stop twirling when it comes to the grooved bead at the end. I think about my two mothers as I clamp on each bead between the tips of my fingers pushing it back with each word. I wonder if they moved the beads as I do? I wonder if they said prayers as I do – sometimes, a one phrase prayer – Mowla show us mercy, and sometimes, a short snap word – Ali-Om. That is a prayer too. I have given the beads names of Vishnu's avatars - Rama, Krishna, Naklank ... and of Abraham's mystics - Issa, Dawood, Musa and Mohamed. When I come to the two faced silver medallion, I pause, as I always do, to call names of Ali Krishna , Rama Satguru-pir, or Hari Saheb or alternatively, Parvati Fatima, holding the silver head.

Haiderali shifts from side to side. I remain motionless and awake feeling the mattress spring jolt underneath me. He is beside me but I feel his mind lives elsewhere. Since his return from Nairobi, he is a different man. No longer do I feel his silent withdrawal from me because I was cruel to his aging mother. I thought now he would think again, and replace my nose siri-button. Does he at all feel the guilt of putting me to shame? I can't tell what his feelings are for they seem to have been absorbed into the horror of Mau Mau. I don't ask about the nose siri-button, and he doesn't tell me.

But Haiderali does try to please me in other ways. Like complimenting my cooking and how well his Friday jamat khana shirt has been ironed, both meaning I am a good wife. Like how he used to say in bed after making love, "I liked that," also meaning I was a good wife. In the beginning, when I was a girl just married, I felt the contentment of 'a good wife' when he gave his approval. What more does an Indian woman want than her wife duty fulfilled satisfying the man's needs? But I have doubts now. Now, when in our mid-marriage years, Haiderali and I learn to live with each other as if all over again, inchoate new codes of eye and word language to show civility not always affection. He even offered to carry the naandi to the jamat khana once. He said it like a friend, not husband. But I did not let him not behave a husband to me, and let him carry the naandi. I worry about him when he is restless like tonight, and when he feels not gratified. Not a man enough. His discomfort creaks on me yet I resent living sub-life of a wife.

Cold water will calm him and help him to sleep. Partly, I leave the bed to be outside. My long dress rasps oddly on the ground. My Bata rubber sandals lap the floor with each step. I take deliberate slow steps towards the clay pot in the courtyard. It is a strangely soundless night on the savannah. There are no hyenas celebrating discovery of a cadaver. No mournful purrs of an aged lion banished from the female pride. There is not even the usual throat crackle of the tree hyrax on the Ol-lerai acacia by the house. There is no chirp of the night cricket nor a croak of the river frog. The twin sounds of the Nairowua night speak to each other and deepen the solitude in the second quarter of the night. Doubts invade me cutting into the stillness around me. Has the loss of my nose button left a hole between me and my husband?

Part Six

Khoja Khoja Centi Moja

In 1947, British India was partitioned into two states. Presumably, the creation of India and Pakistan was based on religions. In truth, argues Narendra Singh Sarila in *The shadow of the great game: the untold story of India's partition (2006)*, the division was drawn to maintain British-US forces on the subcontinent. There was the threat of the powerful Soviets, recently victorious over the Nazis in Germany, descending farther down from Afghanistan into India. India flanked the oil rich Persian Gulf that the West needed to keep under its control then as now.

In the wake of the horrific partition, and the penetrating humiliation suffered by both Hindus and Moslems, causing generations of handed down hatred, accenting cultural, religious and emotional separations, there surfaced a silent Hindu-Moslem enmity among Asian Africans in East Africa. What plagued the old country affected East African Asians. They began identifying themselves either with Hindu India, or Moslem Pakistan. One or the other. This was expressed in common spaces where they met and was no less evident than in apparent emotions that the audience exuberated while watching Indian patriotic films, cricket matches between India and Pakistan, and listening to nationalistic songs and political exhortations that penetrated into the homes over broadcasts from the subcontinent. The nationalist propaganda grew larger in the next decade during the India-Pakistan wars that tailed their independences. Where there was formerly joint representation of Indians in the Legislative Council in Nairobi, there were now two separate representatives, one for Hindus and the other for Moslems.

Amidst the havoc in the wake of changes in the old Indian Empire, and the shift from anti-colonial to religious nationalism, there came the high-pitched call of African nationalism demanding sovereignty. While rejoicing freedom of the old country, many Asian Africans became ambivalent when the tone of African nationalism turned fiercely defiant to British rule in a manner similar to that of Indian nationalism. They knew their jobs, especially with the civil service, the railway and other transport services, and corporations, were adjunct to the Empire. Their businesses and properties were protected by the British law. Many were not certain of those among them, the nationalists and revolutionaries who supported African self-rule. The majority preferred to play the doubting wait-and-see game when change seemed inevitable. But the change came unexpectedly, in haste, no sooner than when the Mau Mau decade ended in 1960. At their famous Sunday afternoon card games in the town's central parks, the recurring question that the Asians asked was: Are we replacing White racism with Black?

In their hearts, the Khoja knew they could not identify absolutely with either India or Pakistan, unlike the Sikhs, who also keep a Hindu-Moslem faith and have developed liturgical script called Gurumukhi that like Khojki, the Satpanth script, is one of the only two sacred lettering from the Landa characters. The Sikhs opted for India. Most Ismailis stayed around both in the old country.

Ismaili Khoja were always looked upon as less Moslem and more Hindu or vice versa, depending on what side of the border they were identified with. The larger Asian African community was so politically and religiously polarized that it could not accept then, as is often the case today, that there do exist significant groups of Indians of guru-pir traditions. These groups profess to be neither absolutely Hindus nor absolutely Moslems as scripted by the two mainstream religious nationalisms. This had been a dilemma in the court rooms of British India where justice was dispensed according to major religious beliefs.

The general curiosity, if not suspicion, of Ismailis being different continued. One reason was that the Satpanthis did not explain who they were while externally they gave civic visibility such as in public health and education. Another reason for the curiosity was due to the practice of creating landmark jamat khanas (prayer halls) yet services within remained closed to outsiders. Then, there was the ambivalence with which the Satpanth Khoja regarded their own ethnicity and origins that did not easily help to locate where their collective political or religious allegiances or origins for that matter, lay in the old country. Sometimes, when they were taunted, the derisions spoke to what thoughts lay beneath. The mocking was reminiscent of the culture of humiliation and difference from the old country that had increased after the independences of India and Pakistan in 1947.

One way the anti-Khoja mocking surfaced was through student bantering in government Indian schools. One such a song, in one variation, was called Khoja Khoja Centi Moja:

Khoja Khoja centi moja	*Khoja Khoja one cent worth*
Khoja Khoja sojah	*Khoja Khoja go to sleep*
Khoja Khoja upaaro boja	*Khoja Khoja lift the load**
Khoja Khoja khoja	*Khoja Khoja disappear*

* Here there is an inference to the low caste manual workers

Ba Ba Black Sheep

My daughter Almas is turning five and excited about the English nursery rhymes she learns at school. She keeps repeating one song in particular over and over again the way children do when they discover rhythm and rhyme. Each line she sings is louder than the previous one:

Ba ba black sheep
Have you any wool?
Yes sir! Yes sir!
Three bags full

Freda sings the last two lines with Almas. I am not sure what it means. I hear 'black' and I know, in English, it's the colour for the night, and for Africans. Sheep are called gheta in Gujarati. Sometimes, we call foolish people gheta because they follow blindly. There is a story I tell children about sheep trooping on like a blindfolded army, and falling over the cliff. But, what's this song about black sheep that my daughter likes to sing?

Their combined voices send sound waves through the house. Freda is an orphan brought up at the Catholic Mission and she speaks better English than anyone else in our household. She can even read and write in English. I hear her plump aa when she helps children with English songs. Almas is the star student of Mrs D'Souza at the Aga Khan nursery. I know my daughter has a good voice. She makes fun of me when I say Maasai sheep are bleating beh-

beh. I walk my fingers in the air showing Almas how the sheep descend blindly to the brook at the Ol Debbie acacia grove following the leader.

"Mrs D'Souza says it's not beh-beh but ba-ba," she corrects me. Kabir smiles from a distance without getting involved in our conversation. When I say how the cockerel in the yard wakes me up with kooke-reh-kook, Almas bursts out into her child laughter right into my face. "It's not kook-reh-kook. It's cock-a-doodle-do." Though she speaks Gujarati with me, Almas says the sounds of animals in English ever since we have been sending her to school. "Weaver birds don't sing chee-chee-chakalee, mummy. They sing twitter-twitter," Almas would tell me. Sometimes, I wonder if she hears the animal voices in English too, like when the sheep bleat beh-beh, does she really hear ba-ba? I can feel a difference creeping between us like an insidious wedge when the sounds of the language change at home. English is changing the rhythm of how we sing and talk with our children. I begin to recognize some English words from my children's animal songs.

As she grows older, Almas no longer likes to sing Gujarati nursery rhymes with me. She follows her brother, Diamond, two years older, who is now embarrassed to sing Gujarati poems he knows so well. Last year, everyone in the family was proud of Diamond when he recited the rain poems of Kalidas on stage at the end of term Parents Day concert at the Aga Khan Primary School. Diamond has even stopped reading the Adventures of Bakor Patel that he had been collecting from his early childhood. I feel as if Gujarati is taken away from my children, yet there are some parents, like Zera Bai and Rhemu Bhai, who are proud of their children speaking in English. They even make small demonstrations in the jamat khana speaking to their children in English. At times I feel uneasy and begin to lose faith in myself when my children act right and confident speaking English to me. The school, the books, the comics, the poems, the films are English now. It's another world they live in.

One day coming back from her nursery school, Almas surprised me. "Mummy, why am I not fair like Snow White?" she asked. I just looked at her because I did not know what to tell the child. Laila Bai's daughter was chosen to be the fairy princess in Almas' class play because she is the whitest of all the girls, is she not? Fairies in her story books are white and dolls are white. Does Almas think I am ugly? Her brown mother is ugly? Who is this Snow White anyway that my bebli girl admires so much?

Thoughts come and go in my head. There is no one at home I can talk to about how I feel about losing Gujarati. Khanu Bai and Mamdu Bhai's children are older, and they continue to speak in Gujarati with them at home while in school the boys speak in English only. They are taught in English anyway. Zera Bai and Rhemu Bhai speak whatever English they know with their children all the time, even in the jamat khana. That's become a little of a family exhibition of their love for Saheb. People wonder and admire how quickly they have become modern.

Gujarati rhymes and rhythms

As the gap between my children and me widens in small ways, I become more like Khanu Bai, assertive about speaking in Gujarati with the children. Diamond and Almas would listen to me speaking in Gujarati but their answers are frequently in English. There are times when I feel frustrated and rebuke the children. Once I hit Diamond with my rolling pin, something I regret to this day. It was out of exasperation.

But what can the children do? Everyone else in the house – Haiderali, Kabir and Zarina speak to Diamond and Almas in English, but to each other they speak in Gujarati with some Swahili. Somehow, Freda feels more comfortable speaking to the children in Swahili, though she knows more English than Haidu does and in spite of Kabir telling her to use only English in the house. Is she also like me? Though a servant, she gives me comfort.

Everything around me is turning English. I think of how Dadabapa's fingers funnelled over my fingers guiding the grey clay pen on my slate. Together we made O આો, the two stroke sound – one at the side and one over the letter. From his fingers, he transferred his love of art-writing Gujarati to my hand like how Ma transferred her love of zari from her fingers into the stitch I made. Like how Ole Lekakeny brought the bead art of the savannah to me bead by bead.

I try to teach Diamond and Almas the music of multiplication in Gujarati. Once they get the rhythm of numbers, they will not forget the tables, and will be able to do calculations when as adults they will run their own businesses. Fluency in numeracy is family tradition. "How will you know how to calculate numbers to the infinite without using paper and pencil like your father and me? Like your Kabir kaka uncle? Math language is every Gujarati's second language," I coax them, but in vain. The defiant pose that the children sometimes lock against me comes not only from their peers, but also from their Kabir kaka uncle and the rapidly changing jamat. It worries me, and I begin to lose confidence in the upbringing of my children. as I had dreamed I would. There are moments when I feel I am losing who I am in the new Ismaili world.

Self-doubting short instances enlarge when they turn into guilt, and my conscience creaks. The jamat wants to be English, and I am stopping my children from becoming modern. "Why am I like that?' Silent questionings in Zera Bai's eyes throw cruel hints. "Your children will not be able to adapt to the world of tomorrow, *chhe nah*? It's the atomic age, *chhe nah*? Gujarati is desi and past, *chhe nah*?" Zera Bai taunts. Her *chhe nahs* sink and rise in tones soliciting confession disguised as questions as if to help me absolve myself from the guilt of ignoring Saheb. She acts like a mullah. She talks to me like she is doing me a favour like saving me from sin. My words stay on my tongue. My head wheels in muted anger.

No sooner than we part, the unspoken words prompt me to talk back. I feel slighted by her self-regard, and the self-appointed teacher to me. Is her faith in Saheb more than my own that she must follow his wishes without a minute-to-think to understand? I am envious. Haidu says that is really faith. Belief without a doubt. Unquestioning belief like Abraham the Prophet's. My thoughts and speech have glued. I look into the sky and search patterns of beauty so I can enter into the blue face of God. The Maasai God is still God. I will enter into her beauty to know who I am.

Haiderali is not prepared to discuss our children's education. I try to talk with him about hiring a Gujarati teacher to give tuition to Diamond and Almas. No response comes from him. From the slight tightening of his lips, I know he is listening, and perhaps, trying to understand as I am - why does Saheb want us to abandon our Indian heritage?

Gradually, sounds of speech begin to change in the house. I can no longer use Gujarati proverbs to teach my children lessons of life. I even stopped reading bedtime stories from the Mahabharata and by Gujarati children writers.

Cowboys and Indians

"True democracy has no colour. It does not choose between black and white ..." I hear Jomo Kenyatta on the radio and turn up the volume. On this Sunday afternoon, the Hindustani Service of KBS – Kenya Broadcasting Service, has replaced Aap ki Farmaish, the prime time Sunday afternoon request show, with Kenyatta's speech. It's quiet time when housewives work - marinating green mangoes for pickling, rolling rice and lentil papadams, preparing chevdo lentils and nuts while husbands nap. After Ma's death, listening to Aap ki Farmaish, the request programme with strings of names and affectionate family messages and tearful songs, has been my routine on Sunday afternoons. In those greetings of loved ones, I remember my siblings, my cousins, Dadabapa and my mother. I know many Indian housewives like me in towns and rural store homes across Kenya, removed from their birth families, would be listening too. That's also the time I keep to clean the smudged spice bottles and to oil lentil dals stored in tins. I would clean and prepare dals, chilies, ginger, garlic and a range of whole spices ready for sun drying. It's all wife's work that I can do leisurely while sitting at the dining table on the house veranda where it's cooler than in the kitchen. And, shu-khar, I don't need to sit on the floor stool. The fat around my midriff and thighs makes it uncomfortable.

Like on most afternoons, the breeze flows from the courtyard rustling through the mango tree and to the house veranda through the door left open. At first, listening to Kenyatta's unannounced speech was not only unusual but also annoying. Now, I am pulled to Kenyatta's voice, "… this land … is a gift from God and I wish those who are black, white or brown to know this." The sincerity in Jomo Kenyatta's speech, the truth that he speaks, the tone of his guttural sentences, his fatherly words like an ancestral beckoning, echoes freedom in my heart. It's exhilarating. It's celebration of liberty in oratory unheard before in an African voice. He speaks with the verve of locked colonial revulsion surmounting over years in detention in the desert of Maralal. He takes me to a dream. I am in love with freedom that Kenyatta brings. Kenyatta speaks to people of all colours to be free from domination. Free of racism. Free of foreign rule that takes away our dignity. That made us the conquered, the subjects and the vernaculars of the Empire. Kenyatta speaks to my heart. My President to be speaks to me. I listen and work.

When Haiderali wakes up after his nap, he will have chai nasto, and then, he will walk to his Sunday card group sitting in cross-legged palothi on the lawn at DC's office discussing the release of Kenyatta and what that will mean for their businesses. I feel he does not care about freedom the way I do.

Kabir is out with his friends – God knows where. In the courtyard, Diamond is playing Cowboys and Indians with Simba. He is creating havoc, pounding an empty tin with an arm size branch shaped like a gun – tha …tha. His new passion is to be a cowboy. He tells me when he grows up he wants to be a cowboy riding a white horse. He must have been a white man in the last karma. The dog, excited, barks incessantly, forcefully, and runs around, yelping with every breath he exhales through his gaping mouth. I look at my son and wonder at his child's imagination that comes from his hope of the freedom he expects in adulthood. Simba is Diamond's friend, and the cowboy's horse. Ole Kitungat, who is sitting under the mango tree reading comics, looks up occasionally, and smiles at Diamond's gimmicks. When Ole Lekakeny retired to rest with his peers at the new homestead that the women recently put up for them near God's Mountain, the missionary teachers persuaded the elders to allow Ole Kitungat to stay at the school's boarding house. On Sundays, Ole Kitungat visits us after the service at the mission church and spends most of the weekend with us. I have cleared a part of the store room in the courtyard for him to sleep and study.

I clean a handful of rice at a time. In-between I pad perspiration beading around my collar with my pachedi-shawl that hangs loose from my shoulder. I spread the grain on the tin senio tray and wait for the concealed insects coated in fine rice powder to move and crawl out. I have an embroiderer's eye that knows how to penetrate and pick out the sly weevil.

"We want to prosper as a nation, and as a nation we demand equality, and that is equal pay for equal work for all …" says Kenyatta.

In the courtyard, Diamond continues running in circles with Simba at his heels. He carries his gun in the left hand and the reins, a sisal rope around Simba's neck, in his right hand. He can command the horse and fire the gun at the same time like in the movie. He watches cowboy movies with his father at Nairowua's new cinema converted by Desai Bhai from his grain warehouse. In a sudden moment, the game stops. Diamond struts to the stack of firewood and urinates, showing off his penis to Simba, rather arrogantly. A slim yellow jet trails termites filling in the cracks where they live. Diamond is amused when the white ants scuttle about in panic and then, he turns around to look at Simba. "You do the same," he tells Simba. The dog crooks his head and looks up, his tongue hanging out like a red strap and his brown eyes still and alert watching for Diamond's hand to jerk like a command to race with him. "Yours is different," says Diamond looking at Simba's penis.

"Shenzi! Silly!" I yell at Diamond, "Stop that! You are seven. A big boy now."

Freda giggles as she mops the floor around the door where dust gathers during the day. She cannot control her giggles. She is still a child. I pretend not to notice her and focus on what Kenyatta is saying, "… If any of you here think that force is good, I do not agree with you: Remember the old saying that he who is hit with a rungu club returns, but he who is hit with justice never comes back …" Wise words from a wise man, an elder, a born leader, a peacemaker, Godsend. Baba wa Taifa, Father of the Nation. The one who will make me proud when he is the President.

"Diamond! I told you before not to pis-pis on the firewood! It's for cooking!" I shout from the veranda, furious because he urinates in the courtyard, and because my attention is taken away from the radio. Kenyatta's words fill me with excitement. He is not violent. He is not Mau Mau, "He who calls us the Mau Mau is not truthful. We do not know this thing Mau Mau." See, I will tell Haiderali, Kenyatta is not violent. He is not Mau Mau, he says so himself. I say to myself. He is like Gandhi. Who said

Kenyatta is violent? A leader to drive us to darkness? To the devil? These are the questions that have been reoccurring in the ever going debate whenever Haiderali, Rhemu Bhai and Kabir meet. These are the thoughts that have seized our minds like fever of malaria since Kenyatta came back from detention. The men should be here listening to the radio.

"Prosperity is a prerequisite of independence, and more important, the beer we are drinking is harmful to our birth right. You sleep with a woman for nothing if you drink beer. It causes your bones to weaken and if you want to increase the population of the Kikuyu, you must stop drinking." Freda and I look at each other and smile in between work, in between listening to long repeated and re-repeated speeches, old and new speeches of the just released from detention Kenya-taa, the Light of Kenya. The one who brings light to my heart. My President!

Diamond's game has more matata noise than play. "Diamond! Stop this tha-tha. It's eating my head. I cannot hear the radio." He corrects me, "Mummy it's not tha-tha. It's bang-bang. Can't you hear?" And he continues with his wild game, trotting about, falling down, rolling on the grass and hitting the tin tha-tha again. He is becoming defiant, striking the empty can with more force than before, and yelling bang-bang at the top of his voice. Is he imagining himself the hero in cowboy comics killing Indians? Is the new language that puts thoughts in the boy's head that makes him play kill the Indians game? I watch Diamond, thinking and puzzled.

Hearing the matata noises in the courtyard, Almas comes running from the bedroom. She is holding a dandia stick. Kenyatta's speech is over and I hear the slim voice of

Lata Mangeshkar strangling through sitar strings. I give my heart to the melody and sing with her. But the children's voices break through the attention I put to the music I love.

"I want to play cowboy. I have a gun," Almas declares.

"No! I am Roy Rogers! You are Indian chief. You have bow and arrows. You don't speak English. You have long hair," Diamond shouts back in English. Both Freda and I smile concurrently looking at each other. How the boy wants to be a man! Turning to Simba, he yells, "Come on Trigger, Giddy up! The Indians are here!"

"Diamond, come and have your tea. I have rolled jaggery in hot chapattis for you and Ole Kitungat. Are you coming? " I look at my two children from the kitchen window with pride, thinking how well they both recited the dua-prayer in the jamat. That's a mark of dutiful parents. Proper upbringing of Ismaili children. It's also our family pride and a tradition.

"I want jaggery chapatti too," Almas shouts from the wall end of the courtyard.

"We will eat later, after the boys," I call back.

The Satpanth Song

The evening of the new moon indicates the closure of the lunar month and the beginning of a new month. It's also the time of asking for forgiveness for the sins of the month, committed knowingly or unknowingly. It is the evening of giving the tithe from the earnings of the month. In keeping with the practice of the Devji Momna family, I prepare an elaborate food prayer platter called the sufro for the jamat khana. I cook the sufro with a heart that's pure, and hands caring for it is a sacrament. I arrange the food on the platter with satisfaction and pride of a grateful vassal offering his labour's harvest to his lord. My feelings in the offering would transcend to Saheb-spirit, the beatific Light called Noor, supreme above all ordinary human-spirits. From him then, the blessings would transcend to lesser spirits called ruh. Ruh, like the ruh of my once mortal Dadabapa, and my grandmother, Sohn Bai, and my mother, Rai Bai. They would transcend like the fragrance of oudh rubbed on warm afterbath body when the pores are open to nurturing of ointments. The perfume itself, like all perfumes, is indiscernible by the skin or other senses but the smell.

I am on my way to khane holding the sufro in hands like a new born baby, lovingly and with contentment of a mother who has just delivered for I have cooked it myself. This evening of the new moon would be for receiving the holy water and su-kreet of sweetened semolina morsels fried in ghee. Both substances blessed with dua-

235

prayers said over them, collectively with one breath, and reverentially with one mind of the jamat making it a holy communion. Consumed together, the power of both transforms the victuals into fare for the soul and heals the repentant. But none of these would cleanse me or bring the peace I seek, for I am an artist, a dreamer of colours like a mathematician conjuring formulae that connect figure to figure in the magic of numbers making patterns that bring him the contentment that only another mathematician knows.

On such an evening in the jamat khana like this evening of the new moon, my insatiable mind asks to be itself away from household chores and men in the family. It would come from the music of the verse, its aesthetic sacred - the guru-pir song that lights the wick, and fills me with ecstasy. Then, nothing matters but the delight of the moment of the song. It would come when the ancient is full in my ears and I see Saheb's blissful face on the wall below the clock donated by Haidu's father. It would touch me, and unlock the imprisoned bird in me fluttering its wings to be free so I find peace. The song's cadence heightens the rass in me, an enchantment that cleanses, and heals as I worship. In its beauty, I see the pulse of zari thread on the bandhani and colours of emankeeki freed by dreams so magnificent that they fill my inner eye. That's the heart's eye, not the mind's. Such is the moment of rass, the moment of ecstasy in the Vedic composition. My worship is the rhapsody of the ginan that is the attar, the perfume of the sacred songs of Hindustan. They are the devotion I know.

I hear Arabic phrases in long sonorous repetitions recently put to Indian worship rites, and I train my ears to know them to know the new faith. But they do not touch me the way the Satpanth song does. That song that lights the wick of the candle in my heart. I try again but the old faith stands before me. Could it be that in the verse of my forefathers, there is an ordained beauty of an awakening that's alien to Arabic sounds? Would an Arab understand the beauty of Satpanth sounds and pictures native to my veneration? I know from Dadabapa the magnificence that stirs me is brought forth from ancestral soul songs of Indians revering Prakash-the Noor-the Light-the Dawn. Is that not the brilliance of Brahma the Creator-the Light-the Noor-the Mystery of Bram Prakash, the ginan? Is it not the Noor I search in the Sufi bard's hymn in Vedic verse pleading my soul's immersion into the fathomless ocean of Light? I will sing the raga to be myself till I hear the call to be one with Brahma the Noor and the dead. I will sing into the haze in my head till it clears. The ancients said one Veda created the music.

Losing Gujarati

It is a Friday and the evening of the new moon that makes it auspicious, and that calls for celebration for the Ismailis. Such a day comes three or maybe four times a year and Diamond is late coming from school. That's unusual. I have already sent this blessed day's sufro to the jamat khana with Freda. My anxiety grows by the minute waiting for Diamond, and I am about to send Kamau to look for the boy, who may be somewhere up on a guava or lukat fruit tree, when I hear Simba barking, excitedly, welcomingly.

"What happened at school?" I ask no sooner than he has his foot on the threshold. I have no time to sit and talk, so I ask while strolling towards the bedroom with my khane pachedi-shawl still warm over my forearm draped in three folds. Freda who ironed my pachedi-shawl is emptying red hot coal from the iron box into the samavat of our bathing water.

"Why are you so late?" Haiderali's question jumps over mine. "You know it's Friday of the new moon?"

"The principal put me in detention," Diamond yells through clenched teeth. I turn around to look at Diamond but instead my eyes fix on the blue ink spot on his shirt pocket, and the fountain pen's golden cover clip. Diamond avoids my look. His eyes shift. You don't want to react to the child's anger annoying as it is. Mee-tho guso *chhe*. It's the sweet anger of an innocent child that would bring a smile to my lips had it been another occasion, and we were not in a hurry to be in time to listen to Aashajee the ginan overture before the dua prayers. I also need to reach the jamat khana in time to find a place to sit in the prayer hall. On such an evening as today, we would sit so close to each other that our folded legs touch one another, and if God forbid, a cramp seized my calf, it would be difficult to stretch out.

Simba's persistent barking calling for Diamond irritates me over the aura of anger my son has brought home on such an auspicious evening.

"Why?" I ask Diamond pretending to be calmer than I am inside.

"Because I forgot and spoke a few words in Gujarati playing rounders. The prefect gave me the Speak English Only disc. Madderchod!" Diamond swears.

"Did you swear in Gujarati? What did I hear you say?" I ask instantaneously.

"No! I didn't swear!" he yelps back.

"Oh! Just for that you get so angry?" I put on a make-up surprise, like a question it is not. I am surprised they have a Speak English Only disc in school.

"Patel Master made me write a hundred lines: I must not speak in Gujarati or Kacchi or Swahili in school." Diamond drops his school bag on the table with an annoying thud and goes straight to the bathroom slamming the door behind him. We hear him swear again at Patel Master, the principal of the Aga School. Simba hears him, barks and then, hops around the mango tree on three legs for a while before he settles down nesting his head between his front paws, whining for Diamond who ignores him today. Butcher Khan's son hit Simba with a stone aimed from his catapult when he found the dog sniffing around his father's butchery. Kamau, following my instructions, tied Simba to the tree.

I watch Simba. An innocent animal detained, and in pain. He is tethered to the tree like butcher Khan's goat I saw on my way to the market. Like Simba, the goat stood there, his brown skin turned golden in the slant of the morning's ascending sunlight. He looked up as I passed by. His eyes shone with innocence like children's eyes. In four weeks it would be Eid, and he would be slaughtered to celebrate Abraham's absolute submission to God. An impious thought came to my mind. What kind of a father was Abraham who would want to slit his son's neck in God's name? What kind of God is God but God who commands a man to show his trust in Him by slaying his child? Was Satan putting such thoughts in me? Or was it the beauty of the goat's coat and shine in his gaze that overwhelmed me? Whatever, at that instant, I say never again will I ask Ole Lekakeny to sacrifice a goat to show my trust in God so He may bless my life.

"Diamond needs to be disciplined swearing like that," says Haiderali fixing his eyeballs on me as if the boy's swearing is due to my upbringing. "He is of Devji family. He carries my family name," he says. I keep quiet. Yes, I know.

Diamond's swearing upsets me too. One more swear word from Diamond, and Haiderali will blow up. I can feel his anger seething augmented by Diamond's own. One more swear word from Diamond and without a thought, Haiderali would slip out his black leather belt from his just put on khane pants, and take a swipe at Diamond in one snap move.

240

"But why are our children punished for speaking in their own language?" I whisper to Haiderali in an attempt to take his attention away from Diamond.

Haiderali does not answer, sniffs a few times, stays still on his chair with khane socks dangling down from his hand. His reluctance to say anything is as good a reply as I would have had, had he spoken.

"It's good for their future. Modern education," says Kabir coming to the sink straight from the bathroom, bare chested with a wet blue towel around his waist. I eye his wet feet leaving splodges of water behind him. Annoying habit. But I felt relieved when he remarked, irksome as it was.

"When he cannot read guru-pir's sacred texts, what schooling is that?" I question Kabir, looking into his eyes the way a woman should not look in a man's eyes. He does not answer; instead, he throws a snap look at me. Does he think I should not argue with him because I am a woman?

At our volunteer Saafai Committee get-togethers, Khanu Bai and I have been talking chup chap under the breath about our children told not to speak in Gujarati in school. Of course, when Zera Bai is around we do not talk about the feeling of disparaging Gujarati pervading in the jamat at this time when the fear of Mau Mau burdens us. However, when alone with me Khanu Bai is bolder, if not honest. She would tell me she feels like a lost sheep - her favourite sentence when unsure of herself. We both know our talk would be distasteful to the community leaders and that would make Saheb unhappy because he appoints the leaders and that makes them sacred in our eyes. No Ismaili wants to make Saheb unhappy.

241

"Our revered texts will be translated into English. We must move forward, Moti Bai!" replies Kabir and then, raising his voice he calls out in Swahili, "Freda! Get me a glass of cold water from the clay pot. Mara moja, quick!"

"Our language connects the past with the present. That's how we move forward," I respond with this standard answer learned from Dadabapa's wisdom. That's when he taught me how to write the first Gujarati alphabet A અ below the line.

"It's not the past with the present!" Kabir pipes out in a woman's voice imitating me. "We move from the present to the future. That's how we move forward. English prepares us for the future. Look forward. Get educated, Moti Bai!" Kabir speaks in Gujarati. However, he says 'educated' in English imposing authority with the deliberate incursion of the word that stands out distinct from the rest of the sentence in the vernacular. In fact, English words in Gujarati sentences intimidate me. I feel slighted, I begin to falter and stop talking.

Difficult to argue with Kabir, I need time to be alone to think. To my dismay, I do not know English enough to spike my Gujarati with words like how Kabir says 'education' and 'modern.' Like how Meeshnari Mohamedali Bhanji Jivraj says 'psychology' and 'philosophy' in his waez sermons mesmerizing the jamat with his knowledge of high English. Now, I wonder if English would be better than Gujarati for our sacred texts. But what I know is that Gujarati gives Vedanta a memory. Gujarati gives Satpanth the wisdom I need to live through these times of changes when African voices and violence put fear in the heart. Most of all, Gujarati gives ginan the melody. Is Gujarati not the music that hosts Islam in the

242

jamat khana? The language that has preserved Saheb for six hundred years in the hearts of the Satpanthis? Trepidations put questions in my head. Doubts, fear and guilt assail me. What will happen when I lose the rass in the pirs' songs that awakens the divine in me? Will English bring home that bond of the native in me with my faith?

A feeling of loss grips me. Haiderali widens his eyes, his face tilts towards Diamond who is now hurriedly dressing up near the ironing table where Freda has kept his khane clothes ready. He won't be late, and so we won't be late. I stare at Haiderali like a sentinel narrowing my eyes and shaking my head to hold his look. Then, turning my head, I pull Haiderali's eyes with my own. My stare fixes on Kabir. My look tells Haiderali how I feel but he shows no response – no stretch of lips, no finger raised and no eye indication, no head movement, not even a little nod at least. Instead, he begins tapping his fingers to a tune in his head. Obviously, he has noticed I have changed, defying men in the house and does not know what to say.

I pass by the kitchen to take live coal kept ready for me by Freda, and carry the glowing clay bowl to the bedroom. Though relieved to be away from my officious brother-in-law, I feel gripped by an agonizing anger that self-questioning ekes out in thoughts. That tells me to go back to Kabir and defy him face to face. After all, Saheb did not tell us to reject our language heritage. Or did he? I don't remember his sacred decree to abandon our mother tongue.

I throw a few strands of oudh sticks over the coal. Spreading my khane pachedi-shawl above the curl of smoke, my eyes fall on Gandhi's biography by the bedside. Bubbles begin to spit sparks on sticky charcoal crumbling to ash.

I stand there before the mirror looking thaat-maat-smart. The aroma of oudh hovers over me as I am all ready to walk to khane. I look down to my pachedi-shawl, pressing the sculptured pleats on my shoulder with my four fingers over and the thumb underneath. I am wearing this particular frock on the chandraat evening, not because it is new or that it looks that extraordinary on me. It's actually quite ordinary, and not even in fashion. I wear it because Haiderali brought the cloth from Nairobi for me when he went to buy beads and the merchandise. I will sing to the mood of the ginans to soothe my heart today. I turn the pages of Ma Gor Bai's hand-written notebook to choose the hymn that would comfort me.

"You are a kasukoo parrot," remarks Haiderali as we leave home. He says it to mean I look beautiful like a parrot in the dress he likes. But also that I talk too much.

I have to be calm. The mukhi-elder had asked me to lead the evening's ginan recital today. I need to concentrate on the song and not return to anger. On the way to the jamat khana, I sing in my head. That helps me to ignore Haiderali's buckwaas, meaning his no sense talk.

244

Anger

The next evening while getting ready for khane, I say in triumph to Kabir, "Gandhi says to lose your language is to be a slave." Like a daily evening drill, we go through the same khane dressing up routine around the dining table in the inside veranda. I speak loud enough for Haiderali in the bedroom to hear me.

"Gandhi also wears a dhoti. Shall we Khoja men folk wear a dhoti too? Shall I walk with you to khane in a dhoti and Gandhi sandals?" snaps Kabir as he makes a knot on his square cut crepe nylon tie. His caustic words bring tears to my eyes. My heart thuds, irritation and annoyance fill me. My feelings are trapped in my thoughts that come to me in colours and shapes, not words. I want to fight, have an argument with Kabir, even slap him.

"See Zera Bai's samosa. Perfect shape!" says Kabir lifting the triangular tie knot under his two bent fingers. He jokes about my friend to make me smile and so trivialize me in the argument. I know this male trick now. I do not smile. He tries to draw my attention to his pinnacled little finger with a long nail like a pointer over the tie knot. To keep one long finger nail is high male fashion among Khoja bachelors of Nairowua that a few like Kabir have managed to uphold without breaking it. I will break that nail on his little finger.

"Churchill called Gandhi a half-naked fakir. How could a half-naked man free India of all the abhorrence of the other caste and religious hate? Look at all the slaughtering between his half-naked gurus and bandaged mullahs let loose at independence! Is India really free? Gandhi should have put on a three piece suit, persuaded his wife to wear English dress, speak English at home. To be free, India has to be modern. That's the key word 'modern'!" Are his thoughts from the book by Subhas Chandra Bose? I too read his biography and I know he is not with Gandhi and moreover, he married an English woman. Kabir circled the air making spirals with one finger pointed up. I don't understand his babbling buckwaas. Happy with what he just said, Kabir hums patting his cheeks with Old Spice aftershave like he was self-congratulating himself. He had shaved in the morning, not now. Sharp scent clouds around the veranda and comes to linger in with the house air already heavy with lifebuoy soap-vapour from the bathroom.

"Nonsense! Buckwaas *chhe*!" I aspirate with as sharp a look as the word itself hurled with contempt. Kabir's cheeks tint red. Haiderali widens his eyeballs as he walks in from the bedroom dressed for khane. I ignore them both.

I take time while pinning a stunning butterfly broach speckled in tiny ruby stones to my pachedi-shawl at the shoulder. Then I focus on straightening the pleats that fan out falling down to the ankles along the gold silk border, width of my palm, hugging my dress.

"You worship Gandhi like a god avatar," says Kabir throwing a look over his shoulder.

"Yes, I worship Gandhi not Subhas Chandra Bose," I say in defiance. His lips twist, and he gives me a compressed side smile, a mixed approval and surprise. Yes, I read his book. But he has nothing to say.

Yes, Gandhi is god avatar to me. My thoughts speak to me. Yes, he has faults. All avatars have faults but Ali the Naklank. *Si-ndio* - yes? Ole Lekakeny would ask to agree. Indians called Gandhi, Father and loved him. But the love between the father of the nation and the father to his son was not there. Gandhi's love for India was like Abraham's love for God. Both so blinded that they would sacrifice the parent in them for a cause bigger than the life of their child.

Then, when I read how Gandhi took a vow to live a celibate, my heart wept for Kastur Ba, his devoted wife still young. Did he ask her before taking the vow of celibacy that overruled his marriage vow? Would Subhas Chandra Bose have asked his wife if he decided to live a celibate?

Bose may have regraded his celibacy vow had he taken one, not fair to his wife. Gandhi expected his wife, Kastur Ba, to tolerate him. So I think about the wives of the two great men having read their separated lives for the struggle for India's independence that united them.

Kabir

The next few months pass by without a word about changing our language from Gujarati to English. The jamat's thoughts and talk are about the Mau Mau and the rising African voices for independence. I have not yet heard the language diktat from Saheb read in the jamat khana. I would have remembered the letter that would have been held over curling incense smoke over the heat of coal, and given to Rhemu Bhai who would have received it reverentially wrapped in a red and green velvet package in his right hand partly over the left. Then with the same reverence, he would have read it out to the patient jamat in slow and clear words. And we would have celebrated that evening together singing a joyous hymn about receiving Saheb's letter.

Expressions on women's faces tell me little or nothing about how they feel losing the language so completely, so suddenly. When the fear of native violence looms over us, how can I ask how parents feel about their children growing up not knowing the religion given to us in verses from the bard's heart? How can anyone ask?

When lost in thoughts, Haiderali would play tabla beats with his three fingers on anything that resonates like a biscuit tin, the table and even a box of matches. I don't know any more what is right and what is wrong. What shall we do? What can I do? Is it right to deliberately forget our language?"

"Moti Bai, think of the changes happening before your eyes. If we adopt English, it will help us to walk along with the modern world," says Kabir. He glances at Haiderali with a side smile soliciting the expected response, and as before, expecting a return side smile, hinting agreement if not praise of his wit. However, to his surprise this time, Haiderali does not respond which pleases me, and I frown back a response, something I had not done before to Kabir. I detest Kabir's man-humour, and this time I show it because of the ambivalence I read on my husband's face. I want to call him Kabiro, like how his friends call him when he acts up. You mzungu white man in brown skin! You coconut! You detest Africans because you fear them like you fear the white DC and so dislike him?

Kabir's actual name is Kabirdin, a Satpanth name that means 'of Kabir's religion.' The one who is the follower of the mystic bard called Kabir of Hindustan who was a weaver's son. When I was little, I loved to hear Missionary Shivji Bhagat speak parables that flowed in his pulsing voice when, and only when, he was in the mood of storytelling, otherwise he was an instructive teacher with a cane in his hand. How in poet Kabir's verses, as in our sacred songs, Vedanta was the warp and Islam's Sufism the weft of the Guru-Pir religions of Hindustan. "When the master versifier died," Missionary Shivji Bhagat would say, "both Moslems and Hindus claimed his body. One to bury him under the frangipani blossoms where they had dug a grave, and the other to cremate him in a sandalwood bier they had prepared. But when they lifted the corpse, lo!" he would pause here, and look into our faces before saying, "the corpse had turned into a bed of roses!" Missionary Shivji Bhagat would wait for a little while to let the picture of the corpse turning into a bed of roses conjure up in our imagination. Then he would say, "Our pir mabap, the parent pir of the Khoja of Hindustan, called his beloved son Kabir, a Hindu-Moslem name. Kabir too became a pir of the Satpanthis, did he not? Half Indian, half Persian that he was. Half a Hindu, half a Moslem, was he not? If not so, then, why are his songs half Hindu and half Moslem? He was a pukka guru-pir poet. We carry the bond of a hushed heritage folded into our language, poetry and the story from India to Africa." That's how Missionary Shivji Bhagat would talk like he was a trance stricken pir, a head full of devotion to Saheb. But the times are such that to talk about the language change seems trivial compared to security of life.

When Simba whimpers in the courtyard calling for Diamond's attention, Kabir yells at Freda, "Go and quieten the dog." Why is his anger put on Freda? Is it because he cannot show his temper to anyone else? He shouts at her as if she were his wife. He walks about here and there with a wet towel around his waist exuding the warmth of his after bath male smell.

Then I hear "Moti Bai!" Haiderali's call betrays his suppressed anger.

"Su *chhe*? What now?"

"A twenty shillings bill is missing from my black coat!" he says raising his voice.

I take a deep breath in and respond in a deliberately commanding voice, "Look carefully again! Search all your pockets! Your trousers too! This is not the first time you have misplaced money!"

"Definitely, the money was in my inner pocket, here," says Haiderali, showing me the inside of the black coat.

"Diamond!" I call out turning my eyes away from Haiderali. Diamond looks smart in his black woollen khane suit and a crepe nylon tie just like his uncle Kabir's. Kabir bought one for him too when he bought his in Nairobi. "I have prepared turmeric paste for Simba's leg. Bandage him when you come back from khane so he does not lick the wound. Now hurry up, or we will all be late for khane!"

Haiderali grumbles, "We have to get rid of that Kamba girl! Kabir spoils the servant. See what she has done now! Look for another house girl if you cannot keep an eye on this one." I don't reply. Why does he say so? I thought he likes Freda. I am suspicious.

The stashed cash in the folds of my bandhani was not enough to pay for my needs, so I took twenty shillings from Haiderali's coat pocket. This time, he noticed it, but for a long time, I have been taking some money from his pocket, albeit smaller bills or coins. I resent Haiderali giving me kitchen and khane money so scrupulously counted that I cannot save from it for my woman's needs, and other little secret pleasures. Like savouring the new Kit-Kat chocolate in town that breaks on your tongue like a crispy crack of Marie biscuit. Zera Bai relishes Kit-Kat, and it was she who recommended to me to taste Kit-Kat just once. Now, I eat Kit-Kat whenever I can, a little at a time, just for the crunch of its biscuit chocolate that crashes on my tongue.

Where is my country?

Coming back from school one day, my twelve years old son surprises me. "Mummy where is my country?" he asks. At home, he speaks in Gujarati to me, though not in the jamat khana.

"Why Diamond? Kenya is your country," I say.

"But I am not black," he answers. "Where shall we go after uhuru?"

"I was born in Kenya. You were born here. Your father was born here in Nairowua. My father was born in Nairobi. Our family has been African for three generations now. We go nowhere. Why do you ask?"

"Just nothing."

"What happened in school?"

"Nothing." Diamond pretends he is not interested in pursuing the topic anymore and begins unpacking his school bag. Clearly, something must have happened in school. He looks doubtful.

"Always remember Kenya is our country," I say again.

"Who told you?" Diamond's question takes me back.

"Mowla Bapa," I reply. He keeps quiet.

"Do you want some chai with chevdo? Biscuits?"

252

"Chai with breadbutter, and strawberry jam in Mombasa train," answers Diamond.

I watch Diamond dipping each slice of butter laden bread into his chai before he takes it to his mouth, careful not to break it halfway. When he comes home hungry from school, he wants his four White House butter-jam slices arranged in a line like wagons of a train. I sit with him today with my cup of chai, hoping he would tell me more about what's troubling him at school. I wait while I dip Marie biscuit in my chaikop, and out before it's soaked too soft, the Khoja way, a skill learned early in life. I would abhor the brown slush settling to the bottom of the cup, dissolving into and changing the sleek Gujarati chai to porridge. Diamond says nothing, concentrating on his train, and avoiding my eyes.

So it is that sometimes, my stories trickle from the sides like silent springs into the river. Stories from the sides are not always heard for they are softly spoken. In whispers, they enter my voice like serene waters flowing into gushing streams that make the river bigger. Thus does my story grow larger from smaller stories, many stories, chup chap stories, meaning hush hush stories.

Patel Master

Two days after the conversation about 'our country' with Diamond, I see the school messenger delivering a note for Haiderali at the bead shop. The note is from the principal, Patel Master. The next morning, Haiderali puts on his buscot.

"I want to come too," I say.

"I will do the talking. Do not say a word in men's talk. Understand?" Haiderali warns me. Haiderali always wants me to be barabar meaning proper as befits a lady, and protects me from local gossips. One of the popular gossips centres on the wife's tongue. Such chatters about women often have origins in the men's Sunday card circle on the lawn of the Nairowua City Hall.

I wear my khane dress, and we accompany Diamond to the school. He will not tell me why we are called to the school. My heart beats fast.

We wait for about ten minutes sitting on a backless bench against the wall of Mr Patel's office before a prefect with a red cloth badge on his front shirt pocket asks us to step in.

"I am afraid, Mr Haiderali Bhai, I will have to suspend your son because he gets into frequent fights. There are complaints from other parents. Two days ago, one fight started by your son, resulted in a nose bleed." Patel Master could not wait to start his complaint, dividing his stern look alternately between Diamond and his father.

He does not look at me, and I feel quite comfortable though concerned sitting there as an observer at men's talk. Above his table hangs a picture of Gandhi, taking a long sandaled stride with a stick in his one hand while with the other, he seems to be adjusting the cloth over his bare chest. "Parents complained to me. They are Brahmins, you know." Among the Indian men folk of Nairowua, Patel Master was better known as the husband of Mrs Patel, the filmi sort of moonfaced teacher at the same school. She is so white like a marble stone that Kabir calls her the Taj Mahal of Nairowua.

Haiderali and I are shocked. Haiderali does not know what to say. His shifting in his chair begins to bother me. He looks at me. My fault? Why look at me? I look back at him - I have nothing to say. I could see Haiderali's first instinct was to thrash Diamond right there in the principal's office, and he may have, had he not heard the principal asking Diamond in a serious tone asserting his authority over both the student and his parents. "Why did you fight with Inderjit?" Diamond says nothing. How could he? He is shaking because of fear of both, his father and the principal. Leaning forward, Patel Master drawls out the same question, this time into Diamond's face. A mixed smell of sweet pan masala and cigarette evaporates out of his mouth with his intimidating words. It reminds me of my religion schoolteacher, Meeshnari Shivji Bhagat.

"He makes fun of me calling me Khoja, Khoja, Centi Moja," Diamond replies breathing heavily. He is on the verge of breaking into tears.

"But is that not who you are?" snaps the principal.

"But he calls me Khoja in a bad way."

"How is that?" quizzes Patel Master with a look of put-on curiosity, narrowing his eyes while also looking askance at Haiderali.

"Like he mocks me that I have no caste and no country, no culture. That I worship the Aga Khan. Sometimes, he says Khoja are Untouchables. He tells me a Khoja is worth a cent because he has no proper religion and no country. He tells me to go to sleep. He walks behind me singing Khoja Khoja Centi Moja, Khoja Khoja Sojah," says Diamond. Tears roll down his cheeks. I wipe his face with my pachedi-shawl, deliberately taking time massaging his cheeks and then the ears.

"Actually, Mr Haiderali Bhai," Patel Master begins, appearing calm and wise, "the partition of India has created some tension among Hindu and Moslem students, and among my staff too, I must admit. But we must be tolerant, as Gandhi says."

"Yes. But why Untouchable?"

"You know the mentality of our people. They say the Khoja are low caste. Nothing wrong with that, don't get me wrong. You claim to be casteless. That is suspicious. Automatically, people think you are low caste. That's the mentality." Mr Patel smiles satisfactorily having given his explanation.

"How can this teasing be stopped?" asks Haiderali angered as much by Patel Master's attitude as by the condescending smile put on him. I see his ears turning red. I put my hand on Diamond's shoulder.

"Tomorrow, in the school assembly, I will read what Gandhi-ji has written about the Untouchables."

"But we are not Untouchables, Patel Master, sir. We are not of chura cleaner caste!" Haiderali is upset.

"I understand, I understand, Mr Haiderali," Patel Master tries to calm Haiderali in a fatherly teacher way. He is, after all, better educated and of no lesser a caste of Patel than a Brahmin himself. "Don't worry. I will read a very appropriate passage that will bring honour to your family. You know the one where Gandhi Bapu says the Untouchables are the Children of God."

"But Patel Master...what do you mean?" asks Haiderali. I shift in my chair. I want to speak. I bite my tongue.

"You must not worry about it at all," interrupts the principal, "let us educate the students and also the teachers in my school on the virtues of tolerance. There have been problems in the school since that Musalman butcher's boy whistled at our Hindu girl, a Brahmin, you know. I will not deny that. Moreover, after seeing that film Naastik the Atheist, my Hindu and Moslem staff look at each other with daggers in their eyes. I will not deny there is tension in the staff room. My wife says, the film director could have done without that scene of torched railway cars, charred and machete hacked Moslem and Hindu women and children. My wife says, Naastik the Atheist should have been banned in Kenya!" Patel Master is carried away by his wife's wisdom.

Haiderali remains quiet, but I can tell from his breathing he is angry inside. I feel like removing my slipper and landing its leather sole on Patel Master's hard head.

"True! True! I tell my wife. But you see, it's a patriotic film with patriotic songs. That's the reality. Let the

257

people decide. India is a democracy, the biggest democracy in the world, you see, Mr Haiderali Bhai. In India people decide," says Patel Master. He appears to have forgotten about Diamond's issue, and why he called us to his office.

"It is better to be an unbeliever naastik than a Hindu or a Moslem," says Haiderali. "That's what the film has taught me." He surprises me. I show him appreciation with a nod, and a half smile that go together.

"True! True! But naastik unbelievers destroy the society because they break the natural law, you understand, Mr Haiderali Bhai? It's the social order that keeps peace in India. Very ancient. Very old, and as the English say, 'Old is gold.' Naastiks destroy the ancient order. They are like communists. Just look at the violence that foreign religions and communism have brought to India!" exclaims the headmaster with an obvious hint at the Partition. Then he adds, "A naastik atheist is, in fact, a communist. No difference!"

"Patel Master, how do you know Khoja were converted from the Untouchables?" Haiderali raises his voice. Diamond watches his father, wide eyed with pride.

"Oh, I see! You see, Mr Haiderali Bhai, it was only the Untouchables of all the Hindu castes who converted to Islam and Christianity," Patel Master speaks as a matter of fact. We are after all, in his office and that's in his school.

Haiderali withdraws because, like me, he does not know anything about the history of conversion of the Khoja, a history about which castes converted to the Satpanth, why, when, and how. Or if at all they did – the thought comes to me. Haiderali remains quiet because deep in him, I know, he feels neither a Moslem nor a Hindu, neither a high caste nor a low caste. The way I do. He is an Indian Satpanthi who does not even feel a convert to Islam. My Noordin kaka uncle would say with pride, how, unlike the Satpanthi Ismailis, the Ithna Asheris converted totally from Hinduism. I wanted to tell Patel Master that Satpanth, the path at the threshold found the words of the pirs of Persia as worthy as of the gurus of India. When the pirs spoke, our forefathers heard Vedic knowledge in their words, home to our songs and thoughts, languages and rituals. Satpanth is my inside faith that is neither explained nor discussed with outsiders. I try to calm down taking in long breaths with words rolling in my head. A brief silence follows as Patel Master expects Haiderali to speak. For a moment, it looks like Haiderali would say something, but since he does not speak, Mr Patel takes over the opportunity.

"Mr Haiderali, may I ask? Do you now belong to India or Pakistan? Where do the Khoja belong?" His eyes narrow showing genuine curiosity and even some sympathy. "This has been a topic of debate among my staff in this school, which as you know, is called the Aga Khan Primary School, the only Asian school in Nairowua, and I tell you Mr Haiderali, nobody has the answer."

Where do I belong? I ask myself. India or Pakistan? Could I belong to any of the two nations born out of the fire of abhorrence of each other's religion that are both mine?

"To both and none," responds Haiderali as he gets up to leave the office, pulling up Diamond by the elbow. I am surprised by his sudden decision to leave, not his answer. Patel Master sees me nodding.

"But that is not possible, Mr Haiderali Bhai. Is it?" Patel Master interrupts before Haiderali would want to say more. He seems to be a different person now. I look at Krishna's statuette that stands among three silver sports trophies on the same table against the wall. Krishna is black, standing cross ankled under a giant hooded cobra, also black.

"In Nairobi, the boys of the Indian High School rioted because the English headmaster removed a picture of Gandhi, or was it Nehru? What happened was..." Patel Master's half-finished sentence stayed on his open mouth as Haiderali leaves without looking back, pulling Diamond by the hand. I follow quickly after them out of the office.

Once outside, Haiderali takes a deep breath and calmly tells Diamond, "Just ignore your Patel Master. Don't fight with these Bania, Musla and Singha boys. They will get tired." He grinds his teeth as he speaks. "Now run to your class and tell me every day what happens in school."

Later in the afternoon, Haiderali tells me he has been thinking about the importance of the day's happening in Diamond's life. That was unusual because he usually keeps his opinions to himself in the house. He says, "Today was a lesson in how to live a Satpanthi, the way of our ancestors. We teach our children by example. But I did not expect we would have to live like this in Africa! We came to Africa to be free."

So change, Moti Bai!

That evening, after prayers at the jamat khana and a good naandi meal at home, Haiderali changes into his pyjamas and sits on the bench under the mango tree in the courtyard smoking the new elegant English cigarette he calls Clippers. It comes in a blue packet with a picture of an English dhow on it. Kabir and I talk on the veranda, seemingly politely, but actually, it's a silent after dinner family wrestling of words. Freda clears the table and takes the plates to the karo to wash. I see from her delayed actions she wants to stay behind to listen to us. I know she will be listening from the karo anyway. Zarina is doing her homework at one end of the dining table, oblivious to what we are saying. After a while, she leaves her books half open to go and sit by Freda, and they talk and giggle. They share secrets that never come to my ears. Zarina's pencils, eraser, sharpener, school bag, compass set, six inch ruler, carbon and tracing papers, will stay scattered on the table until morning when she would throw them all into her schoolbag. Then, without sitting down, she would have her one buttered toast and half a cup of chai, and rush out to school.

"When uhuru bites, Banias, Muslas and Singhas will flee to UK, some will even go to India-Pakistan, but we Khoja will remain behind. So change, Moti Bai! Learn some English to get by! It's never too late," says Kabir ostensibly joking, but he is serious. The kind of seriousness said jokingly. Said in a way that hides his anxiety of uncertainty about the future. Some of us are learning how to dodge around our anxiety by making jokes, and so ease our dilemma for the moment. Who knows how to explain this bewilderment otherwise? I want Haiderali to tell me what to do. Like Zera Bai's husband, Rhemu Bhai, who tells her she must follow Saheb's wishes and speak English to the children. Like Khanu Bai's husband, Mamdu Bhai, who shows his dislike of English that he does not know a word of, with an expression like he had a rotten egg in his mouth, she says. Why do I blame Haiderali? He is a wasi wasi type of a husband who is vague with words. So much so that sometimes I need to wrest out what he thinks through an argument. He knows in his heart what has been the tradition of the Satpanth Khoja, but can he say no to Saheb?

Kabir's tone provokes a quarrel. I need to gather my thoughts and find words to shape them in a way that does not sound rude to my in-law. I take time before I ask, "But we are becoming more English than African. How will that help? Why not adopt African customs?"

"So whose African culture do you suggest we adopt? Kikuyu, Luo, Kalenjin, Turkana, or Maasai? There are more than forty separate African people in Kenya. Each one distinct and proud of its own culture. Be practical, Moti Bai. Can we really adopt or be adopted by any tribal culture?" says Kabir striking a match that he holds like a delicate jasmine flower between his fingertips. Then, cupping the flame with his other hand, he lets it burn down almost to his fingers as if he were defying himself.

Kabir leaves the room humming a tune from the new film called Shaheed the Martyr that he watched in

262

Tanganyika with Rhemu Bhai. The film is banned in Kenya, but we listen to the anti-English songs from All India radio.

Haiderali has been listening to our argument for a while before letting out an audible sigh showing he gives up. In a way, he is indicating he agrees with neither his brother nor me. He begins humming a song from Naastik the Atheist, looking away like he would rather think about other things. From his pensive look, I can tell that like me the incident at Diamond's school that happened some weeks ago, haunts him still. It concerns us more than what we say at home. Perhaps, the same angry thoughts are spiralling in Haiderali's head today as on that day in Patel Master's office. Thoughts that come from anger trapped in a cage of doubts hanging like a cloud over the faith I hold dear to my heart.

Haiderali supports his head with two pinnacled fingers on his forehead, while the cigarette wedged between his other two, glows in the dark dropping grey ash on his pyjama. Could he be thinking what I am thinking? Were not the Persian pirs who came to convert us instead drawn to the creation that honoured the unison of man, fish and animal as God avatars? If not, then how could the bards be inspired to compose such eloquent epics as the Das Avatar and a thousand ginans all in the vernaculars of the regions?

My thoughts circle in my head because I have no answers. Is it Persia's Sufism meeting Bhagti in the Guru-Pir religions of India? I have more questions but no answers really, only questions that remain like residue of my thoughts. My head hurts when I think of how Diamond and Almas will understand the faith when they have lost the language of the faith. Where do I seek the answers? I could ask Missionary Shivji Bhagat, but he returned to India to teach the children of Khoja families dislocated from their homes during the Hindu Moslem rift in the old country. He may be too old now to answer questions, or he may even be dead. Whom can I ask? After the car crash of the three missionaries in Tanganyika, no travelling preacher has visited Nairowua again. I wonder if another learned one will ever visit us now from the school in Dar-es-salaam?

Later, when I bring Haiderali his glass of water for the night, I am finally able to ask him what has been troubling me. "Was there ever a farman edict, or at least a letter from Saheb read in the jamat khana advising us to abandon Gujarati in families?" He looks bewildered. He looks at me like a chained dog sitting puzzled in a corner wondering how to get around, and out of his imprisonment. He coughs to let go his confusion. He whispers a thought I do not understand. Then, suddenly, with a flick of his hand, he gestures to me to leave him alone, turning his face away. Feeling emboldened, and taking advantage of his withdrawal, his meekness, his confusion, whatever his feelings are, I prod him, "Did the parent guru-pirs tell us to pray in Farsi or Arabic? Did they change the sacred to a language foreign to the Indian tongue?"

"No! No! Stop it!" he yells, startling me. The tone of his voice is at once forceful and pitiful as if both threatening and pleading me to stop speaking. He stares at me. The lingering look asks to know what my intention is. Am I trying to be anti-Saheb like my Noordin kaka uncle? I am expecting him to say that.

Instead he says, "Why don't you move over to the Ithna Asheri Khoja jamat?"

"But they are more Arabic than we are," I reply.

264

He gives me a long fixed look, a different look this time, a look to make me feel guilty for asking. I stare back defying him to speak back to me, eye to eye, with honesty, not give me the annoyed husband look again. But he does not speak as if to say I should know the answers to what I am asking. Like a teacher telling the student to think before asking. As if what's in his mind is unspeakable. How can I even put such a thought out into words? What I read is a threat from the fire in his eyes. A shut-your-mouth eye threat.

I walk out of the room and leave him alone, but the question hangs on: Will I ever know who I am when I lose the vernacular that composes the narrative and the verse, the voice that sings beauty to the heart of the native in me? That makes me Saheb's murid. That's Satpanth's soul. I am a singer of ginans, an artist at heart and that is the worship I know. The raga of the ginan secures me to my faith in Saheb. The language that formed the Satpanth is Indian. Did the vernacular not give the Persian pir a melody creating the Sufi path in Vedic hymn? Many questions stir my feelings at this moment of doubts.

Doubts assail me sharp as arrow heads. Was it out of ignorance or was it out of wisdom that our forefathers chose the Satpanth, meaning the True Path that twined Vedic to Islam? I know Sat-guru-pir as the one who came from Ismail the Imam at the assassins' fort on the rock in Persia. Our Saurashtran sages must have debated what the father to son generations of guru-pirs were singing to the folks at dance circles. Would they not have wondered then, consulted among themselves, and put their heads together at the village panchayat councils? Surely, they must have asked how they could keep the divided Hindu-Moslem

265

hearts of the Khoja caste together. "The Imam co-habits the noor and avatars," they might have said, and thus sang the Das Avatar that we hold sacred to this day.

There were no more incidents or fights reported to Haiderali by Patel Master and Diamond was not suspended from school. Needless to say, the teasing in the school continued, but Diamond would not tell his father about the song that Raju and now also Aslam sing walking behind him. He told me, but I had first to promise I would not tell his father. I am a mother, and I know what a child confides in his mother, the father will not know.

Diamond told me sometimes Inderjit too joined Raju and Aslam. Inderjit is the boy who name calls Diamond when he does not fight back. He calls Diamond the meek gathiya boy. And sometimes, Gandhi or Kacchi. Diamond understands gathiya, Gandhi and Kacchi are Punjabi words for a coward, said to provoke him, but he is learning to be a Satpanthi and not fight back. Hindu and Moslem boys, otherwise hostile to each other after the partition of British India, have a common victim in Diamond, the Khoja boy who does not know where he belongs. In this, they are united when they sing, otherwise not. And they are right because Diamond does not know where he belongs in the old country.

Khoja Khoja centi moja	*Khoja Khoja one cent worth*
Nah Hindu, nah Musalman	*Not Hindu, not Moslem*
Ahbi tu sojah	*Now you go to sleep*
Laandh paakarke sojah	*Grab your penis and sleep*

266

The khane librarian

After the meeting with Patel Master in his office, and Kabir's nagging me to change, Hindu-Moslem-Satpanth-Islam storms my head. My mother-love seeks to revenge my son's humiliation. The woman in me no longer accepts Kabir's self-centred male ideas over my own. Yet, my religion tells me to forgive them both. Diamond is not wrong. I am not wrong. My woman's pride seeks a quarrel but my faith practice tells me to let it go. I have thoughts – doubts - bitter thoughts - deeper doubts - hurt. I ponder like a cow regurgitating grass.

I go through old copies of *Africa Samachar* at the jamat khana library where they label and store monthly magazines and newspapers. I like to re-read old articles when I have time before the service starts and sometimes, even after the service. I read because of a thought, sometimes because of the pleasure of recalling. Sometimes, to forget the present like the women who borrow detective and romance novels from the library to read and forget their drudgery. But today it's because I want to fight.

"What are you looking for?" asks the librarian Damji Bhai Jetha, a retired History and Gujarati language teacher at the Aga Khan School. I explain to him what happened to Diamond, and the meeting with Patel Master, the principal.

"Patel Master is a pukka Hindu, and an Indian nationalist. He sees religion and caste with the same eyes. I have worked with him. He sees the Satpanthis the people of a faith, with caste eyes." He goes through a pile of *Africa Samachar* diligently dusting each copy as he reads the title and fans through the pages. A broad smile comes over his face when he finds the magazine that was published at the time of independence of India and the horrendous Partition that followed.

"Read this," says the librarian, "it's an article by Professor Vidya from the University of Saurashtra. It's about Emperor Akbar of India. Aa! He was a lover of art, religions, music and embroidery like you are." Damji Bhai Jetha's remark sparks my curiosity. I smile thank you with a blush.

I look at the picture in the centre double page of *Africa Samachar*. It's striking because its elegance carries the Moghul grace. "I want to look at the picture at home. Can I borrow this for a week?" I ask. The librarian allows me to take the magazine home. He knows an artist looks at paintings like how an astronomer looks at stars.

The article summarized the professor's five hundred page research book that he had titled Moghuls' love of the Vedic.

In the 1580s, Emperor Akbar of Hindustan commissioned the Mahabharata to be translated from Sanskrit to Persian. He called it Razmnama: The Book of War after the great battle of cousin princes described in it. The Emperor called it so because in it wars were contemplated not in terms of strategies and armies but from points of view of human virtues and emotions of moral strengths and weaknesses so compellingly delivered in dialogic verses. In the Mahabharata human strengths are like bonds of kinships, spirituality, compassion, honour, filial duty, humility and forgiveness. Human

268

weaknesses are like anger, revenge, greed, cruelty, cowardice, hate and humiliation.

The article described how the Emperor gathered the best painters in his empire to illustrate the Vedic verse in Persian art. The result was a magnificent collection of Moslem paintings celebrating Vedic religion. These illustrations not only informed but also gave dignity to the book of thoughts on war that resides in minds of men.

The picture in the centre double page of *Africa Samachar* is of a painting of dark Krishna revealing his cosmic form to Arjuna. The prince in the picture is a marksman with a bow, the size of his height, in his right hand and a quiver of golden arrows strapped to his back. If I were a missionary, I would travel to India to see all the 161 paintings in Razmnama that Professor Vidya writes about.

The article concluded that two generations later in 1657, the Emperor's great-grandson, Dara Shikoh, commissioned the Upanishads to be translated from Sanskrit to Farsi and he called it 'The Greatest Mystery'. This, the prince hoped, would invite Moslem scholars to Delhi's royal court to look over the rigid boundaries that encased the Islam that tribal Moghuls came with from the North, and know their indigenous heritage, for they were Indians now. However, Dara Shikoh is better known for *The Confluence of the Two Seas. Africa Samachar* explains the book as a discourse between paths that seem not unlike the Satpanth and several other Gur Pir religions of India that mirror Sufi thoughts in Vedic verse and Vedic thoughts in Sufi verse. Unfortunately, Dara Shikoh's younger brother, Aurangzeb, usurped the throne and killed the crown prince and their sister. Yes, I remember Missionary Shivji Bhagat telling us how Aurangzeb the Moghul threw his own father, the king, into prison because of greed for power, and he massacred the Sikhs and Ismailis alike because both held the Vedas in Islam that he despised as fouling the purity of Islam. He also said it was a woman, a gallant Hindu queen who drove Aurangzeb out of Saurashtra. I saw her in my girl's imagination. A heroic woman in the battle with the Moghuls, wielding her sword with one hand and pulling the reins of her white horse with the other. She would have a gold coronet on her helmet, and the end of her red sari under the metal breastplate trailing in the air behind her like a flag.

Razmnama takes me to pictures in Nooran Mubin, the book on successions and wars of Ismaili Imams, and the peaceful preacher pirs. I have been reading Nooran Mubin from the day I learned how to read. At first, I followed my Dadabapa's finger, and my words hopped along the line like I was walking on one foot. Then, when Dadabapa's finger ran along the line, my words flowed like a stream. It would have been in Sufi Moghuls' India that the pirs from Persia found royal patronage. Then, like the Moghuls they came to be captivated by the universality of the Vedas. The Vedic epics, they must have come to realize, were so vast that they could hold Persian devotions within Indian heritage of the village folks, and yet, not blemish what they knew as sacred. After all, they came and became the pirs of Hindustan, not Persia, did they not? I would ask myself with a smile even as I imagined and dreamed about life in medieval Khoja villages in Saurashtra. If I were a man, I would have been a missionary, I like to tell myself.

After a week when I go to the library to return the copy of *African Samachar*, Damji Bhai Jetha shows me two books.

"You may like to read these," he says. I see one book is about the Moslem Emperor Akbar and the other is on Shivaji, the great warrior and Hindu raja of the Maratha who are like kinsmen to us, the Gujaratis.

While reading these books over a month and half, often old stories told to me by my Dadabapa, Stepmother Gor Bai and Missionary Shivji Bhagat would come to my mind in scattered pictures. Stories about Khoja beliefs in Indian history and myths.

"My mind tells me that the Emperors of India, the Sufi Moghuls of their times, were patrons of Vedic books, and perhaps, of Satpanth pirs too," I say to start a conversation with the librarian.

"Yes. We know the Moghuls translated Vedic books and put them in libraries so Islam may know the land where it had come to nest. So the Hindu-Moslem subjects may live in peace as it is with the Satpanthis," says the librarian Damji Bhai Jetha. His eloquence reminds me of Missionary Shivji Bhagat, and I hang on to his words. "Thus, over time, in their discrete manner, the Khoja cultivated a form of seminal worship chanted in the litany of folklore steeped in Indian knowledge. Then the song gave birth to the Satpanth, a conviction that neither discarded the group bonds of Khoja rustics nor shunned the preacher pirs of Persian knowledge."

It is this song called the ginan that sings to my heart today as it would have to the hearts of my ancestors in the secluded villages of Saurashtra. Having read and

271

talked with the librarian, I feel contented. There is no need to bring up the subject with Patel Master anymore. Moreover, I know Haiderali will not allow it.

Anyway, while reading the library books I came across Rani Tara Bai. Now, I am captivated by the story of this woman who led an army against Aurangzeb the mighty Moghul to free Saurashtra of his tyranny. Her name Tara means Star and I want to know more about her. My heart lies with her.

My story is a quiet one, buried in wanderings into the books I read, and sometimes tangled in mysteries that my faith holds. My stories take me around nooks and corners of untold secrecies, over old stories and under the even older than the old stories. Like how the needle works new stitches over the old, and under the old and even older stitches.

What the parrot pir said to the Queen

Knowing the history of Satpanth does not ebb my feelings. Diamond's harassment in school hurts me. More so because I cannot tell his father or anyone else. Not even Khanu Bai and Zera Bai. My son made me promise to keep the Khoja Moja Centi Moja teasing a secret. The feeling stays in me through the day to the evening like it were a trapped bird fluttering between rage and ache in my chest. In the jamat khana, I put my ache into the evening song tapering into the resonance of the chorale that lingers in the ceiling air as if waiting to merge into the pith of silence of the night sky. But how do I explain to my children that for generations the Satpanthis have exiled their memories to concealment? How do I explain how our forefathers lived in borrowed faith to trick the tyranny of self-righteous religions and rigid castes?

After dinner when Haiderali and Kabir go to the courtyard to smoke under the mango tree and Freda makes a pile of utensils and plates to take to the karo to wash, I walk to the children's room. They are in bed but not asleep. I sing a verse from Das Avatar that Meeshnari Shivji Bhagat made us chant again and again, collectively and individually, so as children, we would know why Satpanth the True Path is the Secret Path.

I remember how the missionary expounded the verse about Queen Suraja of Saurashtra. I say to my alert children, "During the times of pirs and Ismaili gurus, there were demons everywhere disguised as humans. They would sweet talk to children. The demons came from other religions and enemy religions. Their purpose was to capture souls and destroy Satpanth."

With a tone of confidence in his voice, Shivji Bhagat put fear in me to guard myself, and yet be tolerant of other faiths. Now I do the same to my children. "Secrecy is the Satpanth way," I say what the missionary teacher said to me.

Diamond and Almas listen, mesmerized, wide eyed from under their quilts. They ask no questions tonight, unlike at other times when I explained why we must keep Satpanth chup chap, meaning discreet and quiet as narrated in Das Avatar, the epic chant of Hindustan that has kept us together and in secret for so long. It was this song that protected Saheb in the Bombay court against the strong voiced dissenters. Then the judge said the Vedic hymn showed we were different from the Ithna Asheris and the Sunnis, yet Moslems because we believed in Saheb the Imam from the Prophet's house, and we shall henceforth be called the Ismailis. This is how it was through the song that Meeshnari Shivji Bhagat instilled the Satpanth mystery in me when I was little. But it was at home, as it was in the circadian rituals of community worship and living, that I learned how I must keep my faith concealed. Silently, I observed how adults deflected words in talks and how they put on appearances shrouding the mystery of Greater Mystery that resided in their hearts and expounded in the story verses of the Das Avatar. I tell one story from the Das Avatar to my children that I know would flare their imagination with colourful pictures of birds and open blue

274

skies, waters, mountains and palaces as in their fairy tales. As it flared my imagination when I was little.

There was once an Ismaili pir who lived in a citadel on a rock in Persia. He was a pious man and used to meditate every day from dawn to dusk. One day, Saheb appeared to him when he was in deep meditation and said, "Go to India across the border, cross the kingdoms of three Indian rajas and come to Saurashtra. There you will find on the other side of the Ganges, a Queen called Suraja. Speak to her about Satpanth and comfort her for she worries about her soul.

When the pir opened his eyes, lo! He found his green-silk-robe had changed into a shimmering green-feathered-body. The robe's wide open sleeves became wings that he could flap. His red-silk-turban had turned into a red-feathered-crown. He had a hooked nose that touched his lips when he spoke. Yes, he could speak though he had shrunk to the size of half a human arm. His voice was shrill like parrot's talk. The pir, now a kasukoo, meaning a parrot, with a green body and red head, perched himself right on top of the tower of the citadel on the rock, and from there he looked over a vast landscape towards India. Then he flapped his wings and flew. He soared high up in the sky over the mountains and deserts, waters and the three kingdoms. Finally, he spotted Queen Suraja of Saurashtra on the other side of the Ganges. The beautiful Queen lived in a palace with walls made of mirrors and floors of white marble. The pillars were of gold and doors made of silver. On entering the royal bedroom where the Queen was admiring herself before a mirror framed in gold, the parrot pir said to Queen Suraja:

Be comforted O Queen! Accept Satpanth the True Path. Your husband is a demon disguised a king. Be cautious O Queen, in secret now practise Satpanth. King Kalingo must not know or he will destroy you. Saheb will come to Hindustan riding a white horse, Zulficar at his waist, and he will destroy the demon king forever.

And so Queen Suraja did not tell anyone she believed in Saheb, Naklank the unblemished, and continued to practise Satpanth in secret, sing the ginans in secret and pay the tithe in secret. Her husband, the demon King Kalingo, did not come to know or he would have killed her, *nah?* In time, Queen Suraja's faith grew stronger and deeper, and she lived a long and happy inside-outside life, meaning a life of simulation, meaning an Ismaili life, for ever after while she waited for Saheb's darshan-deedar in Hindustan.

The path of telling my story comes from how I spoke about my faith growing up amidst other faiths. I lived inside-outside life like Queen Suraja. Like Remti Bai married to an Ithna Asheri Khoja who in secret sends dua food offerings to the jamat khana. Like Rehema Bai married to Ismaili Khoja who sends dua-prayer money in secret for the box at the silver cradle of Imam Husein's slayed son in the Ithna Asheri mosque. Like the Gupti, meaning the concealed Khoja of Hindustan, both hold paired beliefs. Like Queen Suraja, women know how to survive when what they believe in is denied.

Part Seven

Nakedlegs

While the fear of the Mau Mau gripped the land, it became evident that change in governance in British East Africa was coming as it happened in India, Ghana and Nigeria. At this time there came a wave of modernization sweeping through the Satpanth Ismaili Khoja community. The Evian Conference of the Ismaili leaders was called in 1952 to draw out policies for drastic cultural changes that would project a new visage of the old community in the name of modernity and adaptation to the new era. Like the Evian Conference before on immigration and settlements of Jewish refugees in the new lands, the closed door Ismaili conference sought ways to change the Indian in the Khoja. Through dramatic moves that included a shift of worship rituals to Arabic forms and vocabulary, the community began displaying a character identified by a lifestyle thought to be modern and adjusting to change. All this happened within a decade of the 1950s that ended with the end of Mau Mau in 1960. Then began the rise of brutal state propelled anti-Asian African propaganda.

The Imam encouraged the women to adopt European dress style. He found a way around those who were reluctant at first because short dresses exposed their legs and they felt it was not just immoral but also embarrassing to walk around the town with 'naked legs' as they put it, and without a pachedi-shawl over their chests and heads that they were used to as Gujarati and Kacchi Khojas. The Imam decided to give his signed picture mounted on a board to those women who would wear the European dress. It was a special photo in colour of the Imam and his begum not seen anywhere before. Moreover, it carried blessings written in the Imam's own handwriting. It was like a benediction certificate that the women craved to possess and show off on side boards and shelves in their living rooms. Some had it even framed. It read just one line, as the Imam's blessings usually do, and that was enough:

I GIVE MY BEST PATERNAL BLESSINGS TO ALL
WHO ADOPT SIMPLE COLONIAL DRESS.

A large majority of women, including many in their senior years, put on what the Imam called a 'simple colonial dress'. There were a few, however, who were unable to abandon their traditional dressing and they continued to wear a long frock or adopted a sari as their regular dress.

On Sundays, the Ismaili Khojas gather to celebrate Nairowua's premiers of Indian movies at cinemas - Metropole and Paradise, skipping evenings at the new jamat khana with a tower. They also learn to make rich Mughlai meat curries and biryani with Basmati rice flavoured with spices formerly reserved for festive days. Slowly and elegantly, some families like Zera Bai's shed off desi habits like eating with their fingers, and not using fingers to pinch pick spices and salt out of bottles while cooking. They learn about Western dance and lifestyle that the change from traditional attire for women opened up for the middle class. They learn from magazines and movies, and from the new England-return young men and women. The apartheid, however, snubbed the sudden appearance of voluntary self-assimilation of the Ismailis into European life style while putting aside their own. Nor did it lessen the rising anti-Asian feelings of the African.

Conversely, the Ithna Asheri Khoja women's ethnic Indic dress segued into full length veiling testifying sturdier adherence to the Twelver Shia faith and Middle Eastern religious identity.

Tooko Faraak

It was not that I did not want to visit Zera Bai to see her new bungalow home but I was afraid of her dog. She had assured me that her dog stayed chained to the tree and slept in a crate. As Khanu Bai and I walk through the garden gate, the dog threatens us with several woofs, standing up over a frayed British military coat. I feel sorry for the dog chained like a criminal in one place where he ate and slept while guarding the house. He has a puzzled look on his slanted face like in doubt whether we are friends or enemies. He then barks all of a sudden like he sees someone behind us. A chill runs through me. Frightened, my first words come out in a whispered question, "Mau Mau?" I turn around. Khanu Bai's eyes widen, enquiring What? Then she too looks back at the gate left half open by us.

On the door is a copper plate embossed with two hands joined over a tasbih as in prayer. Underneath it reads: YA ALI MADAD WELCOME in Gujarati. Zera Bai's house help, Grace whom she calls Bhoiti in her Kacchi when we talk, opens the door. The sudden appearance of a black face shakes me up. Standing mute by the door, Grace smiles, and then immediately steps aside in the usual manner of a black servant posing small in an Asian home. I feel relieved moving out of the block of searing heat of the afternoon into the shade of the threshold. Then, stepping over a pool of water dripping from the gunia-sack cloth in Grace's hand, we enter the new apartment-like building that we call bungalow, putting prestige to the residence and its occupants. There are a few more such two and three bedroom bungalow houses on the outskirts of Nairowua. They were recently constructed on the departing Greek coffee and sisal plantations that the wealthier Indians purchased collectively, and sub-divided to erect family bungalow homes.

"It's solid hot. Heat scorches the land," says Khanu Bai stepping into the coolness of the foyer, sunspots daze me. I squeeze shut my eyes a few times to wipe them out. Sunlight through the front door comes into the corridor and stays like a stagnant pool on the gleaming terrazzo, patterned like black pepper on cream. I try to dab the sweat off my brow but my palm is sweaty too. I use the back of my hand.

"Hodi! Hodi! Anyone home *chhe* ...*e* ...*e*?" Khanu Bai yells out like a song elongating *chhe* to draw attention as if from a distance. Instantaneously then, she stretches her neck and peers through the narrow corridor. "There seems to be nobody around," she says yet she sees Grace at the door.

"Hodi!" comes a faint reply from the other end of the corridor. "Come in. Door wide open *chhe*."

Zera Bai is sitting bowlegged on the paatlo floor stool frying samosas. I am carrying a plate of spongy rice dhokra carefully covered over with white crochet net I had knitted for the top cover of our new PYE gramophone-radio. Khanu Bai has a plate of nankhatai biscuits similarly covered. Obviously, she has bought the English powder milk and semolina rusks from naandi at the jamat khana the evening before. She would not say so, giving us the impression she made them.

"Yes, sun-heat solid *chhe*. It burns. I pray for rains when I see blue emptiness above me. If the rains don't come soon, it will be drought again," I say sitting down at the round table in the narrow foyer that Zera Bai calls the dining hall. My hard wooden chair with armrests and a half back faces Zera Bai at the two charcoal stoves glowing in the kitchen. For a while I stare at one side of her kitchen wall blackened with carbon. It looks so much like my kitchen wall. Familiar smell of sizzling hot oil and burning coal from her stove whiffs by me, and hangs in the foyer like an invisible haze. As though instinctively, every few minutes, Zera Bai raises her elbow above her eyes and wipes the perspiration from her brow to the sleeve of her dress.

"Chai will be ready soon. You will feel cooler after a hot cup of tea, heat cuts heat. And hot vegetable samosas *chhe*. I saw fresh carrots and peas at the market. So I said, why not make vegetable samosas today?" says Zera Bai. Then she asks unexpectedly and directly as it has become the manner of her talk suddenly and recently, "When will you two start wearing the tooko faraak? It's been long since Saheb's farman on blessings in adopting the colonial dress, and you are still thinking about it?" Her eyes dart from the sizzling samosas to chai about to crack and bubble through the brown cream in a film of ghee. In a monotonous tone like of a teacher taking a roll call, Musa Ayub the radio host, begins reading a long list of names. Aap ki Farmaish, the song request programme just started.

"To say the truth, I have not even tried one. How would I look in a tooko faraak?" asks Khanu Bai. "Look at my tyres!" She jokes pinching her abdomen under her pachedi-shawl.

282

"You have to start wearing the English dress someday, you know that?" says Zera Bai with such great confidence that it makes me uncomfortable. Perhaps, that's her intention. She does not look at us though, or even towards us while she strains the hissing samosas and then line them one at a time into a bowl drainer.

"Why are you delaying? You know the coming changes are big. We cannot survive if we keep to old ways." Zera Bai's eyes tense, her sentence ebbs into a squeal. She rubs her apprehension on me. "Or are you scared away by *Africa Samachar?*" asks Zera Bai intently changing her voice to defiance. Her eyes widen. The talk of the week after evening devotions has been about a comment in *Africa Samachar* calling us, the Khoja women, shameless imitators of the English.

"Rhemu thinks the editor is a Gandhian nationalist, you know, against Indians wearing English clothes. He makes fun of our open legs, suggesting we have loose characters," says Zera Bai. "He needs a taste of my leather sandal."

Zera Bai finishes cooking, puts chai on the floor. Immediately, the paaht paaht bubbling subsides and the top straightens out without even a ripple. Zera Bai covers the aluminium saucepan, closes the doors of the two charcoal stoves and changes her position. Sitting sideways now, knees raised and together, she carefully lays aside six of the most perfectly shaped triangular samosas that we know would be for her naandi prayer dish that evening. She arranges the rest in a clear glass plate for us. Getting up now from the paatlo stool, leaning forward and pressing her palms on her knees, she sighs, "Eh Mowla!" Then, as she straightens up she says shu-khar in an elongated breath, and

283

immediately starts to hum into the song from the radio in the lobby where we are. Her humming grows louder as she walks out of the kitchen carrying the hit music from the movie Awara into the dining hall lobby.

"Come with me while the chai brews," says Zera Bai with a cheer of a teenage girl in a mood to play pranks. First, she lifts the netted cloth over the PYE radio sitting on the wall shelf, and then hikes the volume as she sings into the song Awara hun … hu hu hu … awara hun.

We follow Zera Bai into the bedroom listening to her singing in perfect harmony with the song from the radio. On the inside of her bedroom door, are cello-taped pictures of actors – Raj Kapoor, Dilip Kumar, Nargis, Madhubala and Meena Kumari, mat black and white cut-outs from Filmfare magazines. Saheb's framed picture is suspended from a nail on the wall above the double bed that has a pink satin bedspread in embroidered colours - red roses and lime green perforated rose leaves. The pillowcases have stencil stitched overlapping double hearts in red with initials Z and R in English. Short, stout and bespectacled Saheb is wearing a long black coat and a tall hat. He is pulling a horse by the bridle and smiling victory.

"Joh - Look! Try this one," says Zera Bai, levelling her eyes at me with a friendly double wink. She takes the frock off the hanger hooked on the handle of her cupboard door fixed to a blue opaque glass painted on with a peacock fanning out its brilliant feathers. "At least try, and see yourself in an English dress. There are no men around in the house." She smiles again shaking her head dole dole and raising her hand with a quick twist of her pointed up fingers like Kum Kum the dancer. She has such grace that you would think she had rote learned these gestures from films like the songs.

"Naakhra *chhe*!" Khanu Bai whispers in my ears referring to Zera Bai's coquetry.

Zera Bai and I are of similar build with a little difference in the waistline - a few more inches on Zera Bai, while on the backside, I am bigger. I can tell the red chiffon dress is made from her sari and the lining inside is from her matching satin underskirt. Roshan Bai, the seamstress of Nairowua, now specializes in transforming saris into dresses. In the jamat khana, you would hear Roshan Bai's mother-in-law grumbling how her home has been turned into a factory for fashioning English dresses out of Indian saris.

I put on the tooko faraak, turn around and look at myself in the mirror on the other door of the cupboard. At first, I blush, my cuffed hands on my lips, embarrassed looking at myself bared. And without the pachedi-shawl, how do I cover those hip and midriff middle age bulges? Moreover, after losing my baby who followed Almas, my body has not returned to its earlier shape, no matter how hard I try cutting down on ghee and butter in my diet. I have reduced from a tablespoon full of heated ghee over my khichedi to only a teaspoon. I only lightly butter my toast. Now I wonder if I will ever lose weight.

"It is so open!" I exclaim. "Hai! Hai! What will people say? A nude passing by their street?"

Both Zera Bai and Khanu Bai burst out laughing like they were expelling series of dry coughs, and then I too feel compelled to laugh at myself. I look a stranger to myself in the mirror. The reflection takes me to the days

285

when as a girl I stood before the mirror with my sister, Monghi, and cousin-sister Malek, chuckling at our reflections in the mirror as we tried on fashionable oversized hand-me-down dresses discarded by the dance girls at the lodge. Meethi Bai would bring the dresses for us, hiding them in her Luo ball basket one at a time so my father would not know where they came from.

"What?" exclaimed my father angrily when one day he did come to know about the dresses. "Clothes from the dancing girls! I will not allow my daughters to accept gifts from that house of sin." He was furious and put a prohibition on wearing dresses that came from Meethi Bai's lodge.

Ma Gor Bai accepted the dresses nevertheless, and had them altered secretly: Lengths were adjusted to the ankles with crocheted borders, sleeves made longer with similar colour cloth, waistlines loosened and darts at the chest opened. Lining was stitched under all the netted sleeves and tops. With the pachedi-shawl thrown over them, my father never found out where the fine dresses that we wore on festive evenings came from. Anyway, girls' dresses were paid for and tailored by Step Mother Gor Bai from her embroidering income.

I throw my pachedi-shawl over my chest and look at myself again in the mirror. It still embarrasses me standing there, my legs nude as if I were in a bathroom.

"No! You don't wear a pachedi-shawl over tooko faraak!" exclaims Zera Bai partly rebuking under her smile.

"And in khane?" I ask. "How will I sit cross-legged in palothi or even with legs behind me on the floor? Head not covered?"

"No pachedi-shawl even in khane," she replies over my questions as if she knew I would ask that next. "I take a stole or a scarf to put over my legs. But at home, you need to wear the usual long dress with all the sitting and standing that we have to do in midst of the family and visitors," says Zera Bai. Then she takes a pause. Khanu Bai and I look at her in wonder and keep quiet. "You have to get used to the English dress. It is the same with me. I am still not completely used to the short dress without the pachedi-shawl over me. But it's Saheb's wish-command that we adapt to the new age. 'Be courageous, have faith!' says Rhemu to me. I tell myself, if wearing an English dress makes Saheb happy, I will do it. His happiness brings baraka to the home."

"Look at me! Joh toh! Hai hai!" I look at myself in the mirror again, first from the side and then from every other angle. "I need time. I look Govi, *nah*? A Mrs Fernandes? A Christian woman, *nah*?" I ask looking at Khanu Bai. I look at my bare legs again, sickly pale from lack of sunshine and soft-hairy, so embarrassing *chhe*.

"Looks bhoonda! Obscene, *nah*?" finally Khanu Bai gives her opinion half covering her mouth under her cupped hand. She puts doubt in me.

"But this is too embarrassing for me," I agree with her. "I cannot wear tooko faraak. Men folk will make fun of me."

"Rhemu tells me that's why Saheb gives confidence certificates to women who put on the English dress. We should be proud Khoja women wearing short dresses. It is Saheb's wishful edict," Zera Bai repeats trying to convince us. "To Rhemu, Saheb's wish is sacred, a command, *nah*?" says Zera Bai with pride. "Only time will tell what does not

287

make sense to us now," says Zera Bai. She waits for a response, but neither Khanu Bai nor I have an answer. "Even the jamat khana caretaker's wife wears a tooko faraak. Look at that - Joh! You two are in the group of the few last stubborn ones. Lagging behind in the world running ahead."

Khanu Bai removes her metal-rimmed spectacles. She looks at Zera Bai in the eye for a moment before saying, "Let the world run ahead, we will catch up." I keep a straight face. Khanu Bai puts back her glasses. Her leg moves constantly and her long dress at the ankles flaps gently.

"My mother-in-law, you know, changed her mind when she saw wives of our elders wearing tooko faraak. Then we both competed for the tooko faraak certificate," says Zera Bai changing the subject. She points to the wall cupboard.

The two photo certificates stand side by side on top of the glass cupboard in the new style that is for display only and rarely opened. It exhibits the finest set of glass crockery in Nairowua just as it was on the day it was unwrapped from Zera Bai's dowry chest. The certificates are made of hard board with a support so they can stand on their own. White haired Saheb sits wearing a bow tie and thick framed spectacles. The begum, his wife, stands by his side in a V neck pleated blue dress. "His own handwriting *chhe*," wide eyed ladies would say, "Saheb writes his blessings to all who adopt the colonial dress."

Zera Bai calls the certificate her own sacred letter from Saheb, a talika-type letter that could be framed and hung in the sitting room. She takes the cardboard certificate reverentially in both her hands and kisses it. "Tooko faraak has freed me from my mother-in-law's taak taak." Khanu Bai and I exchange surprise looks that hint at Zera Bai talking so willingly about her mother-in-law. A recent change. She does not hide for indeed she has faith.

Bai tells Grace to spread the table cloth and bring the new cups and plates from the shelf, and then tea and samosas from the kitchen. Two word commands is all the Swahili she knows.

I wait patiently to hear Zera Bai's next move while I pick at the vegetable fillings that have dribbled out of my samosa and wedged into the folds of my long dress. Khanu Bai burps in appreciation. She has a good feeling of warm chai and hot samosa in her belly as I have.

Zera Bai's day's offering of vegetable samosas sits in an opaque glass plate rimmed with colourful flower painting. Prominent in the two gaps between are bold letters JK in red ink. The samosas will now be on her table while the rice cools, and while the yellow ghee coats over the lamb curry. That's also part of her day's food offering.

From the evenly congealed and translucent film on the lamb curry, you would know Zera Bai uses Mama Harti's ghee to cook. The English memsaheb from the mountain farm makes the best ghee in Africa. Once a week, she descends in her Dodge car from the ranch in the meadows between the hills above Mama Bisekeli's orchards. She comes to town to sell ghee to Asian housewives. English women in Africa drive cars like men, and they even wear trousers like men.

New Wave

Zera Bai is among the first ones in Nairowua to adorn herself in the khulapug faraak, meaning the nakedlegs frock. In fact, she first wore a red chiffon dress one evening with three other intrepid pioneers of the dress change movement. It seems that the women had planned as a team to show their legs all together, and had thus shaved, powdered, and appropriately pampered and prepared the exposure of their hitherto never before seen limbs in public. It was on the auspicious chandraat day at the end of the month when Ismailis congregate to pray, sitting in parallel lines, folded knee to folded knee in palothi. It's the day to offer confession, and pay the tithe thus closing the month. The four women, mukhianis in the hierarchy of prayer meeting groups called mandelis, shocked some men folk like my husband Haiderali who, as he told me later, had to turn his eyes away so as not to have unclean thoughts before prayer time. "In the jamat khana, your thoughts must be clean," he said, "outside is another matter."

The women also shocked Khanu Bai's husband, Mamdu Bhai who we know, has been quietly critical of women who dared to wear short dresses. Khanu Bai told me what he said to her, "Blasphemous *chhe*! Walking about exposing their flesh to innocent male eyes, and that too in the evening! Now, how will we face other men in the bazaar if our wives are seen naked?" Indirectly, he let Khanu Bai know his opinion. To tell Khanu Bai directly not to wear the short dress would have been irreverence to Saheb, wouldn't it? Anyway, who would call Khanu Bai not faithful because she continues to wear the long dress with the pachedi-shawl over her head? She who reads out Saheb's sacred letters from the podium before the jamat cannot be said to be lacking in faith. Moreover, Khanu Bai can recite any farman, the letter dictate from Saheb, verbatim at any time if you were to ask her. She is proud of this, holding the holy texts in her head like a pious Moslem proud of reciting the Quran from memory. Without doubt her faith is pukka meaning unshakable.

Meanwhile, the pious pioneers of the dress change movement continue to instil audacity in each other, some acting behind their ambivalent husbands' backs like a secret society. Later, mukhi Premji Bhai of the Nairowua jamat, himself declared he was on their side because it was Saheb's will and his duty to obey. Once he asked the jamat, "Is it not Saheb's wish for our women to wear simple colonial dress?" Some nodded their heads, some remained still. That's how the mukhi spoke to the jamat by asking not telling them to accept the colonial outfit. And then the men folk asked each other, "Our mukhi represents Saheb, does he not?" Mukhi Premji Bhai was even quoted to have said, "Women who wear the colonial dress are examples to emulate. Like your mukhiani of Nairowua. Like Saheb's wife, the Begum." Needless to say, people know that his wife, the mukhiani of the jamat, was the team leader. But who in Nairowua does not know that she is the one in mukhi's house who wears pants?

Soon wearing the tooko faraak, meaning the short dress, turned into a contest, and reached a peak of its own on Khush-ali days. Gradually, eyes shifted from looking at Bombay filmi magazines for inspirations to dress fashion magazines that came from England and other European countries. Even magazines from the USA found their way to little rural Nairowua on the savannah. Women like Zera Bai sought to catch up with Nairobi, the capital of Ismaili fashions in East Africa. Nairobi fashions in turn looked up to London via women's magazines. Now Gujarati and Goan tailors in the capital's Indian bazaar, and seamstresses like Roshan Bai in Nairowua who worked from home, kept stacks of used glossy magazines like *Women's Own* and other periodicals not so well known, but nevertheless, important for a rare lucky find of a dress pattern different from anyone else's. Periodicals like *the Vogue, Today's Woman, She, Good House Keeping, Wife, My Home and Women's Weekly* – I know the names from Zera Bai who says them like it were a library for her to choose dress patterns from. As for herself, she knows exactly what to wear come the next Khush-ali. Later, even European dress pattern catalogues found their way to Roshan Bai's work table.

In time Zera Bai would scale down her Khush-ali dress to chandraat dress. Chandraats are like Khush-alis too but smaller monthly evening celebrations. In time, her Khush-ali to chandraat dress would step a scale further down to become Friday faraak before becoming a dress for regular khane wear. Finally, Zera Bai's old Khush-ali dress would end up with her house maid, Grace. If not, she would cut it into pieces and use it as a kitchen cloth or duster. In fact, most women follow this pattern.

For many in the jamat to wear tooko faraak was to be like Zera Bai, in step with the women in the magazines. But even as we enter the modern era of prosperity of the 1950s looking at European magazines and movies, I need more time to make the change from my long dress to a short one.

Days go by and I see more Khoja women in town wearing the colonial dress. Some I thought would never expose their legs in public. Gentle coaxing and nudging to change my attire continues from my friends in the Cleaning Committee. At times, the persuasion is annoying, especially so during the period of the celebrations that precede every Khush-ali. Khush Ali, I say, is Saheb's happiness when women compete to don the never-before-seen short dress designs inspired by fashions from Europe and America.

There are those regular Khush-ali days in the Ismaili calendar and those marking Saheb's day of birth and his becoming the Imam of the world Shia Ismaili Moslems. The year has many Khush-alis that keep Roshan Bai, the town seamstress busy pedalling at her black Singer Sewing Machine painted with floral gold vines. The machine boasts it can embroider whatever we want and, moreover, with such precision that human fingers cannot match.

Survival

The Ismaili Council for Kenya has advised the mukhi to bring the evening prayer time forward so we may reach home a little earlier after service. We say a special dua-prayer standing up longer than usual because of the added and repeated lines pleading Mowla for safety of our lives during these difficult times of the uprising against the English. We implore divine protection from the dreaded Mau Mau and implicitly also his guidance on what we should do when the British leave. Images of atrocities flash through my mind even as I pray. Never before have I experienced such intensity during the evening supplication.

Soon after the prayer for peace there is a long talk from the podium on the immediate need for women to adopt western dress and the importance of speaking in English and learning the new dua in Arabic that will be coming soon. Khanu Bai and I exchange quiet looks while listening to the council member.

To speak the truth, Khanu Bai and I do feel a little undecided at times. True, there is uncertainty in the air. True, we look to Saheb for his guidance. Are we being left behind while other women are pushing ahead with the changing times? Zera Bai's taunting is constant. She would look for a space, or create one between our talk, for an opportunity to push a few words in about the blessings of wearing the English dress. Sometimes, I wonder if our long dress embarrasses her when we are walking or talking with her in public? Doubts bother me. Will I have difficulties adapting to the future? The talk of the new age worries me. Our leaders say we need to be equipped for the changes in the country, especially us women. Is Saheb preparing us for yet another migration, this time towards the West where the women wear nakedlegs clothes in streets? Is this a test of my loyalty to Saheb? The test of my unquestioning, unconditional loyalty? And my trust in his foresight? His wisdom is divine and that anchors us when everything else is shifting. Whatever may be the hidden reason, I get no help from Haiderali to resolve the dilemma spinning in my head. Unlike his brother Kabir, Haiderali too may be as much filled with doubts as I am, though he does not say it to me. Perhaps, they talk more openly about strategies for survival at the cards game on Sunday afternoons.

At home, Haiderali and Kabir would joke about the sudden change of appearances of the women in the jamat khana – their untanned legs, their bobbing knee balls at hemlines, and the first time ever revealed shapes of their heads without the ever-present head cover of the pachedi-shawl. On older female heads sit hair buns that Kabir compares variously with wheel barrow wheels, like the one on mukhiani Sherbanu Bai's head to ping-pong ball on Ramba Bai, Zera Bai's mother-in-law. I too would laugh with them seeing women differently through male eyes while affirming my own reluctance to change. I would hear Zarina and Freda also laughing with us in the privacy of the kitchen. Kabir calls some waist lines, no longer screened by pachedis, Dunlop tyres, others would be bolster pillows. The new raised sandals innovatively designed by Mochi Bhai, the town cobbler, are stilts on which clowns walk. But Haiderali does not tell me not to change to English clothes, he does not want to appear not loyal to Saheb. I know he wants to protect me from lascivious male gaze and their put-down gags on feminine body. Who but men would know what's in their minds? But Kabir is not the same. He would gibe at the most unexpected times, "Leave your desi clothes behind and modernize, Moti Bai," he would say. Sometimes, I wonder if it's not because of my defiance to his cajoling that I refuse the English dress?

Undecided days follow. Modernization-adaptation is the only option for survival. It confronts me – speak in English, pray in Arabic, wear the English dress. They storm over me all together, and so quickly at the time when we see our imminent future painted black. Meanwhile, the bond between Khanu Bai and me, the two women who cannot make the sudden change to wearing modern clothes or speak in English at home, grows stronger. We know no English anyway.

For assurance's sake, we re-tell the jokes that men folk bring home. There is a new one each day about this bai and that bai appearing in a short dress in public. Laughter even when faked relieves my anxiety, and probably Khanu Bai's too. We laugh till tears run down our cheeks mocking women in short dresses. First we are amused at how the menfolk perceive the women and then we talk women's secret. Women's secrets inspired by private observations like of shapes of breasts so shamefully visible without the cover of the pachedi-shawl. Khanu Bai told me how she caught Mohamed Mendo's drifting look fix on straight backed Zera Bai who was boldly walking past him with her legs naked and of course without her pachedi-shawl over her chest. Was she unaware she was observed by Mohamed Mendo's stalking eyes exploring her from head to toe? We ask each other. Does her faith make her so blind? Or was it that she enjoys being men's dhingly doll? Neither of us was sure.

"Hai! Hai!" Finally we concur, "That's not a laughing matter. Tooko faraak is not for me no matter what Zera Bai thinks."

"I think Zera Bai evades her anxiety about the future by putting her fate in Saheb's hands," says Khanu Bai.

"She believes she is a pukka murid and we are not," I reply turning my face away from her.

Nowadays, I sit a little longer in meditation after the evening service calming down worries accrued during the day from our assiduous taak taak, talk talk, round round, the unpredictable future. I may even sit for a while in the library reading magazines to clear my head. Haiderali, meanwhile would be talking politics sitting with his friends on the courtyard bench. He would gather the latest news about the Mau Mau. But that is diminishing and is replaced now by news about the fiery speeches of the university educated young and impatient Africans. Many of whom are returning in great numbers from America. Their sudden appearance on front page newspaper photographs wearing European style suits and ties, comes with a new word into our vocabulary. *Africa Samachar* calls them not the freedom fighters nor the revolutionaries or the terrorists, but the nationalists.

Return of rain, colours and bead business

The dry season on the savannah comes between the long and short rains, and this year it does not prolong into a spell of drought as we feared. We had already added one more line to the routine all together evening prayers, pleading with the Merciful One to shower our savannah with rain. Periodically, animal sacrifices are made on Ol Donyo Lengai, the Mountain of God, to cleanse the earth of ills. Thus Maasai ancestors, indigenous spirits of the grasslands, may be calmed and bless the homesteads. It would be the sky that would receive their blessings, and open her calabash to let water pour to the thirsty ground below.

And then when the rains do come, there are torrents. Carpets of fragrant flowers of the wild lay under tree shades. "Honey drips from hives wedged among the branches of acacias - Ol-debbei, Ol-jarbolani and Ol-lerai all male trees. Wild berries, fresh roots for soup and medicine, are in plenty," says Ole Lekakeny. Maasai women bring creamy milk in plenty from their homesteads to the doorsteps of Indian shopkeepers' wives in Nairowua. In the jamat khana the floor tables, recently laminated with marble white formica, gleam with bottles and jugs of milk offerings. "We have removed protective sheaths on the penises of rams and red billy goats, and now we wait for our animals to increase in big numbers," Ole Lekakeny speaks with joy in his heart. "On the plains, the zebra and wildebeest will multiply in great number too. Their migrations to and fro, between the Mara and Serengeti, and the plains at Nairobi, will be in multitudes that will cover the land with patterns dancing on sunlit grass."

I want to travel out of Nairowua. I want to see animal patterns dancing on sunlit grass. I want to see Kilimanjaro, clad in layers of white mantle, smiling from blue height like a grumpy grandfather on an ancient tower who sees peace coming from a distance. I want to be in that moment when Kilimanjaro is awakened by land art. When soft exhalations of contentment in prayers of shu-khar are said in the mountain wind.

Ole Lekakeny continues to narrate, "There are good winds of rainwater blowing down the slopes. There is freshness in the morning air that night drizzles bring to the savannah. The cycle of savannah's rituals will continue uninterrupted, girls' circumcision will soon be followed by their quick marriages, and soon there will be many little feet padding the grasslands, herding goats and singing the rain songs to their teenage mothers. Others will be playing intrepid hunters. Fearless little warriors triumphing over the mighty lion, mimicking adults bragging about their courage in frenzied dances. In their game, they would spear the beast that prowls around their fathers' homesteads hoping to make a meal of a cow from his herd." Ole Lekakeny's words make pictures of his people at this time of plenty. They create deep feelings of affection for the land in me through Maasai eyes. "Each new-born calf is loved by the pattern on its coat. Like the tree bark in horizontal sampu lines; like the gathering cloud pattern awuas; like the strip light in deep dark orok or the first light of sunrise odo sirat. The Maasai landscape is born of art gifted by En-kai. En-kai of the sky adorns herself in pure colours of dawn and dusk that she gifts to humans. Colours are also beaded on her skirt stretched over the beginning and end of day. This is my land, this is my country" says Ole Lekakeny. He holds my imagination to the pictures he makes. "Elders are now keeping an eye for a suitable sacrificial bull for the coming red days of the eunoto ceremonies that everyone knows could even be this year."

Needless to say, Khoja bead merchants will prosper with the prosperity of the herders of the savannah. We will offer prayers of shu-khar, the dua of santosh, meaning contentment and gratitude, while offering fruit and sumptuous fare prepared at home with thankful hands and put on wide platters celebrating abundance. Grumbles about slackened businesses during the dry season of the previous year will begin to vanish from our lips. You will hear shu-khar Mowla more often from shopkeepers expressing satisfaction alongside praise of the Almighty showing modesty and making money. Such is the talk of merchants.

Men and women with ochred skins will bring fresh rain scents of their homesteads' manure, animal sweat, curd milk and soil to the bead shop where I work. They will come to touch and set their eyes on the new stock of beads that I put up for them to see. The Maasai call me Diamond's mother, and sometimes en-tomononi because they say, "She prayed for a son, and God granted her a son."

Husbands

"Your husbands are trapped in dead traditions not faith. Rhemu does not have that problem," says Zera Bai to Khanu Bai and me. We had just finished cleaning the jamat khana and were sipping chai sitting on the bench under the mango tree in the yard. We all know Rhemu Bhai for the khane-sewa work he does with such deep commitment. How inspiring is his reading of the farman letters from Saheb that guide the murids in these confusing times. His reading brings out the familiar soothing tone in Saheb's voice, and his blessings said three times over, calming us down with hope of overcoming the present, if only we lived simply and prudently.

"Rhemu is pukka in his belief. Everyone knows that, *nah*?" I say in compliment. My compliment, however, gives Zera Bai the opportunity she seems to have been waiting for. I notice she has a new locket attached to her chain around her neck. Whereas before her locket had Saheb's picture in colour now it's a gold coin with an Arabic scribble on it. It may be Allah or Ali, I cannot tell and I dare not ask. Her chain is the same.

"It's now a matter of desi ways and modern ways. Your test *chhe*." She continues to say becoming annoyingly assertive, "We must follow Saheb's wish-commands and leave Hindu customs behind."

"Are our customs not religion too?" I wonder but do not want to say it to Zera Bai who may retort. Are our customs really Hindu or just Khoja, which means Indian? I look at Khanu Bai but she averts my eyes deliberately watching two women from the Volunteers Cleaning Committee walking out of the gate.

"To tell you the truth, I feel it in me; I will never wear a tooko faraak. I know it," I say without a thought and having said it, I regret immediately seeing Zera Bai raise her eyebrows. Her expression reminds me of Ma Gor Bai who would show she was in doubt, when in fact, she disapproved. Is Zera Bai testing my love-loyalty to Saheb? She looks at me full into my face like waiting for further explanation. Like a religion teacher at his pupil who has not memorized the day's assignment - a ginan verse or a dua part. Had I not blushed so deeply, Zera Bai would not have repeated that surprise look that played on my guilt. Or does she put on that face to trap me? To expose me? To coerce me to wear the colonial dress? Her unmasked stare makes me uncomfortable. Apologetically, and quickly, I say, "Well, what I mean is just now. I cannot wear tooko faraak just now, you see. I need time and in time I will be joining you memsahebs of Nairowua. Am I not always the slow one to follow?" I say yet inside, I question myself: Do I not have courage enough to stand a witness in public to my loyalty to Saheb? Do I not have the courage to walk in public with nakedlegs and my unveiled head held high up demonstrating a Khoja that I am, a follower of the Aga Khan I am. Call me Aga Khani with contempt if you like.

"We do not always understand the hidden meanings in Saheb's wish-commands, but in time, his purpose will become clear. It will clear like the morning mist. Understand?" Zera Bai assures us once again as we prepare to leave.

"I hope you will not destroy your bandhani," I tell Zera Bai cautiously, looking aside. There is a rumour in town that Roshan Bai the seamstress had cut her own bandhani to make a tooko faraak out of it. It was an unsuccessful attempt.

"My bandhani!" exclaims Zera Bai as if poked with a sewing needle. "Nah! Nah! Never!"

My story is like the savannah. The savannah changes its look absorbing and reflecting the light of the sky. When the sky is dark with rain clouds hanging over it, the savannah turns muddy-mat and dull khaki-brown. But when the sky is blue and bright, the savannah lights up, every blade of grass has a shine of the sunny day. So my story carries words that are sometimes dismal and sometimes cheerful according to how my mood is affected by the news and people around me.

The English dhingly doll

Zera Bai and I sit on Khanu Bai's new sofa, admiring the evolving décor and the new phenomenon in Nairowua called the 'Sitting Room.' A home with the 'Sitting Room' would be envied as modern, meaning like living in England. Mamdu's business in hides and skins, and honey – he buys these commodities from the pastoralists and sends them to Nairobi – is thriving. We sit in the 'Sitting Room' exclusively reserved for just sitting in, chatting, and sipping tea while viewing the exhibits of the family's modern assets, comprising English style furniture that smells of varnish, Phillips radio in the shape of a miniature wall arch veiled in a tight mustard knitted net, and imported plastic and glass artefacts in sets scrupulously dusted each morning by Khanu Bai's domestic help. She calls the man Bhoito whom she has trained from the age of seven when she called him just Toto. Then, there is the miniature marbled model of the Taj Mahal in a glass cabinet. Both Zera Bai and I look at this wonder in quiet admiration now expected of the 'Sitting Room' guests in way of politeness if not marvel. Inside, I feel a distance from the warmth of homeliness that was in Khanu Bai's old house. It's an uncomforting feeling; I cannot easily explain. It's like slipping away from plain living to pretentions of luxury.

My eyes take me to a silver framed photo of Khanu Bai and Mamdu, a copy of the one she had shown us earlier from her box of photos. They are both sitting attached to each other on a bench before this monument to love that has stayed beyond my reach. Khanu Bai presses a button on the glass cabinet and at once, lo! a green glow lights up the latticed marble walls from inside like a spirit shimmering over the grave where would be resting the empress of India, herself a symbol of an Indian's love for his beloved, an emperor's love, India's own love.

"I heard in Nairobi," Zera Bai begins to say, "women walked down Government Road in their short dresses to the *Africa Samachar* office. 'Why are you ridiculing us for wearing the European dress?' they asked Ashok Bhai, the editor, and demanded he prints an apology. But the arrogant editor refused to apologize. They said he told them to get out of his office as he had better things to do than talk to women. The bais then removed their slippers and sandals, and rained down several hard slaps on him," says Zera Bai laughing aloud. "Poor Ashok Bhai had to run to the street."

But I am not listening for my mind is elsewhere where my heart is. "I am filled with sorrow," I confide to Zera Bai before she completes her story. "Kamau has gone to bury Simba in the forest. Diamond accompanied him holding the wheelbarrow and crying all the way."

"What happened?" she asks.

"Simba died last night. In the morning, Kamau found a poisoned piece of meat, half eaten. Someone had thrown it over the wall. "

"Bap-reh-bap!" Zera Bai sighs out exclaiming, "Mau Mau?"

"He was a good dog, dear Simba. Dear to the children. Pray his next karma is full of bliss." We were talking when Khanu Bai rustled into the room from the kitchen. We sit in silence for a while on separate seats.

"Zera Bai, how was Nairobi?" Khanu Bai breaks the silence.

"As usual. Emergency you know, sudden curfews, English armed teenage boys, barbed wires, street arrests – the usual. But there is less fear during daytime if we walk in groups of women. People are getting used to Emergency, and are learning ways to go around, you know, and how to live again. Though not at night," the tenor in Zera Bai's voice changes, "Black faces in the dark terrify me. I see them walking out of newspaper photographs." I feel the same but do not want to say it. How insidious are the images of Mau Mau splattered in the newspapers and leaflets! How they intrude family talk, extend our fears and make the Mau Mau larger, fiercer, more savage with each passing day. At night, when I hear a dog's distant bark, I leap out of the bed and switch on the lights in the kitchen to show we are awake and alert. Everything makes me jump nowadays, especially someone opening the door.

"And the new dua-prayer?" I ask deliberately to get away from the thoughts of Mau Mau swelling in my head. While in Nairobi, Zera Bai has been attending special classes to learn the Arabic dua.

"There is no Gujarati in the new dua. All Arabic, you know. Pure Islam *chhe*," she replies without losing a moment and with a tinge of pride in her voice. She has a teacher look fixed on me. I look down lest guilt shows in my eyes. She acts like the kindly Ithna Asheri Khoja, self-assured in their belief, so much so that they feel it their calling to save their kith and kin, the Satpanthi Khoja, from going astray.

306

"How do you understand what you pray then?" I ask again. This upsets Zera Bai. She raises her eyebrows, makes her eyes bigger, showing annoyance as in a surprised look just awakened out of a sweet slumber by a shout calling her name. Then she begins to lecture me in the manner of showing restraint – she would be patient and explain, not reproach. "The missionary says first, we must know how to say the dua in Arabic. Pronouncing each word correctly in the language of the Prophet is important, otherwise, you may say the wrong word. Arabic has many two meaning words. I just read the dua three times a day from the book. Rhemu fumbles, you know men, but he is determined to recite the dua in Arabic with the whole Nairowua jamat listening. 'That,' he says, 'will be on the new moon chandraat evening when the jamat khana is packed thaso thas.' " Zera Bai smiles.

"But the meaning?" I ask. "Zera Bai! How can you say a prayer that the body does not respond to?" I am beginning to feel I am alienating from Zera Bai like she were from another religion, not Satpanth. Also more importantly, not a Khoja. Yet, I have known her since the first day I crossed over the threshold of the Nairowua jamat khana with my feet patterned red in henna.

"Have patience, Moti Bai!" she retorts sharply. My question has upset her. Then having collected herself, she adds, "Memorize the dua first. The meaning, memorize later. One thing at a time. Have faith in Saheb. The sound of Arabic dua is good for your soul." Zera Bai speaks to me as if I were a child. How can someone tell me what's good for my soul? She sighs exasperated, exaggerating her despair and changes the subject.

"There is a story I must tell you," continues Zera Bai. She speaks about Satpanth Ismaili families recently arrived from South Africa. She observed them in the Nairobi jamat khana as is her habit studying strangers out of curiosity.

"They have large families, the men folk wear goatee beards and young women wear their hair short. Even the women speak English with ease like men, and the younger women dress in tooko faraak with much comfort and grace as if it were always their way. Some women wear hand socks in town and I hear the community volunteers in South Africa wear ties with long dresses and pachedi-shawls over their heads."

"How does that look?" I ask.

"It's their custom. They want to look as official as men on duty," replies Zera Bai as if she knows.

Zera Bai was no doubt fascinated to see this group of Guru-Pir Khojas from South Africa. I think in her opinion, wearing the tooko faraak and speaking in English was a measure of their faith tantamount to loyalty if not devotion to Saheb. "But," she shows doubt over her face when she speaks again, "some also believe in the modern Das Avatar of Sai Baba. I hear at home they revere his picture along with Saheb's."

I have not heard of an Ismaili Khoja family like that before. Khanu Bai too keeps quiet like me.

"Some say it was because of Saheb's persuasion that they left South Africa rather than eternally suffer the indignity of what I heard people call 'apartheid'," says Zera after a thought.

308

"Is it not the same here? European only schools, *nah*? European only bazaars, *nah*? European only back seats in cinemas, *nah*? European only front bus seats, *nah*? European only train compartments, *nah*? European only residential areas, *nah*? European only farmland, *nah*? European only hotels? And even European only toilets at the airports, *nah*?" questions Khanu Bai, her rhetorical nah seeking agreement after every pause.

"People say it was Gandhi-ji himself who taught the two Ismaili Khoja brothers from South Africa to recite the Satpanth dua, you know, the original dua of Satguru-pir. That was the condition that the pious father of the two boys made with Gandhi-ji when he allowed them to join his ashram. The two brothers lived on Gandhi-ji's farm, near Durban. Moslems and Hindus were the same to Gandhi-ji, you know."

"Was Gandhi not a Satpanthi?" asks Khanu Bai.

"Gandhi must have been a Satpanthi. Like Saheb, he believed all humans are equal, *nah*?" responds Zera Bai. "Gandhi says we should follow the path of truth that is the Sat-panth, *nah*? Is it not?"

Khanu Bai and I nod in agreement. Satpanth indeed means the True Path.

"But he must have belonged to the gupti jamat, the hidden community of Gujarat," I say.

"That explains it," responds Khanu Bai before I could say more.

"You know, he must have been practicing the faith in secrecy, otherwise, how did he know our pir's dua?" questions Khanu Bai.

"God is truth, he said. That is the greatest religion. That was Gandhi's religion," I try to explain what I have read in Gandhi's book. "His mother, followed the sister Guru-Pir religion to Satpanth. Child Gandhi played in her lap listening to Hindu-Moslem chants at her temple."

"You know the stone of the jamat khana in Nairobi came all the way from Porbandar, Gandhi-ji's birthplace, *nah*? He must have arranged that with Saheb." It was my turn to add to the truth spoken.

"And Saheb requested the English not to detain Gandhi in public prison. Saheb offered his palace in Poona, *nah*?" says Zera Bai.

"The English agreed but Gandhi removed all the palace furniture from one room on the ground level where he slept and worked on the floor, writing, spinning, and reading there on the floor in just one room. He could have done that in prison as well," says Khanu Bai, widening her eyes. "He lived simply like a guru-pir. A Sufi. He was a mahapir, a great pir; a great soul, a mahasufi. No wonder his picture is in the Nooran Mubin with the Saheb like our holy Imams and pirs, and our holy warriors." Zera Bai and I do not respond because we don't know how to. So Khanu Bai continues speaking with confidence as if to confirm her own words now. "Gandhi-ji must have been a Satpanthi because he believed in the unity of Hindus and Moslems, *nah*?"

So the tale is told about Gandhi-ji and the Satpanth Khoja of South Africa.

My elbow rests crooked on the armrest that is covered with a shiny black plastic mat with a picture of a red rose. There are six of the same, in a set, around the

310

room on armrests of the sofa set. Modern things come in a set. They match.

"This marble design mat on the floor is so clean and shiny, nah," says Zera Bai looking down to the floor, marvelling at yet another new phenomenon called 'the linoleum' that has come to our small town on the savannah. Khanu Bai's linoleum is much admired and talked about among the Khoja housewives in Nairowua.

"Mamdu brought it from Nairobi rolled and stacked up on top of the Merali Bus. It's easy to clean and no cracks wriggling about over the cement floor any more. No need to polish it, you know. It has a permanent shine."

"Your home is so modern, but you are still wearing the old desi clothes. Will you not let go your long frock, your lambo faraak?" Zera Bai comes to the subject of dress change once again.

But neither Khanu Bai nor I respond, sensing Zera Bai's impatience if not her irritation. Silence prevails and that is best at times like this. There is an African proverb: YOU DO NOT CALL A CROCODILE UGLY MOUTH UNTIL YOU HAVE CROSSED THE RIVER. Khanu Bai's dress stirs at her feet. Her one foot is moving on the floor. From the kitchen comes a sudden soft crash, cascading chai overflowing from the pot, sizzling and hissing over the glowing charcoal. Khanu Bai skips up from her chair. "Pirshah! Joh toh! I forgot the chai." She trundles to the kitchen in her long dress.

Khanu Bai sets down three identical chaikops on three identical plastic mats, black and shining. In the middle are pictures of red sparrows sitting on curved handles of flower baskets. The mats stick on top of the round table like they were glued to the glass. I admire how everything is in her house is a set. "Washable you know," says Khanu Bai directing her raised eyebrows to the mats. She has arranged Marie Baring biscuits in concentric circles on a perforated glass plate that sits in another bigger circular but flatter tray, also made of glass. I douse the crunchy biscuit in chai just to the verge of its slumping back into the cup before putting it on my tongue. That's a skill learned early in life. A Khoja skill. Then I do the same with two more biscuits.

Polished Kamba woodcarvings of giraffe, impala, and a morbid Maasai warrior with a shield, one chicken down feather on his head and a spear, carved in black hardwood stands on top of the plastic painted curtain box. A creamy pinkish English dhingly doll sits with sweet-arrogant pose in the middle shelf of a corner sideboard that has sliding glass doors. She is made of hard plastic and has synthetic flaxen curls falling to her shoulders. She is wearing a puffed up tooko faraak stitched on top of a frilly petticoat. On another occasion, I have seen her glassy blue eyes closing and opening with a click clack. English bebli how meethi, sweet *chhe*. She gazes at me with a look of a hungry cat through her outsized eyelashes. I gaze back at her in defiance.

Part Eight

Kanga of the Indian Ocean

Riziki

People in town call me Mouth of Mombasa, but my name is Riziki as you know. My name means Blessings of Daily Bread in Swahili. I live in Mombasa where stories meet and mix like winds from Asia and Africa, and like the people, their arts and their languages. Here, when you walk in the alleys of the old stone town, you know you are walking along the ancient confluence of cultures of the Indian Ocean.

I am Shamshu's mke mwenza, that is to say in Swahili, his wife friend of his first wife who is called Khati Bai. Shamshu is Moti Bai's brother. I live with my mother and grandmother on Mwembe Tayari Street in the house that people say faces the other way from the street that is to say towards the sea though it's not on the waterfront. On this street, there is a market at the bus station opposite the Khoja cemetery where ghosts wearing tall red hats with a tassel rise at midnight. Often they are seen hovering around the War Memorial to African soldiers.

The market itself is known for its morning bustle, and sweet fragrance of mangoes piled high on hand carts and fruit stalls, and also by the fluttering chickens in cages made of forest vines, palm fronds and rounded branches woven into a lattice tied with sisal strings.

I have a son by Shamshu. The boy is called Issa. I get up before the first call to the day's five prayers to make mandazi bread. I take a full tray of mandazi bread to the worker hotels each day just at the crack of dawn over the Ocean, when the dockworkers begin to arrive for breakfast and the air is sharp and cool.

They call me Mouth of Mombasa. They say I have inherited my grandmother Nana's mouth. I also have my grandmother's head that remembers many things. So I must speak, never mind what they call me.

314

Swahili is my language that took form in the sways of the monsoons from Asia to Africa over the Indian Ocean. Riziki is called roji in Kacchi and Gujarati, both languages of the Indian Ocean on the other side in India. My husband Shamshu's people, the Khoja, speak these two languages. Both words, Riziki and Roji, I repeat, mean the same, which is Blessings of Daily Bread. Sometimes, Shamshu, when in a playful mood, calls me Roji as in Kacchi. My grandmother tells me I am that, meaning blessings of food, for I make mandazi bread for the dock workers and with that support the family.

Yes, I can tell stories seamlessly. My stories flow into stories endlessly because we, the storytellers, know how one story informs and forms from another. So we must speak stories over stories, and stories into stories like how my grandmother Nana speaks flawlessly. Like how one kanga in her kasha speaks over many for they, the kangas, are storytellers too.

Sometimes, my words come haltingly. That's when I lose them or mislay them somewhere in my head. Then I look at the kanga and see its pattern and read what it says. My words come back to my head and I talk again. The kanga, too, is a storyteller born of the cultures of the ocean and the land that also gave birth to my language, Swahili. And of course to my people of the double and triple, and even quadruple racial heritages. One way to know the kanga is to first read the meaning behind the saying. Saying like: I LIKE TO BUT I AM NOT ABLE TO - NAPENDA LAKINI NASHINDWA. I had sent the kanga with this saying to Moti Bai who is my husband's elder sister. The kanga is truly beautiful with a red cashew nut tree. "She has been like a mother to me," says my husband Shamshu. I know he speaks from his heart because elder sisters are second mothers. I want to talk with Moti Bai but she does not respond so I sent her the kanga so she knows how I feel. I want my husband's Khoja family to know my son so Issa may know his grandparents. So he may know who his siblings, aunts, uncles and cousins are in Mombasa though they live like our shadows detached from the body. So his grandparents may cuddle him in their laps as they do their Khoja grandchildren passing on the warmth of belonging in kisses and embraces. I want my son to meet his Khoja family so when the neighbours' children call him mwana haramu, meaning bastard, as it happens when they fight, he can tell them what family he belongs to. That he has brothers and sisters too. That they live in a big mansion by the sea and they drive a white Mercedes. But Khoja relatives keep Issa at a distance as if his dark skin and curled hair have a disease that will contaminate them.

When spoken, kanga's words are meant to stir the heart to listen to what the eye says to it. We know how sometimes the heart and the eye stay apart, but the kanga brings them together. Is that not why the kanga is also called Talking Cloth? I do not know whether it's the sounds of the two way flow of winds over the land and the Indian Ocean that take kanga's wisdom to the heart, or if it's the singing of utenzi poetry of the poets of the coast. They make the rhymes and rhythms when their ears are filled with the music of the waves washing the Swahili shore.

One such utenzi, a poem, is called Kasha la Mombasa, or the Wooden Chest of Mombasa. A kasha, like the one in my grandmother's room, keeps secrets of a hundred kangas. To listen to the kanga's secret is to know the kanga. And to know the kanga is to put its colours and words to your body. One part of the kanga wraps me over the womb, and the other falls over my heart like a shawl. So I must wear the kanga in a pair sheltering feelings of the woman in me. But I need not always speak the words it

316

bears. I let the onlooker's eyes trace the kanga's sayings and know their wisdom because words on the kanga are interpreted by the eyes that read them from their own lives.

Sometimes, I feel alone and long for my husband. Shamshu likes his Khoja wife more than me. The other woman, my co-wife, is of his own kind. He seldom visits me. I do not want to think of my children as fatherless or even orphans. Like how sometimes my unkind neighbours would call Issa when we quarrel. Sometimes, they would say my child is Swahili-Mhindi, or even Khoja chotara, meaning Swahili-Indian and Khoja half caste, meaning not a true Swahili. Then I go to quarrel with them. But to Issa, I would sing Kasha la Zamani, the song of the old kasha, the wooden chest of Mombasa that stores gifts of life for him.

My kangas are kept in the kasha, which is my dowry chest. My kangas are my family's pride because they are old and original, every one of them. You could easily tell that because they are stamped MALI YA ABDULLA K.H.E, the trademark, short for Kaderdina Hajee Essak of Mwembe Kuku bazaar of Mombasa.

Kasha langu la zamani kutoka Mombasa

      My ancient chest from Mombasa

Lina ficha zawadi ndani kwa ndani

      Keeps gifts hidden inside inside

Zawadi hizi za nani?

      Whose gifts are these?

When Issa jumps and shouts, "Ni zangu ni zangu ni zangu, mimi - Mine mine mine, me myself," I would wrap him with kangas from the kasha chest. He would run to the mirror and see himself as bright as the star over the Indian Ocean.

Khoja guests

"Wageni! Wahindi! Khoja!" I hear children yelling, "Guests! Indians! Khoja!" And then all at once they are quiet. Their marble game at the doorstep is disrupted. I look out through the window's iron rods and see their enquiring eyes in silent stares fixed on three Khoja Bais.

"Ho...dee! Anybody home?" Happily sing-songs one of them standing at the door. The woman's pachedi-shawl over her head shields her from the scorching Mombasa sun at mid-day. I recognize her voice, familiar and friendly. It's ho...dee of our neighbour, Amina's grandmother, Auntie Khoja. Amina plays with Issa, and sometimes, I leave my son with her when I go to the market with my mother.

"Kaa ... ree ... boonee! There is always someone home to welcome you," calls out my mother with her usual welcoming intonation like an echo of the house. Auntie Khoja steps into the dimness of the corridor. My mother and I smile at each other pulling up our kangas over our heads. The exchange of happy words of welcome relieves us from the tension of the expectation of this visit. Auntie Khoja had informed us a week earlier that Shamshu's stepmother and sister would like to visit us. We three, Auntie Khoja, my mother and me, are like sisters. On Friday mornings we go to the stone market on Salim Road together. At the fete of Eid, we walk around together in fine clothes, similarly stitched by tailor Juma out of identical material and with identical buttons and frills. Every Eid our

318

dresses are unlike those of other neighbours in the Swahili mud town and even from the wealthier ones who live in the stone town of old Mombasa. I open the door to Auntie Khoja, smiling widely at the familiar play of welcome words amongst us residents of Mwembe Tayari. Auntie Khoja's parting lips expose her gold plated tooth, a canine on the left side, envy of the neighbourhood women. Her eyes blink adjusting to the quick change of light. I know she cannot see me for a while standing there in the cool dimness of our house.

"So this is my grandson," says Ma Gor Bai patting Issa on the head and then tugging his cheeks in one long and large pinch. Issa, seated on my hip in a leg embrace around my abdomen, digs his head into my kanga over my chest.

"I would like to take you to my home with me, let's go, hmm?" Ma Gor Bai talks as she walks into the house. I am sure she does not hear my grandmother's warm karibuni welcome from the bedroom on the far side. It was customary to say the boy is such a beautiful, lovable child, so much so that one would want to take him home. So I took it as a compliment to me the parent.

"Ho...dee!" says Auntie Khoja again as she takes the lead walking ahead of the other two women.

"Hodi," repeats Moti Bai in a voice softer than of Auntie Khoja. Moti Bai and I exchange slight smiles that come naturally to us both as our eyes meet. Then at once, our looks escape like those who fall in love at first sight and avoid eyes meeting again lest the secrets of their hearts are made known to the other.

"Karibuni," says my mother, nodding her head while waving to the three guests to come into the privacy of the women's bedroom behind the white curtain with red rose prints. A litany of greetings without handshakes follows, and then finally the guests sit down. Auntie Khoja and Moti Bai sit on the bed opposite the one on which sits Nana, my grandmother, her legs stretched out. Ma Gor Bai gives out one elongated airy exhale, and then with an audible sigh of shu-khar, she brings herself down on the hardback chair touching Nana's bed. My grandmother says karibuni in welcome again, three times over, taking time to take in the look in the eyes of each guest. Having composed herself on the chair after a few shifts, Ma Gor Bai's eyes rove around the room like a bird looking for a tree to perch on. She sniffs frequently tightening her lips to smoulder sudden respirations due to the irritation in her throat. The room smells of Vicks vapour and balminess of aged body covered in sheet. I push the window frame out behind the rusted iron rods above Nana's bed. It creaks before it opens and pivots on loose hinges. As if by instinct, I slip the lever into the second hole without pulling back the curtain. Immediately, a draught of air flows in below the swell of the sunlit curtain. All eyes are set on me as if in expectation of my next move but actually it's to avoid looking at each other.

"Are you well, Mama Shamshu?" asks Nana breaking the uneasiness.

"I am well," replies Ma Gor Bai speaking in Swahili.

"Are you well, Bibi Amina?"

"I am well. Ham-jambo? Are you all well?" asks Auntie Khoja.

320

"Hatu-jambo, we are all well," my mother and I reply concurrently. Nana nods her head acknowledging the exchange of each following greeting, face and head gesture, the langueurs of Swahili welcome that continue at length. Now and then, the bed gives out a painful squeak as she shifts her weight from one side to another.

On the wall above the bed's lotus shaped headboard, there is an alcove in plastered frame of triangular designs. In it is Nana's Quran. On the opposite wall, hangs an English clock between two laminated pictures. One is of grim Kaaba draped in black cloth with a fiery frieze in gold Arabic calligraphy. The other picture is of a winged white horse with the head of a plump black eyed damsel; her long black curls flow in pliant wind as she gallops through the starry night sky. She wears a red and green, jewelled yellow gold collar. She is an angel flying, half woman, half horse. The Prophet is invisible, but he is there sitting in the bejewelled saddle on the human mare in flight to paradise from the hilltop in Jerusalem.

"Are you well?" Nana repeats, looking at Ma Gor Bai as is the custom to ask about health to show welcome, implying she is pleased with her visit. Nana's swollen ankles due to arthritis are under a faded kanga with a large picture of a pineapple in the middle. An even older kanga in lighter colours covers her head and falls loosely over her body. Her back is straight. She is a tall woman. Her skin has the colour of boiled and peeled almond. They used to call her Mama Giraffe when she was young and walked to the market, head held high, back unbending.

"Come to me," says Ma Gor Bai, stretching out her two hands towards Issa. I move Issa around my hip onto my belly and then bowing down, slip him into Gor Bai's

321

lap. Moti Bai touches the boy once on the head, smiling warmly. But Issa does not smile back. Instead, he rolls his eyes first at her and then at the visitors, one after the other, and then his eyes come to me, pleading to be lifted back onto my hips. Ma Gor Bai pulls out a pack of Marie Baring biscuits from her handbag and gives the box, the length of her lower arm, to Issa without a word or a smile. Then, suddenly, I see her suppressing a surging cough with a handkerchief over her lips pressed inwards.

"Greet your grandmother," I tell my son in Swahili. Issa kisses his grandmother's hand, holding it in both his little hands while also holding the box of biscuits pushed in between his elbow and belly.

"What do you say to your grandmother?" I tell my son to greet the elders. Issa keeps quiet, gazing at the strange bespectacled lady who is clad so differently and she also smells so differently from his Nana, my mother or me. Then he looks at Moti Bai and she smiles warmly to him again. His eyes brighten.

"This is my nephew; the resemblance to his father is there," Moti Bai says in Swahili with a Zanzibar accent.

"Shamshu's wife, Khati Bai, will bring him up well. She will make him happy. She will make him her own," Ma Gor Bai begins to say. "And of course, I am there to make sure the child is treated well. When shall we come to take the boy to his father's home?" She talks with confidence. My mother and I look at each other trying to comprehend this not only strange, but also arrogant proposal. My mother begins to move from side to side clearing her throat with slight coughs. I see uneasiness creeping into her eyes.

"We shall live together, heh meethoo? I have a big house, many toys and English chocolates." Issa continues staring at her with impassive looks. Then Ma Gor Bai lets out a sharp, suppressed khokharo before saying, "I will take you to see Fateh Meghji's magic show. You like magic?" Issa does not reply.

I restrain myself from responding. I want to ask Ma Gor Bai, "Does he look starved here? Do we not love him? Am I not Shamshu's wife too? Am I not Issa's mother who you should be talking to?"

"Who does he look like?" asks Ma Gor Bai and replies just as quickly, "His grandfather, *nah*?" Then she asks Issa, "Who do you look like bablo?" I see Issa is puzzled by all the fuss around him. "He has his grandfather's nose and that serious look in the eye without a smile." She speaks in Kacchi now, turning to Moti Bai and Auntie Khoja. "His hair is wiry. Skin a little dark, like his mother's. Shu-khar Mowla, it's a boy, the skin and that bit of kink will not matter much if he is well brought up." I understand enough Kacchi to know this was rude.

My mother adjusts her veil over her head several times and then she brings her hand to rest on her chest, when grandmother Nana, not my mother or even me, begins to speak in long rhythmic unabated sentences. I have heard my grandmother speak like that only once before. That was when there was a dispute with her half-brothers on inheritance of their father's cashew nut farm, something not uncommon between brothers and sisters in our culture when parents die without leaving behind a will trusting the sharia. Nana's voice is controlled, her words guttural and coming haltingly, taking time to shape her irate thoughts in polite conversation as is our custom with disagreeable guests. But her sentences are continuous.

"It is not our habit to give away children and separate mothers from their children." She speaks through clenched teeth. "That is not Islamic. Allah-hu-akbar, God is great. It is not our way to allow our children to accept faiths other than the one we know is the truth. That is the gift they are born with." Nana gestures to me for water. She then drinks a little before saying more, "In our family, we name our children after the prophets of the holy books. Is Issa not the one who made miracles and told stories? Was he not the son of Mariam of the Book? Was he not the one born under the palm tree? Was Mariam, like Riziki, not a mother too? Did she abandon Issa because of poverty?" Nana drinks all the water in the glass and burps, taking time to let the air out.

Nana's oratory strikes me. I know Nana is normally a quiet person and she would not even get into quarrels between my mother and me over small matters of housework when asked to mediate. Ma Gor Bai looks lost. I can see she is taken aback by the Swahili dialogue that refers to proverbs on the kanga, and poetry in the Quran, and stories from the Prophet's life to draw on wisdom and guidance. Nana continues to talk as if she were reciting a passage from the psalms of the Prophet. "We are poor and black, but we are Moslems first, honest and truthful. We have never missed a Ramadan fast and the five prayers of the day. I am old and cannot bow my head down to the earth any more in prayers before the Merciful One." We wait for Nana to catch her breath. My mother waves to the children to go outside and play marbles. They had sneaked in one at a time to stand around the bed, staring and

324

listening attentively, quietly, and insidiously as children do. "When I bow down before God, I can no longer keep my heart above my head. My thoughts below my feelings. Let there be peace. Allah-hu-akbar, God is great! Here I sit in the bed the whole day long where you see me, and here I say my five prayers of the day. God understands I can no longer bow down to touch the earth where I shall return. We believe in God, the just and the merciful, and we trust in Him, the all-knowing and forgiving." Nana pauses, breathes deeply, now exhausted by her own speech. Or is it the anger in her that takes away her breath? That tires her because of the fight with her words that come from her heart and have to be shaped by measured etiquette that we must show our guests? When she speaks again, Nana's voice quivers in poetic modulations as if she were reading the holy verses. "For this we are grateful to God. There is no God but God. Our children are God fearing and know the ways of their ancestors of the Swahili coast. We are given children by God, praise be to Him, so we may teach them the rightful path." Nana stops again and when I think she has finished talking, she adds more words, "Children are the tender roots of tradition. Our responsibility it is to nurture these roots. So be it, as God wishes."

I listen and do not say anything. My mother too keeps quiet out of respect for Nana, her elder and her mother. But I am observing Auntie Khoja and Moti Bai. They do not look comfortable. We avoid each other's eyes.

"I am a party to such a shameful proposal," Auntie Khoja says under her breath in Kacchi to Moti Bai. She knows our Swahili family of matrilineal lineage from the northern islands well enough to know the truth in what Nana has just said. She also knows what Nana said is practised to the letter in our household. Auntie Khoja and Moti Bai sneak looks of concern towards me on the quiet, but my eyes avert theirs refusing to respond.

Ma Gor Bai gathers herself and whispers to Auntie Khoja, talking in Kacchi, "Shall I offer them money?" She touches her breast where she keeps her money in the cup of her brassiere.

"No! Don't, for Mowla's sake!"

"What then? How can they educate this boy? He must be brought up in our community and learn our language and religion. What is his future here? Here, what future is there for anyone within these mud walls?" Ma Gor Bai looks around the room. She drops her lips in a curve making the white bristles above the slack of her mouth stand out at the corners.

"I think we should give them time. You are too quick," cautions Auntie Khoja, biting her lips.

"What time? It's too long already. The boy will never know Gujarati or Kacchi or his family." I see Moti Bai touching Gor Bai's bony hand and holding it, pressing it lightly. I remember how I used to take Nana's hand when I was little sitting by her side in the kitchen when she was upset with my mother. Often it was at night when she came home late from Cinema Majestic.

"Let the father talk to them," says Auntie Khoja referring to Shamshu. Moti Bai nods to Ma Gor Bai looking directly into her eyes the way we never look at elders. Perhaps, she is thinking about her own son, Diamond. Would she agree to let Diamond be adopted by another woman? Would she agree even if her husband told her to give her son to his other wife?

"Shamshu is too soft. Too much love in his head. He does not know how to bring up a family. Soon, he will be a Sunni too," says Ma Gor Bai speaking in Kacchi. She supresses a sudden cough with her pachedi-shawl pressed to her mouth but she has no control over the spasm that shakes her body.

"He will be able to persuade the women in this house he knows so well," Auntie Khoja responds. Moti Bai presses her Ma's hand again, firmly this time, like she wants to feel her bones.

"They have given Shamshu something. Bewitched him!" Ma Gor Bai pushes her lips forward first and then sideways between words. I lower my eyes to the cemented floor. Moti Bai shifts on her chair, adjusting her pachedi-shawl over her head and then covers her plump belly. Ma Gor Bai sits without an expression on her face like a black and white British passport photo.

There is no more talk. We sit quietly sipping black coffee from small bowl cups and eating sweet halwa with our fingers. The halwa is rubbery and has an orange translucent glaze of ghee, and still warm from the kitchen heat. We eat from one plate like it was intended for a family to sweeten their tongues sitting together close to the warmth of their bodies so long separated from each other.

It's the intention that finds my thoughts in my story. It's also the intention that searches the words in the language so full of intricate meanings. When the story becomes confusing, it's like walking through a labyrinth, an adventure, finding the path through thoughts, holding a torch lighted by words.

327

Mke mwenza my wife friend

That evening thoughts come to me facing back. It was a day full of an unexpected meeting of my two families. What I had often dreamed of now worries me. How will the Khoja see me married to their son by nikha? How will they see my dark skinned children with balls of tangled hair in their jamat khana? I massage their coils and curls with coconut oil, and back comb so their hair stands tousled up shinning in the sun. That's the fashion now for children. How will the Khoja jamat accept us? I see old Nana with her greying ringlets, thin and stiff over her wrinkles. Her face talking, her rhythmic coaxing and Quranic verses. Her almond skin glows in the sheen on her bones at corners of her forehead, and she smells of Vicks.

I hear Shamshu at the front door talking to a group of Indian and Swahili boys from the old town. They talk and gesture like girls but are boys. The one who laughs the most and jokes the most with Shamshu wears lipstick and has kohl marks under his eyes. There is teasing, jovial in-between Kacchi-Swahili talk, and laughter, the way our Mombasa men like to chat with these boys playing courtship as if they were girls. Except on Eid days, the boys hang around our house every evening in varying numbers going to and fro their private visits. It's their part of the street anyway. At the side there is an alley where men and women lovers meet later at night, and passing men stand in the shadows to pee.

Shamshu enters without knocking. He has a sprint in his feet, and a wide smile on his face, his eyes narrowing into wrinkles at the corners. He does not hide his elation. He is showing off he is desired by the young men too and feeling two times a man.

Seeing him after three weeks, I am happy. I hold back the anger inside to wait its moment. I am wearing a pair of white kangas with red border and flowers in the middle. I speak to it. I know it's language, and the kanga understands me. I say I know I look elegant. I have features that Shamshu once serenaded in taraab melodies, imitating Juma Balo, my favourite Swahili singer, and gesturing Raj Kapoor, my favourite Indian actor. I pose so he sees more of the side of my face. With his one finger he pushes back the crisp twirl of hair over my ear bringing his lips closer to fill me with sweet words wrapped in saccharine paan puffs. His face without a smile, determined, he pulls my kanga down with one firm tug at the waist.

"Nini? What?" I ask, a shy croak, a faked surprise, intoned mischief tempting his love. My eyes flash pretending to evade playing of hearts, "Nini? What?" I ask again.

"Nini ni nini? What's what?" he asks back in play, feigning male aggression, and smiles, his breath over my face overpowering.

My grandmother has given me a room in her house that is large enough just to fit a single metal bed. Under the bed, we keep our gold ornaments that we wear at weddings and Eid festivities. Otherwise, during the day, the room is kept locked and the key is with Nana under her mattress. Shamshu smiles, loosening his kikoi over the waist.

"Your sister, Moti Bai, has a good heart. I could see that. She is just the way you described her to me," I say. He smiles again. Then I ask in a half awake voice, "But tell me, Shamshu, why did you not discuss Issa's adoption with me first?" He ignores my question.

"I accepted to marry you as your second wife because you had no children with your first wife. That is the sharia. I did not marry you to give away my children to your barren Khoja." I see Shamshu is taken aback. "Both your wives wish to be treated equally. Their rights respected. That is sharia that permits second marriage. I keep my child to myself. Adopt another. A Somali orphan from the war?" Shamshu does not say anything. In the dark I look at him in the face and ask, "Did you marry me so you could take my children for your infertile Khoja?"

Bitterness begins to surge in me like acid from the stomach. If he had the intention of persuading me to give away Issa, then he knows what would be my answer before he starts. Is it why he has come to visit me tonight? To love me as he used to or to love me so I give up my son? Would he ask me to abandon Issa at the moment of my weakness when he is all that my body asks for? He came unexpectedly, and I had not prepared a meal for him. Something Swahili that he likes, like crushed mung lentils in coconut milk or red millet bread, or raw paw paw strands that look like sweet vermicelli but taste different.

Shamshu says nothing. He sniffs between my words. Shapeless shadows of two women in black bui bui veils cast by the street light zigzag within the folds of the curtains over the window.

330

"My co-wife, my mke mwenza Khati Bai, is barren, kweli true? How many years have you been married to her?" Shamshu snuffles and clears his throat. "Six years, kweli true? Dr Fernandes tested her abdomen? He said she is barren, kweli true?"

"Nyamaza – shut up!" he yells out. The echo crashes through the perfumed air hanging in oudh smoke, thick, silent and still in the night. The shout cracks through my heart like a sharp pointed arrow head riling the feminine spirt of my Bajuni foremothers that resides in me as in my grandmother Nana.

"The Aga Khan told you not to marry black women. Did he not?" My words spit out where it hurts Shamshu - talking nasty about the Aga Khan.

"Nyamaza – shut up!" he yells again louder than before. "That was a hundred years ago!"

"Yes, I know, but the Aga Khan's words are eternal to the Khoja. *Kweli* true? It was in Zanzibar he had said that. Was it not? He did not want to see a half-caste jamat when he visited Africa. *Kweli* true?"

When Shamshu shows his male anger to me, I know he has lost his words. He does that to make me feel weak. But he knows I speak the truth that he cannot deny and that I, a woman, can speak back. What he does not know is that when offended, the ancestral spirit in me cannot be quietened easily. The spirit is a woman. I draw my strength from her. "Is that why you do not want your Khoja jamat to know I am your wife too? You are embarrassed of your black wife, *kweli* true? Your own family! You keep us hidden like a disease so you can show the purity of your fair race in the jamat khana, *kweli* true?

331

Shame on you! Shame on your people!" My spiteful tongue will not let go of words flowing through the voice I have no control over. "You two faced Khoja hypocrite! I am black but honest. That's how I have been brought up, that's how I will bring up my children. They don't have to be Khoja."

I click my tongue to let him know my annoyance, and then bite it to stop it, and turn my face to listen to the murmur of lovers in the alley. "I will arrange with Nana to sacrifice a goat for you and distribute the meat to the poor at Sakina Mosque." I speak inside to appease the spirit ancestor with a promise of an offering to calm her down. I pray the promise will quieten her. The night is such that it pleads for peace.

There is no sleep in my eyes, only hurt and hate, the twin sisters that bring wet warmth to the pillow under my cheek. My mind takes me to the pictures remembering the afternoon. I want to transfer these pictures of my feelings to Shamshu. How can I describe my agony? Can anyone describe such pictures that looking back aggravates heart's hurting? I see Ma Gor Bai's eyes roving around the room. Many questions lurk in them. Finally, they come to rest on the dressing table. Standing on it among perfume bottles of various shapes, sizes and colours - gifts from Shamshu, is a studio photograph of me and Shamshu in Raj Kapoor and Nargis side profile pose from the film Awara the Vagabond. Our black and white images are framed in seashells, tinted in delicate pinks by no other than the famed water colour artist at Studio One in Nairobi. I see how Ma Gor Bai's eyes narrow. What is she thinking? That my dressing table with three folding mirrors and a red velvet-seat stool would have obviously come from Shamshu? That it is a luxury I cannot afford otherwise? I

332

am Shamshu's second wife, mke mwenza, am I not? Second wife, but a wife nonetheless. Every wife wishes a modern dressing table of her own, and that she asks for from her husband at marriage. It does not matter how many wives he has, every wife wants her own dressing table. Is it vanity? Maybe, but a necessity for me nonetheless. Would Shamshu's first wife not have a dressing table too? I bet she has. Or is it the studio photo of me and Shamshu that unsettled his stepmother's eyes so much so that she turned her head away deliberately, deftly ignoring the picture and the dressing table in a noticeable way like it was a person with bad breath from rotten teeth that made her wince.

I hear Shamshu's breathing slowing down. His body is calming down from the heat. He's falling into a quiet slumber. His inhales-exhales are becoming even, his lips are a little parted, but he does not breathe through the mouth and I am weeping. I am observing the Khoja women in my Nana's house. I see Moti Bai, wide eyed as in a look of surprise, turning towards Ma Gor Bai who unfeelingly, selfishly, cruelly is asking to take my Issa away from me like she is telling, not requesting. Like it is her right to leave me childless. Ma Moti Bai looks down embarrassed. She is aware how Gor Bai's every expression is keenly watched by me, and I don't say anything.

Later, during the night, my hands come together and cradle over my belly. I cannot sleep. The balminess of the womb lures my hands over my abdomen to feel the pulse of life. I am carrying Shamshu's child. I know it's a girl because she makes me crave for tamarind pulp. I say a quiet shu-kharn for the bliss my husband has given me. His embryo warms my belly yet he has turned cold and distant sleeping by my side. Outside it's the honeyed moment of the second quarter of darkness.

Mombasa in moonlight breathes in the warmth of the staid night air awaiting the cool sea breeze come singing through the port's alleys where ghosts are seen after midnight. I hear the lovers again. He talks of love in hurried words, gasping for breath. She is quiet. I imagine, her kohl smudged eyes in the slit of her bui bui veil sparkle catching light from my window. I imagine, without touching him, she sweeps him into the aura of oudh's fragrance wrapped in the warmth of her veil. I imagine, her henna flowered hands flowing like waves to keep the bui bui in place though there is no wind. I imagine, her sexual hints, unsaid and elusive, allure him to arousal. I imagine she is me. How I lured Shamshu to bed, and yet made him feel it was he, my bwana, my man, my master in control over me.

"Let's embrace, mm?" he murmurs.

"No," she says. A sly refusal.

"Please, my love, just once."

"The midnight shift at Kilindini docks is about to finish. I must go. My father will be home soon."

That night, Shamshu and I do not face each other. The alley lovers will return home taking separate ways. She will walk in the shadows of the back lanes. He will walk along the road under the street lights. Outside, it's a balmy Mombasa night.

The cloth speaks wisdom

Some weeks go by before we would invite Ma Gor Bai to come home again and settle the matter of adopting Issa. The matter was left half-finished and distressing, particularly to me. Shamshu has not come home again, and I have not had an evening with him alone to let him know the feelings of my heart. I know when Issa is seven, Shamshu can take him away from me. That is how the sharia is, but Issa is just three. The thought of the father's right over the child haunts me. I have seen how my neighbour, Halima's two beautiful girls were carried away from her and married to the husband's clansmen in Yemen when they were twelve and thirteen. How my mother and I, and all the women of Mwembe Tayari used to gather at Halima's house to lament as bereaved mothers do, while praying for strength to submit to the sharia that they say is God's law. How we would say it is to God's will that we submit, for that is Islam, and yet we bewail the injustice. Halima never recovered from her loss, and she died a young mother bereft of her children. The husband then married Halima's younger sister. That is custom.

"Please have something to drink," I speak to help break the uneasiness in the room. My voice falters for it has no sweetness. The sort of sweetness that flows like honey from the mouth with words of welcome. My compelled smile screams over my hard sentences, unwillingly putting affection to words to show feelings of warmth I do not have. They turn to cynicism when I ask, "What soda? ...

Pepsi? ... Vimto? ...Snow Cream? ... Tangavizi ... Canada Dry?" The three Khoja women sit in silence nodding limply, gesturing politely, any soda will do. At that moment, abruptly, Nana reaches out and to my relief, opens her wooden chest, called the kasha, that's been at her bedside for as long as I can remember. The kasha, is never moved, only lifted a few inches up every morning by Charo, our house help, to sweep under its squat legs.

Ma Gor Bai gives a box of Marie Baring biscuits to Issa. He takes it, and quickly climbs onto Nana's bed, wedging in-between her back and the pillow.

"The kanga was bequeathed to us, the Swahili women of the coast of Africa by our ancestral slave mothers in the households of wealthy Arab royals, merchants, and sailors of the Indian Ocean. The cloth carries love in it, and sorrows of their hearts. It speaks wisdom in elders' minds, and shows colours in patterns of sea water and migrations. Together, they speak lyrics of cloth art of the Indian Ocean. I hear it in my body when I wear the kanga when I am sad, and seek joy and also when I am happy, and want to show my happiness. Wasikia? To ask do you hear me is to ask, do you feel what I say?"

I see the three pairs of kangas that Nana is looking at have paisley as a motif. All three are in different colours and patterns. I see by the way she holds the cloth, Nana knows her kangas, the art and wisdom words printed on each one that are singularly intimate to her and unique in the town. Though Nana does not read the script, she can tell what is written on every kanga because the patterns and colours on each one of her hundred kangas have a name and memory.

"My mother called this cloth kanga," says grandmother Nana. "It's like the bird from her native Nyika that has grey feathers and white, bright dots. That is how the light glimpses in the dark as glimmers of a bright dots to the eye. Like stars in night sky. A gathering of kangas, make a flock of feathered dots that does not fly, and runs the land." My mother and I look at each other wondering where Nana's parable will lead to. I wonder if the Khoja women, foreigners to our dress, language and song would understand; would even want to understand or care. But I see they are listening, particularly Moti Bai. She, I hear from Shamshu, has an eye of an artist. He would talk about his sister with pride.

"My father called the kanga, leso, by its Portuguese name. There are some kangas in this kasha that my father gave my mother," says Nana. Then carefully, she picks three kangas from a pile of a hundred pairs in the kasha, her dowry chest. During the hard times when Nana had no money to feed the family, she would sell a few of her vintage kangas. And when times were good, she would stock the choicest ones in the market until the memories of the patterns and proverbs faded. Then, she would bring them out again as classics of a past epoch. She would sell the kanga, now valued higher than the new ones in the market because the memories of cloth art held sentiments of the moments in women's lives when they were girls and felt free and valued.

There rises a whiff of stale oudh perfume from kangas too long pressed on top of each other in Nana's airtight wooden chest. Mombasa's heat and humidity have seeped through the stack and given Nana's kangas that exacting musty aroma of oudh, as if the fragrance itself was compressed and packed in the box of African hardwood like a treasure in a museum vault. She then holds the kangas with her eyes concentrating on them like a tray of cups of tea so full to the brim that a little move would spill the beverage over.

"This one is for your eldest daughter," Nana tells Gor Bai. That would be Moti Bai, Shamshu's eldest sister. Affectionately, Nana strokes the patina of pressed jasmines off the fabric. The kanga she holds has a border of yellow blossoms sneaking through foliage of feathery leaves on vines inter-looping. She places it on Moti Bai's extended forearms. Her fingers are curved in as in prayer. Nana keeps one piece of the pair by her side. That's odd, I think, because it's customary to give the kangas in pairs.

My mother comes to sit down on the bed by Nana's side. Moti Bai's kanga print is a garden. A garden that is a reflection of the perfumed paradise as in the Quran. When I was little, colours and floral messages on my grandma's kanga were embedded in my imagination. I was like all the other Swahili teenage girls, excited when a new design of kanga came to town. When I walked along the narrow streets of Stone Town by the old port, and ran from house to house on errands for my mother, grandmother and aunts, I imagined I was treading along lyrics of the rose, kilua and jasmine that fragranced the kanga garden. I was young then and full of dreams. Bringing her arms to her face, Moti Bai brings her cheek to the folds of her kanga on her forearms. First, she caresses, and then breathes in a whiff of its preserved scent.

"This is my second kanga. Riziki sent me the first one with Shamshu. It's red with a picture of a cashew nut

338

tree but this one is so different. May I open it?" she asks, speaking in Zanzibari Swahili.

Nana nods, her head tilted, lips stretched down smiling as if to say, "It's up to you, my child, because the kanga now belongs to you. You do not have to ask permission to unfold it." With gentle turnovers, Moti Bai unfolds her kanga.

Colours maroon, white, and yellow spill over. Thinly pressed brown crispy-dry jasmine flowers drop to the floor. Moti Bai picks up the dead flowers with care of veneration and place them one at a time back into the kasha. "I feel the pulse of the kanga throbbing in veins of my arms," says Moti Bai, speaking in Swahili without the Indian inflection in her voice. Ma Gor Bai turns around to ask Auntie Khoja in Kacchi, pointing to the printed words, "What does it say?" She cannot read the alphabet in another script.

"KILA NDEGE HURUKA NA MBAWA ZAKE," reads Auntie Khoja, "EVERY BIRD FLIES ON ITS OWN WINGS," she says in Kacchi partly to Ma Gor Bai and partly to herself - thoughts seem to come to her as she reads.

Leaves and flowers in three colours embrace the proverb like mother's eyes on her baby breastfeeding in her cradled arms. The kanga is the gift that has unlocked my family, kept hidden for too long from my fair husband's Khoja relations. "EVERY BIRD FLIES ON ITS OWN WINGS," speaks the kanga. That is my fate. But my wings are clipped. I hop around hoping Shamshu will accept me as his equal like the bird hopping around hoping for its cut wings to grow and fly. But in my heart, I want to shout and quarrel with Nana for giving away the legacy that should be mine.

"And give this to your younger daughter." Nana takes another kanga in her hand. It's bright. It's an orange kanga with white, black and yellow prints of star shaped flowers spangled in a spray. It is for Monghi Bai, Shamshu's younger sister. Nana says the proverb aloud, "USIWE NA PUPA LA KHERI MUNGU ATAKUPA," running her fingers on the border that's her palm width with white, orange and red paisleys on a black background. The colours jump out cheerful from a deep dark chasm. Then she hands one piece of the pair to Ma Gor Bai and keeps the other. The kanga imitates the garden, envious like it desires to be God's garden of paradise itself.

Auntie Khoja explains the second proverb, "DO NOT BE IMPATIENT, GOD WILL GRANT BLESSINGS." I look away, annoyed. I understand the varied interpretations of the circumstances when a kanga is worn, given, or received. However, this kanga holds the memory of the Eid day when I was little and sad, because I had no new clothes like my cousins and neighbours. Even the three daughters of the Khoja bhajia masi, the woman down the street, had new clothes with zari borders around the neck, sleeves and hemlines. Each one wore a red nylon ribbon bow clipped to her curled over hair at the side above the ear. Then my dear Nana sang to me, Kasha langu la zamani, the song of the old kasha that stored many gifts:

Kasha langu la zamani kutoka Mombasa   My old Mombasa chest
Lina ficha zawadi ndani kwa ndani   Deep inside, it hides gifts
Zawadi hizi za nani?   Whose gifts are these?
And I replied immediately jumping up as high as I could
  Ni zangu, ni zangu, ni zangu mimi   Mine, mine, mine myself

Then Nana wrapped me up in a pair of kanga from her kasha and sang again:

Zawadi hizi ni za mwanangu mpenzi - These gifts are for my love child.

I walked out of the house holding my mother's hand to the Eid fete like an elegant little memsaheb. The kanga I was wearing was the brightest one with prints of starflower and the writing on it read, "DO NOT BE IMPATIENT, GOD WILL GRANT BLESSINGS". It was the one that Nana just gave away for Monghi Bai, Shamshu's sister.

Every month the microphone on the pickup truck of storekeeper Mali ya Abdulla echoes:

| *Kanga sampuli mpia* | *New kanga design* |
| *Subira huvuta heri* | *Patience pulls blessings* |

A song about a new kanga comes to the streets of Mombasa, and my friends and I would talk about its colours as they first strike the eye. Then we would take turns to decipher the meaning behind the proverb, reading into its nuances and puns keeping in mind the current social or political headlines that break the news on the radio. We would look for the second meaning coded behind the obvious. Was I not the one who said how this kanga "DO NOT BE IMPATIENT, GOD WILL GRANT BLESSINGS", spoke to us to be tolerant of dictator Kenyatta and his clansmen? Did it not appear on the market a month after the President's men abused my people, the Swahili, calling us lazy, homosexuals, witchdoctors, and Arabs, the foreigners who should return to Arabland? We would be patient and wait for God's blessings to strike back at the right time.

"And this one I give to you," Nana tells Ma Gor Bai.

It is the kanga with a white border of black paisley wisps with pointed tips running sideways. The centre has large bright yellow and white discs connected to lines of black dots. Nana recites the proverb on this brightest of the three kangas, "MASKINI NA MWANAWE TAJIRI NA MALI YAKE."

Auntie Khoja explains haltingly as if embarrassed, "THE POOR HAVE THEIR CHILDREN, THE RICH THEIR WEALTH."

"Issa is my grandchild like he is yours. Such children are the intersections of societies where the rich and poor, black and white, Sunni and Shia, Asians and Africans cross paths," says Nana placing the third kanga in Ma Gor Bai's hands. Issa climbs down from Nana's bed and comes to me holding the box of biscuits secure in both his hands. "In Swahili, we have a saying, 'To make a tie on the kanga you need two ends,' " says Nana.

I see Ma Gor Bai nodding. Nana speaks again, "The magic of the kanga is patterned in art that pleasures the eye before you read the words. The wisdom of words calls on the mind to reflect back to the eye, drunk with colours. That is the leso, the fabric whose threads knit women's genealogies. Their stories are memoirs of great-aunts and great-aunt-mothers, stepmothers, sisters, half-sisters, cousins, and half-cousins told in whispers rasping the white ocean sands. There, where the blue sky lisps the sounds of water into our hearts even as our ears are too proud to listen," says Nana and then she pauses, and takes in a deep breath. It's after a long time that I hear Nana the poet lamenting pain. "In the end, it's the feelings that come from the chasm of memories that matter when the kanga talks to you before you touch it. This leso's garden that scents your lap once scented my body when I was young. It pleated around my mother's torso when she danced the cha-ka-cha.

But it was my great-aunt, Bibi Siti, the Storyteller of Lamu, who filled my head with proverbs and my heart with poetry. Her tongue moulded mine, and taught me how to put words to verse. The garden of flowers is versed a paradise in the Quran, and it balms the lips of those who read the Book. Wear this kanga that has caressed bodies of mothers in my family for generations three. Keep our memories in you and honour us. Keep it among your treasures with ocean's aroma at night, for we are one family. One is our respect we share as we do this grandchild. Like two alike pieces of cloth, a piece in each family. She hisses out a long sigh to show she has spoken and has no more to say. After the sigh, I know Nana would lean back to rest on her pillows, and finally say, "Asante," meaning thank you in the manner of closing the talk. Instead, she says, "I pray when you look at these kangas you will find honour in your heart to accept my granddaughter Riziki as your own. Issa stays with the one who gave him birth."

Gor Bai listens with wide opened eyes. She begins to cough as if choked by surprise. Perhaps, she is puzzled.

Nana's plea angers me. I have my dignity and will not ask to be accepted in the Khoja family. I have envy in my stomach that burns. Now, my grandmother has given away my dignity. Why beg for what is mine by marriage? By sharia. She also gave away the kangas, our family heritage to which I have a right. Yet, I know in kanga's garden, relationships are nurtured like saplings brought to bear fruit from another garden. In such beauty, there is eternal peace, and Nana would want her gifts of the cloth that speaks to persuade my husband's family to make peace and acknowledge me as a co-wife to Khati Bai.

Then quickly, as if prompted by a slap on her wrist, Ma Gor Bai removes a tightly knotted white handkerchief from the cup of her brassiere. I watch her as she unknots the handkerchief, and count some old brown, red and blue paper bills showing the side profiles of King George VI. To these bills, she adds three new crispy brown, red and blue bills of the same design and paper with young Queen Elizabeth looking like an angel wearing a pensive half smile and a diamond tiara. Ma Gor Bai selects a few old and new bills that have writings in English, Swahili and Gujarati. She makes a bunch with the bills, and gives it to Nana. I watch grandmother's cheeks tinge red on her wrinkled white skin that glows a sheen.

"Buy a piece of cloth for yourself, and something for the child," says Gor Bai with a smile that anyone would see does not come from her heart. The gift of money, like her smile, has no warmth, and moreover speaks no wisdom.

Shamshu's stepmother does not talk about Issa's adoption again. The three Khoja women drink the sodas in quick squirts in through the straws, and stand up to leave.

"Asante," says Auntie Khoja, as she steps into the dim corridor of rooms with printed cotton curtains at each entrance.

"Asante," says Moti Bai, following Auntie Khoja and looking down.

"Karibuni," my mother replies with a smile, but I know in her heart, she is happy to see them go.

As soon as the door closes behind the three visitors, I walk straight to Nana and I murmur into her ears, "Why did you give away these kangas? You know, I like them very, very much,"

"I am old," replies Nana, "but you are young and you will have more children, and you will have more beautiful kangas. Family means sharing what's dear to your heart. Live with your utu-humanity for the sake of your family. If your husband has four wives, then you must accept all four families of all four co-wives as your own beloved. That is custom," Nana speaks with a firm conviction of her traditions and faith. "Now listen to me, Riziki. A kanga is never old and never forgotten, because its meaning remains in the memory of the gift of your relationship. We offered a kanga today to make a tie. Now it is up to them. Praise be to God. Allah-hu-akbar, God is great!" Nana speaks while handing me the three half pairs of kanga. She gave the other three half pairs to Shamshu's Khoja family.

"I wanted these in pairs so I could wear them. Why did you give them to the Khoja. You know they don't wear kangas! What shall I do with half a pair? " My irritation lets anger slip into scorn, "Half a Swahili, half a Khoja?"

Nana smiles with her loving eyes put to my contorted face. Half teasing me, and half chiding, she says, "Is your child not half a Swahili and half a Khoja too?"

All my life I have watched how new relationships are made, and broken ones mended with this fabric of the women of the Indian Ocean. But I did not expect Nana to give away the kangas in her kasha that I, her favourite granddaughter, the one who looks after her in her old age, who jumps out of the bed at night to hold her hand when her feet refuse to take steps towards the toilet, was expecting to inherit in complete pairs. As a child, I played grandmother with Nana's kangas wrapped around me, and over my head. I wore her kangas when I imitated her gestures like how she cooked sitting down on the floor stool stirring the lentil broth; how she served tea to guests in a tray with her eyes looking down under her kanga over her head. How she covered her hair before men in a kanga hijab. How she tied the kanga around my waist when I was little. She taught me how to dance the cha-ka-cha swirling the kanga to make my man love me when I would be his wife.

So is my story told remembering childhood rituals we created observing adult life. Some rituals are shaped by our belongings, close and personal to each one. Like the kanga. My kangas have many stories to tell. Some are told in words, some in songs, and some we dance when the tale breaks the heart and the body cannot keep still. That's when the secret of the heart kept hidden emerges.

Part Nine

Dance the Kanga

Like the cloth called the kanga and the language called Swahili, the dance called chaka-ka-cha evolved at the western shores of the Indian Ocean where the meeting of the cultures of land and oceanic migrations is seen in the architecture dating back to the tenth century. It could even be earlier but records are lost to time.

Music historians say cha-ka-cha cherishes African, Middle Eastern and Indian musical traditions. The dance rhythm of cha-ka-cha pervades over folk dances of the three lands as does the melodies of taraab, the East African musical genre whose magic haunts ocean waters and continental land like a cheerful spirit.

Ma Gor Bai

In town I am known as Moti Bai daughter of Husein Nagji Padamshi of the bead store in Nairobi and married to Haiderali Devji Momna of the bead store in Nairowua.

It must have been at least three years after my return to Nairowua from Mombasa when I pick up the telephone. It's the operator from the Nairowua Post Office. She says there is a call from Mombasa. Usually, we write to each other and rarely do we call from one town to another. Shamshu tells me he wants to talk to Haiderali, not me. Haiderali is at the table, leaning on his arms stretched out in a circle under his humped shoulders. I don't call him; he looks at my face and comes to the phone panting faint wisps through his funnelled lips. He is just back from his mid-afternoon walk to and from the bank. His wet shirt sticks to his back.

When Haiderali replaces the receiver looking down, I feel my body breaking even before he tells me, "Ma Gor Bai has passed away." I wail, smack my hands on my forehead and then run to the bedroom crying kooth kooth. My stepmother's memories flood into my head like it were intermittent torrents of floodwaters over my body. They echo in my ears. "Eat with me", she would say when I was little and would not eat because she scolded me for not sweeping under the beds or because I resented house chores on some days, and said I wanted to read. Then she would tell me, "I will not eat if you don't." My ears ring hollow, swish-buzz as if I was alone trapped in an empty, endless hall. I weep into the space void of sound. My ears have numbed. Screams from within pierce my innards. I am losing myself in a void. I want to run into the acacia grove to the spirit who will be me and strong. Haiderali comes cautiously towards me and takes me in his arms. For a moment, we lean into each other laying over pillows and quilts. Not knowing how to touch a woman to comfort, he fumbles an awkward caress over my face that ends with a few hesitant pats on the top of my head as he would to comfort Almas when she cries. With both my fists, I clench the compressed lay of his curly hair. It slips - coconut-oil. I tunnel my fingers onto his scalp's sun warmth. I smell into his sweat at the neck, masked over by face sweat leached down over morning's Yardley aftershave. The hot breathing, the heat of his body, his clasp over me, body memories of our just married days stab me like a thunderbolt. Thrusting my hands between us, I push him away, digging my elbows into his ribs, and scream. Haiderali panics seeing me in this sudden state of madness.

It is fast becoming dark as we approach Nairobi. I feel as if the bus was slipping into my awaking morning sleep, half into dreams of my childhood, half in the present. Such were my feelings breaking into thoughts of the past. So passionate are my feelings of the days with Ma Gor Bai that they numb the present. The bus disturbs an assembly of haggard marabou storks picking an evening meal at the cadaver dump by the abattoirs of Kenya Meat Commission at Athi River. The carcass of a zebra by the roadside on the other side of the bus is obviously a kill of a predator from the previous evening. Avian scavengers on both sides of me squawk annoyingly when the bus passes by them. I see the birds take to flight, circle around, and then one by one, return taxiing down to a halt on the cadavers.

"Death of a zebra is not a good sign, *si-ndio?*" Ole Lekakeny would have said had he been with me. "Zebra is beauty. When beauty dies, there is no peace, is that not so, *si-ndio?*"

We stay overnight at my father's one room home on Grogan Road behind the Imtiaz Ali Sufi mosque. The next day, we travel together in the air conditioned Akamba Bus to Mombasa. "New model," says my father. Now he can hold the children in his lap and tell them stories about the invisible animals lurking like spirits behind the bushes along the Nairobi-Mombasa road running parallel to the old railroad. Left to myself, I have time to mourn Ma Gor Bai. I take my eyes deep into the beauty of the land and remain alone in thoughts of Ma Gor Bai over the savannah landscape.

People say Ma Gor Bai died because of her cough that would develop into a ceaseless hacking fit once it started. But, thinking back, I know, she had begun her journey into prayo-pavesa, meaning self-desired death, a little earlier than usual for her age and health. She ate less each day until her breathing became faint and then stopped altogether.

Though she told no one, it was no wonder to me that Stepmother Gor Bai made a decision to commit herself to prayo-pavesa. That was the custom in her old Saurashtra and her family of pir's shrine keeper. She used to say that the prayo-pavesa gave freedom to the aged and the infirm who had neither the will, nor the capacity of the body, or the mind to live on. But it was the guilt that took my stepmother's life, not her health. It was after that terrible accident that killed Shamshu's adopted daughter, Yasmine, that Ma Gor Bai's self-blame became so unbearable that she was losing her mind and saw no reason to live.

It happened at mid-day, when Ma Gor Bai was bringing Yasmine home from school, that the lorry driver carrying stones from the quarry in Bamburi, lost control, skidded along the pavement and hit the little girl. Her palm pressed into Ma's own remained in a firm grip even as she took her last breath. "Why was it not me, Ya Mowla? What sins have I in me that you should punish me, taking away Yasmine from my hand?" When people heard Stepmother lament in this manner, it broke their hearts, and they talked behind her back among themselves to find reasons to soothe their own feelings. That she should have looked out for the lorry. That everyone knows how construction lorries scuttle along Makupa Road. That the old woman is weak on her legs, and should not have gone to collect the child from school. That the mid-day sun in Mombasa blazes like fire, and burns the eyes. When such fitina, that is gossip meant to hurt the heart, came to Ma Gor Bai's ears, often, though not always, through Khati Bai, Yasmine's adoptive mother and Shamshu's wife, she believed it. That consumed her thoughts, and she could not look at her peers in the eyes. She stopped going to her jamat khana cleaning-sewa. Then she stopped going to the jamat khana all together. Thus, it was no wonder that Ma Gor Bai did what she had to. It was the practice she knew would relieve her for she had no more reason to live and Mowla would understand.

Each evening for forty days, I take food prayer tray to the jamat khana. My prayers reside in wheat chapattis, a bowl of curry, a fruit, and a jug of milk. I keep to the appropriate Vedic configuration of sweetened and salted foods in the offering for nourishment of mental and physical health. Each day I talk to my stepmother's photograph, to let her know what I have cooked for her that day. On the tenth, twentieth, thirtieth day, I make mashed mung and crackled rice khichedi, and yogurt khadi with love of remembrance in my hands that were taught how to embroider, and also how to cook wholesome meals for the family and the jamat khana. The fare was Ma Gor Bai's favourite meal in her old age. I would personally carry the tray down Kuze Road to the jamat khana in Mombasa's old stone town by the fish market. A block down was the slave cave at the dhow harbour where our forefathers landed from India. Over the food dish that I was not able to cook for her in her old age, I now offer prayers for the peace of her soul and all those who left before her and are with her now.

It's the beginning of the kite season in Mombasa. Anil and Diamond spend most of the day outside. My sister, Monghi Bai, had come earlier from Kisumu with her son Anil to look after Ma after her ceaseless cough developed into astringent asthma during the last days of her fast of prayo-pavesa. Monghi Bai bought hats for the boys from the Kacchi Bhadala lady who is a neighbour, and who sits crossed-legged in palothi on a platform at her shop in Mwembe Kuku Bazaar. But Anil would not wear the hat because he says nobody wears a hat in Mombasa. If he does, the boys will call him mzungu whiteman. He detests the teasing, that he says will stick with him like kite glue. He says this showing his sticky, flour-wet-white fingers to his mother. She jumps aside. It makes me smile inside while Anil's mischief draws me closer to him. How very much he is like all boys playful with their mothers. Diamond who is

353

younger than Anil, watches him with admiration make colourful kites. Diamond, in fact, looks up to Anil as his elder brother, follows him everywhere, and helps him to unwind the kite string and stretch it, while Anil waxes it, running it through a candle to make it strong. I make glue for the boys with fine maida chapatti flour to paste the tails to the kites and frills that flutter in the sky. The arcs of the kites are made from Khati Bai's fagio broom sticks. Anil would send Diamond to snip the sticks from the broom that lies at the courtyard karo, and that would immediately slap a frown on Khati Bai's face, for it loosens up the tight woven binding on her broom. But she holds back her tongue, knowing how petulant my sister Monghi Bai, Anil's mother, can be when her only child and a son she calls Beta Anil, is reproved by a grumpy aunt.

We had heard from neighbours that Khati Bai, Shamshu's wife, was unkind to Ma Gor Bai, neglecting her old age needs, making her feel she was a burden of mothaj. After Yasmin's death, she would call Ma Gor Bai absakan widow, and say, "The dosi's velvet dress stinks of mildew." She called her 'dosi' meaning old woman, and not Ma that both custom and respect for the elderly requires of the relatives. I know her velvet dress was her wedding dress that she liked to wear on the annual Khush-ali evenings at the jamat khana with her matching zari embroidered pachedi-shawl. That she died sighing nisasa, the hurting groans in rasping exhales of the elderly breathing out pain from their wounded hearts. People say nisasa of grievance is a curse. Now they say in chup chap whispers what we know: Khati Bai will never conceive because of the curse of the helpless dependent whom she called a mothaj, meaning an unloved burden. Not in this lifetime will she conceive and that's a curse, a consolation for the bereaved daughters

354

of Ma Gor Bai. Others, not neighbours or relatives, but stepmother's peers who sat on the bench at the jamat khana veranda each evening with her, spoke differently. They said my stepmother saw little girls at night, ghost multiplications of little Yasmin reaching out their chubby hands to lock grip into her bony fingers, tugging her out of her bed as if to get her out of the way of the trucks hurtling towards them. There are many stories now after her death, stories that explain her death and pain the heart. But what is the truth? God only knows.

I try to keep away from such stories about my stepmother that are told with deep compassion in feminine tones of remorse. Words of sadness and regret about Ma Gor Bai's last days accompany multiple blessings said in shu-khar, meaning contentment. Shu-khar that she died without being a mothaj that is a bothersome dependent, which is not true, but it's said nevertheless, to comfort me. That is custom. I try to be alone so I can concentrate on telling my tasbih beads for peace of her soul. Grief like anger like shame keeps me isolated to myself.

From today I resolve I will not talk of Ma Gor Bai as my stepmother but as my second mother. That is how the Maasai children of Nairowua call the wives of their father other than their own mother. They say they are their mothers too.

Of Cross Eyed and Sheep Headed Khojas of Mombasa

Razak comes to see me. It's a khar-khar-ro visit, meaning an after death comfort visit. Razak, though not an Ismaili is a part of our family. It was his mother Ful Bai, a devoted Ithna Asheri Khoja, who breastfed both him and my brother Shamshu when my mother died in child birth. Milk brothers are deeply respected. Dadabapa used to say mother's milk brought our families together when faith kept us apart. "After all," he would add, "we are all of Khoja mothers' milk."

But our relations go even farther. Dadabapa knew Ful Bai's Ithna Asheri family well because they came from the same village of Haripur in India where they inter-married and ate the caste meals together. Ful Bai's parents, and Dadabapa left Haripur together as a family, and travelled in the same dhow called Nyota ya Bahari la Hindi or the Star of the Indian Ocean. The story is told of how Ful Bai's mother, the one with a bad leg, was thrown overboard the dhow in the night of the raging storm. Ful Bai was just a child and they called her Bebli. However, being a girl, she became a mother to her little brother, Bablo. Bablo was nursed by an Ismaili Khoja mother who lost her baby during the voyage, and he slept with Nanima the grandmother who was coming to Africa to look for her son. Their story lives in my head from the night Dadabapa told me between his cold and hot spells of malaria in his body. It was a bad type of malaria that affects the head. I nursed him for two weeks.

Though we are like a family, Razak and I can neither eat a morsel nor accept a glass of water in each other's home no matter how hot the day, and how much we sweated in the heat because I am an Ismaili Khoja and he is an Ithna Asheri Khoja. Our faiths make it sinful to drink in the other Khoja's home. "Haram *chhe!*" my faith people would cry out with an emphatic *chhe* hushed in breathless horror suppressed with fingers over their lips. It is so because the holy men of our two faiths decreed so. However, when they proclaimed the decree, the holy men did not say to breastfeed each other's babies was haram too. That was the custom among the Khoja over the dissections of religion. Nor did they say we could not drink soda brought to the homes from outside.

"Shamshu does not provide for his two children's upkeep," Razak begins to complain about Shamshu. "He does not even go to see Riziki and the children." Razak is married to Riziki's sister and they live in the stone town near the ancient Bhadala mosque. He has put on weight and wears his hair in a grey fringe around his bald head.

"Saalo Shamshu!" My first thought expressed in a surge of surprise anger. I worry about Shamshu's fleeting morals as a mother would. Elder sisters, after all, are second mothers to their siblings whom they have partially raised. "Does he say why?"

"We don't speak to each other. We had a quarrel." Shamshu had told me that Razak calls Ismailis, Gheta Khoja, meaning Sheep Headed Khoja because he says we are dumb following Saheb like sheep. But I did not know that they had quarrelled, and did not speak with each other.

"Why?" I ask. "You are milk brothers, you know."

"Something to do with money and making a new passport for his friend."

I had heard from my sister, Monghi Bai, who had heard it from her businessman husband, that Razak is the right hand man of the Minister for Immigration selling passports to Asians. In fact, they call him Razak Passport in town.

"Shamshu called me Traansa Khoja." Ismailis call our caste cousins Cross Eyed Khoja because we say the Ithna Asheris look askance from Sat-panth, the straight path. How their quarrel over money has led to hate name calling against their faiths! However, Razak calls me his sister during the conversation, and I call him my brother.

Even today, when an elderly person sees Razak and Shamshu together, he will say, "A picture comes to my mind. I see Ful Bai sitting in cross-legged palothi with the two boys laying head to head in the crook of her each arm, slurping at her breasts as if competing who would finish, and in contentment be the first to burp."

"After all it's one Khoja blood that flows in their veins," his companion would reply in a partial sentence leaving another elder to say more, and sure enough someone would say more, "Like Ful Bai's breast milk."

A third elder would then add his voice, "Property set us apart but we are one milk and blood." Such is the manner of their talk between annoyance and anguish, and the desire to be one again.

True. I also read in *Kacch no Kajio – Quarrelling in Kacch* what the elders remember in their conversations. About a century ago, the court in Bombay passed judgment

358

on the communal inheritance of the Khoja. And then, Saheb, on behalf of one religion, came to be the keeper of community land and buildings in the whole of Hindustan. Yet, the disputed properties were owned by the Khoja caste people and did not belong to any one religion. Thus, out of the quarrels over our forefathers' bequest, we came to be Ismailis bearing the religious appellation, pushing Khoja, our ethnic self, to the back.

Saalo Shamshu! He does not pay for the upkeep of his children! No wonder whenever I ask Shamshu about Riziki, he quickly changes the subject. Perhaps, as they say in the community, he thinks of Riziki as his rakhel bai, meaning his kept woman, the other woman, not his Khoja wife. Ma Gor would not only have thought quietly about Riziki as Shamshu's kept woman, but would have also said it aloud.

Riziki with her children continues to live in Mombasa with her grandmother Nana on Mwembe Tayari Street. The street name says 'the mango tree is ready', meaning the mangoes have ripened on the tree and are ready to be plucked. It used to be a lane where mango farmers gathered to sell their harvest when the English ruled. Today, it's a crowded market street during the day, and a country bus station all through to the night.

Hawa

When the forty days of mourning for Ma Gor are over, I accept Riziki's invitation for an evening of Kesha Ndugu, meaning Wake for Sister, which is all women's all night long gathering to say farewell to the bride.

Riziki's grandmother's house stands nestled in the street among similar houses, lending the particular sand brown texture to Mwembe Tayari. Soft balmy warmth coughs into my face as I step into the corridor of Nana's coral stone and mortar home with a corridor, and palm thatched roof. There is little sea breeze in the month of February in Mombasa, and people pray for rains and accompanying Kaskazi Monsoons that will bring relief from the sweltering heat that stays all night long between walls.

Auntie Khoja is with me. The last time, when I was in the corridor, Ma Gor Bai was by my side. Everything looks the same but for the scents of the evening. The fragrance is warm from lush bunches of pink tinted jasmine buds in coil twisted hair, oudh whiffs and sugared flour of cardamom flavoured mandazi sizzling in oil. Repeated welcomes of 'Karibuni' greet us from many sides. I hear only women's voices. The women have removed their bui bui veils, and are sitting, standing and moving about the crowded corridor looking bright in their family kangas. Each kanga has a saying celebrating marriage or love, wife or blessings of home set in patterned motifs. I have not met any of the women before, but some know me, and they embrace me into their coffee arms in short sleeves, gold bangles and kangas saturated with smoky scent of oudh in a variety of grades. They talk among themselves explaining who I am. They call me Khoja mgeni, meaning the Khoja guest, who is accompanying elderly Auntie Khoja. They know her as their own Khoja resident of Mwembe Tayari. I live in Khoja Flats.

The women of Riziki's family have gathered to bid farewell to her cousin-sister Saida's fourteen year old daughter, whose marriage has been arranged with the son of another cousin called Amin, who lives in Tanga, the old German port town to the south of Mombasa on the Swahili coast. That afternoon in the Mwembe Kuku bazaar, I searched for a pair of kanga for the bride and found one with an apt proverb: MKE NI DHAHABU YA NYUMBANI that is, A WIFE IS GOLD OF THE HOME.

My mind goes to the women's gathering at my own henna night when Meethi Bai and Ma Gor Bai sang the song of the Satpanth bandhani. I share the bride's silent fears and hopes. Her kohl lined eyes look into mine. My heart feels for her. I move closer to her sitting on the mattress.

"Sing and listen to the tales of your family," calls Nana from behind the cotton curtain. Nana, they tell me, is the oldest matriarch and a famed oral artist of Riziki's Bajuni matrilineal clan on the Indian Ocean coast. But it's Riziki who surprises me with her eloquence in measured prose. "My husband and I courted at the ocean coast." Riziki has already started to tell her story and is showing the kangas she had received from Shamshu. I edge closer to her now, anxious to hear the other side of my family which has remained a taboo even to talk about while Ma Gor Bai lived. Monghi Bai too carried the silence and my father just ignored Riziki and his black grandchildren as if they were not family. "We spent the days after our nikha marriage together in the warmth of the Swahili waterfront," speaks Riziki in lyrics now, holding a kanga patterned in brown leaves on red background. "These were times of desires. Desire to be together, desire for a new life; desire to be a wife; desires of a home and children. All woman's desires of the moment of just married." Riziki's sing song sentences lure me to her. "When taraab's music romances with the monsoon gales, the heart palpitates, and promises of the sweethearts fill the ears like sounds of the sea." I hear her voice deepen, becoming lyrical, and coming from the torments of the waves in her heart hollowed of love of a husband. I hear discontent. I hear betrayal. I hear her hurting. I want to hold her hand in my hand and say, "Yes, I understand." Instead, I withdraw to be away from her broken heart and be with Shamshu, my brother. The picture of the Maasai women at the dry river bed scraping water from a hole comes to me. I was returning to Nairowua from Nairobi. How I withdrew from their suffering, their thirst. My palm curls over the edge of my pachedi-shawl crumpling the embroidered border into a ball. I hold my breath.

"Hear me, for I am the vessel of words for your ears to drink from. After our nikha every kanga gifted to me was fine-looking. Every baby in the street was the picture of the child I wished my womb would bear. Every grain of sand had a story to tell about him and me." Issa remains standing, sleepy, and listening while leaning on his mother's knees, his head lies in her lap under the kangas she is showing us. Riziki's second born, a daughter called Salme, about two years old, is asleep at the foot of Nana's bed, covered by a green and yellow kanga on which is a

362

picture of a pineapple and words in Swahili that read LOVE IS GRASS. Pillows are carefully gathered on both sides of Salme, watched over by Auntie Khoja's granddaughter, Amina. Sudden arrival of a group of women clad in black bui bui veil refreshes the room with renewed fragrances of oudh and jasmine. Each one is in a bright kanga and gold. You would think the women are dressed to dance – to show how they shrug shoulders in circles, gesture hands to the air, move the hips as if each one was a bride that night dancing for her husband the first time.

"We went to Cinema Majestiki," says one of them as she lifts her veil and reveals dark Arabic features - almond eyes, sharp chin, and a nose softly aquiline. Her kohl eye makeup runs in a straight line towards the ear. "Ladies Show," she says and smiles. I recognize those uneven teeth and the canine before the front tooth. It is Hawa! We embrace recalling the love of our childhood in the touch of our bodies. Then we sit together hand in hand, and sides touching.

"Nasikia raha moyoni - I hear happiness in my heart. It's the joy of seeing you that soars in my heart," she says.

"Nasikia upendo moyoni - I hear love in my heart. It's the love of seeing you that waters my eyes," I reply.

She asks, "Did the forty mourning days go well?" No doubt Hawa knows about Ma Gor Bai's death from Riziki.

"They went well according to her wishes."

"And her bandhani?"

"Monghi will keep Ma's bandhani. She lives in Kisumu. Has one son."

363

We talk little, but we have many feelings to share in our few words, and the familiar touch of our hands. We continue holding hands, sitting side by side in silence.

"Do you still embroider zari?"

"Yes. Whenever I can. Dress styles have changed you know. Khoja women wear English dresses."

"Modern *chhe nah?*" she asks trapping laughter in her mock question imitating Khoja talk.

Hawa has been married and divorced. When her husband wanted to marry another wife, Hawa said she would not be a co-wife to a schoolgirl. Now Hawa lives with her father, Askari Bakari, in the old stone town near Kuze Jamat Khana. She has two boys, twins. She has put on weight, has a rotund body, and she seems happy. Hawa makes mandazi bread and mbazi beans in coconut cream that she supplies to several dock workers' breakfast cafes at Kilindini harbour. And thus she supports herself and her boys.

"I get up at four in the morning when the Khoja go to khane. By six, I am in the street delivering hot mandazi to the worker hotels when the Khoja are returning from khane," she says.

How a street like Mwembe Tayari where Riziki lives, is like my story that begins somewhere small. Over time, the street changes its face becoming bigger and different absorbing smaller lanes. So does my story absorbing smaller stories grows bigger.

Dance the Kanga

When Nana begins to talk, she demands all attention, so full of feelings are her words. "Legends bend my stubborn tongue to speak. Proverbs of Africa garnish your kangas speaking to your heart," says Nana smiling now. She turns her eyes to me, "Wisdom of the kanga is shaped by old tongues." I respond with a nod. She acknowledges with a return nod. Then, her eyes glide over to Riziki, and back to me, back and forth passing on nods to both. Nana speaks to comfort her granddaughter Riziki, but talks to me as if for her sake. As if to ease her pain, speaking to me. "Men come and go, but we remain in the slippery embrace of misty Monsoon. For centuries ten, the ocean breeze lured hearts of your fair fathers to woo us, your mothers, the black women of Africa."

Nana speaks in Swahili. I am pulled into the music of the ocean. Words with long aa-s and oo-s flow out of her lips like lazy waves lapping over warm white sands. In between, the sea breeze sweeps through palm fronds in silent m-s and n-s. Double syllables - wasi wasi, kati kati, bui bui, sound like clapping oars of the dhow. I feel intimate, native and loved in the tenors of coastal Swahili. For centuries this language has blended oceanic and inland people, and called no one an outsider, Asian or African. It's the language of two ancestral migrations meeting in the kingdoms of Ibadi Swahili, neither Sunni nor Shia yet Moslem. The language that makes a lucid shore belt from the Red Sea to Mozambique. I hear Swahili's richness, its warmth, its lustre in Nana's words. "In Swahili, I am as you are," I want to speak into the chattering room. "Don't call me Khoja guest. I am no guest in Swahili." In the moment of the language, listening to Nana speak, the vast ocean that separates our ancestors vanishes. I turn to Hawa by my side. She knows I am no outsider in Swahili for she is my mama ndogo, that is, my younger mother. Custom requires the child caretaker be respected as a mother too.

"Kweli Riziki ana stori – true, Riziki has a story to tell," she whispers to me.

"Nasikia, I am listening, feeling," I reply.

Two women drummers strike the beat of cha-ka-cha. The dance begins led by Zainabu, Riziki's younger sister. The room whirls in kanga colours, glints of ornaments, silhouettes swing and shadows dance on the wall. In several stylish moves, deliberately exaggerated to accent the rhythm, the women begin to widen the circle into a spiralling rim of quaking kanga wraps tight over their rounded backs. The wraps have so many proverbs, riddles and phrases on them that reading them bewilders the head. Gold rings on dancing dark wrists poise high above the heads gleaming in the light of the sole electric bulb dangling from the ceiling. Riziki stands up to dance, her humming coming from deep within like moans of a wounded doe. Issa climbs into Nana's bed beside his sister, but there is no space for him to lie down. I stretch out my arms for him to sleep on my lap. He half climbs over my knees before I pick him up. Riziki unties, and ties her kanga again tighter below her waist. Her back rigid and straight, she picks steps coming into the cha-ka-cha circle. I bring my hands around Issa and hold him close, my body moving to the rhythm of taraab. My eyes on a forest of coffee hands raised high like

366

a galaxy of shooting stars - feminine gesturing to the spirits of the air. Bare feet decorated in floral patterns of black henna throb over the grey cemented floor. Colours float over jasmine bunches studded into black curls and then hips begin shaking like pulsations of the body. Women are dancing to taraab melodies of the Indian Ocean. I feel the rhythms of Africa and Asia in the stepping thumps of flat soles. My heart throbs with the pace of Issa's breath on my chest. Hawa, sitting by my side, begins to hum into the music. It's a Swahili hum. It's woman's hum. It fills her. Her head moves from side to side. It calls her to the circle. It's a hum a man does not know. The humming evokes the woman in me native to Africa. As Hawa stands to dance, I feel the sensation of the group like droning bees on the acacia. The drum beats become louder. My feet rise on toes and heels thump the floor. Hawa's humming, like a bud, opens into a verse as she falls into the circle. Then, as she completes one round, her verse flows into the chorus like the opening of jasmine flowers clipped to her hair. She dances more, moving her neck in circles, part singing, part humming.

Dance the cha-ka-cha heal your hearts

Your story too will be told in Salme's legend

Closing her eyes, Riziki lets the song fill her body descending to the waist and it moves. Her held-up shoulders in a kanga wrap shake, she sways ready to pick the next step in a new verse. Women sing for the bride and themselves.

"Lala hapa, sleep here," I whisper into Issa's ears. His ear drops to my heartbeat, and I feel his breath again hissing in a rhythm over the rhythm of my heart, its warmth blowing into my chest. I bring him closer to me like he were my own. I feel his curls, soft and cushioned, in my fingers raking through his head. Riziki walks a circle in short half steps with one foot flat on ground, and the other in raised heel, as if hesitant to take the next half step forward. Her waist sways, her backside in brisk shakes. With her eyes closed and head thrown back, she dances the cha-ka-cha, the dance of the kanga. Other women walk into the circle in reluctant one-foot-forward-stop and step, humming into the chorale's timbre and trembling backsides. Each wears a kanga in a pair over a long dress, one tied from the waist down, and the other loosely thrown over the upper body like a shawl at the front. Close relatives of the bride like her aunt Riziki and her sister Saada, cousins and nieces, wear the kangas of identical print and colours called saari za kanga. Women wearing saari za kanga distinguish as the hosts from the guests like me. The guests' kangas read as many diverse proverbs as the pictures on them but all have sayings that are closes to the joy or torment in their hearts that day. Issa falls asleep. His chubby hand slips through the V neck of my dress, and holds my breast. He sucks his thumb with the other hand.

Women clap and sing, "Toa hadithi, pull out a story. Toa hadithi, take a story out." The bride's hands and feet are painted thickly with dark henna and her wavy hair in two braids woven into a jasmine loop, falls in front over her bosom. Riziki sings, juxtaposing the sorrow of an abandoned wife with the joy of telling the hopeful bride how to be a wife:

> *Poetry is written on women's hearts*
> *Like Quran's verse carving prayers on doors*
> *Dance the cha-ka-cha*

Hovering kangas over the heads dip into languid floats below. Riziki continues to sing and dance holding the red kanga with a cashew nut tree over her like an umbrella. It's exactly like the kanga she had sent me with Shamshu. It's probably a part of the same pair. She looks at me and shakes the kanga.

> *So feel my story when you say you are listening*
> *Wasikia, are you listening, also means are you feeling*
> *Dance the cha-ka-cha*

I think she is telling me something in the movement of her eyes from me to the kanga. Again, I read the saying on the red kanga with a picture of the cashew nut tree: I LIKE TO BUT I AM NOT ABLE TO - NAPENDA LAKINI NASHINDWA. I understand it as a welcome gesture to come to the song and dance with her. But no, her hints mean more. How do I receive Riziki's Swahili over the Gujarati native in me? I mean her everything Swahili over everything Gujarati in me. I want to reach there into her half-toned words, her halting step cha-ka-cha, the mysterious proverb on her kanga, her waving hands and the kohl smudged eyes implying the unsaid. The unsaid what? I try to understand, but the Indian in me stops my coming closer with open arms. I see that I can be only part Swahili.

As they circle, some cup clap, some float the kanga over their heads. They move into the rass of Riziki's melancholy song. There is a pause in the singing. It slips into humming, a space to think over the song while they continue to circle without the hands or hips moving. There are no kangas now in winged arms over their shoulders. The rhythm has slackened. Raised heels fall nimbly on the cement without a thud.

I hear Riziki again. Her hoarse voice whispers over the drum beats:

Listen to my story and feel my words in your body
The way you would listen to the smell
Dance the cha-ka-cha

I am shaken awake from Riziki's story by the entrance of a teenage girl nudging aside the door curtain with her elbow. She is holding a tray on which stands six short glasses brimming pink with sherbet. "Karibu sherbati," says the girl bringing the tray forward. At once, Issa wakes up and stretches his arms over across me. I cannot help smiling at Issa. Riziki smiles back to me.

"Let me hold your sherbet," I offer. But Issa has already started to drink, holding the glass to his lips with both his hands, without letting it go. His nose is into the glass, breathing in and out over the pink milk. Having emptied the glass, Issa goes back to sleep. For a moment, I look at the child on my lap. He breathes softly over a line of creamy pink moustache. I look for my handkerchief in my brassiere before his lips get wiped clean on my pachedi-shawl.

"I am happy you visited me," says Riziki when I stand to leave. "Karibu tena - you are welcome to come again. I will return your visit."

"Yes, please do," I reply to be polite but I cringe at the thought of how my brother Shamshu's wife, Khati Bai, would take it, and what the neighbours at the Khoja Flats would say. Yes, I want her to visit us but not like she were some Swahili guest from a mud house in Mwembe Tayari. She must come as a relative. I mean, as one of us in the family. Not as Shamshu's rakhel, meaning his kept woman.

370

"Yes, please do come home," I say again with all the sincerity I can put into my words over my hesitation. Her lips crack into an instant smile and tighten as quickly. She has doubt. Her eyes pose a question. Was she testing me when she said, "I will return your visit"?

It is acceptable in our furtive Khoja talk to say Riziki is Shamshu's rakhel, meaning his kept woman, but not his wife. And never as Khati Bai's co-wife or wife-friend. That is Swahili custom not Khoja. That is how it is said in Swahili not Gujarati. That is how it can be said in *their* language but not in *our* language.

Addressing Riziki as mke mwenza, meaning a wife-friend in Swahili, carries respect that eludes the Khoja mind. Riziki knows that. I read it on her smile though she did not say it. A quick smile acknowledging, yet not believing me. Buried voices contort the lips making them uncertain how to form the words that hurt. I saw it in her dance and eye talk. I saw it in her hand gesturing. I heard it in her invitation that baited a reciprocal invitation from me.

Now I understand the writing on the kanga she gifted me from the same pair she danced with:

I LIKE TO BUT I AM NOT ABLE TO

I turn around and step back onto the doorway where Riziki is standing watching me leave. We embrace. I cry over her shoulder looking away because I do not have the courage to face her. If she visits us at the Khoja Flats and her story is known, Riziki will blemish my family's honour, if not the caste name. She is black. We are not.

371

Part Ten

Era of Great Propaganda Betrayal Hate and Humiliation

Tyranny of Nationalism
Listening to the Other Side

It was from the old white settler grumble around 'The Indian Question' that the nationalists in the 1960s began fashioning the character of the Asian in East Africa. 'The Indian Question' itself was a transcribed copy of 'The Jewish Question' from old Europe. In Africa, 'The Indian Question' was first brought up around 1908. This was about the time when Gandhi, working with the Indian mine workers, had put up a resistance to the apartheid. In East Africa the Indians were also engaged in similar resistance against white racism and rule.

After independence, 'The Indian Question' changed to 'The Asian Question'. Interestingly, 'The Jewish Question' and 'The Asian Question' were debated with similar intentions. Both carried intonations of a threat of shrewd aliens thieving from the natives. Thus their numbers and commerce needed to be curtailed and controlled.

One way to dismantle the perceived or contrived threat was to disempower the Asiatic Kenyans by disgracing them. The President, together with the politicians, thereby mounted attacks on the community calling them corrupt, unpatriotic and racist remnants of the colonial age. No doubt, the rhetoric was an attempt to break the moral resolve of the community to abandon who they were in the sense of their values, pride in their culture, history on the continent and what they had built. They became the well to do nobodies, if not the enemies of the new nation and development. They were even called enemies of Africans. That gave the ethical authority to the upcoming political elites to abuse and loot them. This was not new as it had happened under pogroms against the Jewish communities in Europe and Russia during the fervour of nationalism in the dark periods of their history. The pogroms often targeted the communities' secluded lifestyles as against national integration and therefore interest.

In Kenya, interestingly, integration was reasoned as possible only through blood mixing. But that was one sided, because it would be marriages of Asian girls to African men, not the other way as well. This way of gendered integration in the new political narrative became the trump card of male dominated African nationalism that primarily targeted robbing the Asians of their possessions not necessarily their girls. It may be noted that inter-tribal blood mixing was not demanded as much as the inter-racial marriages. However, the macho type bigotry that developed as a sub-text of insistent anti-Asian propaganda, assaulted womanhood, procreation and the family. All these were held sacred by the Indians. None understood how to use moral demolition through humiliation of wives and daughters better than the African politician. Like the Indian, he was born into patriarchy and knew how to break and dispossess the 'other man'.

To many Asian Africans at the time, the 'mixing of blood' sounded more lust than integration and much less marriage as they understood it. Moreover, the taunting came from older politicians inclined towards polygamy. 'Why don't Asian girls marry Africans?' was a frequent prompt spoken like a threat in political hectoring and layman's speech, intimidating the Asian African women. However, it was not an empty threat. In Zanzibar, it became a reality after the revolution in 1964. Powerful polygamous black army officers and politicians threatened to marry Indian, Arab and Persian school girls by force if the families refused. And they did take the girls away by force. When the families protested, the men were flogged

375

and imprisoned. And when the abused girls' photographs appeared on the front page of newspapers in Kenya, many in the community felt it was an attack on them. "They could be our daughters," they said.

Sometimes, such 'marriages' would be spoken about with arrogance suggesting that was an African cultural practice.[1] True, it was an ancient tribal custom for the conquerors in many parts of the world to seize the women of the conquered tribe as part of the booty. This, and offering young girls in retribution or as reconciliation gestures was in the living memory at the time of independence in East Africa. African nationalism appropriated this ancient practice validating misogyny as culture. The result of such statements from those in authority created deep fear, uncertainties and regrets about holding Kenyan citizenships. If one were to ask the Asian Africans today living in the Diaspora, why they emigrated, many would say, "But we had girls in the family."

As for the women in the Satpanth Ismaili Khoja community, they tried to address the threats against both the Indian women and resentment of their class status by dressing down. They attempted to dress 'simple' as some called it, to avoid harassment stirred by politicians. They wore 'plain clothes' as others said, and some wore just white, without the customary jewellery, especially in the evenings walking down to the jamat khana when they were most noticeable. The short lived self-imposed austerity,

---

[1] It may be noted that after independence, the politicians also bragged about possessing multiple African wives saying it was custom.

however, did not work because the attacks continued. Nevertheless, they tried to 'adjust'.

In all, the anti-Asian propaganda was dramatization about destroying the last vestige of colonialism to gain popular support - politicians worldwide are wont to use racism to win votes. Kenya was not an exception. The Asians, as sub-colonials, had enjoyed a status that was a step above the African during British rule and needed to be taught a lesson as it seemed to be.

Asian two-facedness

Three years have slipped by since uhuru. The Swahili word meaning independence is magical like it were a prophecy of salvation and Kenyatta a messiah. I hear uhuru-Kenyatta, Kenyatta-uhuru like twin words streaming out of lips of Kenyans. Words of promise of prosperity. Words of liberty and unity. Most important, words of hope and dignity. One thing we know is that after uhuru, businesses in Nairowua have never been so good especially trade in farm tools and fertilizers. Landless agricultural people from central Kenya make settlements, and cultivate the expansive homelands of the nomads.

We feel we made the right decision embracing Kenyan citizenship when we had a choice of going to the United Kingdom on our second-class British subject-citizenship passports. Kenya passport is first class for all. It sounds like a deliverance document from servitude of colonial rule and white racism. Moreover, it was Saheb's wish that we should be free citizens of a free country respected by its constitution. The sudden affluence affirms our faith in his wisdom guided by a divine vision. Yet, apprehension looms over the confidence that faith in Saheb offers us. Is it my Indian nature - always doubting? Is it suspicion that Africans would steal my family's new found prosperity? Or is it my Indian race and my Indian caste? Both live deep inside me like proud twin sisters. I dream of my daughter's Khoja wedding with a suitable Khoja husband from an honourable Khoja family. It will not be with a man of another caste or religion let alone an African. Her wedding will be in the jamat khana.

In spite of Saheb urging us to be loyal to the country, I am doubtful about Africans ruling over us. The doubt first set in after the Mau Mau, and now it increases each day from what I see on the TV that stands on the living room table like it were a gift of independence. Outside, we keep smiling to the conceited and openly corrupt politicians, placing garlands of rose flowers around their necks as we do on Saheb's picture. As Hindus of Nairowua venerate temple marbles and bronzes.

"We invite black politicians. Pose for the famous Asian loyalty photographs with them, and bribe the newspaper editor for front page news," says Haiderali. "Wealthy Asians and politicians, business bedfellows, ghand mare *chhe*." He means they are fucking each other's arses. He speaks with bitterness and without shame. Every day, Haiderali must listen to the anti-Asian tirade over the radio like it were a reprimand for his racism. That he deserves the telling-off. Every day, I tell him to switch off the radio but he is pulled to it like an addict who hates his habit but will not or cannot change. Every day, he ignores me. He must listen to it all, every word to the end. Then, he puts his frustration into cynicism that I have to listen to for the rest of the day. The children too are affected by his loathing. That worries me. "Wealthy Asians make the community their in-between gheta, meaning their sheep, foolish followers performing rituals of allegiance to the new chiefs with protruding stomachs - they cannot tie their shoe laces even when sitting down. But we must smile, and praise them in hyperboles at lavish dinners in their honour. Typical Asian two-facedness today!

Shamshu's package

I have little contact with Mombasa after Ma Gor Bai's death. Occasionally, my brother Shamshu sends me mee-thai sweets. Shamshu's package would first come to my father who lives in Nairobi. In it would be six palm leaf triangular sachets of Malindi halwa and two dozen or so Mariakani pendas. It would always be the same. Once my father had told me how he divides Shamshu's package into five parts. "But first I would taste a little mee-thai myself," he said with a slight smile I know so well. The smile that reveals his teeth browned by cigarette smoke otherwise not seen. "I would keep one sachet and some pendas around it in a plate for the jamat khana, for blessings of shu-khar for this gift from my son. The second portion – half a halwa sachet and three pendas, would be for my neighbour, Lalitaben. Actually, the mee-thai would be for Lalitaben's two sons who call me Dadabapa. They accompany me from khane after the evening prayers, holding my hand when the rains are heavy, and the path under my sandaled feet feels like it was patched over the murky gullies with stepping stones, unstable and slippery." My father has night blindness and he feels weak in legs, particularly the left knee that dislocates at the slightest jerk along the footpath by the downhill motor road to where he lives on Kirinyaga Street. It's that street that's behind the stone jamat khana that was the old Grogan Road that connected with Khoja Bazaar along the Nairobi River. That was when I was little and the English ruled. I remember how I carried beads for Dadabapa, my grandfather, along the Khoja Bazaar that

380

was also known as Moti Bazaar, meaning Bead Bazaar. My father rents a kiosk space under the stairs from the landlord Tajiri Njenga to run his paan, newspaper and cigarette street stall on Kirinyaga Road. Upstairs, he rents one room where he cooks and sleeps.

"I keep two pendas and the opened sachet of half halwa portion for myself. The rest I divide into two equal parts, and put them in two identical brown paper bags for my two princesses," he concluded. His lips stretched and seemed longer as he watched me with smiling eyes of a young father teasing his little girl with a penda before putting it on her tongue. As I look at the brown paper bag, I think about my father's lonely life of a widower surviving on modest naandi meals from the jamat khana. I think about the happiness he would have had dividing, and repackaging the mee-thai sweets for his daughters like he were writing a family letter, and connecting with his loved ones who live far away from him.

I see how carefully my father has wrapped the mee-thai in a tracing paper that's probably pinched from the jamat khana store where he does khane-sewa cutting the paper in six inch square pieces. The paper pieces are for the after-prayer su-khreet – a tea spoonful of sacramental fare made of semolina cooked with sugar, milk and ghee.

The tracing paper pack is wrapped in a newspaper when I receive it. My father buys newspapers in bulk sold by weight and uses them for packing loose cigarettes, matches, bananas, bread, medicine and paan that he is famously known for. When he has about two pounds weight of spare newsprint, he sells it to the widow Dolu Daria who sits outside the same two storey building before the jamat khana evening prayers.

You would see Dolu Daria roasting peanuts and grams in sand kept heated all day in a metal karai-basin over live charcoal packed in white ash. A fist size opening glows like a red bulb all night and flares up when she blows into the coal the next evening. So worn out and battered is Dolu Daria's karai-basin that I imagine my father saying to her in mischief as he would have to Ma Gor Bai had she been her, "Your karai-basin was left for you by that handsome Punjabi railway coolie, Zafar Khan, *nah*? The one with buffalo horn moustache. He carried rocks in this karai-basin over his head, *nah*?" That would make Dolu Daria blush, and a smile would appear over her looping wrinkles.

When I am in Nairobi, I watch Dolu Daria's dexterous fingers methodically tearing each double page of the *Daily Nation* into eight squares. She uses a foot ruler not to measure the length of each piece, but rather to press over the newspaper to rip apart a bunch straight and even. Then she rolls the cut pages into neat funnels, so identical that you would think they were made by a machine. Each funnel is just deep enough to contain one handful of freshly roasted mix of peanuts and grams. She makes each customer feel special by topping the funnel package with a loose pick of hot peanuts nimbly measured in one fingertip clutch. Only her fingertips not her fingers, are dyed in orange henna. That masks her nails, aged and grooved. She is too poor to afford English nail polish anymore. But on her bedside table, in front of Saheb's picture leaning on the *Nooran Mubin* with a missing front cover, is an array of fancy nail polish and perfume bottles. They are all empty but the sleek paint and misty tones of perfumes give the impression they are full.

"Before going to khane I take a whiff from the oud bottle. The sweet smell is still there and it makes me feel happy inside," said Dolu Daria to me when we got talking about her life after her husband died. Then she let me sniff into the bottle. It was the good quality, expensive, Arabian oudh that is difficult to get nowadays. The bottle had retained its fragrance, rich and robust, like a refill of the mellowed perfume scent.

During the day, my father sells Dolu Daria's leftover grams and peanuts on commission in the same funnel packages. They give each other company, my father and Dolu Daria, sometimes sharing a naandi meal that they buy jointly, and in secret, at the jamat khana. They get along well, in fact, so well that the neighbourhood boys at the evening religion school have created a love tease song about Hussein Paanwala and Dolu Daria.

Dolu Daria, not my father, looks after the feeble Missionary Shivji Bhagat who is their neighbour. He returned to Kenya with a young wife and three sons when stories of the Mau Mau began to fade. His heart was full of hope of continuing where he had stopped – teaching children at religion school and giving sermons in the jamat khana. He returned to work where he thought he was needed, what he knew, what he believed in, what he was always respected for and what he had learned in his youth at the missionary training school in Bombay. But it was the decade in Africa when we had quickly modernized from Satpanthis to Ismaili Moslems. Now the Meeshnari, as we called him, lives humiliated and without pension. Like the aging jamat bhais, who in their younger days were the devoted housekeepers of Saheb's jamat khanas that we say are his houses, Missionary Shivji Bhagat survives amongst the poorest of Grogan Road, and like them, on naandi meals and handouts. His three sons slipped out of his control and out of the country after his wife passed away. He had set high moral standards for his sons and was ruthless if he heard even a mere whisper about them involved in a fight that was not uncommon among boys, or smoking cigarettes that happened, or skipping the evening prayer at the jamat khana that was possible. "The missionary regarded his family as a model of good behaviour as counselled in Saheb's farmans, and the ginans," said my disgruntled father, a failed post-independence businessman. "The jamat, however, saw the family's poverty and disregarded their ethical living. For that they looked to the rich merchants no matter what."

They say Missionary Shivji Bhagat is a broken man, and has anger of a wild buffalo, unpredictable and often vented out in snorts. That's because he keeps the pain of his humiliation suppressed, I feel, too proud to say he is not a nobody. He was always a proud man. The jamat knows that but they keep quiet. What the jamat also knows, and, in fact, says in chup chap whispers, is that the once zealous missionary has been put aside like a used cooking pot. His knowledge derived from a corpus of ancient wisdom in Indian languages and pirs' songs, is seen as obsolete if not an embarrassment to the modern Moslems.

Missionary Shivji Bhagat's eyesight has weakened from too much reading, his metal rimmed spectacles are as thick as students' magnifying glasses, and his tall frame bent. He walks with a stick. However, his khokharo cough deep down from the throat into a mouthful of paan spices - the chewing habit he retains, is as robust and as recognizable as it was when he was young and my teacher

384

at khane religion school. Whenever I am able to, I send some paan and chai-nasto money to Dolu Daria for my teacher. I wanted to be like him, a missionary. I loved him and I still do

Finally, my father would put the last and the fifth part of Shamshu's package, a piece of halwa and one penda, into his pantry. The pantry in his room is a waist high wooden box frame with rusty wire netting on all sides including the doors. The four legs of the pantry stand in jam tins half full of water with a sprinkle of kerosene film that keeps away the ants that live in floor cracks. My father's habit has been to keep the mee-thai always under an enamel kopo-cup standing in a bowl of water. That keeps the clever cockroaches that fly down from the wall from reaching his sweets. I remember the kitchen cockroaches of shantytown Nairobi from my childhood days. The joints and cracks in the pantry frame was a home for them to come to after a night of foraging around neighbours' kitchens in our courtyard.

The mee-thai pieces would be for my father to relish after dinner and before his last cigarette of the day. The cigarette, I can tell, would be the sigara kali type, made of bitter sundried tobacco that needs constant clearing of the throat with short khokharo coughs between puffs. He calls the box his pinjaroo, meaning a cage as if his food were a beautiful bird.

Shu-khar for the naandi that feeds the aged. Shu-khar for the jamat khana where the elderly like my father can go and find peer company and peace. Shu-khar for Dolu Daria and for how the old look after each other when they are poor and neighbours.

After the dawn prayers at the jamat khana, my father used to visit the neem tree that his father, my Dadabapa, had planted in his Jugu Bazaar home. That was his routine. What he did at the tree, whether he prayed or spoke to it, nobody knows. Then one day Bapa found the developers had uprooted the neem tree. He brought home a large branch that stands withered, crisp and brown under Dadabapa's photograph that's on the wall between the photographs of my mothers, Rai Bai and Ma Gor Bai. He would talk to both of them at different times each day as if they lived with him.

Also in the brown paper bag with my brother Shamshu's mee-thai sweets package, there is a round pack, size of my palm, tightly wrapped in a glossy Filmfare page held by sisal strings pressing into Meena Kumari's kohl blackened eyes. The star actor of the Indian screen looks at me with her vamp eyes from behind the stringed bars as I unravel the twine. A finger size bottle emerges. It's oudh from Gulab French Perfumers on Digo Road in Mombasa. And there is also a round blue tin box of Nivea cream. Gifts from my brother Shamshu. The oudh is authentic.

Crush them like kunguni bedbugs between thumb nails

Haiderali is in the sitting room watching TV, drinking his Tusker beer and listening to Jomo Kenyatta delivering the presidential address at Uhuru Park in Nairobi. The National TV that Haiderali brought home on hire purchase from African Retail Traders is like cinema for free. The station opens at 5p.m. and closes at 10p.m. In between my house work, I try to see what they are showing, and sometimes, we all let go the evening service at the jamat khana to watch the TV. We say the two dua-prayers at home in quick successions more as a routine than supplication.

Today Kenya is commemorating Kenyatta Day. It was in 1952 in October, eleven years before uhuru when the President was arrested and detained by the English. Occasionally, Haidu looks down, shaking his head and listening. Standing in the kitchen filling up the spice bottles, I have my ears put to the sitting room. My thoughts shift between listening to the TV and myself. My feelings vacillate between sadness, fear and anger when I hear my President call my people, my community, my family, collectively all the Asians of Kenya, thieves, looters and whores. He says we are blood sucking kunguni bedbugs who will be crushed between thumb nails. He is in a brown leather jacket, the one he had on when he was arrested and detained more than a decade ago. An artist painted the scene of the famous arrest when the night was blue and

387

starless. When I saw the painting, it filled me with sadness. Its print quietly circulated in the community. I wanted to see it again and again. There was hope in Kenyatta's sacrifice for freedom. Hope in his courage. The sound of the very word Kenya-tta was seductive in its expectation of freedom and end of the white racism. The President was Kenya-taa, meaning the Light of Kenya. True, he looked so bright a light, a star so strong, so kind, an elder so wise, so determined and most of all, a rock against racism. In the picture, even while he walked escorted by armed white and black policemen, he stood sturdy and brave against mighty England. That day when Jomo Kenyatta was detained, I fasted so I might endure pain like he was enduring the pain of a prisoner. I would contain my anger at the colonials with restraint like he was. I was not alone. Lila Ben and other Indian women in her group fasted too. A thousand Indian women signed a petition for the immediate release of Kenyatta when nobody else did. We fasted the way Indians do to show protest and let the people know. We fasted like Gandhi. I fasted and prayed for Kenyatta's release and asked for a boon for my suffering that gods of the avatars are obliged to return. I wanted to be with Ambu Bhai and Lila Ben Patel carrying placards in the street demanding the release of the man we called Father of the Nation. Baba Taifa. But Haiderali would mock me. Now I see the just freed-from-detention President on our new National TV waving his silver handled flywhisk above his head on which sits the Luo elder's cap that I once heard Monghi Bai call ogut teego the beaded head.

I am not sure if I hear it all correctly for the President speaks in heavily accented Swahili over his ethnic Kikuyu. Humiliation stuns my heart. A buzz between words fills the space where numbness sits.

Duguzanguni mwafrika sasa hivi sisi tumepokonya uhuru zetu kwa kabiliana na wabeberu. Na mimi ninasema kwamba serikali yako sasa ata ponda kadiri ya hizo mnyonga damu. Wahindi wanyonyaji kama kunguni, hawa kama malaya. Ee heh…heh…heh.

My brothers Africans just now we wrested our independence after a struggle with the Boers. Now, I say, your government will at once crush these bloodsuckers. Indians suckers like bedbugs, they are like prostitutes.

The President's screed ends with a snigger: ee…ee… heh…heh…heh. The response comes in a tremendous roar of mass applause from Uhuru Park, packed to capacity by hungry people who had begun their journey on foot at dawn from the surrounding seven megaslums of plastic sheeting roofs over cardboard-flattened-tin-wood-panelled-makeshift-dwellings as far as the eye can see. The homes of the undercities are made of the waste from industries, and the discarded stuff by the wealthy of the uppercity. Nairobi is a garden city on the hills. Its head stays high basking in the sun. Belly down, it's dunked in a cesspool.

On the way to the bedroom, Haiderali stops at the kitchen standing in the shadow of the door. I look up. His face tells me something worries him and he wants to talk. He shakes his head looking down, the gesture suggesting I say something to him. Something comforting, something that would agree with his thoughts. Something a mother would say. I have no words of comfort for him. Nor have I anything to be angry about, to curse, or to press more anxiety into his head already filled with worries. I look at him as a mother would to her child in pain. I feel his pain. "I know it hurts," says my look to him. He walks on to the bedroom flicking his half-smoked cigarette into the veranda basin like how children flick marbles with their fingers when they play squatting down on their haunches.

Walking slowly into the living room, I see our new National TV screen glowing a soft white tone. It looks like the glow of the new tube light in the jamat khana. The silver box has become a window for me to look into city politics, and not be seen. Like Haiderali, I keep news time as regular as my daily dua-prayer. I am sweeping bread crumbs on the kitchen floor dropped by Diamond to keep the night ants and cockroaches away. I listen to the TV at the same time, and every now and then take a long peep at Kenyatta's rally. Uhuru Park throbs with thunderous cries of joy every time the President makes a deprecating remark on the greed of the Asians, all of them, even the poor of Kirinyaga and River Roads. All of us.

I see thousands of black hungry people, the city's poorest. Many among them clad in rags are frantically cheering the President they see standing like a god on a high dais waving his silver flywhisk. He gives hope for tomorrow – a promise of justice and equality, for the days when their bellies will be full and their bodies clothed. He is the hope and if only the hungry were patient, they will wait another day to fill their stomachs when the Asians go. They will go, they must go. It is expected. They are not black. The temptation of seeing the Asians go lures from one national day speech to the next. It is alluring and vividly put to metaphors such as ofbedbugs and mirija the straw that sucks up. That is his speech today. Nothing more, same as before. That is his popularity. That's what makes Kenyatta a hero. A nationalist. A god- President. That gives him the power over the people humiliated by poverty and displacement. The slum dwellers will be rich when the goods they see on the shelves of Indian shops are given to them like maize meal from the UN famine-relief trucks. They have seen it before, haven't they? They will possess fine stone homes and drive the big cars parked in front. They will take over Asian duka-stores, well stocked with Sunday best and Xmas clothes, food and even radios and TVs. All that glimmer showcased in uppercity houses where they toil as servants, cooks and gardeners will be theirs when the brown man leaves.

I walk out to the courtyard. The August breeze is cold and I begin to shiver. I am barefoot and have no pachedi-shawl to cover over me. But I opt for peace over the warmth in the house and away from the invectives of our new National TV. The TV is a curse to the eyes more powerful than newspaper pictures. It has an invasive presence we cannot do without.

"Moti Bai!" Haiderali yells from the bedroom, "You will catch cold." He wants me to come inside, he probably cannot find his pyjamas that I washed today.

My tears are absorbed by the parrot-in-cage embroidery on the pillow. My dark mind's eye searches the pattern of the zebra on the blue Kenyan sky galloping over the mirrored shadows running over the savannah grass like the feral wind spirit. I put the hurt in my heart into the heart of Africa and hold the beauty of the land in my eye. Nature is mother beauty, mother love, mother comfort. Nature is the lap to lay down my head and cry into the womb that gave me birth. I see emankeeki's colours. Vibrant colours heaving over the calmness, the depth of blue. The Song of Emankeeki fills my ears turned to sounds

391

of colours at the horizon. I try to reach into it and be the hum in the beads' melody.

Today the melody comes from five musical codes of emankeeki's colours compressed into each other – red-white-blue-orange-green. How can I leave the land that conceived me and made me who I am, Mr President? But all the earth beauty cannot halt the hatred against the President swelling in my heart. My feelings begin running into suspicion of all black people. How they cheer him all together, every one of them, in one voice! Even the poor African joins the rich African to cheer the President. How they adore him like he were a god! How they are one with him! When the President abuses me in snippets of sneers from the podium high up in the park, would Freda and Kamau be cheering him too? Is there no black man who would speak against the President's abuse or at least write a letter in *The Daily Nation* tomorrow? The feelings begin to well in me like bitter fluid from my gut.

I remove the bandhani, emankeeki and kanga from my leather suitcase below my bed to speak to them. To hear what they have to say. To hear the joy they make me feel. Nasikia raha in Swahili is to hear joy. It also means to feel joy. I need the art they hold when trepidations throb in my chest. I need the art they hold when my voice breaks my thoughts, when sleep evades my eyes, when hate consumes me. I want to be with my artefacts of beauty, not because I am afraid she will assault me as she does when I am troubled and the trouble makes me weak. She who resides in me is a coward for she attacks when I fall. But I have come to live with her and let her be where she wants to be with her khelele noises. I call her by her name now. Mama Khelele are you there? Then I laugh at her. She knows I laugh at her because I know when she speaks back, it is buckwaas, meaning empty talk, bulldog threats and lies. I tell her, "What I call you, Mama Khelele, is all you are. A barking dog chained to the post." In fact, I speak rudely to her nowadays when she comes to eat my head, meaning kula kitchwa yangu. Yet I would have to let her be what she wants to be and let her speak buck buck knowing her buck-waas is all no-sense. I know she is not me. We both know that now. She is like any other Mama Khelele in town. The noisy street woman speaking no-sense buck-waas. She would be the mad beggar in the street. She would be the neighbour. She would be the one with whom I volunteer sewa service at the jamat khana. She would be a friend or even a relative. I may even let her dip her bhajia into my tamarind chili chutney, sitting on the bench with her hips pressed into mine. She is all these, the companion I must live with and learn to close my mind to her.

The stories in my head come and go. Some fade away and, if not, I let them go to be at peace with myself. But there are others that will not leave me no matter how much I would like them to go away. These stories stay to build on more stories expanding my imagination and they grow with time.

Wewe mhindi - You Indian

It's Saturday night. Diamond and Almas have gone to see Gold Finger at the new Metropole Cinema. They follow every new English film release like we follow news on the TV. Metropole Cinema is a modern cinema house, as modern as Nairowua can get. It has a sculpted contour of the Empire State Building on one wall and the ship called the Queen Mary on the other. Both in blue plaster profiles raised out from the wall. They are the symbols of great achievements of the modern world we aspire to live in, and imagine we are in step with England even after uhuru, meaning independence.

Sometimes, Diamond and his teenage friends, all Khoja boys, meet at home to watch TV. When they meet, they slap hands with a clack as a kind of handshake and call each other bwana, Swahili for boss, as they swagger and jostle into the sitting room. And they watch everything – boxing and wrestling matches, Perry Mason, Lassie, Little House on the Prairie, cowboy movies, everything American. They avoid everything Kenyan like news and patriotic programmes. In between, they talk about school. They would call their teachers by the names they have given them. Their Hindu math teacher is Gandhi, the Punjabi geography teacher is Dara Singh, the famous wrestler, and the Goan literature teacher is simply named Fish. They call Damji Bhai Jetha, the librarian at the jamat khana library, Steam Engine. The boys also tell English jokes about the Irish and Scots they have never met but they live in their imagination from the English books and comics they read. Their laughter and voices fill the house. They are young and smart, so confident and full of themselves. In fact, they make jokes about almost everyone except the Khoja and the English.

I hear Diamond imitating Kenyatta's tribal Swahili, deep throated and heavily accented. He caricatures political speeches that we, his parents, listen to with such gravity, noting every word to read the meaning behind it. Then, among trusted friends, we would bring up the President's recent harangue comparing it with other politicians' rants during the week. "What do you think? Do you think they mean what they say - force our daughters to marry them? It happened in Zanzibar, *nah*?" We express our fears disguised in casual questions, not debatable in public, softly enquiring from each other in secluded groups. There is no escape from the radio and TV that fill the house with scorn. It's like listening to reversed propaganda against Africans during the Mau Mau days still fresh in memory.

Diamond and his teenage friends name call each other using slurs that they quietly tolerate from their African peers at school. The slurs that would originate from the politicians if not the President himself. Slurs like mhindi mnyonyaji – Indian sucker, mhindi mrija – Indian straw, mhindi kunguni – Indian bedbug. They create impromptu skits, aping Kenyatta's gestures as they do of community leaders especially the mukhi and the missionary. Off and on, I sneak looks from the kitchen across the corridor to the boys. I am amazed at their behaviour and wonder at the attitudes they hold in their conceited teenage heads. I see Diamond standing up to make a speech holding a broom in his right hand raised above his head representing the President's fly whisk:

Wewe mhindi toka, wewe mhindi mwivi, wewe mhindi malaya
- You Indian get out, you Indian thief, you Indian whore.

Is it because his friends are in his house that Diamond acts like a chief? Or is it simply that he clowns so he is liked? What will happen to Diamond if our house help reports him to the secret police? Fear grips me. I need to reprimand my son after his friends leave. I need to tell Haiderali.

How quickly and how well the boys have learned English, and think English as if they were born with the language on their tongues. How did it happen so quickly? I mean how did we change so quickly? How did we become English so quickly? Parents like Zera Bai and Rhemu Bhai are proud of their children speaking only in English. As if they would become English and rich and go to England like it were their motherland. But what I know is that speaking in English means coming from the educated elites. English is a civilizing language, a cultured language, the language of those whose children go to England to school. English is the language of progress. English is the language of the leaders and most importantly, it's the language of the future as Kabir would tell me. Saheb too speaks to us in English.

Soon, Diamond will be writing his Cambridge School Certificate Examination which is set and marked in England by ghost teachers he will not know. When I look at the Kilimanjaro on his table made of books piled on top of each other, all written in English, I am as astonished as I am bewildered. I had a clay slate for writing my first Gujarati alphabets and that too was shared with my sister Monghi.

There is this new age word called 'Education'. We say education in English in a sentence in Gujarati creating disparity between home and school. Old and new. Between generations. Between the rising power of one language and the diminishing one of another. Between tradition and change. Between being Indian and European.

And 'Modern' is another English word we use nowadays in a sentence in Gujarati. Modern, is a proud word aligned to being an Ismaili, not Khoja nor a Satpanthi, for that is Hindu from the old country, if not backward. Khoja describes the Ithna Asheris, our cousins, who opposed being called Ismailis. They have not just retained the old caste name but are insistent on calling themselves Khoja. We are not them. Their women wear veils. Our women wear short dresses without hijabs and saris on occasions. Yet, both are descendants of the same Khoja forefathers of the greater Lohana group. We say we came under the fold of Pir Sadardin. He was Persian, a guru of Islam, some six hundred years ago in India. We listened to his songs partaking deep Vedic knowledge in folk hymns of Saurashtra venerating the Imam at the assassin's fort on the rock in Persia.

Some say the singing bard was an Ithna Asheri, others insist he was a Sunni. Some say he was a Sufi yet others would say he was a guru and pir both. He was like an avatar with many hands yet no two were the same. Each Khoja held a different hand and said he was like this. Or, it may be that he gave one hand to one, and another to another. It did not matter to him what matters to people.

Paper Citizens

Having returned from the jamat khana and eaten, Haiderali and I watch the 9 p.m. news while waiting for the children to come home from a birthday party. After the news, there is a documentary by a team of Danish architects on unplanned settlement in Nairobi. We see thousands of poor people moving into the city and settling in the river valleys where the grass is tall and lush, where the sacred fig trees flourish among the riverine acacias that glow at sunrise like beads on bodies the nomads of the plains. The rivers of gushing water that were closely protected by the colonial government for the health of the city are now turning into ripples that straighten out into fetid pools once the rains stop.

"Where are all these people coming from?" I exclaim aloud. It's the first thought that comes to me. I am astonished at the mushrooming growth of family homes each one the size of my kitchen. Each one made of tin and wood panels with plastic sheeting for roof. The crowds I see on the TV, protesting, looting shops and throwing stones when the university students riot, live here in this other Nairobi of shacks.

"These are rural people...lost their land to droughts ... and the rest to politicians," Haiderali replies in hesitant sentences between munching chevdo and licking over his lips relishing the spice dust. I turn around to look at him, my eyes deliberately widened in a false surprise look of What? like the mature Indian actor in love scenes playing the innocence of little girls that bring smiles to the audience. But his mind is on the TV and he would not turn around to see me. His left hand, limp like a rubber glove, rests on the edge of the bowl of chevdo. His fingers dig in searching for the peanuts buried into a variety of lentils and nuts. He then rubs off the fried peanut skins in the bowl before his fingers bring the shelved nut to his tongue. He does that in one unconscious move while his eyes remain on the TV. In spite of my taak taak complaints, he still would not use a spoon while watching the TV and eating. Or at least use his right hand. I see cream on his chai beginning to film in wrinkled lines. I do not remind him his tea is getting cold and stiff kaarak.

"We have land grabbing disease in Kenya. It's an epidemic. It has seized our new royal families. Made the hyenas sick in head and round in stomach," he says without moving his eyes away from the screen. It's a new way of speaking about ministers mixing cynicism with half-truths between name callings – royal families, big fish, Mercedes Benz, hyenas, vultures, pigs. I also hear his friends, both Rhemu Bhai and Mamdu Bhai, speak this kind of snide language. "Now the helpless and landless are crowding into the city hoping to find something to put into their empty stomachs. This is called mandaleo or development. It's the American puppet's rule." He talks like Kabir now but Kabir is not around to see how his brother has changed. Perhaps, Haiderali learns politics from his Sunday card games. But my husband can change his mind. Today he says this and tomorrow that. He is wasi wasi meaning unsure of what comes out of his mouth as if feelings in his heart speak over reason in his mind.

399

Talking under his breath, Haiderali's sarcasm lapses into sighs in long audible exhales. Kind of sighs of being in doubt and then sighs of resignation or sighs of despair or sighs of giving up that make thoughts turn bitter, churning them inside the head like curry bubbling phat phat in the kitchen pot. In all they are sighs of hopelessness. Hurting sighs from him hurt me. "We are paper citizens, *nah?*" he would repeat with scorn and then look at me. When my brother, Shamshu, who has incidentally groomed friendship with the Minister of Immigration, hears Haiderali scoff at the politicians or the President in this way, he calls my husband a racist. He tells me that Haiderali admires the English colonialists. That Haiderali is not loyal to Kenya. Sometimes, they have an argument and will not speak to each other for months.

"There is no peace for the acacias and animals," I add, repeating Ole Lekakeny's words softened by apprehension that sits on us these days like a black cloud. Recently, Ole Lekakeny has been lamenting the felling of the acacias for fuel by Kenyatta's agricultural settlers and sundowner fires at the new tourist lodges on the traditional pasturelands of the nomads within the expansive savannah game parks. Then, it's no secret about poaching of animals for ivory and skins by the new royal families magically created by maendeleo, meaning development. Created like instant coffee also new and magical.

I ask my husband what's troubling him, and then quickly say before he can answer, "But where shall we go so we can have something to put in our stomachs?" He keeps quiet and does not get annoyed with me interrupting his thoughts with questions he cannot answer. A mosquito

400

buzzes around my ear. I throw a hand towel over my ankles.

"There is a new law called Africanization. We will have to move to Nairobi. From next year all Asian shops will be restricted to operate in the cities only," he says. "Africanization means leaving your beads to the MP, Moti Bai."

I keep quiet. Haiderali's reply deepens my anxiety. He reads my face and I can tell by the way he shifts on his sofa that it makes him uneasy. He puts his pain on me knowing it will hurt me and that will pain him more but he cannot help making us both miserable. What has become of the country? How did it come to this? Then he takes the chaikop to his lips and quickly puts it down. The tea has turned cold. He does not complain. He does not tell me to have the tea warmed up again or make another fresh cup. He keeps his lips stretched and down, sulking disgust and sipping chai in drops.

I had first heard about the new law called Africanization on the Hindustani Service of the Voice of Kenya, and later I heard more from the talk in the jamat khana. *Africa Samachar* has made no comment on the new law so far and how was it that Africanization and Paper Citizens emerged like twin brothers, both words said in English, at the same time in all the vernaculars of Kenya over the radio. Talking with Khanu Bai and Zera Bai is like listening once again to the news commentaries about Asian greed, their money laundering crimes, their segregationist behaviour, their blatant racism, and their clannish habits shamelessly refusing to marry their girls to Africans. Is that being racist? Are we immoral? Are the accusations characteristics of paper citizens? Makes me doubt myself.

Makes me question myself inside and the value of my Kenyan citizenship. Or is it guilt? I begin to feel different. "It's not me," I tell myself. It's not my people, it's the other Asians. Not Ismailis. It's the Hindus and Punjabis.

Nevertheless, I feel insecure in my own country. Insecure in my brown skin in black country. Do I belong here? Am I colonialist, and I didn't know? Misgivings about black people creep into our evening talks after the jamat khana service like an insidious worm boring between words no matter how small and insignificant may be the matter.

Failed race

Little incidents with our house helps or shop clients or the vegetable vendor, are related with such passions that they put alarm into the heart. They become larger than they are. Thoughts become nightmares. How do Africans see me at the vegetable market? How do they see me when they come to the shop? How do my house servants look at me? How do they look at my clothes when theirs are tattered? Each time I put food on the table, my eyes shift to Freda. Is she watching? How do her eyes see? I mean what do her African eyes spell out to me that my Asian eyes cannot see? What would she be thinking eating the leftovers from the serving bowls? Leftovers from the table are like my old clothes I give her when I have no more use for them. And I call that generosity when talking with Khanu Bai and Zera Bai! Boasting how kind and caring I am to my servants. I do not see my kindness as mollifying my guilt but I am so much affected by Kenyatta that I now ask myself, "Do I really own the house with a sitting room and sofa set when I exploit them?" My racism, my exploitation, my oppression – the accusations are getting under my skin. I retort. They have little thieving habits. Freda sulks, she is lazy, she puts up quiet reluctance to work after dinner – all words mean the same - she is not a good servant. They are Asian words, Asian thoughts. Are they the characteristics of my race? A race that failed to integrate and develop Kenya? Immoral brown skinned words are like discarded peanut peels. Asian race sins. I have fears. Are Freda and Kamau waiting for me to leave so they can occupy my house? My kitchen too?

403

What will happen to my beads? Just a few months ago, I felt safe with my two servants, but now a wall of distrust has fallen between us. It's like during the Mau Mau days. But there is a difference. Ten years ago the governor warned us to be careful of Africans. And today, the President warns the Africans to be watchful of Asians. What we own belongs to Africans, he says. I start locking cupboards at home and then the bedroom door, limiting Freda's movements in the house. Kamau does not enter the house. His work is in the courtyard and the karo. Where before, I did not padlock the inside veranda in the evening when we went to the jamat khana, now I ask Freda to take her evening chores - shoes for polishing and kitchen utensils for washing to the courtyard before we leave for the evening prayers. Sometimes, I panic when she looks at me dressing in fine khane clothes.

"It's Africanization of paper citizens," Haiderali mumbles. "It's your skin, not your citizenship that matters as it was under the English. We thought we were equal to the English because we held blue cardboard British passports. But they were the citizens of the United Kingdom and we were their subjects. Now we live in a country where democracy means all citizens are equal, but Blacks are more equal than Browns."

"They call us 'paper citizens' as if we are not humans," I say quizzing Haiderali. He does not reply for a while. His silence confuses me. I speak in anger. "Whatever it is, paper citizens or blood citizens, Nairobi is not a safe place to bring up children. Is it not to Nairobi that the landless are moving ? Can we not live here in Nairowua?"

"Every Asian shopkeeper is moving out because he has to, not that he wants to," says Haiderali and then he asks, "Whom shall we sell the shop to?"

That night, Haiderali is restless in his dreams, turning sides and whimpering like an abandoned puppy. Full moon's light wedges in through the parting in the curtains. He moves closer to me and clamps his hand on my arm. He is shivering but his grip is tight. In the firmness of his touch, I feel he seeks refuge in me. I place my other hand on Saheb's photograph under my pillow over my tasbih. I seek refuge in him.

"Look! Look!" Haiderali startles me. He is shaking in the dead of the night pointing to the shadows on the wall. Is he is seeing the politicians or the Mau Mau coming to loot him? Or is he seeing Kenyatta and his MPs turned into the British Black Watch soldiers pointing machine guns at him? "Lock the front door!" he screams. His eyes are wide open yet he is not awake. Quietly, as if he were conspiring with me, he says, "Use the back door. Get the children. Run, the back door. Quick!"

I pull the curtains over the gap in the middle where the two sides come together. He snores lightly and calls me Ma. I press his sweaty head to my bosom.

Africanization
Africanization Africanization

On the radio, I hear Africanization, Africanization, Africanization, Africanization. The words howl out of the parliament and spread around the country in Punjabi, Gujarati, Kacchi, Hindi, Konkani, Swahili, Maasai, Kikuyu, Kamba and Urdu. Africanization is a threat yelled out of the radio and whispered in conversations.

"Asian civil servants dread this word. Railway mechanics and workers of the vast apparatus of the fallen Empire hate this word. The father to son trade apprentice trained generations loyal to their trade and employment feel betrayed," says Haiderali.

I expect letters to the editor and editorials in *Africa Samachar* about this bigoted policy but nothing like that appears. Haiderali says Asian leaders will do something, say something to the community, hold a press conference, have community meetings. They would hold their heads high and hire a lawyer to demand their rights. India will do something. Great Britain will do something. I expect all the Asian communities to break the walls around them and come together. Go to court to challenge the government and the Constitution of Kenya. We have a history of resistance to injustice, do we not? Did Indian lawyers not defend Kenyatta and the Mau Mau detainees? Did Indian railway workers not strike for equality and freedom? Did Indian workers not shoot Isher Dass, the lawyer who turned against them siding with the English? But there is silence.

"Our leaders hold British passports. Their children go to schools in England while they make business deals with the politicians here," says Haiderali a month or so later after the announcement about Africanization. He speaks with bitterness and looks at me like he was trying to read my mind. "Africanization makes me feel nobody in my country," he says. Haiderali feels despondent, and more so after reading Kabir's letter that arrived today

"You read Kabir's letter about the situation in the Congo, and you see Kenya in it," I say and then add, "The silence is so unlike the Indians when the English ruled. When the English ruled, Indians protested in the street."

"We were poor shop keepers making ends meet, and workers then. We had the courage to protest because we had nothing to lose."

At the vegetable market in Nairowua, there is a striking absence of Asian women. Fair Mrs Patel is not seen again in her dazzling sari. Wives of government officers and bank clerks are not there anymore. But most business men have remained in Nairowua hoping to negotiate an arrangement about their family stores and homes with MPs and senior government officers. Will they pay for the properties we developed living frugal lives and saving? They would ask each other. Will the politicians pay a fair price? Who else can we sell our stores to anyway? They are the only ones who get foreign aid money, and bank loans. Some shop owners in nearby towns are even thinking of accepting the politicians as their partners, giving them free shares. What option do they have? If not, they say, there is still the alternative of working out some monthly or yearly chai payment. That would be bribe money for the favour of trade licenses. Licenses for the commodities like beads that their forefathers had introduced, and gradually built commerce in the new country.

Meanwhile, months of uncertainties pass by. Our husbands continue to meet at the Sunday card circle and wrangle thought plans out of each other. What they would have said openly a few days back, now they are reluctant to speak about. What are they thinking? Tight lipped card players eager to meet hoping to pick up hints from the pool of secrecy and scheming. Who is planning what with which politician, and more importantly, will he stay or leave Nairowua? Where is he going? How did he manage to take the money out of the country? How did he bribe his way out? And most important, who are his contacts in the new government?

Every evening we pray communally, and in earnest. Where once we sat cramped with folded legs pressing into each other, now there is room enough to stretch out and relieve the numbness in the calf. I listen to Saheb's farman dictate to be loyal citizens to the black government. I look up to his picture, and I pray over doubts that haunt me like thought demons. Is it a visitation that torments me? Or is it my imagination? Such doubts weaken my faith. I pray for my faith to remain unstained because of Africanization. I pray for the will to follow Saheb's farman. I will tell Haiderali we must be loyal to Kenyatta's government and not talk against it no matter what we see or hear. We must overlook corruption that's so visible and intrusive. We must close our ears to anti-Asian abusive talk that are so audible. We must pretend there is no Africanization. There are others like Zera Bai and Rhemu Bhai who too are badgered by doubts that worry me and Haiderali but their faith is strong. Zera Bai tells me to have trust in Mowla and reminds me of the story of Abraham, the Prophet who put his trust in God and a knife to his son's neck.

"Come to the jamat khana regularly. You will see everything will be alright, inshallah." Nowadays, Zera Bai ends her sentences with inshallah, meaning as God desires. Having left all her worries to her trust in God in this way, she will not say more. Like her husband, Rhemu Bhai, she has developed a new way of getting around problems by closing conversations with inshallah – God willing.

Though I try, I cannot be like Zera Bai who leaves everything to God and be at peace. When the path ahead appears blurred, she says, "Inshallah! God willing!" She means Allah decides everything. Partly, she speaks showing off how modern she is, and partly, that she is a pukka Moslem. Or it may be she avoids a conversation that may break our friendship.

I pray for these days of uncertainties to pass. Saheb will talk with Kenyatta and explain our situation. He will tell Kenyatta about our absolute loyalty to his government and the uneasiness we feel about Africanization. I do not always understand Saheb's plan for his murids, meaning his followers, but I have faith.

One thing I know, I will never be like the murids in Tanzania who disgruntle like croaking crows gathered at the mango tree in Nairowua jamat khana yard. When their properties were nationalized, they said Saheb misguided them. Some youth turned to communism to belong to their birthland and Nyerere's party. Others emigrated, and some told their children studying abroad, "For God's sake do not return."

A story is told of how one murid smashed Saheb's photograph when he lost his new house still under construction to nationalization. Some call it nationalization others say it's socialism yet they mean the same. With his house, Kurban Bhai Dhanji lost his hope, and that broke the man. He did not understand Saheb when he put his tasbih aside, and so lost his soul too, and then he began drinking alcohol. Another man called Firoze Bhai Mohamedali, they would say in the same breath, collapsed and died of a colossal heart attack when he heard his house was nationalized. Such are the stories that Tanzanians bring with them ploughing worries in the Nairowua jamat. They say they come to visit their relatives in Kenya. However, we know the Tanzanians come not to visit their relatives but to smuggle out cash and family jewellery dipped in used oil, and clogged in spaces in their car engines, and secret compartments specifically built under the seats. On the way back, they smuggle Kenyan KCC butter, Kenyan KCC ghee, Cadbury chocolates and such other imported eating luxuries that socialist Tanzania no longer allows its citizens to relish.

It is not easy for the jamat in Kenya to hold back the feelings of their kith and kin in Tanzania. Now they re-tell the Tanzanian dilemma in foreboding voices that go around the community like fever, and swell the growing suspicion we have about the mind of the African. Should we prepare to leave Kenya too? Should we stop restocking our shops too? We express our doubts openly to each other seeking out opinions but like good businessmen never giving away our intentions. To tell the truth, those Indian businesses with a politician patron have never done so well when the British ruled.

"What really works under Africanization is window dressing," Haiderali says to me. "Putting up a black face on your premises is the new line of entrepreneurship. It's official but for me it's too risky now to go into partnership with our MP. He is greedy, arrogant, drinks too much and marries too often. Can I really trust him? Rhemu Bhai tells me I should use the MP's weaknesses if I want to stay in Nairowua. As for him, he is leaving. This much he revealed to me."

"Window dressing is like keeping a paid receptionist at the desk," Zera Bai would explain to me. "In that way not only do we sidestep Africanization but also honour Saheb's farman." I know Saheb's counsel to us is to bring Africans into partnerships with our family businesses and retain Kenyan citizenship. Kenyatta must have told him so.

In my story my faith wrestles with doubt. We learn to speak differently like a painter using many colours. Like putting one colour beside another, and waiting to see how it looks when the paint dries. Then, painting over with new colours, and waiting again. Faith and doubt are like opposite colours that stand beside each other and wait. Sometimes, one brushes over the other until a new thought changes the mind, and starts believing or doubting again. Then one begins painting all over once more.

Sisi ote rafiki iko chhe - We are all friends

Haiderali retires to bed, earlier than usual. It's after a long time, maybe even years since I have seen him clutching the tasbih in his fist. It's the tasbih I had made for him threading each bead with a soft prayer whisper alternating Pir Shah with Ali OM. Pir Shah-Ali OM, Pir Shah-Ali OM blown over each other over the yellow amber beads. That was when I suspected he was turning into a Moslem, influenced by the dark kohled eyes sparkling behind black veils. I do not hurry with work in the kitchen tonight. Diamond and Almas came home late and are already in bed reading Superman and Beano-Dandy. The comics arrived this evening in one package with the Merali Bus from Nairobi. I see a grumble on their faces. Their favourite TV show, Lassie, is replaced by a documentary on the life of President Jomo Kenyatta. It's a recent narrative about the valiant freedom fighters, the Mau Mau, Kenyatta's arrest and ultimately independence of Kenya. It exults the President as the liberator as if he led the heroic rebellion against the English. The house is quiet but for Freda humming gospel music between clings and clicks while she washes pots and pans at the karo in the courtyard.

Switching on the TV, I roll up my legs on the sofa, lean back, and look forward to the late night comedy hour on the Voice of Kenya. The News Hour is just finishing as I catch the last part that's dancing at the City Hall. This spectacle is followed by commercials: latest models of

412

saloon cars - Mercedes Benz, Volvo, Peugot and BMW. Then come more modest musical commercial for the ordinary folk: Asparo ni dawa ya kweli; Sanyo Juu, Sanyo Tops and finally the sing song Sugua Rob, the new muscle pain ointment that is now competing with eternal English Vicks on the shelf in our store. The entrance of Mzee Tembe, Kenya's top comedian is accompanied by laughter and hard clapping hands in the studio. The excitement of the audience at the studio floods into my sitting room. Freda tip toes from the karo and stands behind me, bright eyed and keyed up to what's to come. I watch her from the corner of my eye.

"Mangi! Mangi!" calls out Mzee Tembe acting the Indian. Enter Mzee Pipanga acting the servant Mwangi.

"Wewe apana fanja kazi majuri - you are not doing good work," blurts out Mzee Tembe the Indian in grossly caricatured Swahili. Mzee Tembe, the Indian, is dressed clumsily in a white Gandhi dhoti and a Nehru cap, stereotyping the Gujarati Bania storekeeper of the old society now a rare sight in Nairobi. Laughter and clapping from the audience fill the studio.

"Lakini bwana, mimi nasikia njaa – but sir, I am hungry," replies Mzee Pipanga acting the African servant.

"Jaa? Wewe iko jaa? Saa ote wewe tho na sikia jaa. Hapana kazi iko, lakini jaa iko – Hungry? You are hungry? You are hungry all the time. No work but hunger is there" says Mzee Tembe the Indian storekeeper. The studio audience roars with laughter.

"Bwana, sisi ote rafiki iko neh? – Sir, are we not all friends?" asks Mzee Pipanga the servant imitating his Indian master.

413

"Rafiki tho iko sawa sawa, lakini kazi iko pia. Nani fanya kazi yako kama sisi ote rafiki iko? Yes we are friends but there is work too. Who will do your work if we are all friends?" retorts Mzee Tembe the Indian.

So the drama continues with heightened glee from the audience. By now the viewers are on their toes, jumping with uncountable excited outbursts. Freda's suppressed giggles break into open hilarity. I feel like there is a mass organized mockery of the Asians – of all the centuries old migrants over the Indian Ocean: the Khoja in various employments, Hindu Gujarati traders, Sikh carpenters, Goans clerks, Parsee professionals, Punjabi house builders, Kacchi brick layers, Memon merchants, and Bhadala the sailors. The contempt strikes me in the heart. Brutal humiliation in the glowing moment when the nation celebrates freedom with fireworks that dazzle the night sky. My confidence in myself - my heritage, my morals and my history in Africa – the Asian African history wasted. It's diminished. Shattered like glass with one blow. Who am I? Where do I belong? I am so ashamed of who I am.

"Switch off the TV after you have finished," I tell Freda as I leave the room for some cold water from the fridge. Freda also likes to watch I Love Lucy, which follows the comedy show before the station closes down at midnight. Meanwhile, the Swahili comedy continues, creating larger than life cartoons, making the Indian shopkeeper extraordinary – his monkey gestures, his comical speech, his hilarious attire, his amusing face parodied like he were a circus clown put on stage to entertain cheery spectators. Intoned, his deceit exposed. It was the Independence Day TV special.

My heart is heavy and my legs feel weak to carry my body when I move into the bedroom. Haiderali is asleep with *Chakram* on his belly. When he lies on his back, his abdomen looks so bloated that one would think he keeps a calabash under his pyjama pants.

Laying down my head on the pillow, I let my mind glide over into the open blue sky that I watch during the day. The bed is no longer a mediation between me and Haiderali. Mediation that comes from the warmth of the body of a man and his wife. Mediation that comes from the feelings that human touch transcends. I see engoiteeko the zebra galloping over feathery clouds.

From above, I watch over the Maasai landscape, the splendour of its geography flowing over me. My zari in crispy silver rosettes on the bandhani shines from a distance of my marriage day over the horizon. It sleeps under my bed. It shines in my imagination awakened by the picture of its art-wealth, the weight of its border falling from over my shoulders in two parts. Yet the weight of its border holds it over my shoulders hunched forward as was the bride's decorum. A custom to show modesty. I think of how stitch in stitch is like a walk of the sewing needle on the silk road. The stitch has a rhythm of a walk. It has the rhythm of beads on the emankeeki, of colours of the kanga. Colour to colour dances in kanga's garden paradise. Bead in bead gives thread a verse in the stuffed darkness of my suitcase binding the three relics of peace. I stay bewildered in the wonder of the mystery of Light in my three objects on woman's body. In it I will seek comfort from the hurt of the day when Kenyans across the nation are cheering the President while he jeers me like Mama Khelele in my head.

I leave the bed, walk to the kitchen shelf and take the tall green bottle with a partially scratched out label of English vinegar. I drink a cupful of the tea I had prepared with forest herbs and roots that Ole Lekakeny brings to me to keep Mama Khelele quiet in my head. It's bitter, she does not like it. I drink more. I hear our new national anthem:

Oh God of all Creation
Bless this our land and nation
… Let all with one accord
In common bond united
Build this our nation together

A sharp click. Freda switches off the TV halfway through the national anthem. The soft tube light glows brighter and then vanishes. The house is dark. Freda rustles passing by me. Silence. My mind returns to the afternoon's hurt. Humiliation is hard to accept. It twirls around in my head in rings of withdrawal-fear-anger-repugnance-revenge. Can beauty in the artefacts in my English suitcase take away these feelings? I don't go to them tonight. My heart weeps. The national anthem chimes like an echo mocking me in the darkness.

Oh my country! Oh my President!

Kenyatta - Saheb photograph

It's a routine now that in the evenings after the prayer service, we sit in the yard on separate benches for men and women and take in long breaths of the evening air that blows over the vast expanse of the savannah. More women join Khanu Bai, Zera Bai and me after visiting the khane library. Frequently, we hear the same stories but told differently in varied tones that come from mottled emotions. Haiderali and I are affected differently.

We are home just in time for the 9 o'clock news. After a quick naandi dinner, Haiderali and I begin talking like trusted friends. More often than not, we comment on what we have individually heard and from whom to start a conversation. He is interested in what the women say for that would reflect on what the men, their husbands, would have said in private husband-wife talk that they would not say when talking with other men. Haiderali speaks in broken sentences, half said, expecting me to complete as if to test my opinion or what I know before he says more.

His reluctant sentences more often than not charge arguments that I know, and I know he knows, come from buried anger from worries and fear. What begins with cynicism levied at the government, blankets over all Africans. Black government, black politicians, black voters, black servants, black people. "After all gola *chhe*," he remarks. Words he would not say in public. But secrets of

417

the heart roll out between Haiderali and me like a mist we expect the other to clear. Our anxieties are spoken in hazy expressions over supressed emotions. Wasi wasi worries. I expect more from Haiderali, the head of the family. "You save my beads corner from Africanization. No, that's not enough. You must save the entire shop as it is and our home in Nairowua," I speak out in annoyance lashing out words at him, the man of the house.

"Why attack me?" he asks in a calmer voice. "Tell your President to save you. I am a mere Asian, a Haiderali not the Kenyatta."

And with friends, the only thing we seem to discuss without holding back thoughts is news about Asians who are deported. Who is caught laundering money; who is making the most money with the President's clansmen as his partners, and who killed his daughter because she eloped with an outsider. Yet, there is rising unemployment, famine, and poverty in the country. More important news to talk about. There is also the question of shifta bandits in the north to discuss. Haidu gets his news listening to scratchy All India Radio, a habit he has cultivated with much pleasure, since he acquired the new transistor radio with a two feet long silver aerial. He no longer listens to the Kenya Broadcasting Service.

In every sentence that they speak in the parliament, the politicians say Asians are detriment to the economy and development that is modernization. In today's news, while debating in the parliament, the MPs made it clear that getting rid of Asians must start in the governing assembly. Then only would Africanization slither down to every tier of the society from the civil service to transportation and commerce. "African MPs who cultivate Asian business partners pamper them like their mistresses," said one parliamentarian. But would the MPs let go of free money? The latter they say are mere papers and paper is not land which is Blackman's country or blood that is black. Africanization has roots in African customs and African philosophy that is communalism or African socialism. That is to say wealth must be shared. Indian businesses must be fully African owned. Indian girls married to Africans.

Every evening, I find myself repeating to Haiderali like a mantra, "England does not want us. India will not accept us. There are no more railways and roads to make. There are no colonies to develop. Where shall we go?"

"So what should we do?" asks Haiderali.

"You must buy KANU party membership even if you do not feel KANU at heart. KANU is Kenyatta's party after all. Get it tomorrow. I watch the TV and how Kenyatta hymns venerate him. He is god, present everywhere. Omnipresent Light of Kenya."

"We must hang a photograph of the President in the shop, the one with a fly whisk raised above his Luo beaded head," I say.

"Huh! As if he loves Luos like his own Kikuyus!"

"And frame your KANU life certificate too. Hang it under your President," I say.

"Shall we then remove Saheb's photo?"

"Nah! The President's photo is not a replacement for Saheb's."

"How will the two photographs look side by side?" he asks.

"In Mamdu's bicycle store there is a photograph. A family photo. Half smile on college-boy Saheb in high-collared Indian coat standing with Kenyatta the wise, the Father of the Nation. Let's get one like that, Haidu. It shows we are loyal to the President, and Saheb is his friend."

"You mean it shows we venerate both side by side?" he asks. Is he mocking me, or does he mean what he says? Who knows how Haiderali thinks nowadays! A man so full of pessimism spits out disdain with every word. All my coaxing and cajoling cannot fend off such hatred that swells from bitterness in him as if the 9 p.m. news spawned a hurricane of rage in him. I would try reasoning but his scorn does not lessen.

I make cucumber salad and slice oranges for him to eat at lunchtime. I make fresh lime juice for him to drink first thing in the morning and yogurt before bed. I have a list in Ma Gor Bai's own writing of all the vegetables, lentils and fruits that cool the temperament and I cook accordingly. I do not keep mangoes in the house anymore and that upsets Haidu immensely, especially when mangoes, his favourite, are in season and you see the tree in the courtyard weighed down with succulent red and yellow cashew shaped orbs. But what can I do? Mangoes are hot and induce heat in the body. Like red meat that I avoid cooking as well.

"OK. Baas, baas, fine, I will ask Rhemu to bring that picture from Photographer in Nairobi, framed and ready to put it up at the entrance. Or do you want it with your beads on the veranda?" Haiderali scoffs again. He does not like to be told by me what to choose. Like teenage Diamond, he snubs me as if my request for the picture is a parental command. I ignore his words. I know he will bring the photograph for the store.

I look around to see where Freda is. Is she listening? I don't hear her working.

"Freda!" I yell out, "Where have you been all this time? And where is Kamau today?"

"Sijui, I don't know," she replies from the doorway.

"I did not see him yesterday and now today also. How can someone just disappear? Who will do his work now?"

I have noticed that though he gets upset and becomes even foul with his words, Haiderali does pay more attention to me, much more than he ever did before. Is he losing his head-of-the-family confidence? The Khoja father, Khoja husband, the Vir of Kacch Kathiawad. He of Saurashtra. Haidu has lost some of that man in him that lessens me. Or is it sweet pee, the disease runs in his family from his father's side? It kills manhood before it kills the man. Did diabetes not kill his father and grandmother too? Can he protect his property as a man should? Can he protect his daughter as a father should? Though, now I can speak to Haiderali without fear, it makes me feel insecure. I feel unprotected. Displaced. I am losing the confidence I felt in him. I am losing my wife confidence. My wife presence around him. My wife joy.

I look forward to going to the jamat khana where I can put my anxieties into the ginans that are the sacred songs of Satpanth Ismailis, and to Saheb. That has been the tradition of my ancestors that has held us together.

421

Suspicion and fear of Africans heave in me like a turmoil from within. During the day, I keep it compressed roaring in the pith of my belly. After the evening devotions, I know the confusion I hold will leap out of my mouth like a whirlpool of words when I meet my friends. Moved by our fear and anxiety, Zera Bai, Khanu Bai and I will snap into each other's half said sentences - taak taak complaints and buck buck buckwaas, which will not always make sense, but will be said nonetheless to sooth our anxieties. Such is the confusion in our heads. We look forward to our evening talk though it gives no solution.

Sometimes, my story stretches and recoils like an elastic band. It inhabits me in my anxieties so much so that often I tell my story to myself. Anxieties speaking into anxieties are like pictures mirroring pictures.

Wait-and-see

It's another Sunday night some weeks after Kenyatta's damming speech. Haiderali comes home at supper time looking more tired than before he went out for fresh air and talk with his friends. I am back from the jamat khana. My head is buzzing with new anxieties shafted over the old. Today, I did not wait for Haiderali to come to khane with me. I needed to go even if alone to be away from Kamau and Freda. At once, I want to tell Haiderali how I sensed panic in voices of women when we talked about the President's speech at Uhuru Park at mid-day. But on seeing the expression on his face, I keep quiet, at least for now.

Haiderali stammers, spacing his words as if he is not sure of what he wants to say to me. "If you want to live in Nairowua...then I will have to give out a part of the business ...as Saheb says...alternatively a large monthly chai money to our MP ... That's what Magan Bhai is doing now so he can live in Nairowua. 'Buy time while I save enough money to send my children to UK. Don't hurry,' he says, 'wait-and-see'. The MP even got him a Kenya passport, though he is not born here like I am, and I suspect his wife and children keep their British passports. Magan Bhai would send his children, daughters first, one at a time while waiting for the vouchers for his parents to enter England. Then no one would suspect. Meanwhile, he will be sending money out of Kenya through the MP's wife who is his legal business partner. Finally, he will wind up his business and hand over the keys to the MP and leave. He plays 'wait-and-see' game, he tells me. He will remain a citizen of Kenya and keep the British passport as well. The British will ignore that as long as his money flows into UK. He tells me even if they are category B second class citizens of UK, that's better than category A first class Kenya citizenship. Good strategy! Wise man! Why did we put all our eggs in one basket becoming Kenya citizens? I don't understand what is happening. Do you? As long as you and the children are safe, I can live anywhere and like Magan Bhai follow 'wait-and-see' plan from day to day. Like Magan Bhai."

"We shall live together. Give the MP a share in our business. Lower your head a little. Let your ego go for the sake of our survival. Grovel to him like your friend so we can live in peace and together. Our children are too small to be sent away to a boarding school in UK. Can we afford that anyway? We are no longer British." I speak in whispers as if it was always my habit. We have learned to speak softly like thieves whispering in the dark when we talk about our future and politics. It's like how it was during the Mau Mau days.

Children have also adopted their parents' behaviour, but they speak more in coded language. It's a culture of fear, a culture of silence, but more a culture of 'wait-and-see' what happens next that pervades our home as it does the street, the market and the jamat khana. It's all about play acting to survive the times like this. I feel like the Gupti, meaning the Hidden Khoja of Hindustan. We hide our thoughts and who we are. We distrust each other in the jamat as if we are enemies; as if someone amongst us may report our conversation to gain some business favour from the new DC or the police commissioner or the MP. The distrust has grown so much that even among friends there is not the same sharing of secrets as before.

I see anger in Haiderali's narrowing eyes. "I don't like anyone interfering with my business. I want to be my own master as I have been. We had nothing but a handful of beads when we came to Nairowua. We struggled. We, not the MP, built this business and the town." Haiderali spits out words at me as if I were the MP whose sight repulses him yet he cannot do without him.

"Is it not also Saheb's wish that we give a share of the business to Africans, work in partnership and teach them to trade?" I ask hoping Haiderali would calm down and not put his frustration on me.

"What Africans? Freda? Jennifer? Ole Lekakeny? A worker, our servants to be our business partners? Our partners will be politicians – well connected to renew the licenses and by-pass Africanization. They make the law and they show us how to break the law," says Haiderali in a way he expects no answer when he has no answer himself. Then he keeps quiet and puts his palms flat on his forehead. "Window dressing," he mutters after some thought. "Buying time. You have to grow up in a duka-store in the bush to understand business in Africa. You can't make instant businessmen like instant coffee out of a Member of Parliament who grew up a cowherd." Haiderali now speaks calmly but his tone is laced with scorn. It's his sweet-pee illness that causes that kind of irritation fused with bitterness.

"You should not have eaten so much kheer. The doctor said no kheer at all. Kheer has sugar," I reprimand.

"My sweet-pee is not bad."

"Then why ants in the toilet?" He ignores me.

After a while, when I hear showers approaching, I go outside. I speak to the rain in the poem of Kalidas. Feminine poems. Love poems. Mother poems. Poems of rain and fertility. Raindrops sing the rhythm of affection. Poems of joy. Mitti attar, the fragrance of the moistened earth enters me. It will carry me into honeyed dreams when I go to bed cold and sprinkled on like rose water on a festive evening in the jamat khana. I am wet but not wet enough for a towel rub.

Before Haiderali begins to snore, I take his hand in mine, and rub my thumb over his wedding ring. Ma Gor Bai, my second mother, had goldsmith Patni of River Road in Nairobi craft the ring laid with one ruby from her necklace. My thumb rolls over the dot size red stone embedded in gold not raised and not as big as on my ring. My fingers caress over Haiderali's hair around the ring and over his knuckles. I listen to the raindrops becoming heavier, and then a gale sweeps through the showers carrying the sound of drops away with it. An icy chill runs through my body like a seizure. Turning to the side, I push myself closer to the warmth of Haidu's bare chest pulling his hand over me and bringing it to cup over my breast. Suddenly, he shuffles as if awakened from a nightmare and jerks his hand away from me. A brisk awkward bounce and he turns around facing the other way, away from me.

"Saala Gandhi!"

426

Najmu Chotara comes to town

Then one day as if by a miracle, as if it were an answer to my prayers, Haiderali comes home jumping. A rare sight. "Najmu Chotara wants to buy my shop! Najmu Chotara wants to buy my shop!" He repeats. "Najmu Chotara half Maasai, half Khoja wants to buy my shop. He is the biggest bead merchant in Narok town," says Haiderali. I absorb his excitement and breathe out a sigh of shu-khar. But then other thoughts come too. Do I want to give away my beads yet? Do I want to give away my little corner of afternoon quietness and live in noisy Nairobi?

"Half Maasai *chhe*?" I query.

"I know his family well. They used to break their safari in Nairowua and stay with us overnight when I was little," says Haiderali. "The Maasai respected Namu's father, old man Govindji Bhai. People said he was a convict who married a dance girl but she died of a bite from the black mamba of the Spirit Rock, leaving him with twelve children." I nod. I have heard the name of Govindji Bhai before. He was one of the three prisoners on the dhow in my Dadabapa's story. He was the one who stayed back in Kenya when the other two returned to India after the British left. "Ma disliked the dance girl but Govindji Bhai and my father helped each other to stock beads, and they loaned money to each other when times were hard. They were good friends like business blood brothers. Govindji

Bhai married again. This time to an uncircumcised Maasai girl, a Christian convert at the mission. They have one son, Najmu. Ma used to say the black mamba of the Spirit Rock sunk its teeth into Gulzar Bai because she was full of sins. There is a legend about the black mamba of the Spirit Rock, how it seeks out sinners."

"My Dadabapa knew Gulzar Bai. They came to Africa on the same dhow," I say quickly, as if I wanted to add to the excitement, like wanting to give my testimony to Najmu Chotara's family reputation. That he would be a good buyer, meaning he would pay the right value for the shop and that he would pay although he was half African. "I knew who Gulzar Bai was. She came to my second mother's satsang at home. Gulzar Bai lived with Meethi Bai at the lodge in Nairobi." I was about to say my red velvet dress with white lace neck and sleeves that Haiderali liked so much when we were just married and young, once belonged to Gulzar Bai who had brought it with her from India. Meethi Bai gave it to me after Gulzar Bai's marriage. No one had a dress like that, and it was my favourite Friday khane dress before Diamond was born and my waistline changed. I wore the long dress with a red silk pachedi-shawl held with a butterfly glass emerald broach pinned to my left shoulder. I bite my tongue.

"Najmu's family is connected to the MP's homestead through his mother," says Haiderali. Then he sits down at the dining table on the veranda, puts his hand to his forehead, "Like Najmu Chotata, I too was born here. I too speak Maasai. I will die here in my home. My ancestors are buried here and so will I. We put up the first shop in Nairowua and founded the business. Others came, but we started." Haiderali's voice slips into a shrill, "Shall I

428

sell the shop?" He is not sure now if he will sell the shop to Najmu Chotara. That's like him nowadays. Wasi wasi *chhe*, unsure of himself

"Kabir writes the situation in the Congo is not peaceful either. We should not go west he writes. There are revolts of the army. He thinks the problem is that Congo is rich in minerals and that interests the Belgians and the French, and of course, after independence, the Americans are everywhere. They compete with Russians. The second scramble for Africa comes from both East and West," says Haiderali like he were reading Kabir's letter to me. "Congo is more difficult to understand than Kenya. But Kabir says business is good over there if one is prepared to take the risk of security. The country is like under a permanent emergency."

"So where shall we go? Saheb wants us to remain loyal to the country of our birth. How can we when we are driven out of the towns we live in? Towns we developed. When the cross lines of red, white and blue flag descended on the 12th of December, the straight-lines of red, white and black flag ascended. I see the same colours. The army brass blasted Funga Safari. Your safari is over. Pack up and start marching out. So goes the song. Soldiers swayed colobus monkey skins on their heads, waving goodbye. You saw how it was on the TV, *nah*? The applause thundered loud enough to deafen the ears of the sky. Yet we could not hear. Are we stone deaf that we cannot hear them telling us it's time to pack our bags and leave, funga safari?" Doubts torment me as I say these words from the pictures on the TV playing in my head. Doubts come when I don't see what road lies ahead. Haiderali has two minds. Wasi wasi *chhe*. That adds to my worry. A man must be strong in mind and definite with words. But we must remain loyal to Saheb. That is tradition. That is the faith of our forefathers. That is our strength. The strength helped us to live through the jeering of the Ithna Asheris and Sunnis. They said we are not Moslems like them. But who said we were Moslems like them? How every Moslem thinks he is the only pure one! The pioneers survived, holding on to the faith. We must remain loyal to Saheb. We must remain loyal to the country of our birth. We must remain loyal to the citizenship we hold. But the citizenship is not loyal to us. But the country of our birth is not loyal to us. Will the faith be loyal to us and see us through this quandary? I begin to question my belief. Do I sin? Or do I too have two minds that many of us have come to during these times of uncertainties?

"Pack up? Quit Kenya? Never! There will be no homeland for us Khoja now. There was hope when the Jews got a country of their own. Not any more, after all that trouble with Palestinians. Wish the Jews had accepted some part of British East Africa instead. They would have let us stay," says Haiderali. After a thought he asks, "Would they have?" I hear the words on his tongue come from the unease in his heart.

"Hold on to your faith like a drowning man holding on to the rope," I say. Words come from my mind partly to comfort my husband and partly myself.

But I know much of what he tells me today is thought over information from his card game friends. Fear and hate confuse him, makes him undecided. His voice cracks into a shrill note. He needs me to comfort him with words or at least a nod to show concern. To be with him.

Unlike his brother Kabir, Haiderali does not read *Africa Samachar* or Gujarati magazines from India. All he reads are jokes in *Chakram*. His English is not good, so he avoids English newspapers. But he listens carefully to his friends.

When I meet Zera Bai and Khanu Bai, we pluck words from each other's tongues before the sentences are complete. What we hear from each other are the same thoughts we have heard from our husbands. The men have no solutions. Moreover, they have grown distrustful of each other especially those card players who 'sleep with ministers' as Haiderali says. Business whores, he calls them. No one expected Africanization that came as surprisingly as did nationalization in Tanzania. They happened so close to each other that both Khanu Bai and Zera Bai think Kenyatta and Nyerere conspired together. After every second sentence Zera Bai would say, "Gola *chhe*. After all they are black." The assault on our citizenship spurs loathing. Repulsion rolls over our tongues. Is it because our forefathers came over the ocean not land that we are not equal citizens? We ask.

"Gola nu raj *chhe*," we concur, it's black man's kingdom. Thus we assuage our fear with repugnance like eating sweet mee-thai over a bitter pill that we reluctantly swallow because we have to – there is no way out of this trap.

Part Eleven

Changing Face of the Land

Haiderali decides to keep the shop and buy the trade license with chai money, meaning bribe that the MP would collect from him around Christmas time each year. That's how they have agreed. The bead business, however, is affected by new roads. With the new roads come bus and lorry traffic. And with that come the goods and agriculturalists. The new settlers are Christians and do not wear beads. Nairowua no longer looks like a semi-pastoral town with a string of Indian shops, a market square by the country bus stop and the DC's office, the health clinic and a church on the outskirts. In the small wayside kiosks where before there were only some dangling lines of tobacco in plump banana leaf packs on twisted chains also made of banana leaves, now there are Maasai beads as well. Fewer Maasai come to look at the beads that Moti Bai puts on the rack each morning, looped in strings. She now works on the beads alone because Ole Lekakeny has moved out of Nairowua to live with his age mates at the seniors' homestead near Ol Donyo Lengai, the sacred mountain that echoes voices from the earth.

Moti Bai would watch with dismay how the trade in beads is slipping away. The trade that Haiderali's great uncle, Jadavji Bhai and the itinerant Khoja foot merchants, apprentices to the business king, Allidina Visram, brought to the savannah. Bead Bais would tell you stories of how they lived frugally, with persistence laid in the hope that the beads would be known and appreciated one day. And then the thrill they would feel when they saw the ethnic people come to their bead displays. How they would step over their store's thresholds, suspicious of the hairy Ol-moindi as the Maasai called the Indians. "Ol-moindi have heads like colobus monkeys," Ole Lekakeny jests how his people, the Maasai, see Haiderali and Kabir straight black Indian hair.

The artists of the savannah would reject some colours and cling to others as if they had always known them. They could now touch what was given to them by their ancestors in metaphors and stories of colours so they might know e'sikar, meaning, the joy of beauty. Ole Lekakeny would say that was the Eye Knowledge remembered in Maasai body, geography, the sky and the legend of creation.

The strange people with colobus monkey heads, who came to Maasailand in carts and on foot, put the pastoralists' love of nature's art into their hands. The beads spoke of lessons in humanity in the grammar of osotua that is beauty and it also means peace, human relationship and blessings. How their eyes studied memories of splendours in pictures of the mind and dreams. How they read the displayed beads in the Indian's store and recalled the diorama in the Eye Knowledge of their ancestors. How in bead talk, they would hear distant tales of their walk after descending from the sky, a journey over time so long that babies born along the way became warriors, married and had babies of their own. When they became grandparents, they would cut a branch of the African hardwood tree with bright green leaves that shone the Light and strip off the bark, smooth it with sandpaper plants and carve out a knob to hold in tight fisted hand. Then they took short steps and slow steps to continue the walk, and as they walked, they named the geography of the continent in colours along the valley of the mighty Nile. The colours marked their route, how long they walked and where they came from. When they settled and built houses, they put the memories of colours to beads in combinations worked into the rhythm of their footsteps, songs and dances like how the Satpanth Khoja recall their origin in the colours and patterns of the bandhani and the su-astik. And so they remembered the great walk that they call the origin like how the Satpanth Khoja remembered their coming to Africa as a voyage. All are stories of crossings of continents that brought them to where they are.

Now, Haiderali concentrates on selling ploughs, farm tools and fertilizers to the growing small-scale cultivators of maize, beans, bananas and potatoes. Though there is nascent resentment against the new settlers in the air, there are fresh vegetables on the table. Contrary to fears that independence would bring an end to Indian businesses, the changes, in fact, bring great prosperity. Plans are made and money collected to build a new jamat khana of stone with a tower in place of the old wooden building with a red tin roof.

The MP acquires more trade licenses for Haiderali to sell a variety of goods. Haiderali decides to keep the scanty bead trade going on the veranda partly because it's a shrine to how he started the business. "Beads gave us roji that is our daily bread. Beads are sacred like how the tools are sacred to the craftsman," he would say. In time, the bead display becomes a little sanctuary for Moti Bai and no more.

But Haiderali is a man of two minds. Every now and then, he would remark with regret that there were hardly any customers coming to the store to buy beads. Once, he even said he wanted to change the name from KHIMJI DEVJI MOMNA AND SON BEADS AND GENERAL STORE to KHIMJI DEVJI MOMNA AND SON FARM TOOLS AND GENERAL STORE.

The wealthier section of the Ismaili Khoja community in Nairowua, send their children to the former Europeans only high cost schools. They drive in cars even over short distances that they used to walk to, like to the jamat khana in the evenings. They put the food prayer offerings of naandi in the boots of their cars, so they would not have to hold them in their hands and leave pungent smells behind in the car.

American churches – the Methodist, Seventh Day Adventists, Baptist, Pentecostal, Lutheran, Latter Day Saints, Full Gospel, Jehovah's Witness, and even more appear with such competitive zeal that one would think there was a religious carnival racking the countryside. Loudspeakers blast sermons in Swahili and Maasai. Hymns crack through the African air over the natural echoes of feral life and wind hissing through the acacia trees. Open air evangelization rallies break the peace on Sundays and even on market days in remote places amid growing poverty of the homesteads due to restricted fenced pasturelands and privatization of the once community owned land. Kabir, who is Haiderali's brother and Moti Bai's brother-in-law, calls it an 'American Spiritual Invasion'. Sarcasm embeds his thoughts in all matters nowadays, even religion that he calls 'a CIA outfit'. At the shallow pools along the Nairowua River you would see white priests holding long metal and wooden crucifixes dunking heads into the water, praying with fervour for salvation of the heathens while looking up into Nairowua's blue sky where there once resided the multi-coloured God of the savannah. But En-Kai is still there if you put your eyes to the sky, and think differently like you were a native of the land before the Indians came to make the iron road that ruptured the country, and before the white men came speaking of new religion. The new religion they speak of is so removed from the land that it says the Maasai will need to die to live again, and leave this land of beauty to them, so they may know peace. To the Maasai eye, peace is beauty of the land and the sky, and you must be alive to know it. But the white men insist peace is found only in the dead man's country.

At the baraza meetings, the new black DC-in-training, they call him Bwana Rungu, waves a club in his right hand as he talks to the people. He ridicules Maasai dress, rites and the tradition of wearing beads as dead customs against development. He calls them anti-maendeleo, meaning anti-progress habits of the past if not outright primitive, meaning un-Christian, if not dirty and uncivilized. There is even a threat to ban the use of ochre on bodies, age group graduation ceremonies and wearing of beads. You would see the new government officers coming from upcountry dressed like the departed English officers in khaki suits, sunhats and sunglasses, yelling out 'Development' while demonstrating their power, arrogance and superiority over the ethnic people. And then they collect money for ghost harambee, meaning fund raising, meetings.

Then, when the police begin harassing the Maasai coming to Nairowua in their ethnic attires, the men quickly don English khaki pants just before entering the town, and they drop them as quickly when they leave the town, neatly folding them up before tucking them into their shoulder bags kept ready for the next visit to Nairowua. Thus they avoid confrontation with the law of independence.

The Maasai have not heard of God's revelations yet they have humanity. They have never harmed the Indians or ever stolen anything from them over the generations that they lived among them.

438

Mukhiani of Nairowua

Within five years of independence, the population of Nairowua changes significantly. Now there is a growing number of small-scale vegetable farmers coming to the town. They come by country buses from the fields carved out of the pastures of the nomads, and allocated to them within a hundred mile radius of Nairowua. Haiderali's investments in ploughs, farm tools and fertilizers begin to pay off. With the flow of more money than we had ever had, my life begins to change. When Haiderali comes home, with a new car, a brand new Morris Minor, we stand before it for a photograph dressed in our best khane clothes. I learn to play bridge. Saturday nights' supplications over, and we meet at the Aga Khan club to play cards in mixed men and women groups. We even enjoy a little gambling. Haiderali keeps a bottle of Tusker beer in a brown paper bag near his feet under the table. We rotate who would buy the naandi dinner for the group.

It was at the card game that Guli Bai Musa Jina, asked me as if casually, "What business does your son's friend's father run?" I know Diamond has a new friend, Amin Jeraj. He has even brought him home once. But we know his father, Jiwa Bhai Jeraj, does not run a business; he has always been a teller at the Barclays Bank since it started in Nairowua.

"I don't know," I lie looking into the cards fanned out in my hand.

"Where does the mother sit along the wall seats in the jamat khana?" she asks again. Guli Bai Musa Jina annoys me.

"I don't know," I say again. She knows Jiwa Bhai Jeraj does not have a title that would permit his wife to sit with us, the titleholders as we are known in the jamat. It would also be the wives of the titled who would wear the bandhani on celebratory Khush-ali evenings.

"Is it not proper for Diamond, son of the community council chairman, to go out with Jiwa Bhai Jeraj's son?" I ask Haiderali when we come home tired and ready to go to bed. He nods, does not say anything, pulls up the quilt to go into the bed. I want to say more. "Not that he is not a well behaved boy. It's because of the parents. They are not so poor to be on welfare, but still not so well to do to be titled." I would not want Diamond's friendship with Jiwa Bhai Jeraj's son to take away the newly acquired class from us when I am just beginning to enjoy some prestige in the community. Anyway, I let it be for now, and will gently prompt Diamond not to be seen often with the boy.

There is no mention of replacing the diamond siri-button that was on my nose. Haiderali must have pawned it to pay for the loan he owed Rajan Lalji, the bead supplier in Nairobi, taking away my dignity to save his. Perhaps, he wants me to look modern like Zera Bai who removed her nose button because her husband, Rhemu Bhai, told her it was a Hindu custom.

But Haidu does allow me to make a gold chain with amber beads. That's all in high fashion. Perhaps, it assuages his guilt.

440

I take the opportunity to order a gold set that would go well with Almas' dowry that I have started to get together, and one for Diamond's wife when he marries. This is custom and Haiderali does not object. Both the gold sets have modern designs that look like miniature frames of structures under construction. Now when the times are good, I keep the children's gold ready and in the bank. That is custom too. Haiderali also purchases a Life Insurance Policy from the Jubilee Insurance Company in Nairobi and he jokes with me how I would be a rich widow should he die. But in my heart, what I wish most is for my Haidu to be appointed the mukhi of Nairowua. Then I would be the mukhiani of Nairowua. The road is paved for that. Haiderali gives generous donations to the various religious functions as an anonymous member of the community, though everyone knows who the donor is. If not, a persistent enquiry through eye gesturing and hissing whispers would weed through the suspects, and yes-no doubts until the anonymous donors are located. I can tell by women's furtive glances towards me as the donor's wife. But I keep on looking straight, pretending I don't know who the unnamed donor would be. But I know, they know I know they know. The anonymity when emphatically announced to the jamat through the microphone, provides the essential grade of humility, a requirement for those aspiring to be leaders. For my part, I spend more time in the jamat khana doing sewa service work here and there. That's most noticeable to the jamat and most gratifying to me. When you work for the community, using your own hands doing something as low as cleaning floors like the servants in our homes, it brings humility. That humility is closer to God than any other virtue. I also make larger and more elaborate food prayer offerings of rich spicy Mughal dishes that are difficult to pass by unnoticed. I lay them out on Dutch ceramic and Pyrex glass platters. My dinnerware is easily distinguishable from the cheaper Chinese plates of other housewives.

I continue dreaming what I would do when I will be the mukhiani of Nairowua. What clothes I would wear. What perfumes I would wear. What jewellery I would wear. What I would wear on new moon chandraat evenings and Khush-ali nights. And what I would wear on other days. How I would sit facing the jamat and receive prayer offerings over fare prepared by them. In return I would gift blessings to the jamat on Saheb's behalf. I would receive whispered confessions of each murid facing me on bended knees and palms joined.

"My name has been forwarded to the Council for the position of the next mukhi of Nairowua," Haiderali speaks to my dreams. We have just come home from the jamat khana. It's time to eat and then watch the 9 p.m. news. But …" he stops talking.

"But what?" I ask.

"Moti Bai will you not try wearing short dresses. Khanu Bai and you must be the only ones in the Nairowua jamat who keep to desi clothes."

"Should it matter how I dress?"

"Some say as leaders we would not be good examples. Leaders ought to show they follow Saheb's farmans. You know a long dress does not look proper on a titled lady at the wall seat in khane. Have you seen any? Will you not try, just sometimes, if not all the time?"

I withdraw into myself. I feel small. Should I start wearing short dresses? The embarrassment of exposing my body to the male gaze will make me feel even smaller.

"Varas Khan Bhai made a comment," continues Haiderali, "Even a bride wears a short dress at her wedding nowadays. The men laughed. They laughed not because he made fun of you but because Varas Khan Bhai who is on the Council said it. They laughed to please him."

"Tell Varas Khan Bhai to put on short kaptura pants at the next new moon evening in khane. I will wear a short dress if he wears a kaptura!" Haiderali looks at me with a smile. "And ask him when will we have a woman on the Council?"

"That's a strange thought!" says Haiderali his smile changing to put-down man to woman laughter. "You want to sit on the Council with a pachedi-shawl waving over your head like My Flag?"

I will keep on dreaming. I live inside and outside the world of dreams. Dreaming is like telling my story to myself. I stand inside my story because it's about me, and outside because I am the storyteller. Dreamers are storytellers too. Or is it that storytellers are dreamers too? Sometimes, they imagine what they have not seen.

Freda's son

I am tired of the talk filled with fear-suspicion-
hatred all put in one conversation that's been around for
months moving round and round in chee-chhe-ru circle.
These are restless days not knowing what to do. In my
head, I go over my talk with Zera Bai and Khanu Bai like a
repeated drum beat. Whatever I am doing in the house, the
talk is there, taak taak drumming in my head. Mama Khelele
has quietly retreated. Perhaps, she is confused too, as I am.
I mean the real me. But one thing I know, I become
stronger when my thoughts become clearer and because
they are my own thoughts. Haiderali will have to listen to
me. His wasi-wasi doubts, changing plans every now and
then, takes us nowhere. I must say to Haiderali again and
again, taak taak, "Give the MP chai money and let us buy
time. Add milk to instant black coffee. Bribery makes it
brown." He does not even look at me when I speak like a
drum stick, taak taak.

"Where did this chai business start anyway?" I ask
changing my tone.

"Ask your brother. Shamshu mocks Asian leaders
coaxing the community to go to Kenyatta's chai parties.
Have tea with your President who loves you, and leave your
wallet for his hospital project," Haiderali scoffs, he is in a
scornful mood again. "Everyone knows it's a ghost hospital
but can an Asian refuse the President's invitation to chai?"

"Chai is better than deportation or moving to Nairobi."

"Where shall we go?" Haiderali repeats my words, talking to himself as he gets up leaning forward, bent like he has stomach pains. He moves towards the courtyard toilet slowly talking to the ground, "I am a brown citizen in a black country. White England will not accept me. I chose to be Kenyan."

"But you did send your brother to the Congo," I call after him. Haiderali does not reply. I hear him muttering to himself, "Kenyatta saalo mari ghand mare *chhe*. Kenyatta fucks my arse," he repeats. "Yet I must hang his picture on my store wall! Buy life membership of his party. The only party allowed. Saalo! Calls Kenya a one party democracy!"

"Don't talk like that! We have growing children at home!" I shout after him, but I don't think he hears me or cares to hear what I say. Diamond and Almas have gone to the movies, thank Mowla. I know Freda is giggling somewhere in the house though I do not see her or hear her. My suspicion eats me. I know she would have her ears projected to our conversation wherever she is, squatting at the karo washing dishes, standing on the veranda ironing our khane clothes, polishing shoes, mopping the kitchen floor. Haiderali does not care about family respectability in front of servants. I feel I am losing my self-respect, and with that, my authority over Freda. I need to find another house help. I should not have employed her again after she went to her rural relatives to deliver her baby. But Haiderali insisted we employ her again. He would not listen to me. Will another servant be any different? Freda and her son live in the African township of Majengo where there is a

445

community of servants, bois and ayahs working in Asian homes. The grandmothers look after their daughters' children while they come to look after ours. They support each other within their ethnic bonded families living in tin, plastic and mud houses. Like Freda's family is Kamba, and close to other Kamba families of Majengo.

Haiderali often asks about Freda's boy and I suspect he pays for his upkeep. He asks me to send used clothes, biscuits and mee-thai sweets to the boy like he were one of our own. I have not even seen the boy. Haiderali talks about Freda's son like he knows him.

"Is he your son?" I question Haiderali one day on the way to khane when I know he would not shout back at me in the street.

"Are you jealous?" he questions me back and then immediately adds, "Poor Freda works for you all day. This is the least you can do for her."

He puts guilt in me over my suspicion. I keep quiet all the way to the jamat khana that evening but inside I am burning.

While walking home after worship, I feel no night wind. That is unusual. I miss the sensation of cool air in my nostrils. Breathing deep, I would control its inflow as I walk, and feel the cold nip inside bringing calmness to my mind. Haiderali walks alone ahead of me and Zarina.

At a distance we hear the battered Merali bus roar into Nairowua, its tyres grinding on the chipped stone road like a grater, grating out a ball of red dust that hangs in the still night air. The whirring machine quietens as the bus moves towards Rhemu Bhai's bicycle shop and the new BP Petrol Station next to it. It will stay there for the night. It

446

will be cleaned inside and washed outside. Arriving passengers' bustle softens into the second quarter of the night as they, tired, late and hungry after the day-long safari, walk home. Some would have cloth bundles on their heads and children at the waist. Some would be holding plastic bags in embrace or over their shoulders. Some carrying metal suitcases in both hands. All walking home towards the African township as we quicken our steps in the opposite direction towards the Asian part of the town.

The Exodus

I am shaken awake out of my dream in the middle of the night. Wet with perspiration and anxious, I hear myself gabbling. Peering through the haze in my eyes, I see the shadow of Haiderali standing bent over me like a tree. He is in pyjama pants and shirtless looking at me with a glass of water in his hands.

"What's the matter?" he asks, "are you seeing Mau Mau?"

"Diamond is lost. People are running on the runaway to the airplane. BOAC has arrived and is leaving. They are rolling away the staircase but the doors are wide open." My words are incoherent. I hold on to the disappearing picture in my mind so I do not lose Diamond.

Haiderali sits by my side and helps me sit up. I guzzle water in gulps spilling some over my chin and feel its coolness sliding down my throat and over my throat in concurrent flows.

"Diamond is sleeping in his room. Su *chhe* – what is it?" asks Haiderali. He seems more confused than surprised. He has never before seen me like this.

"I was dreaming we were at the airport with the crowd stampeding towards the airplane leaving for Great Britain – men carrying luggage, women in saris holding babies, old people leaning on the young. All in heavy coats, blankets and shawls. Others sitting in wheelchairs smothered in cloaks."

"You have been looking at too many pictures of the exodus," says Haiderali going under his quilt. He turns around, and in a short while he is exhaling air scraping through his throat. Exodus is a new word in our vocabulary. The insidious word has crept into conversations and into my dreams. It's the word in English that carries foreboding pictures. Pictures that alarm and terrify us. Pictures that assault families viewing the nine o'clock news on the TV before they go to bed. Pictures that they see again in newspapers when they wake up the next morning. Pictures that one would think are deliberately put there to cause panic in the community. Pictures that demand we leave quickly. Exodus is like the other word called emergency full of images that swell fear in the heart and the fear eats into words. Emergency was less than a decade ago when the Mau Mau roamed the night.

Because I do not read English, I look deep for a long time into pictures of the Asian exodus out of Kenya. I try to understand. The luggage they carry is in all sorts of makeshift packages and suitcases. One old woman is even carrying her kitchen pot with her. It's probably her favourite utensil without which her pilau would not be the same. She is like me who measures the recipes by how the ingredients spread in the pot. So it has to be the same pot. The expressions of their faces and gestures are all the same – they exude anxiety. A collective community apprehension – Gujaratis in saris, Punjabis in long tunic-shirts over loose pants, Goans wearing short dresses, pervades the airport departure hall like a colossal aura as it does in our homes. I also look at the five p.m. Swahili news on the TV and listen to the follow up commentary on the exodus before going to khane. The airport faces haunt me. They are my people. I think I could be that woman in the sari sitting on her

449

suitcase holding her son and daughter in each arm at the airport lounge. A tin of travel food sits by her foot. I am that mother of children. I could be that woman in a sari pressed in among the tired mob at the British High Commission. They have been standing for weeks at the door waiting to present their papers and secure the visa before the deadline to enter Great Britain clamps down on them. What used to be a single tidy line has swelled into a mob of desperate and nervous families. Their mood aggravates as days go by. The new legislation now requires a voucher over the visa to enter Great Britain. The process is tedious and slow. The British High Commission people are suspicious of every Indian as if she were a criminal. They even stopped the flights. Some sleep there on the pavements in the rain and the cold highland night air of Nairobi harassed by the police. Mr Patrick Shaw, ex-British now Kenyatta's most feared police henchman, patrols the pavements with a baton in his hand and a gun at his waist, pushing the crowds back as if expecting a riot to flare up at any moment. In the scuffle that he creates, he thrusts at a defiant woman. She does not move. He shoves her with force this time tearing her sari blouse. She is a small built Gujarati woman and he, a Goliath of a white man in khaki police uniform. She is shamed. Next day her picture appears in *The Nation* newspaper. She has filed a court case against Mr Shaw. She demands her right. I am her.

Kenyatta deports the storyteller

Days of anxiety seem not to pass quickly. Rhemu Bhai's bicycle shop has a large sign in red letters, SALE. Khanu Bhai has moved to Nairobi. Her sons have already started school there in the big city but her husband is in Nairowua hopelessly trying to sell his business so then they can go to Canada. He needs to show that he has cash in hand to get the visas. Mamdu Bhai buys naandi for his evening meal and warms the left-overs for his lunch the next day. Once in a while, I send him a pile of chapattis or a jar of mango pickles, Khoja gum paak, thepla and such foods for chai nasto, meaning teatime snacks.

"Every time our Nairowua MP comes by the shop to collect beads for his girl friends or farm tools that he never pays for, he drops hints, intimidating me," says Haiderali. "He tells me if I need my shop license renewed next year, I should put his name down as a part owner. He knows I am in a tight place. He knows now as a Kenya citizen I can go nowhere. Saalo golo madderchod *chhe*!" Haiderali lashes out a terse abuse calling him a black motherfucking bastard. Rarely have I heard him use words, such abuse, so much hate of Africans. "But I have to keep a smile on my sorry Indian face, give him a cup of tea and agree with him that all the corruption in Kenya that we see nowadays was actually started by the English and the missionaries. I want to ask our Honourable Minister, 'So

Africans just aped English corruption like the English dress, English religion, English language. Is that right, your honour, *si-ndio*?"

"Leave him alone and don't talk like that in the house, Haidu. Freda understands Gujarati. Keep your voice down," I try to caution Haiderali but he does not listen. Saalo man!

He repeats the abuse in defiance. He speaks to his hate. "Drives through Nairowua like a mad bull in his black Mercedes. Thinks he owns everything here. Saalo! He does not care how my family will survive, the first shopkeeper family who built this shop, this town. Saalo!" Haiderali lets out his anxiety in abuse, and then pauses abruptly as if to think again. "The MP tells me plainly that because this is his ancestral land, everything that stands on it is his. That's African custom and African custom is law now after independence, he tells me. That I should know that. He says that's the social law. It is ancestral law. The Constitution is just paper. Saalo madderchod *chhe*!" Haiderali cannot stop snarling angry frustrations in the air like a lion trapped in a cage.

"Don't talk like that! Don't you hear the news? Do you not hear what people are saying? Are you deaf, Haidu? Asian citizens like you are deported when they talk like the way you do, just the way you do. It shows lack of gratitude for the citizenship they gave you. It's disloyalty to the President. President the father, almost a god to some. He is their Saheb. You will be called a racist, a traitor, and deported or killed like Pinto if you speak like that about the MP."

"Now you too speak like your brother Shamshu. Are you also hired by the minister to sell passports to

Asians?" says Haiderali. He knows the sarcasm and mention of my brother's name in that way would quieten me. Saalo! My husband *chhe*! Spoils my family name.

"Kenyatta deported a white man, Robert Ruark. I read it in *Africa Samachar*. He was a storyteller. Even a white man can be deported in twenty four hours. What about an Asian like you? You will be at the airport within an hour. Your shop confiscated."

"Was that lack of gratitude or loyalty, or was it the fear of hearing the truth that your white storyteller was deported?" he asks before I could say more. "Imagine, deporting a storyteller! No brown or black writer, our own storytellers, stood up for him. Did they? Yet, they say all writers are of one colour. They read the colour of his skin, not the ink of his pen. Hypocrites that the writers are under their skins!"

"When will you learn to control your tongue? Think of your family Haidu!"

"I am thinking of my family!" Haiderali barks back at me. "That's why I put on the famous Asian welcome grin for the minister on my wretched Indian face! I even give him tea with four heaped spoons of sugar that he likes. Chandu Bhai of the neighbouring shop would put a garland of roses around the minister's thick neck when he steps into his shop, wishing he had poisoned the flowers. He is desperate to sell his spice and grocery business. There are no Indians left to buy his spices. Most have joined the exodus. He tells me the minister wants his house that's attached to his store with everything intact in it – 'You walk out, I walk in,' he tells him. He does not want his business. At the card game, Mamdu Bhai asked Chandu Bhai where he learnt to act. What film, henh?" Haiderali bursts out laughing and continues to laugh as if to ease the worries consuming him. "We had a good laugh," he says wiping tears in his eyes before they roll down.

"Why are you talking about Chandu Bhai? How will that help? How does that concern you? I don't want to listen to your BBC. What about us right now? What shall we do? Where shall we go? Do you care about me? Your children at least? Do something. Why are you ignoring me?" My anxiety speaks in relentless questions. I cannot stop asking, blaming, mocking Haiderali with questions, taak taak. Is it me or Mama Khelele the avatar of the angst in me speaking on my tongue? Who am I? Is there any point talking with Haiderali? Is there any point asking? He is so full of loathing. He speaks to his worries weighing on him not to me. I worry about him on top of all the other worries I have. I worry about us all. I am the mother. One rash word and we will be thrown out of the country. Deported? Join the exodus? But we are not British anymore. Is Freda listening? I am losing myself. I feel exasperated worrying. I rush to the kitchen. I must start cooking. Cooking what? Where are the pots? Where is Freda? Is she hiding somewhere chuckling at me? The look in her eyes has changed since the hounding stories of the Asian exodus have been circulating. Or am I imagining? Am I suspicious of the woman with whom I must live? The woman I depend on to maintain a living that I alone cannot.

Doubt

When Haiderali comes home, it's almost 9 p.m. TV news time. He has gone to meet his card circle friends on a weekday which is not usual. I missed the communal dua-prayer evening at the jamat khana waiting for him. Now that he has come home, I will start warming up the food once again. I was expecting him to come home earlier at the usual dinner time around the 9 pm TV news. I don't like warming dinner for the second time. It's not more work that frustrates me, but the taste of food changes. Being away at dua time is annoying as it is. I look forward to an hour of chanting and peace at the end of the day that only the jamat khana can give.

"Facts or rumours," says Haiderali running his hand through his thinning hair, "What is what nowadays? At last Magan Bhai told me he thinks keeping Kenyan citizenship and retaining his wife's British passport is a wise thing to do until the cloud clears. Be loyal to both white and black. We are brown, the colour in-between. That's the natural way. Our home is in-between. He told me. His MP friend from Nairobi does not care about his wife's citizenship, nor Magan Bhai's for that matter. As long as he gets his money every Christmas, he will renew the wholesale trade licence immediately. He is a Nairobi MP, moreover a Kikuyu of the President's tribe. He laughs at the Nairowua MP, a Maasai. Calls him small fish."

"But Saheb wants us to be loyal, absolutely loyal to our country," I say.

"That you can do if you are wealthy, circling around like a halo of leaders. Then you can carry passports in separate pockets," says Haiderali. I ignore him.

"If we follow Magan Bhai, it will be like we are not loyal to Saheb," I say. "That would make me feel guilty."

Haiderali says no more, not because he does not know what to say, but because he prefers to keep quiet about such matters. Or is it because I am a woman? He knows I take our conversation over to Khanu Bai and Zera Bai. And they bring their conversations with their husbands, Mamdu Bhai and Rhemu Bhai, to me. That's the unsaid basis of our trust. We tell each other what we conclude after bringing together all the suggestions, cues and doubts that we gather from the words, tones and behaviour of our husbands. Khanu Bai and Zera Bai know their husbands as I do Haiderali. Though the men go to Sunday card game, and talk to each other, each one thinks and is planning differently depending on what deal he is negotiating with his godfather politician. They are a group of five who need each other to listen to their anxieties. They speak selectively so as not to reveal their deeper secrets and deals they make with politicians. This they share only with their brothers if in joint family businesses, not with their wives. As for us women, what choice do we have but tell each other what we think, and how we are not listened to?

Nowadays, when we talk among ourselves our words are laced with predomination and suspicions. In the evenings after the prayers, and sometimes, at the volunteers' meetings, we listen to each other's fears and uncertainties. Our talks juggle around keeping a balance between lack of trust in an anti-Asian government and loyalty to Saheb. Zera Bai interprets Saheb's counsel in a way that dispels doubts so people like to listen to her and ease their worries. No one wants to break their faith at this time when they need assurance from their belief. Like when Saheb says, "Do not put all your eggs in one basket," Zera Bai is sure he means we should have two citizenships like eggs separated into two baskets. Or that some in the family should prepare to migrate, and some live in Kenya. "Like the Quran," she says, "Saheb's counsel can be interpreted in many ways. Whatever way suits you is the best one for you for the time being." She would emphasize for the time being. If we show we don't agree with her, she would be quick to say, "Saheb sometimes says what he does not mean to say so the government does not come to know what he is advising his community. There are spies, and those half Ismaili half Ithna Asheris who come to the jamat khana like detectives."

Zera Bai would be prompt to come with an answer if she expects a doubt coming from me. "Everything is possible when you follow what Saheb says. He knows and will make it possible for you. Just have faith in him." She minimizes my faith in Saheb over her own. "His words always have two meanings." She would say like she understands Saheb better than I do.

I switch on the radio and listen to the Hindustani Service on the Voice of Kenya. The news headlines takes me by surprise. India slams her door on Asians from East Africa, her centuries old travellers made orphans, from re-settling in the old country. "They are not Indians," says India, "for they are either British or Kenyans." India looks at the passport and not our ancestry in her villages when she was British too. I know there are those in the jamat

457

who regret abandoning British citizenship and the old tradition of loyalty to the Empire that gave us security though not equality. They say the English would never abandon their subjects no matter how beneath them they saw our way of living, eating and worship. We had got used to be treated second class, and were happy with the refuge we enjoyed as the coloured subjects of the United Kingdom. But there are some ungrateful and disgruntled ones like my Noordin kaka uncle, and now Kabir as well, who are not happy, and want more. Others like Magan Bai who have a politician-partner-godfather are learning to play the new game with a new government. Will Haiderali be wise, listen to me and put our local MP's name to our business and not sell it to Najmu Chotara? I want to live in Nairowua.

I am lost in thoughts churning over what the radio says and what she says and what he says, and what contradicts what each says to the other. In the turmoil raging in my head, I forgot to cover the pot with little water standing in the inverted lid. The smell of burnt rice flows over to the sitting room. Haiderali sniffs aloud as if suddenly the flu has caught up with him. He clicks with partially sealed lips like mother hen calling her chicks. I have heard that snide clack from the side of his mouth before. How do I tell him at this hour that the pilau when re-heated sticks to the bottom and burns the pot? How would he know or even care to know when he has never entered the kitchen leave alone cook? It's his fault coming home late that the pilau got burnt.

The next day a word for word translation of Kenyatta's rant takes up all the fifteen minutes of the news time on the radio. I feel debased listening to my President's address said in Hindustani. The vernacular service, my own home station, assaults me. I am confused, sad and angry at once. His degrading screed in an Indian language now, akin to Gujarati, my own vernacular, seeps into my blood like snake's venom. I am pained when my President says I am milking the economy. That I am not loyal to him. That I am greedy. That I don't belong to him. That I don't belong to Kenya. He disowns me. My body breaks. His words are vile. I feel demolished when he calls me a whore. Where shall a whore go? How can I look at the vegetable women in the eye tomorrow? How does a whore look at people in the face? How do I face Freda now?

I clutch my tasbih pressing my fist to my agonized heart. I wait. I hear myself breathing heavily. I look into Saheb's eyes, start counting the beads, pirshah, pirshah, pirshah. It's my mother's tasbih with broken beads. I put my future in my faith in him.

Then thoughts enter without a warning. They sneak into me through the cracks in my prayers, breaks in-between pauses in my murmurs - pirshah, pirshah, pirshah when I take in long breaths.

Wewe mwivi	*You are a thief.*
Wewe malaya	*You are a whore.*
Wewe si-kitu	*You are nobody*

Oh my President! Hysterical taak taak whispering in desperation echoes in the pith of my ears. What will happen now? I despair. Gloom fills my heart. I rush to the shower and push my head under cold water. My body stiffens, it shivers, my teeth chatter eating into my talking thoughts, freezing them.

That night in bed I clutch my tasbih, and at once begin rolling it. The fear of my slipping confidence in the President, then in the country and finally in myself overwhelms me. The fear of my children's tomorrow grips me. The shock and distress of exodus plagues me. No prayer words come to me, yet I keep moving the tasbih. The feel of each bead passing through my fingertips calms me, for fingers on tasbih carry memories of peace.

My body pulls towards Haiderali. He puts his arm around me. He understands. I want to believe he does even if he were dreaming with a pillow between his legs about his other woman. The woman in the black township or Freda. I press my tasbih in my fist in hope for a better tomorrow. Prayers give no solutions but they give assurance of help.

I turn my head now towards Saheb's picture. It's dark. I cannot see it. But I gaze where it stands for I want surety from him that my prayers will be answered. That they will bring peace over the anxiety that stabs into thoughts in my mind.

Part Twelve

Two Enemy Tribes
Communists and Asians

Following Kenya's independence in 1963, freedom-development-democracy was the song of the day. It fired a promise of equality and nationhood in the heart of the land. It was in such an atmosphere created by the mystique of nationalism that two enemies of the state were exposed and brought to stand before the people. One was the godless communist and the other was the corrupt Asian who has become a citizen.

The era of the Cold War in the Northern Hemisphere from 1960s to 1980s affected the resource-rich eastern Africa that was also strategically important with a shoreline that stretched from the Red Sea to Mozambique. The West panicked when socialism began securing ground in Angola, Mozambique, Somalia, Ethiopia, the Congo and Tanzania. The possibility of ambitious Somalia extending its socialist ideology into Kenya through territorial claims of Greater Somalia threatened western investments and military bases. The 1960s and 1970s decades-long guerrilla warfare called the Shifta War generated intense racism against the Cushite groups of Kenya, particularly the Somali who are Moslems and are said to have migrated from the Red Sea region. Generally, they have sharper features, slim physiques and are lighter skinned. That makes them different from the Bantu who originate from West Africa, and the Nilotic groups who came from the north down the Nile. The racism against ethnic Somalis that began as war propaganda, has become so embedded in the mainstream society comprising the majority Bantu and Nilotic people, that it lasts to this day.

Proxy wars fought on behalf of capitalism and communism, were managed by dictators and for that they were handsomely rewarded with power and wealth by the superpowers. While recoiling from the double guilt of slavery and colonialism, and shocked by the momentous rise of civil rights movement in the USA and black consciousness elsewhere, the Western media helped to groom a Kenyatta. He was the proverbial African elder, a wise man from the fables, saviour of the black people and restorer of African wisdom and dignity that chastised the apologetic West's arrogance and racism. While he mouthed 'African Socialism', Kenyatta was a capitalist at heart and corrupt. Moreover, Kenyatta would rein back the advance of socialism to facilitate extending of corporate enterprises and foreign army stationed in readiness to fight the communists. At home, Kenyatta was a ruthless despot who grabbed land and committed more massacres, especially of the Cushites, detentions without trial and torture during his 16 years of rule than the British in a hundred years.

With the emergence of a larger post-independence class of white expatriates, who brought in massive aid money, and the corporate staff who partnered with the political elite, the state-engineered racism faded from anti-European to anti-Asian. A handful of Asian Africans had just entered industrial and banking sectors built on generational knowledge of local businesses that in many instances were created and held within families. They had developed commercial networks that were beginning to bloom across eastern Africa, and they made capital. The domestic capital may have been seen to challenge foreign investments and ambitions of the latent African bourgeoisie.

One significant product of the state propaganda against the Asian Africans was that it brought the diverse communities of various religions, hitherto exclusive even to each other, closer together. Collectively, they made an undesirable race. Like their Asiatic identity, and an African passport, they all shared a future together as aliens under the black government.

The Hospital Massacre

Months of uncertainties and anxiety from not knowing what to do, what will happen next, seem not to pass. It feels like all the days are one. Seasons of heat and cold are one. Days wet and dry are one. Time seems to be at a standstill. Same conversations and same uncertainties swing to and fro like a pendulum on the crescent curve.

We were late that evening coming from the jamat khana because Haiderali and his card group were talking, standing in a circle by the mango tree away from the rest of the jamat. They talked longer than usual while their wives waited in the cold with food plates in their hands. It looked like some kind of men's emergency meeting that could not wait till their Sunday card game. So I waited patiently with Zera Bai and Khanu Bai at the bench near the naandi table that should have been the bench with wrought iron lion feet that Haiderali said he would make in his mother's memory. It's been many years since Ma died and Haiderali has done nothing about the bench in her memory as he said he would. Whenever I remind him of what he promised himself, he tells me he knows. Or that he has not forgotten. Or he would ask a curt question: kem mathu khai *chhe*? meaning why are you eating my head? meaning kula kitchwa, meaning why do I pester him?

The news on the TV is about Kenyatta receiving foreign ambassadors at the State House and then about him receiving donations from the Asian business community for the never ending construction of the national hospital in his

464

home village of Gatundu. Everyone knows by now that all the donation money that the President receives like for the annual famine relief fund is a blatant lie. Gappa *chhe*. It's actually bribe money legalized as charity. Haiderali's eyes peer into the TV like trying to recognize who is who in the Asian businessmen's delegation at the State House.

"There are two types of Asians. One type you are looking at on the TV queuing up for a photograph with the President at the State House. The other type is the undesirable group who opposes Kenyatta. They do not survive," says Haiderali. Then he surprises me with a question, "You heard what happened to Pranlal Seth? He joined the opposition party and was deported? He was a citizen. Make me some tea."

It is not unusual for him to interrupt me while I am watching the TV and ask for water or tea, hand towel or even a basin to wash his hands. When I say something during news time he yelps out, "Su *chhe* – what is it?" meaning I am disturbing him.

"Pranlal Seth was that small built man who went around Nairobi from home to home, persuading everyone to become Kenya citizens at the bang of independence," says Haiderali, "He was a strong KANU man." Haiderali pauses again. "A lawyer in Kisumu, close friend of Zera Bai's father." He pauses the third time. "Pranlal Seth was among the first Asians to become Kenya citizen," he says and pauses again before finishing the sentence, "and among the first to be deported!"

"Zera Bai told me he was a communist and a friend of the opposition party Kenya People's Party they call KPU."

465

"All communist Asians from Kisumu should be deported," says Haiderali unexpectedly and as if he changed his mind about Pranlal Seth. "They launder money, and send cash to the communist party. They damage Asians' name. Kenyatta protects us from the communists."

"Where are these communists coming from?"

"The Congo," says Haiderali.

"See what happened at the Lake Hospital! Monghi Bai wrote the President killed only Luos, many Luos."

"Odinga is their leader, a big communist. Sent his son to Russia to study, did he not? To learn communism in Moscow. Anil, your sister's son, tells me Kenyatta would never have massacred the Luos without a nod from America. He says the Americans do not like the Russian hospital project there on Lake Victoria in the middle of Africa. And they detest Odinga's Kenya People's Party. KPU as they call it."

"Maybe, but see what Kenyatta has done! Ole Lekakeny tells me spilling human blood angers the land. Humiliation of a proud people has planted deep roots of tribalism in the country. That's trouble. It's easier to wash off blood on your hands than the earth that is the heart of the people. He says history will not be the same."

Haiderali sounds confused, which is not unusual nowadays. He keeps two minds, thinking mind and talking mind. He talks this way and that way and confuses me. He talks wasi wasi. He talks unsure. What will happen next? Everyone I talk to in the jamat khana is just as mystified as we are as husband and wife. The common question on our lips is: Who are the communists? Where shall we go now when the elephants fight? When the government and communists fight?

"Kenyatta has two enemies, communists and Asians. We two should unite," says Haiderali, "Kenya Asians and Communists Bhai Bhai *chhe*!" I know he is referring to the recent India China alliance. The alliance between the communists and a democratic nation carries the slogan Bhai Bhai, meaning brotherhood. Is he being cynical again? He smiles to me as he used to with that desi filmi look, meaning Indian love-sick look as in films, like when we were young, and just married and imitated actors. Then he puffs out scattered laughs like giggles exhaled in his breath as is his habit when mocking.

Sometimes, when Haiderali is not hiding his thoughts from his words, he talks in broken sentences like he is finding something lost in his mind. Like he does not quite understand what he says or that what he says is not what he means to say. And sometimes, he speaks to me louder than his normal way of speaking as if to hear himself would help him clear doubts in his own head. I suspect what he says comes from thoughts arising from what he has heard from his card game friends, not from his own head. Najmu Chotara, knows African customs better than others, but not everyone trusts him because he is a chotara, meaning half half, half black half brown, half Maasai half Khoja. He knows Asians are playing a losing game and he wants to gain from their losses. Haiderali now suspects that's why he joined the card group.

Next day Ole Lekakeny comes to the shop. I notice he has changed the copper earing in his earlobe for a plastic Kodak film spool container. That would be for his tobacco now. Though retired, he comes and spends two or so hours

467

on his crate where he used to sit. I have kept the crate standing sideways as it was in the same place opposite my chair. When I tell him what I had heard about the hospital massacre in Kisumu, he says he knows. News travels quickly from mouth to mouth and from clan to clan, tribe to tribe. News travels from eyewitnesses to homesteads like savannah fire across grassland. He tells me this is not the first Kenyatta massacre. There are others like of the Samburu people who are cousins to his people the Maasai and of the Boran pastoralists of the Northern desert who are like his own kinsmen. Massacres are committed by one man, Kenyatta, that the world praises as Africa's wise old man, the liberator. Kenya-taa, the Light of Kenya," says Ole Lekakeny. His are words full of disdain. Such words coming from an elder impale my heart. "But here we know, and our fellow nomads know, it's not true. We say it's the Kikuyus who kill, not Kenyatta." He stops to think before he says more as if speaking out his thoughts deep down from the home of fears would put a curse on him. As if some wandering spirit would hear him and know his heart. "In Africa, blood is thicker than water. If anyone from another tribe hurts me, my people will rise against the man's tribe, not him alone. Kenya is a tribal nation." After a while he says this, "We live in Africa that calls for revenge of spilled blood. The earth needs to be cleansed. That's justice, *si-ndio* - yes? Luos say the Kikuyus are killing them, not Kenyatta. And Kikuyus keep quiet. They do not condemn the slaying of citizens at the hospital because they cannot condemn Kenyatta, their chief, their blood. They would say to condemn Kenyatta would be to condemn the tribe, for they are all children of one ancestral mother, *si-ndio*, is that not so? Are they not as we are? A tribe in one homestead. Just as all tribes are. Kenya is a tribal country, *si-ndio* - yes?

468

Massacre is the mother of humiliations for it strikes the heart of the land. To humiliate one people is to humiliate the earth and that is all people."

I keep quiet. I have many questions but asking them would bring out more questions. Am I ready to listen to more when I have not yet brought together everything that the old man just said to me?

When Ole Lekakeny speaks again, it is as if to caution me of the coming changes, "Kenyatta is afraid of the strength of the Luos. They are gaining ground. They are getting ready to avenge kindred blood lost at the hospital on their own earth in Kisumu. Revenge is natural, *si-ndio* - yes? Revenge saves your honour, *si-ndio* - yes? Luos are educated and they know Kenya. What is the cure for humiliation but revenge?" Ole Lekakeny takes a long pause twirling his banana leaf pouch before he opens it. He pushes a pinch of snuff up into his nostril and insufflates before exhaling through his rounded lips. He repeats, a pinch of snuff up into his other nostril. I watch his body calming. "Kenyatta knows. His men are holding night meetings under the mugumo tree pledging loyalty to him. Oathing in way of the Mau Mau. The English know Mau Mau rituals have changed hands the way they wanted it under a new chieftain. But Kenya sleeps. Kenyatta is master of planning night crimes." Ole Lekakeny waits for the expectant sneeze but it does not happen, and the moment passes after three aborted gasps. "Pledging loyalty to the land, and to each other of the pure blood of the Karinga Society as they call. The Karinga are not chotara, half castes. The Karinga are of the royal House of Mumbi of the uncontaminated tribal blood. The Kikuyu do not take kiapo oath to defend Kenya's Constitution. They take the oath to defend Kenyatta. Kenyatta took to the oath to defend the Constitution and all the people of Kenya. He lied."

When I return with a cup of tea and breadbutter sandwich for Ole Lekakeny, he says, "Kikuyus say Asians are dead root stumps. They trip them. Kenyatta will uproot the nuisance left behind by the English."

Ole Lekakeny puts deeper fear in me than my women friends. Kenyatta will not defend us. Kenyatta betrayed his oath. Kenyatta is a liar. Kenyatta the rogue President. Savagery pictured in Ole Lekakeny's words begins to inhabit me. Panic grips me, and I begin to sweat.

At night I have nightmares. Machete hacking, machete maiming, machete killings, machetes … machetes … machetes. Hacking people, cows and even dogs. Kikuyu machetes. Machetes raised over my head. Mau Mau days return to my head.

I pick fear from the feelings my body remembers from those dreadful days of the Mau Mau. Such feelings remain when everything else changes, and the days look peaceful on the outside. But the old story evokes what resides deep within and puts them into the new.

Chai Oath

A knock on the back door startles me. It's two hours after midnight. Three more knocks, spaced evenly. They stop. Quiet. Then they come again, three sharp hits. My stomach cracks. The knocks are louder this time, rising above the raindrops pecking on the tin roof. Stop. An eerie silence fills the room.. I sit up on the bed snapping my eyes open shut staring into the hushed night. Who's there? I hear more knuckle whacks like serial thumps of pestle pounding into a stone mortar. Or are they echoes from Haiderali's nightmare – sounds of Mau Mau breaking the door? I am awake, I tell myself. My breath shallows. My body tenses. Fear alerts me to remain still. Haiderali growls, "Su *chhe* – what is it?" He has woken up and is annoyed, disturbed at this honeyed hour of his sleep. But he will not go to the door. Coward! I hold my breath walking to the door with the police whistle clutched in my fist.

Putting on a throaty male voice, I ask "Nani - Who is it?"

"Ole Kitungat," comes a weak voice over the patter of raindrops on mud pools.

Ole Kitungat is wet and shaking. Raindrops sparkle in his tight-curled hair like they were beaded into it. Misty cold breeze from outside gushes in through the open door. I begin gasping air in and out to quieten my raging heartbeats. It's a stormy moonless night.

"What happened?" I ask.

471

He does not answer. He walks past me to the back room where he stays over the weekends. I see fresh bloodstains on his shirt at the back.

"Are you hungry?" I ask so he may say something, but he does not answer. I do not pursue with the questions on my lips. He closes the door on me. I knock lightly with the heel of my palm. He opens the door just a little, and speaks in whispers through the slit. I cannot see him.

"Chai Oath! But I am not a Kikuyu! Secret oath, kiapo. I am not afraid. Kamau was there. He was the overseer. I saw him and put my elbow over my face. I was afraid to look at his face. You are my mother, mama. Keep it secret. But you know I am not a Kikuyu, mama. It's not my kiapo, the oath. It cannot kill me. I am not afraid. Kenyatta cannot kill me with his kiapo, it's his blood oath. I am not a Kikuyu!" He says, repeating words hurting him inside. I feel his Maasai pride is wounded. It's like the oath was meant to take away his being like forced integration into the larger Kikuyu culture and identity.

"Tell me more, my son. I am your mother. I know you are not a Kikuyu. I will keep your secret." He opens the door just an inch more. His raven eyes in unshed tears glisten. He wants to say more, but then suddenly, as if pushed by a spirit within, he closes the door on me again and clangs shut the stopper from inside. I hear him singing. I understand more Maasai now than when I came to Nairowua as a teenage bride.

Are we birds that we should live on trees
While they stay below and hurt the land
Where our ancestors lived in peace, they weep now
Healing their pain, cleansing the land, is for the youth

Silence. I hear sobbing.

I worry about the boy but he will not speak to me. Horrific images of the Mau Mau from newspaper photos less than a decade ago crowd into my head. Now I know they have never left me. How can they? Mau Mau memory is recent, not yet erased. Can it ever be erased? Memory of slaughter returns at the sight of blood stains. Machete hacking. Humans and animals alike. The word oath itself, kiapo in Swahili, sounds like a threat of some foreboding violence. Some witchcraft secrecy. Sorcery. Death. Infatuated by some wicked wandering spirit. Madness. Any one of these can be the result of kiapo. Anxiety creeps in all over me like a serpent crawling in through my ear. As if possessed, I kick off the quilt and pull up my dress to the thighs. I undo the hooks on my dress. I am sweating maji maji. Water water over me. Haiderali disturbed in his sleep, curses as he wakes up.

"Everything tik *chhe*?" His voice cracks through the tension I feel as he asks if everything is OK.

"Everything barabar *chhe*," I whisper if everything is fine.

Heat in my body burns my eyes. I rush to the karo and splash my face with cool water from my cupped hands under the running tap.

Fear of the Communist Tribe

I don't tell Haiderali about Ole Kitungat. But he knows the boy came at night. I don't tell Haiderali whatever I hear from Ole Lekakeny on the same day when he comes to the shop. Haiderali has to be in the mood to listen. Otherwise, he may shout at me because I listen to buckwaas, meaning no-sense talk. He blocks such talk. Or he may be so shocked that he would go to the bedroom, bolt the door after him and go under the quilt.

It was not until the next Sunday morning when I tell Haiderali about the Luos and Kikuyus, and the chai oath. About the big conflict fermenting in Kenya and how it worries me. On Sundays Haiderali opens the shop for two hours in the morning from ten to noon, and sometimes, he comes to sit on Ole Lekakeny's crate in the pale sunlight and cool air. Against the sun, the capillaries in the bowl of his ears appear red. I hoped he would take Ole Lekakeny's words to his card group friends that afternoon. The talk with his friends would help contain his feelings, whatever they may turn out to be. Haiderali gave no immediate response. But he listened carefully to me before walking away, giving me the impression he had heard that before.

Khanu Bai is like Haiderali too. She listens without even a nod. Nevertheless, I will tell her things that linger in the head. I would tell her the feelings I keep about Haiderali that grate on my heart. Sometimes, when she does not respond, she makes me feel I am lying or that I am too sensitive about little things. Or is it because such news disturbs her too, so much so that her mind refuses to believe it? Some people are like that. Speaking to Zera Bai would increase my worries because she would start talking about this and that, other things and fears unrelated, small issues she has with her house help and African customers at Rhemu Bhai's bicycle shop. She is known to invent incidents and if not, embellishing what she hears from the radio. "She is capable of that," Khanu Bai would say to me, "it's anxiety that makes her that way for she was not like that before independence." Zera Bai often ends talking with words like, "Leave it to Mowla. He knows. He will guide us when the time comes." Time comes for what? To leave Kenya? Go where? Her talk is jem tem, meaning this way and that way, not straight and to the point, especially when she talks about Africans. She brings out her mixed feelings of fear, suspicion and hatred. Again, she would jump back to the days of Mau Mau stirring up old panic of the night runners that sits on my heart like a rock. It would be like she were waiting for an opportunity to speak out all the kept inside worries from all the past incidents pervading the minds in the community. I don't need to speak to her. Her anxiety rubs on me and makes me feel the same and at the end of the day, I quarrel with Haiderali.

"Kikuyus follow Kenyatta and Luos follow Odinga. Both tribal chiefs," says Haiderali some days later to my surprise. He does not talk politics with me. He was having his breakfast and spoke between sips of chai. Obviously, another idea from the Sunday card circle on the lawn at DC's office the previous evening. "But your nephew, Anil, says the two tribal chiefs are directed by their paramount chiefs, America and Russia." I did not know he has been speaking politics with my nephew over the phone. I was wrong, for these words come not from his card game friends, but my own nephew! Saalo Anil!

"How is that?" I ask, puzzled. Haiderali has made it a habit of half speaking nowadays. That's the trend in town today, nobody wants to say everything they know openly or completely. Half speaking is like saying just enough, like giving hints and letting you complete their sentences. Haiderali puts the blame on Anil and leaves it there. I think he has been probing Anil because he wants to know what the boy from the university thinks and then he can proudly carry it to his card game group like his own ideas. And that Anil is another one. Politics excite him, and he cannot stop preaching and showing off how much he knows, and how ignorant the Asians are. Saalo, gaando *chhe*! He is crazy.

"Anil told me America and Russia are the mothers, the matriarch elephant mummies of our dictator Kenyatta and his brother dictator, our Somali neighbour, Haile Mariam. Anil carries your favourite Noordin kaka uncle's family trademark. Rebellion runs in your family blood."

"Does your brother Kabir not talk like that too? Does he have my blood or yours?" I retort, and cough as if to lessen the confrontation. But my chest is filled with sickness. Words are heavy to lift when weighed down with anger. My breath is partially expressed through words, more fully with a cough. Haiderali keeps quiet for a while. He did not expect this from me.

"My brother Kabir is poisoned by your Noordin kaka uncle, his father-in-law now. He was not like that before he married your cousin-sister, Malek, was he?"

476

I did not expect this from him.

"Yes, he was. Only you did not notice," I respond fatafat, meaning immediately. "But Haidu, are Luos not communists like the old man Odinga and young Tom Mboya? And is it only Anil? All university students are led by some Professor Karl Marx?" I had heard the name mentioned by our MP on the radio but I am confused. "Who is he?" I query. Anil had also mentioned him once. "Is he a professor there? I wish Kenyatta would listen to our MP and arrest Professor Karl Marx at once. It was Headline News on the Hindustani Service at lunchtime. They have done nothing about it, yet Luos are burning with rage. I know the rage of humiliation is the worst of all the rages. It kills. It demands revenge. It demands blood. I wonder now if that makes you communists? Diamond told me a Luo boy in his class smashed Kenyatta's portrait. Diamond saw it, and he told Diamond not to tell anyone about it."

"Diamond should not open his mouth. You too should not open your mouth too wide when you talk with other women. Don't talk jem tem. We do not know who is who nowadays," says Haiderali. I hear his concern. "The Honourable Minister is right. Dr or Professor, whatever Marx, whatever he is called, should be arrested and deported. I don't know if communists are a new religious group or a party, but whoever they are, they are a dangerous people. See how the communists massacred Arabs in Zanzibar, and forced fair looking schoolgirls to marry them. They came all the way from Cuba with weapons to make coups in Somalia, Ethiopia, Mozambique, wherever they could overthrow governments. Kabir writes there are communists in the Congo too. He writes like he

477

knows them well, like the only hope for Africa is with the communists. I don't know what has got into his head. Sometimes, he calls them Russians and sometimes Cubans, and sometimes, even Chinese. And sometimes, simply university students. Then sometimes, he calls them Lumumba's army, though the President was assassinated just as he was elected. Kabir calls it a CIA thing, whatever that may be."

"I think CIA is a new virus that affects the brain and people go mad and kill for no reason. It comes from an African monkey in the Congo."

"Yes, like all fatal viruses these days," agrees Haiderali.

"A minister was also assassinated in Kenya last week. Was he a communist too like Pinto and his Goan comrades? Was he like Makhan Singh and Balwant Singh?"

"Did you see the photograph in the Daily Nation? Students rioting. They are all communists," I say. "Who else would do that? I don't like it when the President abuses me, but I don't like communists either. Kenyatta is right. If they are not controlled, Russians will take over the country like in Somalia." The story is in *Africa Samachar* with a map of Africa divided into red and blue. I know such a story makes Anil happy and he follows the news with fervour. He encourages me to read more so we can discuss. He says there will be bloodshed in Kenya like in the Congo, Zanzibar, Ethiopia, and Somalia. He does not seem to care about the people anymore, let alone his own people. Yet, he says he cares about all the people equally. Saalo, communist *chhe*! Saalo, Mau Mau *chhe*! What worries me is not just what Anil speaks but what would the Khoja jamat say about him. How they would ask sugar coated questions over the

478

intrusive ones: "But he is so young. Hot blood *chhe*." Followed by, "I have not seen your bright young nephew in the jamat khana recently, hm?" I know the hm is a masked question appearing to be polite when they want to ask, "Does he not believe in Saheb anymore?" or "Does he say his dua-prayer?" or worse "Is he a naastik, meaning an atheist?" Such questions come from community curiosities, and return to fatten the gossip worming into conversations.

"You talk like you are in Kenyatta's cabinet. Are you his head minister's double?" Haiderali scowls out sarcasm. But he does not understand how bewildered I am about what's happening in the country. We all are. The times are such that nothing makes sense any more. The English were better. If they were racists, they did not hide it. They would write clearly: EUROPEANS ONLY even on toilet doors. Imagine that! Our words like our thoughts change like chameleons, and they go in circles inflating at every turn like balloons at Eid fete on the cricket ground of the Moslem Sports Club.

The next day, Haiderali reads out a paragraph from Kabir's letter that puzzled him as much as it angered him:

We Asians look at Africans like birds released from dhows by our grandfathers when they were lost at sea. The birds showed us the way. They were our guides. They showed us where the land was. Then they came to rest on palm roofs and trees, and the coral walls of Mombasa, and saw us arrive safely. They watched over us, living among us but we ignored them because we said they were not like us and they were black. We did not see them as beings who rescued us from the storm. We thank God not them in our daily prayers for the food on the eating mat. We only saw how they could be useful to us and we thanked God. What we forget is if it were not for the birds we would never have known Africa. We would have drowned in the Black Waters. Without them we would never have loved Africa the way we do. Our pioneer fathers would not have survived without the fresh milk and meat, corn, berries, roots and honey they brought for us. We have to adjust, my dear brother, and know our history. Let me tell you one more thing: Communism has room for us all to live together, and live well.

"What's come over my little brother?" he asks me as if I would have the answer. Then he tears the letter into small pieces, crumples each piece in pressed fist and throws them up like dead leaves blown into the air by a sudden rush of wind during the November monsoons.

My story closes old patterns and opens new ones. Travels, jamat khana talk and letters from distant lands sew patches into the old fabric. Not all stories survive, though. Fear and honour steal some. Some, we put away for reasons not said. Others, we lose because we forget how to tell a story. When later, the question is asked, "Who are you?" We look aside.

My nephew communist chhe?

Nowadays, whenever my sister calls from Kisumu, she complains about her son Anil, as little sisters do to older sisters even when they are adults and married. Like how she used to complain to me about Shamshu, who would frighten her with cockroaches that he would hold upside down by their whiskers, still alive and moving. "Anil agrees with Minister Shikuku and Minister Matiba. Imagine that!" Monghi Bai would say, and repeat to emphasize how much it shocks her. "Anil angered his father when he told him Asians are milking the economy. We corrupt Africans, we halt development and we create poverty, he said. These are his exact words. We segregate; take money out of the country. We do not give our girls to Africans to marry. Imagine an Asian boy saying that to his father! Asians are this and Asians are that - his list of the evils we do is endless."

When I told Haiderali what my sister said to me, his reply was, "Anil goes to the University of Nairobi. What do you expect him to say? He thinks like an African."

Irritated by his reply, I ask, "Kikuyu or Luo or Maasai?"

"You know they are all communists there at the university. All of them, Kikuyu, Luo and Maasai," Haiderali's words don't waver. His anxiety speaks.

"Are you saying my nephew is a communist? An Asian? Khoja boy a communist?"

"Anil is in the travelling theatre, is he not? They go around the countryside performing Mau Mau plays. Acting like barbaric guerrillas. Do you not see their pictures in *The Nation*? Their plays are written by communist professors. Maybe Marx himself."

"Mowla Saheb! What has become of my nephew! My own blood! It's Kenyatta's anti-Asian ranting that drove so many out of the country, and now the youth are turning to communism. Anil was not like that. He recited the dua before the congregation when he was just six years old. He used to sing ginans. His mother told me Anil lost face at the university when they called him an Asian, meaning not a Kenyan."

"Anil despises his own race. It's kaal yoog the dark age. It was predicted. Communism is Godless," says Haiderali.

"That boy hates Mulji Bhai. Anil quarrels with his father because he wants the employees at their petrol station to be paid more. He is like Makhan Singh. My sister tells me how Mulji Bhai bribes the trade union men every time they come to settle workers' complaints. Father and son fight all the time. It's an unhappy home. Monghi Bai tells me her husband is driving their son to the communists."

"Just a minute ago you said Kenyatta is driving Anil to the communists," says Haiderali.

"Yes, that too. We are cowards. Asians are cowards. We speak in whispers. Each day, we go deeper into silence, letting fear creep all corners of the community,

482

making room for hate to fester in the hushed spaces of words held back."

"If you speak like this you will be deported! You are an Asian woman after all. You will be deported like Seth and Shah."

"That's better than being killed like the Luo woman at the Russian hospital in Kisumu! I will live wherever I am but what about your children? Where do they belong? Think of your family! Forget about me." My anger speaks interrupting Haiderali. Frustrations shape my words.

"Anyway corruption is good for business," Haiderali sniggers.

I ignore him, and say, "Anil has become a communist. But his mother says he comes to the jamat khana in Parklands in Nairobi. He volunteers tutoring children. That makes my sister happy."

"Nah! Nah! He goes to the jamat khana so he can date Khoja girls!" Haiderali jokes. "Do communist girls at the university not like him?"

"Women are not communists. Anil says he is a volunteer because he wants to help children from poor Khoja families dependent on reluctant community welfare."

"But for his upkeep and coffee at the Hilton, where he meets his friends to talk about communism, he takes money from his father."

"The parents are spoiling him, I know," I reply. "But what can they do? He is their only son."

"Does that make a difference?"

"It makes a difference. Yes, it makes a big difference when your only child is a boy. Communist or not communist, he is still their son, good son or bad son, still a son. He is their blood. They gave him a Satpanth name, Anil, with such hope. He studies literature at the university."

"Anil cannot be a doctor or a lawyer or even an accountant. Reading books is his job. What kind of a job is that? A job for lazy communists?" Haiderali questions.

"He writes as well, you know."

"Oh yes! He writes in the university newspaper. 'The police are rioting on the campus' he wrote under that photograph of riot police in gear. The Special Branch came to his room at midnight and ransacked it. Did they not? They were looking for communist books and found Chinese Mao's poster. He was taken for interrogation, was he not? He was released only after Mulji Bhai gave a bucketful of chai money to the commissioner."

Haiderali tells me what I already know. I avoid his eyes. He knows I don't like him to remind me of the incident that my family hides from the jamat's ears. It would bring shame to the family.

"Anyway that is past now," I interrupt hastily before he can go on. "But where shall we go? We have young children. We can't go to Nairobi. There are communists there at the university. They riot and create violence in the city." I feel trapped in my own thinking, not really in the argument. I am afraid of violence. Remnants of fear of the marauding Mau Mau around my house return.

Haiderali puts the cup of tea to his lips. It has gone cold, his face distorts in a frown. He gulps it down anyway,

484

for the sake of it, without tasting, the way he swallows a tablespoon of Milk of Magnesia on Sundays to pass out worms he collects eating in Majengo. I nag him to take the medicine; otherwise he would not.

"Your politics eat-my-head – kula-kichwa-yangu," says Haiderali. He sounds troubled and annoyed. His look tells me he does not want to talk about anything. Yet, he speaks, putting his words into whispers like a thief on the veranda hiding from the light. I have to strain my ears to catch what he says between pauses. "Now Saheb tells us not to put all your eggs in one basket... But this wisdom comes too late for me." With that sentence spoken in anger or by mistake, he steps over the doorstep like he was sleep walking.

Haiderali has not had his usual holiday afternoon nap. He does not say where he is going; he does not even say he is going out. I presume he is going for a walk with Rhemu Bhai. Who else from his card group is left in town? Zera Bai is in Nairobi with her children waiting for Rhemu Bai to sell the business and their bungalow before joining her. Then they are going to Canada. I suspect the walk had been pre-arranged. There is anxiety in the air. They are the remaining two fellow Ismaili shop owners in Nairowua playing the wait-and-see game with the government and Africanization.

As they walk they will talk about their usual subject which is politics and shop matters. The sun is hot. It's too early for the two to play cards on the patch of green grass at the DC's office.

Since the day I married Haiderali, I have been hearing about shop matters albeit in parts. Shop matters like how to evade taxes, where to get counterfeit goods, the

485

price of gold, the stock market, and most importantly how to launder money through trusted goldsmiths. All these have been handed down to the sons and nephews from their fathers and uncles, grandfathers and great uncles in joint family business networks.

"Security of business capital is family security. It comes first," says Haiderali to me. "We are a business family and business is survival for us like rain is for the Maasai pastoralists. That has been the Khoja merchant's way of life whether he is a Kacchi or Gujarati. Business is my country."

My story rests in folds of memory, in legends of the land. My story comes from many stories. When the broken stone mill turns, it echoes a song. Its rhythm follows the shapes of rice, and hardness of a variety of lentils. Follow the rhythm of the story like how you listen to the rhythm of the grinding mill crushing seeds of many kinds.

Funga Safari

In the morning, at around ten, Mutiso, my house help, sits by a heap of clothes at the wash place called karo. He sits on his haunches, holds the round club in his hand and begins thrashing clothes under cascading water. I hear intermingling sounds from the courtyard: sloshing water and singing. He is singing the popular worker song nowadays that has a repetitive regimental rhythm like of soldiers on a march. It's called Funga Safari. It's time to pack up for the safari, so goes the song. And that's an order from the owners of the land.

Funga safari, funga safari.	*Pack up for the safari, pack …*
Amri ya nani?	*On whose orders?*
Amri ni yetu	*Our orders*
Amri ya wenyene inchi hii	*Orders of the owners of this land*

More and more, I feel victim to the common humiliation of the brown race. The humiliation has put the rich and poor Asians in one class that had divided us before. When the President and politicians slam us equally as 'the Asians' the condemnation herds us together. At times, my nephew Anil looks confused but will not say so. The communist pride in him stops him. Even the castes have come nearer though marriages are strictly along bloodlines. The humiliation levelled at us all, collectively, make us aware we are one people - Punjabi, Khoja, Gujarati, Kacchi, Parsee, Goan and Sikh. We all are one - Asian Africans.

Sometimes, I think Mutiso understands Anil's 'Struggle' to mean struggle against the Asians of Kenya. After independence, there are no English to struggle against. At least they are not as visible as the Indian in the well-stocked shop amidst poverty. What is this struggle against the rich about, if not against the Asians?

Sometimes, Anil explains about the multinationals, and sometimes, about how Kenya's plantations and minerals are owned by companies from Europe and America. But this is not evident to Mutiso. How can he see the owners who live overseas? Moreover, he knows the big companies in Nairobi have black managers and that to him is shared wealth. But Asian houses, clothes, and their shining cars are not shared with the Africans. At the same time, I feel sorry for Anil for the discrimination he says he suffers at the university from his fellow Kenyan students and the ridicule he tolerates from his communist colleagues because he belongs to the business race. Sometimes, Anil comes home to study with his three friends. But it's more like they are holding secret meetings, the way my Noordin kaka uncle used to with his Punjabi friends when I was little. Sometimes, I wonder if Anil will ever be accepted as an African that he wants to be. That he says he is. Sometimes, when he talks about 'the Struggle' that I think means communism, I see he tries to show he is equal with our house help, Mutiso. But can he be his servant's equal even under communism? Sometimes, I think he feels guilty coming from the Asian business family and so tries to be what he is not. Anil says all his black friends from the university are not his brothers. His real brothers are in 'the Struggle' with him. Can they really be his brothers? Sometimes, I don't understand what he means.

488

However, when they come home, his African show great respect for me as Anil's aunt. They call me grandmother shosho. I like it. It makes me like them too. I make khado chai for them. I cream thick layers of yellow Blue Band margarine over soft Supa bakery loaves. for them to eat the way young boys like – a big soft bread bite together with a big gulp of hot chai that melts the margarine in the mouth. The mixed taste of bread, margarine and tea stays on the tongue and slides down the gullet with the satisfaction having had something good.

Part Thirteen

Two Nairobis

Within a decade after independence, rural poverty and urban worker slums grow exponentially multiple times more than Nairobi's modern buildings and luxury housing. Then comes the compelling pillaging of national wealth: land, mines, animal ivory and skins. Corruption, always, if not often pronounced the Asian disease, is now eventually seen inhabiting Africans of elite families and politicians, and their networks of kinship patronages from the State House to the villages that operate like ethnic cartels.

Hence, coupled with power and rule by bloodline, corruption considerably undermines the judiciary and democracy. The brutality of the armed police and the para-military is blatant and visible when meted out on the defenceless street people. The street people, often the residents of the mega undercities, live without clean water, light and a decent meal a day. So they come to the city centre and spend the day, some looking for casual work and some for food. The government, however, cannot control the militancy enflaming the slums where they sleep. The resistance is so palpable that no policeman will dare enter these cities, and interfere with the dwellers' freedom to live away from the state's brutality.

Thus at the turn of the 21st century, the picture of the black working class in Nairobi is not different from that of the brown working class a century ago, as they were building the road, the rail and the city, in all, the modern Kenya. In 1902, Nairobi's Medical Officer, Dr Spurrier, had noted in his report to the municipal council:

As regards the Indian Bazaar ... Damp, dark, unventilated, overcrowded dwellings on the filth-soaked and rubbish-strewn ground housed hundreds of people of most

492

uncleanly habits who loved to have things so, and were so let. Here was the soil, the "good soil" for the reception and free propagation of the plague once introduced.

Kenya's Minister of Health today would describe the slums as damp, dark, overcrowded dwellings of filth-soaked and rubbish-bestrewn homes to flying toilets.

Here is the soil, the good soil for the reception and free propagation of crime, cholera and AIDS.

The Minister of Health would echo his colonial counter-part who was speaking about the Indian working class of Nairobi in early 1900s. Such is the cycle of capitalism, brown bodies are replaced by black bodies in Kenya's cities, but the stink, the rats, the diseases and the poverty is the same.

"But the truth is," Anil, Moti Bai's left leaning nephew, a student at the University of Nairobi, would talk back to the Minister on the TV, "you want to sell the land to the developers and eat your piece of the independence cake out of their misery."

The City of Nairobi, like a gawky witchdoctor of Africa, is notorious for seducing victims of wars, famines and land grabbing mania into the decoy of its sham wealth and rented modernity. At night, the Kenyatta Conference Centre, international sky-scraping hotels, banks and multinational corporations, all boasting post-colonial development, glow over the squalid workers' habitats like a conference of fireflies over sewage dumps.

It's a thirty foot high concrete bougainvillea clad wall that surrounds sixty eight Ismaili Khoja homes in a community housing estate and shields them from diseases, crime and the stench of poverty that blows with the wind from the fetid valley below. Here, in the Old Highridge

Ismaili Housing Co-operative, Moti Bai lives with her nephew, Anil. She left Nairowua soon after Haiderali passed away. At first she lived with Diamond, her son who worked with an accountancy firm in Nairobi. But after his marriage to Rosie, Diamond moved out with his wife. They have one son called Rahim and are preparing to immigrate to Canada.

From her window on the fourth floor, Moti Bai can see the squalid slum sprawling along the Muthaiga River Valley and the stone wall of the German ambassador's bungalow where the bald headed eagle nests. Through an arterial network of paths, tin shacks and plastic-mud-cardboard shelters, the Muthaiga River Valley mega undercity joins other comparable valley subcities that crouch below the belly of the handsome capital city seated on crests of five ridges that boasts of unceasing real estate investments. Moti Bai's house-help, who is called Mutiso, uses this labyrinth of workercity paths to come to the Ismaili estate on the ridge, crossing over colonies of the urban unemployed, and the labour force. Together, they comprise Kenya's political nerve centre and hope for change.

My grandson Rahim

My heart breaks when Diamond leaves for Canada with his family. Rahim, my grandson, is almost five years old. In the mornings Diamond used to drop him at Mrs Mwangi's Day Care here in Parklands, and Mutiso, my house help, would bring him home at midday. Rahim was my joy in the lull of hot Nairobi afternoons. How I would hold my eyes on him to memorize the details on his face – his curly hair and those black eyes that said to me, "I love you grandma." We ate, napped, and played together until the evening, when Diamond came to pick him up along with the food tiffin. I was quietly happy that Diamond loved his mother's cooking more than his wife's. But it created unhappiness in the family, adding to the growing tension between Rosie and me.

"Mummy, Rosie's chapattis slack and her curry does not have that vermillion film under the ghee. The sauce is fine, the flavour hivi hivi, so so," he would say, turning his palm and head simultaneously from side to side, "the potatoes break, the onions undissolved float like dead worms, the …" Diamond would go on.

"Mowla knows how many times I have taught your wife how to make decent curries," I would say. This is my mother-son moment. True, many a time I have shown Rosie how to cook curry my way. I had shown her all the ingredients, going through the cooking systematically. However, I would leave out some subtleties the way we do when exchanging recipes. Like I would not tell Rosie, I add potatoes just when the curry simmered. I did not tell her I threw in a few strands of saffron after switching off the heat and before spraying over the last batch of cilantro into the pot. Only then, I would let the sauce sit in the stillness of its inside heat with the lid on so the steam would hold in the flavour of cilantro and saffron over the spicy sauce. Even my ordinary meat curries have that richness of taste that Diamond loves. My curries look like the ravishing Khoja kaleo curries. The ones cooked in waist high iron cauldrons over slow wood fires at the open air kitchen for communal meals. The ones we have with pau loaf never with rice or chapattis. That sort of curry. Rosie adds more tomato puree to get the redness and her curries turn out like Pep Tang tomato sauce, as Diamond would say.

"I do not understand why Rosie's curries look so stale thick tomato paste. There is no finesse to it, so jaat-like. So unlike Ismaili cuisine." I would add on more such words if given the opportunity, but that would depend on Diamond's mood because sometimes, he could suddenly change and start talking in favour of his wife. How her mince meat pies are delicious, how her pasta is mouth-watering and how her this and how her that of English cooking is the best in town. Then I would be quiet and try to ignore him. He can suddenly switch in favour of his Rosie. It's been like that between us since the day he got married. Diamond told his sister, and she then told me that on the wedding night, Rosie took an oath of her devotion to Diamond like a good Indian bride that an Indian expects of his wife like in the movies. She made him feel a god, he said, when she sang to him behind the locked door:

496

Tuhi meri mandir	*You are my temple*
Tuhi meri pooja	*You are my prayers*
Tuhi mere deveta ho	*You are my God*

Diamond said Rosie's song was sweeter to his ears than my lullaby and was at once aroused. I did not sleep that night.

Rosie and I don't see much of each other. They live in their own maisonette at Ngara Ismaili Housing Co-operative. Sometimes, I can see the tension of strained relationship between Rosie and me on Diamond's face. Like when his heart hesitates between anger and love for me. At times, suffused with mother's envy, I lure my grandson closer to me when I cannot bring Diamond to me. I see Haiderali in my grandson Rahim, especially when he manipulates me because he wants sweet su-khreet I make for the jamat khana on new moon chandraat evening.

"You cannot have sweet su-khreet because it's for Mowla Bapa," I would say.

"Just a little Ma. Mowla Bapa will not see," he would reply. And so the conversation goes on and he wins in the end.

"You spoil Rahim with too many sweets," Diamond would tell me, echoing Rosie's taunts behind my back. "Then he does not eat the soups his mother makes for him."

"He is only a child," I would reply, though inside, I would be happy.

Rahim liked to play the warrior in the afternoons. Mrs Mwangi had been telling him stories of African warrior heroes and the patriotic Mau Mau freedom fighters. After independence, heroes in children's books changed skins –

497

from white to black. When he had had his afternoon nap and a glass of milk, Rahim would run to the courtyard. He would remove his shirt, poke a feather in his hair and become Shaka Zulu. Mutiso made him a bow from the fagio stick broom, and some arrows from the same river reed broom and taught him Kamba archery - how to shoot the arrow with two fingers without using the thumb. Rahim was quick to learn. Sometimes, I would think he must have been an African warrior in his last karma. While ironing my khane clothes for the evening, Mutiso would watch Rahim at the great battle of the plains fighting the English and laugh aloud.

"Why am I not black?" Rahim surprised me one afternoon as I was getting the tiffin ready for Diamond.

"Because Mowla Bapa made you brown like your daddy and me," I tell him. He looked at the picture of Saheb on the wall as if he were there.

"I will tell Mowla Bapa in my night prayers to make me black with muscles like Shaka Zulu," he replied and went back to the garden to play the warrior.

Once I asked Rahim the inevitable question that adults ask children, "Who would you like to be like when you grow up?" I was expecting him to say, "Like my daddy." Instead he replied, "Dedan Kimathi," to my horror. Dedan Kimathi was the feared leader of the Mau Mau.

My story is told in loops, pining pains of my heart. Hear the silent wailings of my mother's heart. I lose peace to save my vrt meaning my mother-pride and that's the family way.

Intermarriage integration

I have laid out Anil's supper and covered it with white cotton crocheted cloth. He is late coming home; he caused a furore in the jamat khana when he hit Abdul Cowboy.

"Why did you punch Abdul Cowboy?" I ask Anil as he steps into the house.

He hesitates to answer showing me he does not want me to ask him, "Because he hit me first."

"Why?"

"Because I called him tatooro," Anil whispers taa-too-ro, meaning big penis, elongating the vowels and sulking.

"You know that's abusive. You must apologise to him."

"Why?" Anil asks staring at me, "He called me tatoori first. We were arranging seniors seating when the chair I was carrying hit his knee. He cried out. People turned around. It was an accident. "

I know it's an insult among Khoja boys to call someone tatoori, meaning small penis, meaning, not a man enough. The name calling often leads to fights, and complaints to the mukhi by the parents of the victim.

Once when Anil came to Nairowua with his mother, he captured the admiration of teenage girls in khane. How they loved to hold the chubby ball of a boy in their arms, and pinch his pink cheeks on his brown skin! Anil would kick himself free from their embrace, and throw back the sweets they gave him. Because of the girls' attention, the courtyard boys, with whom Anil played football with his bald tennis ball, teased him and that aggravated his anger.

Anil hates his height. He has taken after our Noordin kaka uncle whom people called dhururu, meaning five cents because he was short. The mukhi elder did not reprimand Anil, and some volunteers were visibly seen to be happy after the incident. Fatma Bai the rich widow who is my neighbour, tried to put shame on me through her looks across the naandi table. I could see on Anil's face that he was happy, even proud that he hit Abdul Cowboy who is known for his bullying of the volunteers.

That day, I had roasted eggplant in ash of charcoal and neem leaves, and I had made dry chapattis on clay plate that I normally use to make black millet rotlo bread. In a side plate, I put some yogurt, one green chili, green coriander chutney and half an onion, peeled and sliced in four squares. Anil likes his raw onion this way that he learned to eat from Punjabi boy scouts on a camping trip.

"We expect three chartered airplanes carrying Ismailis for Saheb's darshan deedar from Toronto-Vancouver-Calgary," Anil says the three names like they were one city. "You will see the jamat khanas as packed as they used to be before the emigration started," says Anil. I notice he likes to talk in numbers to me. That is a new style of talking with numbers spoken in English.

"They immigrated to Canada, nah?" I actually want Anil to tell me more about Canada. The fear of emigration haunts me like a pestering ghost that you know is there, but

500

cannot see. Like Khanu Bai and Zera Bai, I would have to go to Canada sooner or later. Parents immigrate to where their sons are. That is custom. That is expected.

"Yes auntie-masi, the majority have immigrated to Canada. It's the second home of Ismailis of East Africa," says Anil with an abrupt laugh, silently cynical, "Multiculturalism, you know. We like that."

"What are you talking about now?"

Anil tries to explain, "In Canada, you can keep your culture and religion. You do not have to show you integrate by intermarrying with the white people or the Aboriginals. Saheb is a friend of the Prime Minister and visits Canada. They both like multiculturalism."

"No intermarriage? Then how do you integrate?" I think of what Khanu Bai used to say, "We are guilty of not intermarrying with the blacks in Africa and we shall pay for it one day." Some of my community volunteer group friends agree with Khanu Bai, yet they would rather accept the punishment than have a black son-in-law in the family.

"Politicians don't talk of intermarriage integration in Canada, yet they promote multiculturalism," says Anil, scooping yogurt from the bowl with a cupped piece of chapatti that he uses like a bowl spoon. He eats quickly and then I notice his ears begin to redden. His eyes shift. His mood changes. The feeling of triumph over Abdul Cowboy evaporates. It's the word politician that upsets him.

Anil is upset because two weeks ago, he was slapped on his face by an MP at his father's petrol station on Kenyatta Avenue. Anil visits the petrol station during his free time to check on the accounts and while he is there he helps around to get to know the customers and, 'to keep an eye' as his father Mulji Bhai says. Stupid Anil, without fear, though politely, asked the minister to pay for the petrol. Anil had filled up Bwana Benz's car personally, full tank as he was asked to. Any talk of politician nowadays, flashes back this particular memory in Anil and he gets annoyed with whoever is with him.

"You Asian exploiter! Mhindi!" Minister Bwana Benzi bellowed at Anil who was sitting down on the ground holding his cheek in his hand, humiliated before his staff and onlookers from the street. The minister then drove off without paying and scoffing as he called out of the window of his Mercedes Benz, "Out of Kenya! You Asian whore! And leave this petrol station to me!" The MP jeered to the delight of the staff. Already, a small street crowd had gathered at the petrol station.

That night after supper, Anil tore up his Kenya passport and stomped on it right there in front of me in the kitchen. He then walked out without picking up his shredded document. The radio was blaring out a patriotic song that's become the signature tune on the Voice of Kenya.

| *Haraaambee!* | *Haraaambee!* |
| *Vuta pamoja!* | *Together we pull!* |

"Haraambee! Eeh! Haraambee! Eeh!" Anil imitates Jomo Kenyatta, rolling up the *Daily Nation* and lifting it up to his ears the way the aging President raises his fly whisk at political rallies. "Tu-voote paamoja! Eeh! We pull together! Eeh! Njenga in-chee, build the nation." Anil mimics the President's Kikuyu accented Swahili, "African peasants leave your farms to me, Indians leave your shops to me. Tu-njenge in-chee paa-moja. Let's build the nation together - Hee...hee...hee."

Anil's imitating the President puts fear in me. What anger! What scorn! What if Mutiso hears him? Anil talks like my Noordin kaka uncle who lives in the Congo. His daughter, my cousin-sister Malek, is married to Haiderali's brother Kabir. I receive long three to four page letters from cousin-sister Malek every three to six months. "One page per month, or two," we joke between us. I would read Malek's letters in parts, and some lines I would read again for she writes like how she talks, intensely.

Kabir was persuaded by my father to convert to the Ithna Asheri faith and he even fasted and prayed with him during Ramadan. Surprisingly, he actually fasted the whole month from sunrise to sunset! When we quarrel over small husband-wife nothings, he mockes Saheb to hurt me. He sees Satpanth with Ithna Asheri eyes. Sometimes he calls me Aga Khani with contempt on his tongue. It's like when my parents argued over small things and their squabbles came to their beliefs. Kabir would say Satpanth is not pure Islam. I would ask him 'What is pure Islam then? To be an Ithna Asheri? Would the Sunnis not call you a heretic?' He would keep quiet, and return to Saheb calling me a hotchpotch faith believer and sometimes a mishmash. I tell him I am happy with my hotchpotch and mishmash religion like he is happy with his pure Islam. I had learnt to say that from my mother and that, she told me, was the Satpanth way to keep peace in the divided Khoja family.

But then one day Kabir surprised me again. He said, 'I did not stop paying the tithe called dasondh to Saheb so I would have to pay the tithe called qhum to the Ayatollah!' He said, 'The tithe is called by a different name but was still the tithe'. He made me laugh when he said how from an Aga Khani he became an Ayatollahi. 'Like the English say,' whispered Kabir to me, 'jumping from the frying pan into the fire.' Now, he has

503

stopped going to the Ithna Asheri mosque altogether. My father does not speak to Kabir. I hope this coming Eid, I will get them to embrace each other so we may live like a family in this small town of Goma. After my mother's death five years ago, I invite my father, my brother Bahdur and his family for lunch every Eid. But Kabir worries me. It's not good to live without belief in God no matter what path you take. Nowadays, he talks of 'the Struggle' like it were a new religion.

How time flies! Sometimes, I wonder if we will ever see each other again, my dear cousin-sister. Let's keep praying, so we may meet just one more time in this life.

In another letter Malek wrote that Kabir's mind shifted between believing and not believing in God. Sometimes, he gave money to the communists. But he worked hard at his Coca Cola depot – he has a franchise to supply Coca Cola in the province, and that otherwise he was a good husband to her and she was happy. However, she did once hint how often she cried because she could not conceive.

I worry about Anil after reading my cousin-sister Malek's letter. What will become of Anil? He acts like his uncle Kabir. It's dangerous the way he speaks. What shall I do? Should I not tell his parents to caution him? We live in uncertain times. I say to Anil, "There is a Gujarati proverb, SHOW YOUR IVORY TEETH ON THE OUTSIDE AND CHEW WITH THE REAL TEETH INSIDE. We must live like the elephant nowadays." He smiles to show he finds me funny, maybe, even old and senile.

"What if Mutiso hears you imitating the President?" I dare to ask Anil. Someone has to challenge him. He behaves like Diamond when he was a teenager.

"He won't report me to the CID. He is a worker and naturally on my side of 'the Struggle'." Anil replies as usual talking about 'the Struggle'. It's always 'the Struggle' for him. His head is filled with 'the Struggle'. 'The Struggle' comes readily to his lips faster than God's name. He lives in 'the Struggle'. He is blinded by 'the Struggle'.

Anil even talks about 'the Struggle' to Mutiso! Anyway, Mutiso is the only one around the house who listens to him. Besides that, Mutiso is always pleased for time off his chores and for some education from a university student. Anil reads in Swahili to Mutiso from a book called *Class Struggle in Tanzania* and he says to me, "It's by a Khoja called Issa Shivji."

"What a nice Satpanth name he has!" I tell him. "He has both Abraham and Vishnu in one name. He must be a true devotee."

Or Anil would read from *How Europe Underdeveloped Africa* or from the one he likes the most called *The Wretched of the Earth*. He names these books like a daily mantra, and so often, that they pulsate in my head like the prayer in Arabic. Both unintelligible. Both foreign to my ear but to Anil, they are sacred. He reminds me of Zera Bai.

Anil would go on and on about 'the Struggle' until he would have no breath left to speak. He would even drum communism into my head, though I understand little of 'the Struggle'. Mutiso has no questions to ask and agrees with an elongated 'aeh' for 'yes' to everything Anil says to him. And that makes Anil feel accomplished.

Mulji Bhai and Minister Bwana Benzi

About a month after Anil's incident with the minister that was followed shortly by the incident with Abdul Cowboy, Mulji Bhai and my sister Monghi Bai, arrive from Kisumu. By now, Anil's two stories are told in many versions as they circulate in the Ismaili jamats in Kenya and Canada, and like the stories of street robberies, and thefts by Kenyatta's family, they reach to a point where it is difficult to know between rumours and truth. Kenyan and Canadian side of the families share mixed versions of facts and fiction first over the telephone, and then in their respective khanes toned by what they have heard and what they imagine. They exchange such stories over their anxieties across the continents and oceans. Kenyan family stories are followed by talk about the falling value of the shilling and incidents of growing violence in the cities. While Canadian Ismailis talk about layoffs and recent divorces of senior couples married decades ago in Kenya. They talk about how their children grow up not respecting elders, and sometimes, about an incident of racism on their street. Then almost concurrently, they compare the price of gold in the bazaars of Nairobi's River Road and Vancouver's Main Street or Toronto's Gerrard Street. All blending stories Asian African and Canadian.

"Beta, you should not hit someone in the jamat khana," Mulji Bhai tells Anil who keeps quiet looking the other way. "And you asked Minister Bwana Benzi to pay?

506

Never ask a golo minister to pay!" Mulji Bhai's voice carries muted anger, mixed with sympathy-love such as that of any annoyed father towards his son who has brought shame to the family. "From the President to the clerk behind the counter, they expect chai from citizens whether they are brown or black. It's the new way to show your loyalty to government officers and respect of their positions. You must have surprised the minister, you fool, bhoot *chhe*! In fact, he must have felt insulted to have slapped you like that." Like a guarded Indian parent, Mulji Bhai's fury from the fear of retaliation by the minister is directed to his son who is the victim. Yet there is father love and father empathy for his son in his reprimand. Will my trade license be confiscated? This might as well be his thought underneath his ire. Mulji Bhai's face distorts with anxiety when he speaks. Monghi Bai brings him a glass of water from the fridge.

His father's words upset Anil. He is still nursing his humiliation and perhaps, even thinking like Rama of taking revenge on the demon MP Ravana in some ghastly manner. To make matters worse, Anil is laughed at by his co-volunteers behind his back. News of the two incidents spread. That makes him feel small, and he hates everyone including his father now.

Partly, I blame myself for urging Mulji Bhai to come and talk to his son. Perhaps, I should have waited a little longer for Anil to calm down. But then he told me he had been to see Manji Brothers, the Khoja street gang, for help. That worried me. He even told them he would like to join them, but he said they just laughed at him. He then went to the Azad Brothers, the Punjabi inner city gang operating from old Grogan Road, a stronghold of tough Asian youth.

507

Children of mechanics, sign writers, carpenters and ironsmiths. But they too laughed at him. A university boy? How can they trust someone like him who has not grown up a Nairobi school drop out from the Asian ghettos of Gorgon Road and River Road, or even from the outskirts of Eastleigh?

"Were you trying to fight corruption with an MP? You fool! Bhoot *chhe*! You will see one day how we can benefit from corruption. If you want to run petrol stations, befriend the politicians. You said you wanted to run BP and be independent, didn't you? The President and other ants that latch on to the American elephant's leg will survive. The rest will be flattened. We need well connected politicians like Bwana Benzi to carry on with our business." Monghi Bai brings a second glass of fridge water for Mulji Bhai. He takes it from her hand before she puts it down. "We will get back what he takes from us. That's the law nowadays, that's new Kenya. You harvest what you plant. Corruption is the fertilizer. You can reap tenfold from what you plant into the minister's belly."

"But how do you benefit from this pot belly of a minister? Big fish eat small fish. He will eat you too," Anil says with contempt. He is not listening to his father. His head is full of communism.

"Don't you talk like that to your father, son!" says my sister and begins to massage Anil's shoulders. He does not resist.

"Every brown businessman needs a black godfather to protect him. Secure his license to trade for next year. That's the unwritten law now. Like the English movie about the Mafia gang you were telling me about. If you need to run a business, you need a black godfather." Mulji

Bhai tries to control the heat in his head. He gulps down fridge water again. I am listening from the kitchen and dicing onions and tomatoes for the evening meal. "Be practical and keep safe for Mowla's sake," says Mulji Bhai, his voice breaking into a cry of plea. He gets up to go to the washroom saying, "Never ask a politician to pay."

"Now listen, Anil," Mulji Bhai begins with a softer tone no sooner than he sits down on the sofa in the same place, "beta, my son, have you not heard about our President asking the American ambassador for a gift of a private jet? That's chai for exchange of all the favours he gives him, like the American navy in Kenyan waters. Like big mineral and trade deals for American corporations. Like keeping the Russians out. It's business, fair exchange on both sides. Both sides benefit. Learn how to make deals." Mulji Bhai then slips into whispers explaining how to do business to his son. I want to hear that but cannot hear him anymore.

"Yes, yes, I know all that. That's why the Americans need to keep dictators in power. Kenya is an ant crushed under two superpower elephants with their tusks locked in Cold War. But how do we benefit when the minister does not pay for the petrol?" Anil asks almost yelling out in anger.

"Don't you talk like that to your father, son!" says his mother showing annoyance in her eyes fixed on Anil's face.

Monghi Bai had told me later how much her husband Mulji Bhai feared for his self-righteous son, and how he has sleepless nights. I understand Anil is their only child. Who else can Mulji Bhai trust but his own blood? In

509

this economy of 'big fish eat small fish', as Anil calls it, who do you trust but your own blood?

"Sons and fathers have fought each other for generations," I console my sister. "But in the end, they are one blood and will be one, you will see."

She looks up at me as if to say, "Yes, I know but ..." and says, "We must get Anil married. Family responsibility will leave him no time for 'the Struggle'." Innocent mother love. Distressed mother love. Anguished mother, she thinks of the only solution known to her. "How can I save my son from communism? How can I stop father son quarrels?" Her look asks. Unlike me, Monghi Bai reads little. Persuaded by Indian films, she believes marriage of her erring son will put him in line. "What do you think of Kassam Lalji Velshi family? Their daughter has just come back from Canada. Raised in a boarding school in England and educated in Canada," says my sister, and then she asks again, "What do you think?"

"Hm," I reply not sure what to tell her. I know Anil detests wealthy families, and especially the Canada returns who call him Eneel that he hates. And worse, calling his father Melji Bhaai. Mulji Bhai himself, however, may be thinking of a safe business family alliance. A Kassam Bhai Lalji Velshi daughter would raise his status in the community. Mulji Bhai may even receive a higher jamat khana service title that will qualify him to put on a golden turban and red robe on Khush-ali day. My sister Monghi Bai will wear a bandhani shawl over her shoulders. Moreover, a girl who speaks Gujarati with an English accent is a person of modernity, not local and well educated. She is above those others who speak with Asian

510

African inflections, meaning local English. She is everything that Anil's parents aspire and what he despises.

I agree with Anil for I feel the same, but how do I tell my sister? You find the same admirable qualities in each of Kassam Bhai Lalji Velshi's five daughters. Qualities that appear like the girls are living in a cloud as if they are white fairies in children's picture books. Qualities that blur them to a distance from the community in Africa. But I say nothing to my sister who is drifting into the wealthy Ismaili city women's company, and the exclusive afternoon ladies bridge club. I was in such a group too, but we were the village type - rich, yet country folks. "Like Tanzanians," the Nairobi ladies used to call us, "desis in European dresses and two-stripe slippers."

Aati! Asians also build Kenya?

After the incident with the MP, Anil uses the word kario, meaning he-black, more easily than before when referring to black politicians. The word used to enrage him when he heard me say it. He even called me a colonialist-racist once. His rebuke hurt me. After all, I am old and his aunt. He loses respect for elders when communism fills his head and words like colonialist and racist blurt out of his mouth like fire.

"I supported Kenyatta, though I had never heard of communists before you started speaking like Nyerere. I supported Kenyatta because I hated the arrogance of the English," I say to Anil. He cracks a sudden put down laughter as if I am lying.

The jamat continues to mock Anil's stupidity for asking the minister to pay for petrol They say, "He lost an opportunity to expand his father's business when the minister wanted free petrol." Some call Anil, Karl Marx, others call him Mao. The petrol station incident has, in fact, become a joke, which infuriates Anil, exaggerates his humiliation and diminishes his confidence. This affects any position of responsibility he takes up in the community. As for Mulji Bhai, he is worried about losing his business. But then, happily, an opportunity comes by and Mulji Bhai makes up for his son's foolishness. Minister Benzi approaches Mulji Bhai for a harambee donation towards his daughter's education at Brampton Community Fashion Design School in America. Mulji Bhai seizes the chance to go meet the minister and apologize for his son's hot bloodedness in person. The visit pleases the minister to no end. Coming home after their meeting Mulji Bhai looks pleased with himself.

"I said to the MP that the youth nowadays have no respect for the elders, and he agreed wholeheartedly," says Mulji Bhai. " 'Yes, yes, look at the university students. They riot all the time. They spend more time in streets than in classrooms', was his reply. Then he advised me about the need to discipline children from very young age, especially boys, to respect elders."

Finally, their conversation led on to Mulji Bhai offering such a generous donation for education of the MP's daughter in America that the next day it made news.

Asians contribute to build Kenya. Mr Mulji Bhai, a Kenyan of Asian origin, led the harambee drive for education of Africans.

Hearing about her husband on the radio, Monghi Bai blushed. When I teased her, she reminded me of how I blushed when I met the English governor at a garden party who praised Haiderali's family as the pioneer shopkeepers of Nairowua who were building Kenya. She remembered. How we joke about ourselves as sisters do!

Needless to say, the MP pleased Mulji Bhai. Not that his patriotism was acknowledged by a high ranking government official, but that, he now felt assured his business would be safe. No doubt, the MP's comment would have sent ripples of self-congratulating smiles in Asian homes across Kenya. How they would be talking about the remark for many days to come, dispelling wasi

wasi, meaning unsure, thoughts about leaving Kenya while reassuring themselves of their determination not to emigrate to Canada.

Anil hates what his father did. But Mulji Bhai boasts about how he finally gained a right business partner. Bwana Benzi would protect him from other black politicians who had already threatened to grab his cotton business in Kisumu and the petrol station in Nairobi. "They did that to Mukhi Akbar Karmali Jessa," Mulji Bhai would repeat like a mantra to overcome fear. "Mukhi did not co-operate." Meaning, he ignored the politicians' proposal to partner with them or at least offer a handsome monthly bribe.

During the following weeks, my sister Monghi Bai prepares elaborate prayer food dishes every Thursday to take to the jamat khana that's about ten minutes' drive away by car and about half an hour by the seniors' khane bus from the Old Highridge Aga Khan Flats. Often she would say a prayer of shu-khar in way of contentment for the gratification for having locked into partnership with Minister Benzi during these blessed days of 'coffee boom'. A God-given opportunity has fallen in Mulji Bhai's lap. It so happens that Minister Benzi is of the same ethnicity as the President. That makes him a powerful ally in the smuggled-coffee business. In fact, any illicit business is risky for an Asian without the support of a well-connected politician. "The 'coffee boom' earns us more money than the BP petrol station on Kenyatta Avenue in Nairobi and the cotton ginnery in Kisumu combined," my sister confides in me.

Sometimes, Mulji Bhai needs to stay in Nairobi for weeks grooming his relationship and the coffee business with Minister Benzi. They go hand in hand. My rich sister's visits to Nairobi bring honour to me. Now no bowl of kheer pudding goes to khane without a distinct embellishment of peppering of crunched almond and pistachio mix. People notice. I feel proud of my family's prosperity. At times, my sister orders clothes from England when Mrs Betty Benzi, a family friend now, goes on overseas shopping sprees with the wives of other MPs.

"Here, try this." One day, Monghi Bai gives me a brassiere she got from Mrs Benz. "It does not fit me. It's from Marks and Spencer in London." Then she goes on to say like it were a bye-the-way comment, "Minister Benz asked Mulji Bhai to put my name together with Betty Benz's on their Toyota importation business. Government contract, you know. But, he chose Anil's name instead." I see envy filling her eyes. It's the same look she had when Meethi Bai gave me the ruby ring she had promised Monghi Bai. "Mulji Bhai joked he would not like to see me become like the ministers' wives – rich and powerful mamas of new Kenya. Then partly while teasing me, and partly in mockery, he added that the mamas belonged to the liberated business women's NGO that's patronized by the elephant queens from the royal family." I have heard people say they don't see elephants anymore along the Nairobi - Mombasa road because of massive poaching. But who would have thought that women from the President's own family were behind the killing?

Anyway, I have never felt as important as I felt comfortable wearing the English brassiere to the jamat khana. I put it on only on the evenings of the new moon we call chandraat when we dress up, and have a small celebration.

Part Fourteen

Second Era of Great Propaganda Betrayal Hate and Humiliation

Tyranny of Ethnic Nationalism

While the Soviet Union was breaking into smaller nation states, marking the end of the Cold War, stories of horrific ethnic fighting circulated in Kenya. Cartoons caricaturing the cultural minorities ridiculed them as some sort of primitive and un-Christian savages, making them nobodies and not wholly citizens. Thus, their claims for justice for the stolen land, torture and killings were dismissed. Ethnic group identity names like Turkana, Maasai and Pokot became ethnophaulisms not unlike the words Asian and Somali in the prevailing political and mainstream speech. TV shows reinforced the prejudice through caricatured ethnic accents, cultural mannerisms and dress. Again, these were not different from the post-independence comics of Asians and Somalis.

Any minority protest or resistance against the oppressive regime was branded as banditry and addressed with brutal force resulting in cultural humiliations of mainly the pastoralist groups. Words like 'tribal warriors', 'bandits', and 'ethnic cleansing' found their way into the media and then mainstream talk, inciting fear, ridicule and hatred among the diverse nationalities. This was not unlike the British propaganda that separated one ethnicity from another during the Mau Mau era of the 1950s. Often, one would hear the minorities say how the President, black as they were, was not different from the English, if not worse.

The culmination of the government's insults put on the demographically smaller ethnicities were the massacres. Traditionally in East Africa, ethnic killings are viewed as the ultimate collective disgrace when not only the cultures, but the homeland, considered sacred where the ancestors reside and where peace trees have roots, is humiliated. To the people of the land, their communal and decisive loss of dignity is tied to the earth. The earth was stolen before their eyes and desecrated with human blood. Ethnic poets and storytellers gave expression to how their people were shamed, condemned and dishonoured through heart rending verses and narratives, creating a body of resistance oral literature. The resistance oral literature was reminiscent of the Mau Mau songs that mobilized the young men in the late 1940s and the 1950s against colonial rule, and importantly, for recovery of their stolen land. Over time, this clandestine oral lexis became folklore that captured the hearts of young men who would be organizing against the oppressive regime to protect their resources, honour and identities. To this day, the repressive state cannot stamp out the intensity of ethnic feelings over claims for land, and for calls for justice for the massacres by the State. Thus, healing of the communities remains incomplete and tensions persist.

In contrast to the resistance arts of the rural communities, the official culture was State manufactured, and focused on the ruling ethnic group's expressions. These were exclusive if not overwhelming and imposing on those outside the Presidents' kinship community. An example of such a culture was the numerous eulogies sung and danced at political rallies performing homage to the dictators as instruments of liberation, modernization and development. The more dictatorial the regime became, the more intense became the veneration drama that subsumed loyalty through awe, admiration and fear of the despots. The presidential dancing troupes were trained to sing rhetorical tribute songs that in time became hymn-like worshiping a god. Wherever the President went, there they appeared overdressed in ethnic consumes. Such performances consumed TV and radio time as national culture.

In defiance and in contrast, the ethnic resistance arts created in isolated and rugged landscapes of pastoral Kenya, were collective, participatory and spontaneous. They expressed feelings that came from the impulsive heart as is the nature of oral literature, and they sought justice. The dissident culture, however, also sowed seeds for the corrupt politicians to emerge like warlords, exploiting and manipulating the humiliation, and fostering violence against the ruling ethnic group. Thus, when the suppressed rage against postcolonial greed, looting and humiliation came to the fore, often described as ethnic nationalism, it was horrendous.

Meanwhile in the urban centres, the first two president autocrats, Kenyatta and Moi, brutally suppressed freedom of artistic expressions and began systematic persecution of writers, journalists, dramatists, lawyers, intellectuals and visual artists. They banned artwork and historical plays in ethnic languages that spoke to the memory of truth, and reached the hearts yearning for justice and promise of democracy as in the Constitution.

Jomo Kenyatta, the first President of Kenya left a legacy that thrives on fear of ethnic and racial pluralism. Kenyatta's bequest also established a compact structure braced by patronage and rule by tribal kinship as integral to governance. This has led to violent rebellions and ethnic tensions that continue to this day especially during the election times. The world arms market that had flourished during the Cold War bringing increasing prosperity to the North and devastating impoverishment and violence to the South, has never thrived better than after the 1980s when the Cold War ended, the Soviet Union disintegrated and ethnic conflicts escalated.

Fatha Dakitari

It was during the same week soon after Mulji Bhai and my sister left for Kisumu, that Fatha Dakitari came to see me at the Old Highridge Ismaili Housing Co-operative. A surprise visit but I was glad to see Fatha Dakitari, a man from my small home town of Nairowua. As he stands at my door, first I note his hair. How white it has turned. His blue eyes have sunk deeper into the face, pale white on wrinkled neck. But his smile is the same, genuine, almost comforting. As he steps inside, I become alert to his foreign presence. A white man in my home makes me feel small like he was my patron. I want to impress him with my clean home, Indian food and clever talk that would show how intelligent we are. I try not to show any sign of nervousness. I look into his face and into those eyes, blue of the deep ocean. He reminds me of the governor I met at the garden party at his bungalow on the hill in Nairowua. That was after the war, I was a young lady with my husband by my side in a smart English suit and tie.

"Six months ago there was a terrible massacre in Kariobangi Korogocho. I am collecting money to build a home for the orphans," he says sitting down.

"I know, it was on the TV news," I reply quickly. Mutiso told me how, one evening machete wielding Kikuyus descended on Luo residents in the twin slums singing songs reminiscent of the Mau Mau. He said they were the Mungiki. The previous year it was the reverse.

521

Luos clubbed Kikuyus at Kibera, the largest slum in Nairobi. He said the Luo gang called itself Taliban.

I warm the left over dal bhajia from yesterday's naandi. Fatha tells me he is too old to work as a surgeon anymore and now lives in a mission house at St Mary's in Nairobi and writes poetry. "A surgeon needs sharp eyes and steady hands of a young man," he laughs pulling his lower eye lid down with a finger showing his eye ball in blood red veins and then opening his palms before me the way beggars on Kenyatta Avenue stretch out their hands and thrust their palms towards you. His hands have loose skin ripples on the outside but inside his palms are colourless, white, and glassy smooth.

"I will soon retire to Ireland. There is a home for old missionaries there near my family farm," says Fatha leaning back on the sofa. I serve him tea in my Blue Willow bone china tea set. It's the one with Chinese landscape drawings painted on in blue ink that Haiderali had bought from the auction when the white coffee farmers were leaving Kenya, some for South Africa, others for England, Australia and Canada. I keep a small napkin toowal on his plate. As soon as he takes a bite, Fatha snaps his tongue smarting with tamarind sweet and sour chili chutney. It is such an unusual click clack, so loud and so unlike an Indian's that's often a compliment to the perfect taste of the chutney, that for a moment I thought his tongue was singed. But he continues dipping bhajia in the chutney after every bite and click clacking.

"With no government in Somalia and corruption of border guards, the slums are saturated with AK 47s. Then we have politicians inciting tribalism everywhere, especially now at election time," says Fatha Dakitari as if he was confiding in me. "There are massacres even in the cities now. We forget so soon the massacres of the Mau Mau days," says Fatha Dakitari shaking his head. Images of Mau Mau have not disappeared from my head. Such pictures do not die. They feed into new ones, refreshed, and seem not unusual except that every new picture is uglier than the older one.

"And don't forget Idi Amin," I add. He comes to mind.

"Yes. It's the same pattern. First, you hear broadcasts on the radio demonizing Asians. Asian hate speeches, then their expulsion, emigration - exodus. People celebrate and dance in the streets but before long, the carnage begins. Black bodies float in the rivers and lakes like logs," says Fatha.

That's true. Fatha speaks the truth. How is it that my nephew Anil does not see that? Fatha is not an Asian but he sees it. First it was hatred of the English then it changed to hatred of Asians. Now that has transformed into fellow African's hatred of each other. Is it not like that? Fatha says it so clearly.

"A politician shows his loyalty to his tribe with vile words towards another tribe that he says eats into their cake. It has become a custom for politicians to build their popularity by spreading hatred of others. That's the politics of Kenya today," says Fatha, speaking in Swahili.

"Will our writers and artists in exile return?" I interrupt Fatha. He raises his ungroomed eyebrows like he is surprised to hear me speak about writers and artists in exile. They came to my mind. Snippets from Anil talking to Mutiso about writers and artists who have fled overseas to escape racism and detention without trial. Personally, I know nothing about all the hoo-ha about these people of 'culture and conscience' as Anil calls them. I think they are communists like Anil, but I do not say that to Fatha Dakitari. I say simply to impress Fatha as if in compliment to his passionate words. As if to assuage his feelings. To show I feel the same and understand him. "Imagine the President banishing our storytellers into exile!"

"Once I heard Marjorie Oludhe Macgoye, the poetess of Kenya, read from her book. She is called Daughter of the Lake. She is white like me, a white daughter of a black country, lamenting the detention of storytellers. But the politicians do not listen to the rhymester's grieving lyrics. No other writer of any colour stood up to protest the detention of Ngũgĩ wa Thiong'o. She did. All alone. The only one in Kenya."

"Because there are no writers left in the country to protest!" I react, nodding my head in agreement. I agree though I do not understand everything said by fatha.

"There are young poets, artists, and writers who play hide and seek with the dictator. Nagging him till he can sleep no more. Storytellers spring like grass flowers as they always do wherever there is oppression," Fatha Dakitari assures me speaking in faultless Swahili. Oppression? I have heard that word before in my house. Fatha speaks like Anil, half reflecting to himself and half talking to me through deep thoughts.

"There will be no tribal wars if Kikuyus and Luos intermarry." My comment surprises Fatha. He keeps his eyebrows raised for a while looking at me. I begin to feel uncomfortable. I know Asians do not marry Africans, but surely, Africans could marry each other to integrate and end the violence. After all, they are all black.

"Will they intermarry? Should they not integrate? I don't know if this will ever happen. But for now, I know the new President's tribe is machete-ing the old President's tribe. No one is taken to court or charged with murder." Fatha Dakitari's tone shows he does not really want to talk about this to me. Is it because I am a woman? Is it because I am Asian? I cannot make out. Fatha reminds me of Kabir. But they are not the only ones. This happens with Anil too. It confuses me and I forget what I want to say.

"The situation at present is how to cope with the orphans of the bloodshed," says Fatha. "We have formed a multifaith committee to look after the orphans."

We keep quiet and concentrate on drinking tea. Fatha studies the picture of Saheb on the wall.

"Is that the Aga Khan?" he asks.

"Yes," I reply, blushing. He knows Saheb!

"He is a very wise man, and handsome too," says Fatha. I blush. "He is among the richest men in the world," he adds. I blush again. Saheb has wealth that is his abundance, he has wisdom and beauty too. God's blessings. He is the rass in guru-pir's verse. To me he is the divinity, the bridegroom in the halo of light and the dazzle of brightness. He is the flute player Krishna, and the final Indian avatar, the unblemished Naklank of the divine descent of the Arabic prophet, the just warrior, the storyteller Mohamed. The pleasure I get from Fatha's words fill my eyes with water.

"Reminds me how my mother used to fix her eyes on Virgin Mary when suffering became unbearable for her.

525

My father was an alcoholic and often we had no food in the house. We were nine children, and we lived like orphans. My mother used to tell us what her grandmother told her about the potato famine and how her family survived looking at the Holy Mother. They continued to live on their farm in Ireland when every relative and neighbour immigrated to America. My mother brought us up gazing at the picture propped on the altar shelf on our wall at home. I remember the picture leaned back on the Bible. That's how I became a priest in love with the picture. Just looking at the Virgin. The picture was my salvation, my hope, and it became my life and joy. A gaze at the holy picture without words is still a prayer," he says in his self-thoughts the way old people talk. But I nod as if he talks to me. I know such talk. I too put my eyes into Saheb's in the picture. I understand holy pictures.

Turning his eyes towards me, Fatha shakes his head with two fast jerks as if thrusting himself out of the pain of the past. Changing the subject, he continues to say, "Mr Devji was a good man, and handsome too." I nod and blush. Yes, Haidu was a good man, and handsome too. "Diamond is handsome, too, like his father? How is Diamond? " he asks.

"Diamond immigrated to Canada with his wife and son," I respond with a smile, though a tremble in my throat betrays something in me. Loneliness? Separation? Fear? I too will have to follow him one day soon. That is custom. Parents follow their children. Fatha does not say anything and ponders. He puts his hand on my shoulder, then drinks more tea, eats one more bhajia dipping it in tamarind sweet and sour chili chutney without a drop falling like how an Indian eats. His eyes first narrow, and then squeeze into their sockets. The sudden sharp tinge of fresh tamarind soaked in chilli has his tongue smarting again.

"And how is Zaibun?" he asks, looking into his notebook for the name. I had gone to the Catholic Mission Hospital for my second delivery as well. Fatha knows Almas as Zaibun because he was the one who wrote her birth certificate at the hospital. Her Ugandan passport carries her birth name that is her legal name though a misname, a kisirani name that was fated to be her tragedy.

"She lives in Canada too with her two children. Both boys." My eyes nip in the warmth of tears as I speak. My small mother, Ma Gor Bai used to say, "When the heart aches, it's the eyes that cry." I take a quick swig of hot tea and then gulp in some more, letting the heat glide down my throat. I wanted to close my eyes just for a second to smudge and spread the tears under the lids preventing them from rolling down. Instead, I leave to wash my face.

"How is Ole Kitungat?" I ask when I return.

"He is the top student at the high school. He will make a good scientist one day. This coming school holidays, he is going to be busy working as a research assistant to an intelligent girl doing her PhD on the Maasai beadwork around the Kilimanjaro area. I knew the mother of the girl. She used to work at the mission in Nairowua. I think she married someone from the Aga Khan community."

That must be Govindji Bhai's granddaughter from his Maasai wife whom he married after Gulzar Bai died. Haidu told me the black mamba of the Spirit Rock sunk its teeth into Gulzar Bai's ankle when she went to collect eggs from the chicken house.

"He is a good boy."

"And how is Naaras Nasira?" I ask.

"Oh! Mama Dakitari is a grandmother of many children."

Fatha smiles broadly now when he speaks. "After she retired from the maternity ward, Mama Dakitari started an organization that's active against the circumcision of girls. It's an NGO, unpopular with the elders, but Mama Dakitari is a determined and fearless lady. She has some success with young girls in schools," says Fatha Dakitari. After a while, he adds proudly, "The hospital has expanded, and it is entirely run by in-house trained African staff. Before I retired, I made Freda, who worked for you, in charge of the hospital laundry. Before that, she washed clothes and linen from the priests' house, when Nduta, her mother, retired. Freda is a smart lady, meticulous about keeping records. Her handsome son, Iqbal, is in Grade Seven at the mission school. She has not baptised him."

Hearing about Freda's son fills me with a passing resentment. Haiderali died, but he left me with a dark spot on my heart - envy of the black women whom he loved over me. Or is it that I am envious of Freda because she has what I lack - a handsome son who lives with her, a job that brings her respect, and no doubt also, admiration of the Nairowua community? Or is it her income as a woman, her independence and security of having a home that I begrudge? It may be because she has a country, and a language she can call her own, and I don't anymore.

Fatha dips one more bhajia in the sweet and sour tamarind chili chutney. "Hmm ... lovely choot-ney!" He shows he loves it, taking his time to say it, before he speaks again, "Oh! I forgot to tell you. I met, your servant, Kamau. That was some years back. When he was working for you, he said, he was arrested, herded like cattle with other revolutionaries, and put on a truck with barbed wire sides. They were taken to the notorious Mau Mau detention camp at Manyani. Kamau looked feeble. His hair was all white, because of fear, I assume. Something haunted him. At times, he lost words and began shaking, shouting curses and fighting with some invisible beings. 'Nightmares trouble me even during the day,' he said when he calmed down. Mostly, it was Kenyatta he abused." Fatha pauses to finish his tea.

"Your tea must be cold. Some hot tea?" I ask.

Fatha raises his hand to say no and continues, "You know the President did not honour the revolutionaries after independence that they had fought for, and suffered. He left them to die impoverished in their old age. Kamau came to the hospital for treatment of his soles that hurt when walking. He had no pads left due to torture. There was not much we could do for his feet, but then, the nuns asked if they could take care of him. As he was being led to the mental home, Kamau turned around, and asked me about you."

What Fatha just said about Kamau hit me like lightning. I picture Kamau, a young, good-looking man with a bushel of black hair on his head, washing clothes at the karo, laughing and singing. I don't know what to say. I feel overwhelmed.

"This is for the orphans' shelter. The mission takes care of the destitute, and the castaway better than anyone in Kenya," I say to Fatha as I give him one of my yellow gold bangles. He accepts the bangle in his right hand cupped over the left.

The bangle is one of a pair made of twenty two carat gold with a yellow tint - difficult to find nowadays, that Haiderali's mother had given me. I did not wear the bangles, their touch on my body brought bad feelings of kisirani in me but I kept them in the hope of giving them to my granddaughter. I would tell my granddaughter the story of her great grandmother Ma Jena Bai. Now, there is only one bangle left from the pair to tell the story.

"I was very happy to see you again, eh … eh. Really very happy indeed," says Fatha as he is leaving. He emphasizes very happy, saying it again and again. He does not remember my name.

The next morning Mutiso is at the karo singing a church hymn. I hear repetitive callings to Yesu, meaning Jesus.

"What worries you this morning?" I ask.

"Last evening I saw a man hacked with a machete as he came out of the matatu taxi-bus. What happened in Kariobangi Korogocho will come to Mathari Valley. I live there. I did not sleep. I have a family."

"Have they caught the killers?"

"No."

"The government will find them. Bring them to court."

"You cannot find your lost goat if you look for it with the one who has eaten it."

530

Storytellers of Kenya

After Fatha Dakitari's visit, my thoughts take me to the storytellers of Kenya. Anil talks about them as some kind of heroes. Fatha knows about them too. I know Kenya nurtures storytellers that speak for her people at various times in history, but I had not given much thought to them before. Was my Dadabapa not a storyteller too? And Noordin kaka uncle, and small mother Gor Bai as well? Was Ole Lekakeny not a storyteller? Now I know storytelling is the breath of the land and it will always be there as long as the land breathes. No dictator can stop storytellers from speaking and singing. Sometimes, Anil comes home with friends who sing beautiful songs that tell stories about the land and also about greed and corruption of the politicians. They make fun of the politicians calling them vultures and hyenas and also pigs with red heads. Sometimes they sing a Swahili song called Pambana or 'the Struggle'. Often, they sing and talk in Anil's room behind closed door. I serve them tea and Supa bread with a thick paste of Blue Band margarine.

Now it's with different eyes that I look out to the valley below from my bedroom window. Sitting in my armchair on the third storey apartment of the Old Highridge Ismaili Housing Co-operative building, I wonder if there are any storytellers below sitting by the open fires of the slum dwellings? The morning sun shines bright, warming the tin roofs that creep up to the thirty-foot high concrete wall shrouded with a lush green canopy of

531

bougainvillea that flower white, red and magenta the year round. Somjee's bougainvillea, they call it. A cracked and illegally re-fixed pipe diverts some of the water from the main City Council line to the shacks and vegetable shamba-gardens of the backcity dwellers. Many of the shanties are owned by politicians and people favoured by the President. On the strength of his signature on a scrap of paper, the President allocates a plot here, and a plot there in the riverine forest that sustains the health of the river. One more word of hatred by the politicians against Asians during this tense time of national elections, and hordes of hungry people from the valley slum below, like the one I see from my bedroom window, will fall on us, looting, raping, clubbing and wiping clean this wealthy Ismaili estate that leans on the wretched of the city. *The Wretched of the Earth*, as Anil calls them.

At night when the moon is full, I see the roofs reflecting dull moonlight between dark shadows. When there is no moon, I watch open air kitchen fires like boat lamps spotting a sea at night. It was on one such moonless night, at about midnight, when I was awakened by screaming mothers calling after their children. In the silence of the night, the sky glowed orange. The slum was on fire. I heard excited dog barks and anguished shouts of both women and men. Noises and voices like they were next door neighbours. I imagined the scene while the estate slept.

I heard a clamour rising to a crescendo but I could do nothing. I saw nothing. In the morning when Mutiso, whose relatives live there, told me what happened, a cold shiver ran through my body. He said mobs of young men came from the neighbouring slum on Kusi Lane to loot the victims of the Muthaiga slum. It's the women I heard yelling curses while they fought back the youth to stop them from pillaging their ragged beddings, dented utensils, cardboards, plastic sheeting and maize flour. The poorest of one undercity were fighting against the poorest of another of Nairobi's undercities. One mud-sack-cardboard-tin family cabin pitched against another mud-sack-cardboard-tin family cabin. Slum dogs yelped with greedy pleasure sniffing rancid garbage in the rotting in the clogged river flow.

At midnight I listened, imagining what was happening during the fire that blazed through the slum in the valley below. The women fought the looters. I imagined mothers standing over their goods and keeping hawk eyes on their children, some wide eyed and awake, some laying on the dust deep into child slumber, all guarded by older children standing like night watchmen under the sacred fig tree of the valley. Poverty has stolen the soul of the country. Now I understand Anil when he says Kenya's utu, meaning humanity, is stolen by the corrupt government reducing us to a man eats man society.

The coming Friday, being the last Friday of the month, I will invite Seven Little Virgins. I will fry potato chips and make beef patties, put them in white buns from the English bakery and serve them with Pep Tang tomato ketchup. The girls will like what they call beef burgers. I will ask Anil to bring a tub of vanilla ice cream from Snow Cream downtown Nairobi near his university. He will do that for me. He never says no to anything I ask for my manta meal for the little girls. It is my manta prayer wish to continue feeding the Seven Little Virgins once a month until I unite with my grandchildren in Canada. It helps to soothe the pain of separation with the hope of uniting.

How I dream of Rahim and little Zahra who was born in Canada, playing on my lap! I will help Rosie in the kitchen and make kheer and puri that I will serve with my own hands to my family. I long to mash pilau, roll it into balls and slip the rice balls into Rahim's mouth. I would chew the tough meats a little and make it tender for the children. I will teach them to say shu-khar to Mowla Bapa with each ball of pilau I roll into their little mouths. We will have a family photograph in the studio with me sitting in the middle, Diamond and Rosie standing behind me, Zahra on my lap and Rahim at my knees. I will send the photograph to all our relatives around the world. I will send the photograph to Zera Bai and Khanu Bai. This photograph will close my photo album. I will carry the album with me to Canada with my bandhani, my emankeeki and my kangas from Riziki and Nana, her grandmother whom they called the Storyteller of Mombasa.

The Struggle

I wake up worrying about Anil. The night's heavy downpour has pattered down to a soundless morning drizzle. I see Mutiso sitting at the karo reading what looks like a page from Anil's university notes. Next to him, slithering up the glass wall of an open jam jar is a squirming globe of plump ants, tiny honey tubes attached to fluttering wings. Broken and delicate translucent wings cloud the bottle. Mutiso has been foraging the ants for his lunch. Gushing water from the tap overflows from the wash bucket. He is oblivious to my approach. I come to shut off the tap.

"Aren't you washing clothes today?" I ask at once. Mutiso looks up startled.

"No, mama, I am reading a little only. Then I start washing."

"Reading what at this time in the morning?"

"Pambana."

My stomach splits. Last evening, women in the jamat khana were talking about this paper called Pambana, the revolutionary underground newspaper also called The Struggle. On their way to dawn prayers, they said they saw hundreds of white cyclostyled leaflets strewn along the muddy paths trodden daily by bare feet house servants from the valley slums coming up to their domestic chores or to look after children at the Asian mansions on the ridge. I know it is treason to possess this leaflet that the government has condemned as communist. They say its Chinese or Russian propaganda inciting hatred towards our good President and his good ministers, our good government and the wealthy who provide jobs to the poor.

"Where did you find this?" I ask.

"In Bwana Anil's trousers," he replies, picking up Anil's khaki trousers from the wash bucket.

"Put it in the stove," I say. "No, give it to me."

I press the paper in through the stove's door and watch it burn as the chai is about to boil in the saucepan. Then I prod into the carbon flakes with charcoal clippers mixing the black specks, cinders and grey ash in with the hot coal.

Anil has secret habits of my Noordin kaka uncle carrying night papers. Kabir too had started reading the banned magazines in Nairowua.

I wonder how Kabir is doing in Canada. Does he have a job or is he looking around to start a business? When President Mobutu expelled Asians from Zaire, Kabir and Malek settled in Quebec. Malek wrote me a long letter to say how cold it was in Montreal and that the jamat met in a church for the evening prayers. She wrote that some Satpanthi Khoja in Quebec were from Uganda, but many came from French Africa – Zaire, Rwanda, Burundi and even Madagascar.

That evening coming home from khane, I begin my routine rounds of the house, sighing prayers as I move from room to room - pirshah, pirshah. I cannot trust leaving this to Anil. My dress shuffles at my ankles. I check to see if the windows are fastened behind the iron grill. I must feel the handle is tightened on each window.

In the night, whenever gunshots ring in the neighbourhood, I wonder whose house is attacked. Under my breath, I whisper pirshah, pirshah, pirshah. Then I do a second round of checking the locks on all the doors and windows. I must tug at each handle and jerk the lever again during the night. Finally, I pass by the red light and look at the panic button blinking. I pray into the fear in my heart as I lie down and hear the wind from the slum valley blow whisper into my ears. I say shu-khar into the night facing Saheb's picture on the wall invisible in the dark. I know he is there.

I tell the story a little at a time when the spirit of the story teller awakens the tongue and haunts me like an ancestor clamouring to be heard. Then, I know I must let go the story I hold in me. But not any story, just the one that needs to be told at that time.

Part Fifteen

Between shifting mantras

Silence is the language of God,
all else is poor translation.

Jalāl ad-Dīn Muhammad Rūmī (1207 –1273)

Prayers of shu-khar in anticipation

In the days that follow, I prepare myself spiritually before Saheb's coming visit. The missionary says a murid should make herself worthy of his darshan-deedar through prayers of gratitude. I offer long prayers of thankfulness, stand up tasbihs of shu-khar-santosh for I feel fortunate for receiving his propitious presence. The prayers and my joy in expectation of seeing Saheb ease the fear that comes from what I see on the TV. I see the growing brutality against those asking for a multiparty government. There are angry people all around us who call themselves Saba Saba. University students are incensed, rampaging through the streets, burning trees and stoning cars. They are looting Indian shops and defying the ban on democracy, because, as Anil says, "The President is divinely installed by a mother called USA to rule Kenya with his one and only party. Americans like to keep Kenya stable. The media in multiple ethnic languages copycats what he says like the ten headed demon king Ravana." Anil has an annoying habit of throwing a jibe here and there when he is watching the evening news with me. It's irritating. It's what my Noordin kaka uncle used to do listening to the radio in those days when the English ruled the land.

That evening in the jamat khana, both Khanu Bai and I admire Zera Bai in secret, because she can adapt so comfortably and so quickly to being modern and English.

She changed to wearing the English dress almost overnight and says her dua in Arabic.

Now, Zera Bai actually can lead prayers in Arabic before the jamat wearing a nakedlegs dress without a head cover! She is bold. Both Khanu Bai and I have privately concluded she does not understand her dua. "But that's the modern way," she would say with a confident smile as if she knows the modern way and we don't. What is exactly the modern way anyway? Wearing European clothes? Speaking in English? Praying in Arabic? No sooner than the member from the Education Board gave an impassioned speech in the jamat khana telling us to drop Gujarati than some parents launched into English speaking with their children. Into their half-Gujarati-half-Swahili sentences, they now inserted the few English words that they knew. In the prayer hall I would overhear them talk to their children in sentences like "At home mayai nu saak *chhe*" and "Lala after dua. Tomorrow school *chhe*."

But one thing we are sure of and that is Zera Bai will adjust well to English life in Canada. Unlike Khanu Bai, Zera Bai looked forward to emigrating. She can also bake a cake and decorate it with soft white cream in fluted spirals, like the wedding cakes behind the glass counter at the English bakery. Some cakes even have a dhinglo white man and his dhingli white bride standing in the cream holding hands. But most of all, we are happy because Zera Bai will finally be with her grandchildren in Vancouver.

"Every night after the evening dua, Rhemu and I hold the photographs of our grandchildren when the desire to hold them in our arms grips us," Zera Bai would say. "We would tell them stories. I imagine breaking a penda and putting a bit on their little tongues, a little at a time so I could stretch the moment of joy seeing them eat the penda. We would tell them stories of African animals, each animal – zebra, giraffe, impala, elephant, dik dik – would be a finger of my hand. The elephant would be the thumb, the giraffe would be the middle finger; dik dik, the little finger of course, zebra the index finger, and the ring finger would be the hopping impala. Rhemu would walk his two fingers on their arms, over the shoulders, and round their little round bellies. We would imagine Shazia and Sameer giggling at the African animals walking over their soft bellies. And we would smile to each other. Only then do we sleep each night holding the photographs in embrace." Zera Bai would often repeat this same story to me and Khanu Bai.

When I visited Zera Bai to say farewell before her long safari to Canada, she said to me, "When Rhemu was ill with malaria and he thought he was going to die, he had his photograph taken with the photographs of our grandchildren. Sitting on the sofa with a blanket over his pyjamas, he had Shazia's picture on his left, Sameer's on his right. Each day we live in a dream of living with our grandchildren."

After Zera Bai and Rhemu Bhai immigrated to Canada, it was Khanu Bai's turn. She had no choice but to leave Kenya because her boys emigrated from Nairowua after their father, Mamdu Bhai, died and they were not interested in continuing with the hides and skins business and living in Nairowua. Actually, Mamdu was shot when he hesitated to hand over his car to the AK 47 wielding gangsters near the Supreme Hotel on River Road when he was visiting his sister in Nairobi. It was a brand new

Toyota Corona. People say it was his dream car for which he had been saving all his life that took his life.

Today I wear the earrings that Khanu Bai gave me when I went to say Ya Ali Madad, meaning May Ali Help You, farewell words that also mean a blessing. Indians understand the meaning of receiving and giving gold - it's more than the money value of the gold. It's about affirming the bond of relationship, sometimes a gesture of forgiveness and reconciliation over the bitterness in families, and among friends especially at partings and marriages. The saffron yellow of the metal is the auspicious rock colour from the earth, its light does not lose the warmth, it does not tarnish or its worth lessen. It's like my friendship with Khanu Bai. Our relationship is golden; it will grow in our memories as we age.

In accepting the gold, I made a promise to myself to gift Khanu Bai a gold ornament in return when the opportunity came. It need not be immediately. That is the faaraj, meaning the obligation of reciprocity that will hold the memory of our companionship until we meet again. That is the Khoja way, and it's as ancient as the Mahabharata.

Between shifting mantras

At night, I take the new dua booklet near my tasbih beads under the pillow beside Saheb's picture. Zera Bai gave me this green booklet with a loud whisper into my ear, "Know your dua." She used to attend a special class on the new daily prayer in Nairobi taught by a young man called Kamru Missionary. People called him Kamrumeeshnari like it were one word much to Zera Bai's annoyance. She would call him Missionary Saheb Al-waez Kamrudin Bhai with equal emphasis on each letter. Anyway, Kamru Missionary taught her how to say the new dua in Arabic "without the interference of the raga", as Zera Bai put it. It's so unlike the way we have been reciting the Gujarati dua in a voice personal to each reciter in the rhythm of the language we all know. I sang to the Indian in me when I prayed. Like who I was. Music and language were one, close to me in my worship, the inheritance of my Saurashtran ancestors.

Zera Bai told us how through painstaking repetitions she mastered the Arabic verses reading in Gujarati alphabet from the green booklet. "I used to get up at four in the morning to learn the dua," she would say. But she has a good memory and can impersonate young Kamru Missionary's Arabic like it were her own tongue, carrying forward his tones and shades of accents from Kacchi that is both the preacher's and Zera Bai's mother tongue. Moreover, she told me one day in no less austere words than a hasty command, "You should now pray without the music of the Indian raga singing in your head, Moti Bai."

And when I asked her, "Such a thing possible *chhe?*" she retorted raising both her eyebrows in an overstated surprise. It was almost like an angry religion teacher's look of astonishment made to put shame of wickedness to the pupil for doubting about God if not a slap across the bewildered pupil's face. Zera Bai's eyebrow gesturing conveyed an intimidating question, "How can you even ask such a thing?" Then taking her time over an extended sigh, indicating exasperation, she said, "Everything is possible if you put your mind to it. Be a pure Musalman, Moti Bai. Leave your Hindu-vera behind you. When we crossed the Black Waters, we left our castes behind, and with that the old religion, and all those Hindu-ways." I knew she meant my Indian habits and Satpanth, the religion of my ancestors. Does she really believe in what she tells me? Or is it a put on, a show to say she is in step with the modern age? Acting modern.

Thoughts of the day when left unspoken and supressed because of fear or shame, return at night yelling to be heard. They ask me, "Does Satpanth not live in the vernacular? Do I not call to the indigenous in me in worship?" I felt like I was losing the ground under me, so much so that I never talked about the Arabic prayers again to Zera Bai, or in fact, to anyone else. Not even to Khanu Bai. What hurt me most was Zera Bai's sorry look and the clenched teeth smile that made me feel not faithless but worse, not loyal to Saheb.

It so happened that one evening at the prayers, sitting with my legs folded in palothi listening to the Arabic dua, my pachedi-shawl over my head, my eyelids down, my head tilted slightly up, the way I sit to listen to the sacred song of guru-pir, panic seized me. I felt the melody of worship in me had vanished from my jamat khana! I could not hear it in the new dua-prayer. The sacred was broken. My jamat khana was suddenly foreign to me. At that moment like a flash, I resolved to learn the new dua in Arabic lest I lose my worship altogether, and with that, lose Saheb. I will put Satpanth to exile. Into concealment of shame for it's not the true religion. I have to be a pukka Moslem.

Now I think of Zera Bai every night when I read to learn to pray. When the opening verse of the new prayer is said without the familiar poetry of the raga, it rings brazen in my ears.

> *Bismillahahir-rahnanir-rahim - In the name of Allah, the most beneficent, the most merciful*
>
> *Al hamdu lillahi rabbil 'aalameen - All praise is due to Allah, the Lord of the worlds*
>
> *Ar-rahmanir Raheem - The most beneficent, the most merciful*

I try to sing the Quranic verse in the raga of the Saurashtran chant with the hope that it will bring music of worship back to me. I cheat but that's what I know. I repeat the lie. But the verses in Arabic stand at a distance from the codes of my heart. I keep reciting. Bismillahah contests with the hum of Gujarati dua in my body's memory trained a Satpanth from the day I learned to speak. I say each line over and over again:

> *There is no God but God*
>
> *There is no God but God*

I tell myself, if I say these lines for a long time, every day, three times a day, concentrating completely like I did to learn the math table, Arabic's beauty will unlock and its rass will seep into me. I try to block the meddling of the

Vedic melodies of the ginans in my head. It's the old religion nagging the new one on my tongue.

Again and again, I strive to recite the Quranic verses the way Zera Bai said I should. The lines do not stir my feelings like the old dua in Gujarati verse but I continue. The shine and shimmer in the words do not come forth the way it does in the song of guru-pir but I try. The pir parent of Satpanth was Saurashtra's bard when the Moghuls ruled. His words shine in my heart like my bandhani's zari florets in my eyes. His melodies are my dua to Saheb like the emankeeki is to the Maasai when they sing. How do I break my heart from my mind? I will try to wean my stubborn heart away from the Satpanth like a baby from the breast. I will try to know Arabic sounds reading from the green booklet and draw make-believe feelings from them. But they come bashing to my ears every time I roll my tongue to say them. Hard memorized repetitions without a melody that I can recognize. I can barely say them aloud, let alone remember them. Another attempt.

Bismillahahir-rahnanir-rahim - In the name of Allah, the most beneficent, the most merciful

Al hamdu lillahi rabbil 'aalameen - All praise is due to Allah, the Lord of the worlds

The stanza muffles on my lips. I fumble. My tongue trips over words awkward to its turn. Forgive me, Ya my Mowla Saheb, for I sin! I cannot follow thee yet I thee love. I know each word though foreign to my ear, is still a prayer. I must try again and not deny Arabic because I do not understand it. I must respect the faith of the new age.

Zera Bai's voice rings in my ears: "Arabic's radiance will come with practice, patience and perseverance. 'Remember the three p sisters', said Missionary Saheb

Kamrudin Bhai." Zera Bai says the three p sisters - practice, patience, perseverance in English like an English schooled missionary and explains the rest in Gujarati also like a missionary. "You will learn in time. For now you need to keep the new prayer words in your mind, even when your body doesn't feel them. More Arabic in you, closer you are to God. It's a matter of practice, patience, perseverance," she repeats the English words looking into my eyes like an impatient religion teacher waiting for his pupil to err so he may have an opportunity to belittle her and show his authority.

I want to tell Zera Bai my worship is of the poet in me. My worship is the melody. It's the canto of the Satpanth ginan. The verse that lights my heart like a match to the wick of a candle. That's what evokes the asal, meaning the origin, in me, and I sing with my ancestors for we are one in the chorus offered to Saheb. I want to tell Zera Bai my worship is of the ancient in me. It is the native artist who evokes the images, patterns and colours, all are one in my devotion.

And when I ask Zera Bai why we do not read the Quran in Kacchi or Gujarati, she sighs, as if to say, "What can I tell you now? Your ignorance exasperates me." Then, straightaway, she would start explaining like I were a child, "Learn to pray in Arabic like how we learned to calculate math tables in Gujarati. Did we not train ourselves to memorize the tables before we knew how to calculate?" She sings in tal beat rhythm, "4 times 2 equals 8, 4 times 3 equals 12 , 4 times 4 equals 16. Right, *nah*?" At the tip of her tongue is the implicit question, "How ignorant can you be, Moti Bai?"

Zera Bai looks down on me. I feel it. Makes me small but worse, unfaithful to Saheb. I cannot recite modern prayers because I cannot commit Arabic words to memory, and its sounds do not take to my Indian ears. My ears do listen, but they hear differently. Can my tongue shape words that the ear does not hear as it should? Guilt bites me. I try again. Am I naastik non-believer? Am I no longer a Satpanthi? Saheb's murid no more? His devotee no more because I cannot pray in Arabic? Was the religion of my ancestors a lie then because they did not pray in Arabic? When I cannot see his avatars in the divine sounds that the vernacular in me summons, I do not get the fulfilment of devotion. Doubts break me for I love Saheb. Saheb is my faith. Tobha, tobha, – forgive me, forgive me. Shall I deny Arabic or deny myself? My conscience conflicts. One night, I say I will not pray in Arabic. Another night, guilt overwhelms me. I try out Arabic prayer once again.

My guilt torments me. Fear of no longer knowing Saheb in worship torments me. Doubts assail me. Is it shaitan, the devil who speaks in my head? Is it Mama Khelele? Then I ask myself: How can I memorize the dua in Arabic when I cannot not even pronounce Allah? Zera Bai showed me how to say Allah circling her red lipstick lips through which hurried out an inflated Aal-laah. It was partly a throat exhale, partly a word said with the tongue flicked from the palette. Do I even hear Allah as an Arab does, so I can say it how he says it? Am I reluctant to change or simply lazy? Self-doubting questions fill me before I close my eyes to sleep. But sleep evades me. I need to sing the old dua in Gujarati, in parts, in its raga to break the current of qualms rushing into my head so I may sleep.

550

In time, after months of rote recitations three times a day, I can read the Quranic verses in Gujarati script from the green booklet. However, I am too embarrassed to say them before anyone, not even Anil. Though Arabic words now sit on my obstinate tongue, heavy as they are to lift them up into a verse to sing, its melody is yet to reach me. But I feel satisfaction in my heart for I have followed Saheb's wish. That would please him and that is my faith. It's the faith I know, not Arabic, that's just a language, or the Quran, that's just a book I cannot read. Nor the new curled-over letters into letters like tangled knitting strings that they tell me are the sacred sounds of 'Allah' and 'Ali', and 'Bismillah'. In my heart, it's Saheb's smile, his picture on the wall that matters.

So my story closes the old and opens the new that we adopt and make it our own like copying dress designs from women's fashion magazines that come to us from England and America and we call it modern.

Shika!

We were on our way to the evening worship in the seniors' khane bus when a boy in a tattered yellow and black Tusker T-shirt and khaki pants hurtled out of the roadside bushes running alongside the bus. My look fell on him. His eyes pleaded me to save him. He had Supa Bread loaf under his crooked elbow. Someone behind him shouted, "Shika, catch him!" one more shout repeated like an echo "Shika, catch him!" And then a cascade of cries poured around the bus as if falling from the sky. "Shika, catch him! Circumcise him! Mwivi thief!" In no time, there were a thousand voices sang a chorus, "Circumcise! Circumcise! Thief! Thief! Shika! Shika!"

Yelling reverberated in the neighbourhood and as many people with knives as with sticks, emerged as if from the grass. Others came from the walled Asian houses along Wangapala Road on the high ridge that skirts the Muthaiga Valley slum. Within minutes, a crowd surrounded the boy. They called him the uncircumcised, meaning he was from the Lake region and therefore of the other ethnicity that supported the opposition party. Blood streamed down his head to his muddy bare feet cracked with lines on both the heels, his toe nails were invisible under caked dirt. Through the window of the slowly moving bus, I saw four men shoving the screaming, pleading, remorseful boy to the ground. The louder he screamed the greater was the laughter. Then came the bellowing, "Lace him! Lace him!" Delightful, almost a celebratory excitement filled the air.

552

Some shouted back, "Leave him! He is circumcised! He is one of us!" But their pleas were drowned in the cheering that thrilled the mob as they jumped around the writhing flames like warriors spearing a ferocious beast that they had already vanquished.

I put my face into my pachedi-shawl patting sweat over my forehead. The bus had stopped unable to steer away from the crowd around it. Abdul, the driver tells us to keep the windowpanes up. Then he gets up to lock the door and makes a round to check our windows tapping his finger on his lips as he passes by. No words, not even pirshah, could come out of my mouth. My fingers would not count the beads of my tasbih running through them. Even today, I sweat whenever the boy's face in an inferno stands before me, his eyes beseeching me to help him. We sat in the bus, hushed, shocked, terrified, and I did nothing to save the boy, afraid even to open the window. I remembered when returning to Nairowua with six month old Diamond in my lap, I did not, but I could have thrown water in my Fanta bottle to the two Maasai women standing in a hole digging brown slime. What could I have done now that would not have put me and other seniors in the bus at risk? I ask myself in consolation.

Gradually the bus moved away from the horror to the jamat khana in Parklands where tonight, we would be celebrating Saheb's coming visit. The anticipation of his darshan-deedar surges joy in me, wiping away the screams of the slum boy rolling in flames. Saheb's voice will fill the jamat khana and flow over the turbulence. For the blessings of Saheb's visit I would say lakh lakh shu-khars, meaning hundreds of thousands of words of gratitude, from my heart.

553

That night my body tries to quieten the fear over the double guilt in my irresolute Indian head. I try to put Arabic prayer over Gujarati supplications etched in my mind. I put them into the horror of unyielding images. But the pictures of the mind harden like layers of old paint. The crust is difficult to scrape off with words even holy words. My body feels isolated by the Arabic prose that lies clothed in Gujarati script in the little green book under my pillow beside my tasbih beads. Yet, I must continue, for my love for Saheb is deep, and as true as his picture by my bedside. I see him wearing a colourful Indian turban. He smiles. I put his face before the horror of the boy in the fireball. I put his picture into my guilt and into the fear in my eyes as I close them closing the day as Zera Bai would, repeating verses in Arabic reading from Gujarati letters. Saheb's being stills me. Soon he will step on the African soil, onto the red carpet from the street, and walk under the chandeliers lighting his passage along the corridor of old stone jamat khana of downtown old Nairobi. His presence will fill the ancient stone building and our hearts.

My jamat khana

The stone jamat khana of my childhood stands at the corner of two roads: Moi Avenue that used to be Government Road, and Tom Mboya Street that used to be Victoria Street, and it faces Biashara Street that was the Indian Bazaar, leading to Jugu Bazaar, which is Jugu Lane now. Here stood Dadabapa's bead and blanket duka-store where we lived in a tin house on granite stilts and granite stone steps where I would sit in the sun and dream what I would do when I was an adult. When Saheb enters my beloved jamat khana, it will glow in the African night. It will flare up a thousand electric bulbs, arching every window and door blinding the darkness. Baitul Khayal, the hall of meditation, will shimmer regal again under the copper diadem tower that keeps watch over the sleeping city sitting on five ridges and five valleys. I will venerate Saheb like Radha venerating Krishna. His appearance, my holy communion in the house of ginans, flowers and his images, my jamat khana:

> *I will venerate thee with showers of rose petals*
> *Nay with fresh jasmine buds*
> *With tuberose nargis*
> *And rich fragrances of sandalwood*
> *Nay my Lord, prince bridegroom*
> *I will venerate thee with showers of pearls*

I think of how Nairobi slumbers at night, resting its weary head on the soft shoulder of the Great African Rift Valley awaiting Saheb's visit. The ancient valley, where the woman was born and from where began the great migration of the human race to the five continents so it says in this month's *Africa Samachar*. The night comforts the city's weariness of its many changes that I have seen in my lifetime due to maendeleo. Maendeleo in Swahili means going ahead that is also called development or becoming modern. Maendeleo has created a sparkling upper city of Corporation Empire when the other one faded. Nairobi is capital city of skyscrapers of steel, concrete and glass. Concurrently, I also know from TV and newspaper pictures, there also exists an undercity that spreads in maendeleo's shadow. The city that hosts the descendants of rural cultures strained by poverty, loss of land and conflicts. The three blights are countrywide and common to all no matter what the ethnicity. All this I pick up here and there, and listening to everyone around me especially my house help Mutiso and Anil, my angry communist nephew. When we go on the Sunday afternoon drive he shows me rich people's homes where there were once forested river valleys. Then he shows me the slums thriving like maggots in the wealthy's waste on the other side.

A very fine chance

Returning to my post, a space allocated to me as a volunteer of the women's Saafai Cleaning Committee, I stand behind the scouts in khaki uniforms lined up on either side of the red carpet rolled out for Saheb. The red carpet will take him and his entourage of robed and gold turbaned elders, and their wives in silk saris, to the prayer hall on the second floor.

The music that's played today has its own mesmerizing nostalgia of bygone days. It educes a celebratory note, the repeated monotonous thuds of the scout master's drum recalling memories of marches of such previous visits of Saheb when we were little, curious and joyous. Then the long awaited shrill from the scoutmaster's whistle, identical to the one used by the Kenya Police, streaks through the air like a siren. At once, the band strikes up Noor-e-Rasul-illah, the tune that stops my breath. The tune that salutes Saheb. The tune that celebrates Noor the Light. The tune that calls upon the Light of God's Prophet to shine on us. Stillness grips the air all around.

Saheb steps onto the cushioned red carpet rolled out from his car door up to the elevator. He enters the passageway. Abruptly, all camera flashes stop, as if the batteries died. Prayer of the salwat in wind murmurs flow like gentle ocean waves washing around him, repetitively lapping and overlapping in a current of whispers. My lips move in unison with the words of many, inhaling exhaling, each breath a purifying thrust of air in-out, out-in. I prepare for the first instant of his appearance. It would be the most auspicious instant of his darshan-deedar, the mystical meeting brought to my expectant eyes taking in the first glimpse of him that would bring serenity over the turbulence that surrounds me. My body is still, my breath abated. Saheb to come, Light to manifest. Then it happens. The moment of his emergence into the corridor of chandeliers like a crack of soundless lightning, lasting a split second of radiance between day and night. That radiance touches me; watery warmth smarts my eyes. It is as if Saheb's picture by my bedside comes to life through the halo of lights arching the door. A frisson runs through my body. When Light fills the heart, the eyes cry. I trance standing still, falling into nothingness as if I were at the portal of life and death. He comes closer, the distance between me and the living picture shortening. I curb the hysteria seizing me. He passes, the garb of avatar. The one who would reveal his true self at death when the cloud of mystery of Satpanth vaporizes, for who knows if the pillar she holds in darkness is gold or silver or mere stone? He turns around to talk to elders walking behind him, their heads bowed, hands clasped in front left over the right, and eyes intently lowered. In a split second, Saheb's luminous glance turns lucid. It enters me. I feel it seizing my body. A powerful yet gentle brightness transcends his look and a current-like sensation like no other sensation grips me rippling through my body. All in a second. My hand gesturing over my face in an Arabic mantra waits at my lips transfixed. I stand riveted in his brilliance. As pure a warmth as of a new-born baby at my breast skims over me. It's not the warmth of sunlight nor of fire, a star nor water. It's the feeling of warmth in the body and mind combined that comes from without yet does not touch any of the five senses as I know them. Is this the moment of Light? The numbness, the radiance, the absolute bliss of Light in a split second yet timeless? Is this what missionary Shivji Bhagat described how it would be when at death the lesser light of the mortal soul merges into the bigger Light of Divinity?

So hypnotic is the moment that it brings together the dead and the living into the aura hanging in the corridor of the jamat khana. Before I know what happened, Saheb passes me adorned in a robe of deep cream silk and interlocking Indian paisley and a black silk felt hat. His picture merges into the picture of older Saheb in a halo of avatars at Dadabapa's altar. There is calmness in his measured steps and movements of his hand, falling and raising again to the forehead in salaam - spreading peace and blessings. He walks like a cresting wave over his murids awakening a noble moment of meditation into those hearts that know him. Then, he disappears into the prayer hall where they sit, holding in their breath in expectant silence, a gathering of the Satpanth Khoja of an ancient order of Hindustan in an African city. Still ancient, and still hidden, after two hundred years, or even more, in the new country.

Dadabapa used to say our spirit fledges in Saheb's darshan-deedar and the Saurashtran song that nourishes it. He spoke like it were an intonation, "The sight of darshan-deedar and the sound of the native ginan are the stewards of the spiritual in the desolate heart of Africa. Today, it is so as it was when I arrived at the old slave port of stone town Mombasa. As it had been in the old country so it is in the new."

Standing spelled by the vision just vanished, I feel another sensation from without grip me. I sense Haiderali. Then immediately Dadabapa fills the silent space followed by Ma Gor Bai, Meethi Bai, and my own mother, Rai Bai, whom I had hardly known. I see them all, beyond the five senses. They linger in the moment of grandeur and say nothing. Their aura hovers around me until I am suddenly awakened by Zubeda's hysterical saar saar nose sobbing beside me. Inside, I say shu-khar for the prostitute's sins are washed away seeing Saheb and she cries with joy and in gratitude and freedom.

Then, a commotion coming from the prayer hall surges like a tide on the full moon night. It alerts me. Another flow of whispers in waves of hushed awe comes to my ears: Widow Hir Bai is at Saheb's feet in dast bosi, the ancient gesture of reverence of the Satpanth murid as in the ginan:

At Saheb's feet the murid veiled
Sati breaks her string of pearls
Picking each bead she venerates
Head bowed so low to the ground
So many, so long picking pearls one one one
Thus she thee venerates
Saheb at thy feet

I tell no one how when Saheb turned around, the Light of his darshan-deedar eyes shone into me. I am blessed, enthralled. I tell no one about the spirit presence of my family. We congratulate each other, whoever we meet. We are all blessed with a shared feeling of a very fine chance of darshan-deedar, and we reminisce comparing with other fine chances in the past. We call each other the fortunate ones, kissing, hugging and congratulating again and over again. We agree that this time, we had the best of all the fine chances. A sense of contentment fills me. In my

560

heart, I believe it was meant to be that in that one unexpected fleeting second, I would rise to a new plane. Sometimes, what one prays for all lifelong happens in a split moment. It was like a dream. I count my tasbih beads whispering shu-khar-santosh-shu-khar-santosh over and over again. The prayer helps me to be humble, and contains my brimming pride within me so it does not light up my face and attract the jealous eye.

The warm air in the jamat khana corridor is still and dense with perfumes, Arabic, Indian and European. Incense and breath mix with the humid heat of bodies, armpit sweat over deodorants under tight sari blouses, stiff shirts beneath woollen suits, and dresses wrapped over in shawls and sweaters on this tropical night. Outside, the jamat khana glows with a thousand bulbs. Each arch of the window and doorframe of the three storeyed chiselled granite structure is lighted like it were a spotted outline of arches sketched on the slate of Africa at dusk. The glow runs in four directions through street corridors illuminating the hungry and homeless huddled below shop windows. Some are already submerged under palm mats, gunia-sacks, cardboard boxes, plastic sheeting and what not. In their makeshift dormitories, they will wait out the cold of the highland night air of Nairobi in solitude when the celebrating Ismailis have gone to their plush suburban homes and the lights are switched off.

Part Sixteen

Snap of the umbilical cord

By the late sixties, the Asian in Kenya was the man *In a Brown Mantle* as Peter Nazareth, the writer, titled his 1972 novel that prophesized the expulsion of his people. For the larger skilled, small shopkeepers and office wage earning class, who maintained the service, commerce and communication infra-structure of East Africa, it was an enigma. "Where do we belong?" they asked. In other words, "What is our identity?"

It was now obvious what they had been doubting and what the elders had been asking at their Sunday card games in the park, "Are we exchanging White racism for Black?" They had finally to accept that they were indeed Paper Citizens. That the Constitution like their citizenship was mere paper. That racial prejudice in East Africa, mirroring the nationalist polemics around 'The Asian Question', was put to law as was 'The Jewish Question' in Europe. That, like the debate on 'The Jewish Question', the debate on 'The Asian Question' was empty of any meaning. Except to weaken and break the communities, directly or indirectly, compelling many to leave.

During the previous two hundred years, Asian families had been moving around the three East African territories in search of opportunities and for social purposes such as marriage. Consequently, they had forged strong ties across the three regions of the British Empire and affection for East Africa as a whole as their homeland. What happened in one state affected them all. Today, they are collectively referred to as the East African Asians.

A culture of silence, fear and secrecy enveloped the East African Asians during the post-independence pogroms that aimed to deprive them of their roots, properties and livelihoods. Within their closed groups, some Asians became suspicious of each other, while others came closer together, tighter as sets of trusted friends more than they were ever before. The worst was a sense of betrayal felt by the old generation who had worked to build modern East Africa and dreamed of a home for their children. Yet, there were others who imbued the harrowing guilt of being sub-colonials, and racists, and accepted the condemnation of the nationalists. On the other hand, fear and hate, and heightened racism fermented in some minds as they looked for a way out. The community that stayed back, befuddled as the times were, spilt into several ways.

Some strategized to survive in their birthland out of choice or compulsion because they had no option while they waited a window to open to emigrate. They were the 'wait-and-see' type who would ask 'what to do now?' and 'where to go?' Some wished to leave, but had no escape routes i.e. no visas to go to another country, no families abroad, and not enough skills and finances to pay for airfare and resettlement. These groups were ridiculed as 'sitting on the fence'. Paradoxically, when they did attempt to emigrate, they were condemned for lacking in loyalty to the black government, implying they were racists. That validated further national condemnation of the race unwilling to accept African rule and integrate which had come to mean inter-marry. Some, on the other hand, went into partnerships with the politically connected elites and, like them, became millionaires.

By the late 1960s, the word 'Asian' had come to connote a breed of crooked, disloyal, racist and greedy humans - all four adjectives were adjunct to the moral failure of a race to qualify as residents or citizens of an African country. They were openly referred to by Swahili hate words such as wanyonyaji and mirija, both meaning suckers, which came to be synonymous with the word Wahindi, meaning Indians. Thus, it was not surprising that there was celebration in the streets of Kampala and smiles of approval all over East Africa when Idi Amin announced the expulsion order to the Asians. That was in August 1972. By November of the same year Uganda Asians, as they were known, were landing at the airports in North America and Europe, and in camps as refugees.

Almost all the young and upcoming Asian African novelists, poets, journalists, and intellectuals, the first generation writers in English, the language that addressed modern East Africa, slipped out of the country. That created a disruption in the stream of vibrant discourses on novels, drama and poetry at the moment of the community's transition from vernacular to literature in English. Some, mainly of theatre and poets societies, struggled to survive and pursue expressions under the despots who had clamped down on all intellectual and artistic creations that were even mildly critical of misrule, racism, the growing poverty and corruption.

In all, the dislocation of the writer from his/her heimat was so devastating for Asian African literature that it has yet to fully recover in East Africa. Now, after almost half a century, there comes from the Diaspora under the rubric of Asian African Literature, narratives that should have been written at home. The home that came to be the Home Between Crossings.

Canadian immigration

Finally, the day for the abhorred interview for my Canadian visa has come. It's a misty mid-August Monday and the kathak music of Pakeezah from the evening before at Shan Cinema fills my ears. Pakeezah, the dancing butterfly at the khota-prostitution house in British India. Tha-thai-thai-taak, aa-thai-thai-taak. Red-white-blue-green, red-white-blue-orange. I see the pattern omuatat of the savannah in the sound of music in my ears. The rhythm of colours and patterns of raindrops appear on the bright bougainvillea bushes flowering along Uhuru Highway. I put my fear into the beauty of sounds of colours while Anil keeps regurgitating words like an unsatisfied bull so I would remember one or two if not all of the provinces of Canada: Nova Scotia, British Columbia, Saskatchewan, Manitoba, Alberta and Quebec, Ontario and Newfoundland, New Brunswick. My interview is by a white lady with woolly flaxen hair, taller than I am by a foot.

This is yet another encounter in my life with a white lady face to face. Receiving a manlike smile from Mama Bisekeli in the bead shop in Nairowua was the first time. Meeting the DC's wife under a wide brimmed hat with a yellow ribbon that flopped over the side in two loops was the second time. That was the first time ever that I stood close to a real white memsaheb who looked like someone from Woman's Own magazines next to seamstress Roshan Bai's Singer Sewing Machine. That had made it a memorable day in my life that I would talk about as if I had met the Queen of England. The third was when a white woman shouted at me in the toilet at Nairowua airport.

It had been a Sunday afternoon and as usual on that Sunday afternoon, we went for a drive to Nairowua airport to see the airplanes taxiing down and flying out like vultures on the savannah. Two-year-old Diamond was in my lap drinking his milk from the Fanta bottle, and listening to his grating over the grooves on the bottle with my house key. As the car came to the first bougainvillea roundabout of the airport, Diamond pressed his hand down on his groin muttering excitedly without stopping, "Pish pish...pish pish." Haiderali speeded up and parked at the departure gate. I jumped out with Diamond at my hip frantically looking for a toilet. I found one in the lounge where white travellers were seated with open books and newspapers spread under their noses, their bags by their side. Entering a clean little room, I was removing Diamond's pants when someone from behind screamed in mixed English and Swahili: "Toka! Toka! Coolie! Can't you read? Cho hi ni Europeans only! Mzungu tu! Mzungu peke yake." I stood there like a stone statue. I felt Diamond's hot urine spreading over my stomach through my dress. That was my third encounter with an English woman. Now, I poise for the next one.

My first impression of the visa lady was how small she was from the other European women I have seen in the streets of Nairobi. She had made her own lips with red paint like Meethi Bai and Zera Bai, though they both have plump Indian lips. I thought she should have some kohl under her tired brown eyes. Surely, a mid-skull parting would be more suitable on her hair than loose open hair without a hairpin for a lady of her age. She walks quickly, taking short steps, tapping her shoes and throwing her chest up with each one step thrust forward in the little space of the office. She gives me a comfortable chair to sit on. That surprises me. Never before have I sat on a chair before an English person. She is respectful, I say to myself. I feel embarrassed about the dotted line of blisters on my neck left by a Nairobi Eye - that modest looking fly I had unknowingly slapped coming home from Shan Cinema last evening. It was in the car and it was dark. I pull my pachedi-shawl over my neck that exposes my hand.

"Nice henna on your hands, Mrs Devji," she says. "Did you paint it yourself?"

"Yes," I reply, nodding spontaneously, partly shocked and partly feeling uncomfortable by her comment on the henna on my hands. I slide my hands under my pachedi-shawl. I begin to feel better, my fear lessens but the lady's speech puzzles me. Her talk is toneless. I cannot make anything of it like if she is happy, kind, or angry. I can see that Anil who has accompanied me is confused too. I conclude the lady is suspicious not believing whatever Anil says about me. She does not smile, but does not look angry either. Anil keeps on smiling and he looks foolish, almost begging to be heard and be seen a good and honest man from a good and honest family of a good and honest lineage and community. He is accompanying his good and honest aunt who wants to join her good and honest children in Canada. Anil tells the lady that both my children, a boy and girl, have jobs in Canada. I, myself, feel totally lost and wish to be redeemed from this emergency. I take refuge in the highest orders of prayers both in Gujarati and muffled Arabic, running words over the tips of my fingers under my pachedi-shawl.

As the interview continues, I slip my hand inside my pakit purse and feel the tasbih. Its touch fills me with calmness, but I dare not show the tasbih as this would upset Anil. The lady appears to be talking to the paper in her hand, silently making marks. The paper in turn appears to talk back, silently. She draws a line across the paper, crumples and squeezes it in her fist, takes another printed sheet and starts to make marks on it again. The paper and the lady seem to work as a team like a spirit who talks from the calabash to the medium in a language not understood by her client. She asks, Anil answers. This ritual goes on for half an hour. I keep counting prayer words on my indices to influence her marking good for me on the paper.

Two fighting elephants
raise dust

Anil slams shuts the door of his cream Toyota salon, calls the immigration lady by some name – a racist? Did he say that? He screeches out of the parking lot. He is upset and feels slighted. The white woman seemed to ignore him, a university graduate from a wealthy Asian business family.

We pass by the President's office on Harambee Avenue, tall buildings, men in suits, women wearing straightened hair walk in stiletto shoes on even pavements. Harambee Avenue, clean and modern. We drive along Uhuru Highway towards downtown Nairobi. It is chilly. The midday sun is just appearing, quickly clearing the mist. Our breath is fogging over the windscreen so I begin to wipe it out with the edge of my pachedi-shawl. Immediately, Anil stops me with a quick flick of his hand lifted up over the steering wheel. Suddenly, I hear a crash close to my ears. I duck down without a thought or looking back, both my palms pressed to my ears. My pachedi-shawl slips down from over my head. Simultaneously, a knock at the back of my seat throws me forward. Startled, my lips pressed inwards stifling a scream, I turn around wide-eyed. The back window is smashed open.

"Wahindi! Asians! Wahindi! Twanga!" From somewhere outside, yet from everywhere, the same shouts repeatedly reach my ears. More stones rattle on the

571

Toyota's shell. Anil accelerates. The window by Anil's side is a myriad of frosted crystal lines radiating fractured sunlight from a hole in the middle as if intentionally created so by a glass artist.

"University students are on the rampage again!" He speaks through tightened lips. His eyes look wild, bright with a flame of some innate joy and compulsion. Blood drips onto his trousers from the back of his hand on the steering wheel.

"But why do they hate us?" I remove my tasbih and begin counting, pirshah, pirshah, pirshah.

"They say we support our despot, the President," says Anil staring ahead, "Moi partners with Asian mbwa kali class to keep off Kikuyu tycoons. He wants to create Kalenjin tycoons using his Asian cronies. We are always happy to play the game to keep the tribal balance, and make a little more money than yesterday." Anil's eyes are fixed on the road. He talks his anger to the tarmac.

There are crowds moving between the cars and side crossings. Some in rags are scurrying around the bougainvillea looking alarmed, alert and lost. Having passed the next roundabout canopied in lush olive green bougainvillea, spotted in full orange bloom, Anil begins to speak again, "They see us Asians, you know, collectively as one tribe like their own, the entire community of cronies of the dictator. Kumanina!" he curses, "bedfellows of corporations!" Anil lashes out abuse. I keep quiet, not because of my nephew's buck buck babble, but because of the fear of the angry crowd around us. "Western NGOs preach democracy and western corporations manufacture tyrants. Then the tyrants buy their weapons to quash democracy. Wajinga stupid! Our so-called leaders, brown millionaires, bedfellows of black politicians, bedfellows of corporations. Kumanina! Thriving kunguni bedbugs thriving on workers' blood!" Anil rages with hate, his ears turn red, his eyes widen as if awakened all of a sudden from a dream by the rock through the window.

Pirshah, pirshah, pirshah. My heart races. It's difficult to understand Anil. His anger adds to my fear from the heat in the street. I continue telling my tasbih. I do not wish to talk more lest Anil loses control of the car, and hits someone on the mob-filled road. I see terrified beggars and the homeless; many children are in rags. Then I see armed policemen and the military. They are jumping off from black armoured trucks like ants running up to swarm onto a piece of cake. Anil slows down. A throng of street children dash by my window – running collectively, sniffing glue, running again, stopping, sniffing glue, looking back, startled and running again. I see a girl. She may be twelve or thirteen years old, running in the crowd barefoot. She is wearing a headscarf like a married church lady and has a baby in a yellow flower picture kanga tied so tightly to her back that the baby does not bounce with her strides and leaps. I gasp without a sound when I see the girl's emaciated body.

"Poor slum dwellers resent us as their mothaj. We should leave Kenya and keep our dignity," I say almost in a whisper like a prayer said over fear.

"What dignity? What mothaj? It's my right to live here! I was born in Kenya! So were my father and my grandfather! I will join 'the Struggle' and help build a socialist country. I have friends from all tribes. We think alike," Anil barks back like a dog disturbed while eating. Again it's 'the Struggle'. He is obsessed with that word.

"There is an African proverb, WHEN TWO ELEPHANTS FIGHT, THEY RAISE DUST," I say. That's what Haiderali used to tell me when I spoke for Kenyatta and his people and against the English. We were one then snarling at the whites like angry cats. Now, anyone who hurtles slogans against Asians is called patriotic. In a way, Anil talks like me when I was young and just married. But I don't understand his modern politics when he says 'it's not tribe but class'. He always talks of 'the Struggle' in this way. I would tell Anil, "When their Struggle is over, the warriors will shake hands. You, an empty brown lunch bag, will be thrown out with your 'Struggle' in it when they have eaten enough. They will say dust itches their eyes. Dust is brown like you."

I see an indignant mob burning tyres at cross streets. Anil swerves and takes another route. I see street boys and girls playing hide and seek with the police. Stealthily, they recede towards their sanctuary under the Museum Hill Bridge. Some boys are stalking a terrified group of mamas, Nairobi's vegetable and fruit vendors. They wait for a chance to grab their kiondo baskets and fill their empty tummies.

Then through the splintered glass, Anil yells out something into the air. He is excited, but at whom is he shouting? Then I realize he is yelling at me, looking the other way through the broken window. I didn't hear his words, but his anger angers me.

"Whose side are you on? Kikuyus, Luos or Kalenjin? Even if you feel like a Kikuyu in your heart, Anil, you will never be accepted a Kikuyu. If you feel a Luo or a Kalenjin, you will never be included among them. You can neither be received as equal in the Kikuyu-Kalenjin-Luo tribal power war triangle, nor in any of the other forty African communities. It's your brown skin, not your Kenyan heart that matters. Or for that matter, your blue passport."

"Nonsense, Moti auntie masi! You think like a tribalist, a racist! A typical Asian! Khoja gossip!" Anil's rudeness shocks me. Once, when I complained about Anil's rudeness to his mother, my sister Monghi Bai, she told me it was not only Anil. All university boys talk like that to their elders. She regretted that his father, Mulji Bhai, did not send Anil to an English university. "Because of his stinginess, my son's mind has been poisoned by communists. My only son, tobha Mowla! What may I have done in my karma to deserve such fate?" She repeats this every time I talk to her about Anil's behaviour. She blames herself as Indian mothers do taking the sins of their sons on themselves. And if not that, on their bad karma. Monghi Bai even fasts, hoping the penance would cure her son. So I stop complaining about Anil to her. I feel the pain in her mother's heart. The discordance in her heart that mother-love cannot layer over mother-guilt-shame.

"The battle is not among Kikuyus, Luos and Kalenjin. It's not tribal but class war. A war against corruption. A war for justice. It's 'the Struggle' between the rich and the poor! Look outside! Who is throwing the stones? Are they Kikuyus, Luos or Kalenjin? The poor look alike, they fight as one. They fight the power-wealth greed Kikuyus, Kalenjins, Luos, and the in-between Asian bourgeoisie. Like my father they scuttle from one black godfather to another in the three tribe power war triangle, depending on who is in business at the State House. They will cast a vote for their godfather's gang, sponsor his election, and we shall call it democracy!" says Anil. His self-loathing has hardened into self-hate of his people. Even of his family. "Then White House will clap for us because their sponsored thug is elected! They will say Kenya is the most stable country in Africa. Just look at the stability outside!" says Anil. "The wealthy flourish because of ethnic clashes. We have learned to dance in the balance of the tribal triangle and grow fatter bellies, build fatter temples, gamble more, do more kotha mid-night clubbing."

I do not understand Anil anymore - all his buckwaas, meaning nonsensical talk, about class and 'the Struggle'. Anyway, I will not talk again to such a disrespectful nephew. Saalo, thinks he knows everything because he reads books at the university. He has no respect for the many years I have lived and known politics from the time of the English raj long before he was born. Anil has no respect for the elderly or his own kind anymore. He is the new Mau Mau.

The chaos persists in the streets, though in scattered pockets, while in the car, Anil and I are skirting around it. "Put on the cassette of guru-pir's songs," I ask Anil controlling myself. The sacred verses will calm me. But he ignores me. I wish I knew how to insert the tape and press the right button. It's the man who knows how to use the tape recorder and drive the car.

Uhuru Park means
Freedom Park

We pass by Uhuru Park. It's dappled with grey-blue-khaki-green-metallic spots. Uniforms, helmets, shields, and swinging batons. Line over line of Kenya riot squad and Kenya paramilitary in heavy boots are munching into the crowd on the green lawn like caterpillars eating their way through. Robots chasing a scattering of fleeing women. The grass itself is strewn with head scarves, slippers, kangas, sisal baskets, bananas, bofolo-bread lunches, porridge thermoses and even pieces of torn dresses. The stampede raises dust. Shrieks tear the air apart. Some women are running with arms raised over their heads before the routing militia. Sharp feminine screams and woo woo cries of mixed fear, pain, and sheer shock pierce through the broken glass windows of the Toyota. The noise is pregnant with emotions of something frightening about to happen like an explosion over the city. I move closer to Anil. He throws one surprised look at me and then his eyes are back on the road ahead.

I see the militia chasing a terrified group of women into All Saints Cathedral. They beat them, dumping the limp bodies into caged vans as if they were already corpses. The charge of batons and rifle butts is systematic, almost mechanical like some pounding factory engine. I cover my eyes. I cannot see the reality of what normally I would stare at in newspaper photographs. The Daily Nation pictures have come alive today running before my eyes! Anil drives on, tensed as he is, he remains alert and cautious. Then sudden alarm replaces the fury on his taut face. "Kumanina motherfuckers!" he spits out abuse. "Moi's militia is attacking mothers! Kumanina motherfuckers!" he hurls abuse again and again. Pirshah! I look deep into Saheb's laminated photo that my sister has glued onto the dashboard in Anil's car with instructions not to ever remove it.

I see the street girl with a baby in a yellow flower kanga running in a panic with the crowd. She crosses the road in front of us. Looking out through the windowpane, I catch the fiery stare of the girl as she turns her head to look at me. Noticing a rock in her hand, I lean back on the seat and then slide half down. For a moment, I thought she would fling the granite into my face. For a moment, I felt I was peering through her eyes at me, the mhindi, the Asian behind the glass, an Indian dhingly doll. My black eyes clicking at her poverty, her sickness, her shame. The one from the outside of the impenetrable upper city's wall of wealth. The dictator's people. The people who represent the powerful who collude with the ruthless military. They are responsible for her animal existence. Someone from them raped her. Someone who is her child's father. Someone who gave her the blotched pus marks on her face. Someone who is the cause of her running like a yelping slum puppy. An orphan of the rich that she is. Does she think I am that object of her spewed curse? I cringe out of fear and partly guilt.

In seeing me through her hate stare in this way, it seemed right the girl should want to throw the rock into my face. My bloody rich Indian face. Bloody rich Indian eyes. Bloody rich Indian car. Bloody rich Indian clothes that glitter. I duck further down, frightened and in shame, pushing my head deep between my knees until my back hurts.

Anil drives on, without taking his eyes off the road, without a break in his mumbling string of abuses in mixed Gujarati, English and Swahili, the way Gujarati Asians in Africa speak in three languages punctuated by *chhe*. Saalo police kumanina *chhe* - saalo MP kumanina *chhe* - saalo government kumanina *chhe* - saalo America kumanina *chhe* - saalo imperialist kumanina *chhe* - saalo kumanina what not *chhe*. The crowd's energy invigorates him. The wild vigour in him is palpable. I can feel it. It fills the car. Tension builds up inside the white Toyota as it builds up outside. We drive in the midst of it. He is on their side. With the mob. With the 'Struggle'.

"America says Kenya is the most stable country in Africa. You see stability outside?" Again Anil mutters the same sentence through lips that do not seem to move, "Women in the streets have taken over what defeats the men." I am quiet and horrified, sitting in the battered shell of the Toyota. Was Mary Muthoni Nyanjiru, who hurled a rock at the English, not a woman too? Anil, though hurt and bleeding, is disgorging foul words at politicians in a strangely elated way as if he were celebrating violence around us. Is this 'the Struggle' he talks about? Is this 'the Struggle' he has been waiting for? Does 'the Struggle' mean such chaos? Is 'the Struggle' another word for violence?

When I peep up, I am taken aback seeing once more the girl with the baby in a yellow flower kanga. She is standing across the road far away at the bougainvillea fence. I see her, her one foot forward as if she were about to leap over the fence. Instead, she bends backwards, takes a decisive aim and hurls a rock at the riot squad. A policeman is hit, he bleeds and falls. Others panic and open fire in the direction of the girl. Bullets clamour around the Toyota. The side window glass crashes in a combined split-sharp explosion. Within minutes, there are bodies strewn across the sidewalks. A few lay on the tarmac of Uhuru Highway, also called Freedom Highway of the capital city. Pirshah! My eyes search for the girl. I see the yellow kanga partially visible behind a bougainvillea bush. My heart thumps hard. I feel numb. Sick in the stomach. I begin to sweat profusely. My mind screams inside me but my tongue is frozen. As if by instinct, my eyes come to Saheb's picture on the dashboard wanting reasons, not peace. Would the girl in yellow flower kanga be an avatar of Mary Muthoni Nyanjiru? Would she be the woman who hurled a rock at the white colonial on the day I was born? Would the women at Uhuru Park be multiple avatars of Mary Muthoni Nyanjiru? Would they be Njokis, daughters born again as their names would tell you, to fight dictatorships and oppression?

Anil turns into Kenyatta Avenue, drives along Moi Avenue towards University Way, his eyes darting in a circle from the mirror on the right, left, back, the road in front and back to the mirrors. Jacaranda elf trumpets carpet the pavements purple. They look so beautiful I want to lie down and press them to my chest. In Rani Bagh, the garden of old Queen Victoria, once the Empress of India and East Africa, stands a faded weather beaten white pillar of a stout veiled woman. She waits alone in pachedi-shawl and long faraak, neglected, forlorn and forgotten. Some say she is the Virgin Mary and make a sign of the cross when they pass by her. Some wonder who the lonesome mother is. Some say she is the patron saint of the beggars of Nairobi for the

580

beggars come to rest at her feet. Others would not agree. They say she is the patron saint of thieves and pickpockets. They take a break when the sun is hot or to evade bribing the police, and take refuge in her shade. Most, however, say she is the comforter of the poor. Under her gaze, a black evangelist in a meticulous three-piece suit booms through a microphone reading the Bible in English. His assistant similarly dressed, echoes the verses in Swahili through a second microphone. "The Kingdom of God is nigh," they bellow, oblivious to the bedlam across the other street along Uhuru Park. Uhuru Park? Freedom Park? That's a mockery. Call it Martyred Mothers' Park after today.

Once I am home behind the safety of bars across doors and windows, and with askari-guards patrolling round the clock, I breathe a sigh of relief. The day is over. Shu-khar! I wash my palms of the henna painted flowery letters in Gujarati: Nova Scotia, Ontario, British Columbia, Saskatchewan, Manitoba, Newfoundland, New Brunswick, Alberta, Quebec. The names will not go away immediately, but I wash my hands, to wash away the day.

Humiliation of disowning motherhood

The next day after the evening prayers at the jamat khana, women gather in groups to talk about the incident at Uhuru Park. There is horror in their eyes. Anxiety in the air. We had all seen the *Daily Nation* photographs of the riot police hounding old women. Some had watched the news on the TV before they came to the communal supplications at the jamat khana. I tell them I was there and what I saw. They come closer me. Even those I don't usually talk to come to listen to me. How Anil's hand was bleeding and how the Toyota was pelted with stones. How the car window crashed like a drinking glass falling on the concrete floor. How a bullet zipped in shattering the side window. How lucky we are to be alive. They listen in silence and shock. But what horrifies them is how President Moi treated the mothers protesting in the park.

"Does he not have a mother?" asks one.

"Would he have treated his mother like that?" asks another.

"What if he were detained without trial, would his mother not have come to Uhuru Park to ask for his release?" asks the third.

The ones who read the *Daily Nation* and listen to the BBC, filled in bits and pieces that described the event in more detail. Their inhales and exhales spoke unsaid fears and shocks. Their hands in silence shifted from over their hearts to the lips from where would have come words of anguish had they not been so shaken.

Someone asked, "Where do we go? Whom shall we speak to? Everyone lives in silence and fear." Then someone else said, "When old mothers are not respected for the traditions they hold, it's time to emigrate." No one replies or says if she has applied or is intending to apply or has the visa already to immigrate to Canada. That is always a tightly kept family secret.

Later in the evening, I look at the photographs on the front page of the *Daily Nation*. "MOTHERS OF DETAINED PRISONERS WITHOUT TRIAL FLEE," Anil reads out the heading aloud looking over my shoulders and then continues on his way to the kitchen. Yesterday comes back in my eyes. I see them. They flee before the brutal charge of the riot squad and the paramilitary. Helmeted, armed and shielded in metal, the machine-like army of young men assail the old mothers in cotton dresses and head scarfs. Putting the newspaper pictures together with what I saw yesterday is like bringing two pieces of a torn photograph together. First, the women herded together like trapped animals, hugging each other in one tight embrace. A combined hug in unison out of fear. Of comfort. Of courage. Of unity. Of solidarity of mothers. I felt I was in that circle of human embrace. Some whimper for mercy, others sing hymns. Aged mothers thought the President would listen to them, for he has a mother, too. Then one of them steps forward before the contingent of young armed men and she begins tearing clothes off her body. In Africa, it is a taboo to see a woman, who is the age of your mother, so distressed that she unclothes herself surrendering her dignity to a young man the age of her son who, by custom,

583

is her son, too. It's a gesture of wounded motherhood that many do not understand. A gesture showing there is no more utu or humanity left in society. Of showing self-inflicted humiliation that says it's not worth being a mother. It's the humiliation of sacredhood of the womb, meaning the giver of life. Shame and sin would fill the eyes of the onlookers. I saw Draupadi in the arena naked and conquered by the villain princes, and Krishna could not save the women's honour. In Africa, to see your mother's nudity is shame to the onlooker and a curse. Everyone knows that it pains the land when the mother forfeits her honour to her sons' gaze. Dadabapa used to say the land is the Mother. Dharti Mata. If you insult a mother you insult the land. You insult your birth. It's rape. More mothers come forward, ripping clothes off their shrivelled frames, spitting curses and disgust, tearing away headscarves, casting away mother love in rage now forfeiting the dignity bequeathed to them by nature when they gave birth. They are surrendering in defiance to the rape by their sons. It's the defiance like of Gandhi surrendering to police brutality with open arms. They sing hymns in unison daring the armed men to come, touch and further dishonour their parents until they are satisfied. What more have they to lose when they have lost all, meaning their self-respect? Some policemen cover their eyes, others turn back and yet there are some who advance without shame. They would say they had orders. Or they are not of the same tribe so the curse would not harm them or that they are Christians now. That these are not their mothers. They don't believe in superstitions and primitive customs. Never before, not even under the English raj, not even during the girls' circumcision unrest at Mt Kenya, were the mothers of

584

Africa reduced to such humiliation as under a black government.

The loss of being mothers to their sons penetrates to the hearts of those who Anil calls activists. I saw it in the eyes of the slum dwellers and student rioters through the car window. They cast their eyes down and shook their heads, and left, and came back with more stones. The loss of motherhood means barrenness of land. It's like shaming fertility. If you were to listen to the mothers, they would tell you all sons born to the land no matter what tribe are their sons. That is custom. It's the heritage of Africa. The land will not forget this mother's day of shame. Of the great humiliation of life held sacred in the mother's body for that is the tradition.

In my story humanity is called utu as in Swahili and it comes from mtu, meaning human. Utu is the quality that makes a being human and tells us who we are. That much I know growing up in Africa. I will remember 25th of February as Kenya's Day of National Shame and Humiliation.

Canada suddenly a homeland

Three weeks later, after the interview at Kencom House for the Canadian visa, I receive a letter from the Canadian High Commission stating the interview was successful and I could go ahead with preparations to emigrate if there were no major medical problems. Now, Anil and I talk about the interview over and over again repeating the moments when we were nervous, which have now turned into moments of triumph. That same day, Anil calls Diamond in Vancouver to tell him about the trials and triumphs of the interview, and how nice was the immigration lady. He may even apply for a Canadian visa, but the problem was that he had a degree. "A mere plumber or a seamstress has far better chance of getting a visa to Canada than a university graduate, a major in African literature moreover." I heard Anil tell Diamond.

That evening, now once again, Anil and I talk about the interview as we sit down for a small supper. I am having my usual chapattis broken into pieces soaked in a glass of full cream KCC milk with about two spoonfuls of sugar. This meal is now my regular menu at night. Unwrapping the creamy pink striped wax paper, Anil cuts into the stone cold butter from the refrigerator with the sharpest kitchen knife he could find. He then places the chunk on a slice of spongy Supa Bakery toast still warm from the toaster. The butter melts into transparent veins running to the edges as he bites into the toast. Quickly then, licking from below, he

586

stops the drip from falling onto my tablecloth. Next, he dips the toast with the layer of butter into his chai and slurps it into his mouth. I look at him and once again I am reminded how we are trained to let the toast soak up the chai just right before it becomes soggy and flops back into the cup, *nah*? This is a skill acquired in families through practice and patience from childhood. It's an Ismaili skill like navigating through crowds on a celebration night, juggling steamy cups of tea in one hand and hot plates of curries or pilau, paper napkins and plastic forks underneath without spilling either on the gorgeous saris or equally gorgeous Punjabi dresses shimmering zari jug mug in cramped social halls of the jamat khana.

"Hmm. You can best taste the salt when KCC butter is frozen hard," says Anil. He eats a second piece of breadbutter in the same way, dipping it into the chaikop through a floating film of ghee. I go to my room.

Alone in my bed, I break into cold sweat. Fear and guilt churn into each other when they come together and possess me like a jinni taking control of my body. I feel overwhelmed. I cannot breathe. Sliding into my Bata rubber slippers, I paaht paaht my way into the silence of the night to the fridge, fill a full glass of cold buttermilk chaas and let it slowly slip down my throat. I feel its coolness settling in my belly. Then I sit down at the table where Anil was eating his toast about an hour ago. I drink a second glass of cold buttermilk swig by swig this time. I am afraid of leaving home, my land, my people, my everything around me. My life. The only place I know is my home and my jamat khana in Parklands. My coveted niche at the floor table where I sit cross-legged, counting money and giving out change at the naandi place every evening. It's my

587

volunteer-sewa service that fills me with contentment. How can I be away from all this? Most of all my daily routine is set by history. I have seen the jamat khana in Parklands built and rebuilt; renovated and re-renovated with its arches and palm trees, and rose gardens lovingly cared for by women volunteers I know. They are my friends. Am I deserting the poverty, crime and misery of the streets and valleys of Nairobi? I cannot do much about the problems so colossal but still a part of me. I grew with them. How can I now step out and leave the country decaying? How can I say your poverty has nothing to do with me? Black poverty and Brown wealth are two sides of the same coin. I feel guilty for being brown and selfish.

At night, I listen to drunken brawls in the valley's undercity. I hear wails of a wife beaten, a hungry child crying below my window and I feel the night's pain. Their wretchedness seeps through my ears and into my body like a sting of a wasp. Wasikia, to ask do you hear in Swahili is also to ask do you feel. I feel the pain of the city. Its rotten sores stink. Wretched city! Wretched of the city! Goodbye, wretched Nairobi! Goodbye wretched Kenya! I have nothing to do with you anymore. I am not one of you. My grief dissolves into anger. And anger into withdrawal from all that I once loved so dearly.

The loss of my birth city carves into me not because of its misery, but due to my migration, and it is bitter and I curse the city's wretchedness instead. That's how I feel today. That's how I felt about Haiderali when he collapsed and died, and I cursed him the next day. It was my grief that abused him. He died on the new moon's evening we call chandraat, and the Maasai of Nairowua say it's the evening of the green moon. Like how the pastures are green after the rains when the grass, sprouting out of the dry and dead grass, is fresh and young. So does the crescent moon emerges young and green after the death of previous month's moon.

My story wonders. The eye deceives the mind seeing only the new but the memory knows underneath the new lays the old. My story is like that for it walks the trail over the old paths making the new.

Kini and Ntinti

After my medical examination for the Canadian visas, I visit Kini at Kenyatta General Hospital. I have cooked porridge with milk and maize flour and added spoonfuls of sugar to it. That's how Kini liked her porridge when she came to visit me in Nairowua with Ntinti. Sweet and milky. Now she is in Kenyatta General Hospital, resting. Neither the Maasai herbalists nor the Kikuyu spirit healers or the white doctors at the Mission Hospital could cure her. The illness is one that lets other illnesses enter into the body and stay, and it has no cure.

Some say the sickness spreads rapidly on the savannah, like a pestilence. My heart is heavy. Images of the two girl brides with their emankeeki bouncing on the edge of their shoulders, surge before me. Now I see Kini at Kenyatta Hospital lying like a famished calf of the savannah, de-adorned of her emankeeki and her leather clothes decorated with beads. How proud she was of carrying such beauty on her. AIDS they say is like the Ol-ameyu famine that eats the flesh.

We hold hands and leave them, and hold them again. Her feeble arm loops as she lifts it but has no strength of a firm handshake pressed into my palm as it used to. Her throat is thirsty, her skin scorched cold and crackled like the vulture's neck on the acacia tree.

"I cannot return to the land because I have been bewitched. The earth does not want me," says Kini.

"Nobody will touch me. Only Ole Lekakeny visits me. He walks leaning on a stick, and comes with his granddaughter, but she does not come into the room," Kini speaks in short sentences whatever comes to her dying tongue.

"How is the old man?" I ask before she says more.

"Last time he came when the moon was white and full," she replies. "He said he will not come again because it was not easy for him to travel anymore. He said he was in good health, his teeth were strong and his eyes as good as of a young man." Kini stops talking to cough. Her body shakes with each spasm laboured up her throat, dry and windless. The cough leaves a whizz in her chest, but she tries to complete her sentence, "His legs are tired and they refuse to walk. He brought me sour maziwa lala milk that had slept over the night in that smoked calabash." She lifts her hand, and points to the calabash on the side table. It's long, an arm length gourd with beads embroidered on leather top. It's like the one she used to bring the sour milk in for Ole Lekakeny at the bead shop in Nairowua.

"Where does he live?"

"At the elders' homestead at the foot of Ol Donyo Lengai where the ancestors walk at night and leave their footprints."

"Can Ole Kitungat take me to see Ole Lekakeny? My nephew will drive me close to the homestead."

"Ole Kitungat is in the outside land. Send him milk, he is a young man," she tells me.

"Yes I will. Who can take me to the elders' homestead?"

591

Kini does not reply, and we fall into a silence. She closes her eyes.

"I will come again to see you."

"Soon?" she opens her eyes and asks in a whisper to keep the cough down.

"Yes, soon," I lie.

"My people do not accept me and they do not want me to return home to rub my curse on others who are pure. I will not return to pollute the land. Only Ole Lekakeny came and his granddaughter did not enter the room. But you are from outside. My curse will not affect you." She comforts me while she cannot comfort herself. "Ntinti died of the curse, and she gave it to me." Kini astonishes me with her remark about Ntinti.

I shake the thermos flask well before leaving it on the table while waiting for Anil to arrive and drive me away from Kenyatta General Hospital that stands like a portal to Kibera. Kibera, they say, is the largest slum in Africa and probably, accordingly, also has the highest concentration of HIV infection among the poorest of the world. My body cries within. Why is Anil so late?

Haiderali

It's 2nd of November. Five years ago today Haiderali collapsed and died. It was chandraat, the evening of the new moon and the jacaranda trees were in purple bloom. The Maasai at Nairowua call such an evening, the night of the green moon or young light over the aging darkness. Like green shoots growing under old grass. I was busy looking for his khane socks when he fell down while he was dressing up. Heart attack I thought.

I sat at his side and tried to wake him up calling out his name and convincing myself he would wake up, wide eyed awake and frightened of his own nightmare of collapsing and dying. Like becoming a shadow of life after life. My tongue began to thicken. So heavy to lift to form the words knocking in my head. I found the mukhi's telephone number and called him. He said he was coming with his wife. I waited sitting on the floor, wringing my hands.

Fear of the present and memories of the past come together, filling my head like a patchwork of fleeting feelings through the time we lived together. At first, I sob dooskha dooskha. "Friday is an auspicious day to die," I console him consoling myself. "You died before becoming a mothaj, for this shu-khar a thousand times."

As always, I fast when chandraat falls on a Friday. It's custom. My sorrow, the suddenness of death — the uncertainty before me, my feelings of helplessness made me half delirious. Why was the mukhi taking so long? I was losing my mind to the distant past. I was young again. I put my pachedi-shawl over Haiderali's head the way he used to imitate Raj Kapoor throwing my pachedi-shawl over his head, and making actor eyes seducing me into courtship, then a song. I was his Nargis, he used to tell me. Eternally his Nargis, he said. Never aging Nargis, always beautiful Nargis. But today, those eyes are silent in deep meditation.

"Where are you?" I ask. "Do you not want to speak to your Nargis anymore, henh Haidu? Will you not sing to me?" I tried to tease him out of his sleep, tease talking with slanted eyes like Nargis in Awara. No response. I tried his favourite courtship song:

Tu mere dil ka moti hai, abhi dil torke maat jana

You are the bead of my heart, do not break my heart and leave me.

"I am your Moti, nah!" I ask. He would not reply. His face calmed into meditation. His lips relaxed into a smile. The husband's smile of indifference to wife's nagging that I knew so well. A half hidden smile like he had a secret from the other world that eluded me. Like the ambiguous smiles on the pale faces lying on the floor in the jamat khana awaiting burials. Relaxed, all knowing smiles, at peace at the threshold, and unmoved by the sobs of the friends and relatives. I see white hair in his nostrils that I had not noticed before.

I say to him, "Haidu, do you remember that day you asked, 'You are my Nargis, mm?' "

And I asked, "You are my Raj Kumar, mm?"

You asked, "You are my rose, mm?"

I asked, "You are its fragrance, mm?"

I smile mukh mukh within me. How he would run a rose over my face to loosen the stiffness of fear that gripped me when he touched me. He would run the red rose around my neck, and over my arms and across my chest before he slipped it in my cleft. I let it stay there in warmth of my body through the night's love. In the morning I picked up the crushed petals and put them on my dressing table between perfume bottles.

"I will cook six varieties of curries and three of rice to make sufro prayer tray for you. You will be so proud of me, henh Haidu?"

I feel overwhelmed, seized by fear and insane with sudden distress. Widow's self-blame assails me. Am I an absakan outcast? No! I will not accept that. A nobody? No again! Did he die because of my bad karma? No! I open my eyes wide to escape accusations of my culture. To defy them. Memories long curbed return with vengeance taking advantage of the weak moment.

I remember when you complained about burnt rice, I shouted back at you to cook yourself next time, and you kept quiet … It was not my fault that I slipped in the jamat khana and lost your baby. It was a boy. I know you wanted a second son. You wanted to try again but I refused. I should have tried to have a second son for you … the MP of Nairowua killed you, I know. You refused to sell the shop and our house to the MP. You refused because of my beads, my afternoon meditation and my home. I know though you never said it. He hassled you. You started drinking. He sent thugs to the shop. They looted and carried away the tools and furniture. You had to sell the shop and our home to Najmu Chotara. The MP was furious and we left Nairowua quickly. You wanted that and we left Nairowua quickly. We did not even go to the graveyard to say the farewell prayers for your father and mother. You drank even more than you smoked in Nairobi, and we quarrelled every night.

"You sleep with black prostitutes", I shouted loud enough for the neighbours to hear. "You will bring diseases home to me!" You loathed me but I know your anger was tempered by alcohol. You have a kind heart and you gave me everything I needed. You know how stubborn I become when angry. My anger is not like yours that comes quickly and goes quickly with alcohol and sleep. My anger stays in me because it is fired by the envy of the woman in me who hates other women who love you too. I am your wife. The women in Majengo took you away from me with their black magic. Believe me Haidu, had I had means to support myself and our children, I would have let you be with the life you wanted. But I was trapped in your house, a mothaj of my marriage.

In the evening, like every evening of 2nd of November, I stand the photograph of Haiderali, my young Haidu in English sports jacket, against Nooran Mubin and confess his sins on his behalf. On his behalf, I ask for forgiveness three times over. After three short sentences of repentance, I sprinkle holy water on his picture at his forehead, three times over accepting forgiveness on Shah Pir's behalf. Then I go outside to look for the Maasai night watchman who is from a homestead around Nairowua.

"Will you take me to see an old man from Nairowua who lives at the elders' homestead at Ole Donyo Lengai?" I ask him. "The old man worked with me at the

596

bead shop in Nairowua. I will pay you. My nephew will drive us there. Do you know him?"

"Yes, I know him. He died on the last evening of the green moon."

My hear sinks. I stand speechless for a while before I talk again, "I will give you some money to give to the elders to sacrifice a goat at God's Mountain." My response comes without a thought, like an instinct. I had vowed never to sacrifice a goat again. "This will be the last time," I remind myself. "It will be for peace in the homesteads of Ole Lekakeny's descendants."

The watchman stares at me with his unbelievable brown eyes. Then he smiles and nods approval.

"Peace among the children makes the ancestors happy, *si-ndio* - yes?" I ask.

"*Ndio* – yes," replies the watchman in a quiet tone almost shy but pleased.

"I will also give you money for a large calabash of honey beer for the elders," I tell the watchman. "They will remember him when they gather. They will sprinkle some beer on the Maasai earth, an offering to invite Ole Lekakeny's spirit to join their circle. They will tell him they meet in his honour. That the beer they drink and the sacrificial goat meat they eat are in his honour. That he is remembered and always welcomed in their group. That will make Ole Lekakeny very happy. *Si-ndio* - yes?"

"*Ndio* - yes," replies the watchman with a smile.

"Tell the elders the goat must be unblemished. No scars and with straight horns. Its skin must be spotless and white. Sawa sawa - agreed?"

"Sawa sawa - agreed"

Yelling in the valley slum below my window and behind the thirty foot tall wall, steal my sleep. I keep awake listening to the anguish of women. It's past midnight and my heart weeps. The picture of the two Maasai women scraping water from the hole in the dry river bed comes to me. Pictures of the angry girl in a yellow kanga, and distressed mothers of detainees in Uhuru Park fleet through my mind. What can I do to stop their agony? What can I do to change the behaviour of politicians? The images do not leave me.

The next morning, I give my yellow gold bangle to Anil. It's the last one of the two from my mother-in-law.

"What's this for?" he asks, wide eyed.

"For 'the Struggle'," I reply.

First Anil jerks back. Then he slides the bangle through his hand, and pushes it up close to his elbow under the long sleeve of his shirt to keep it safe. And then he gives me a hug.

My story runs like the Nile. Many rivers flow into the Nile from many directions and change its waters like how my story changes when other stories merge into it, and keep moving all together.

Magendo Days

Minister Bwana Benzi is now the Minister of Trade and Commerce, and a business partner with Anil's father Mulji Bhai. They first started a partnership with illicit trade in coffee from across the border in Idi Amin's wilting Uganda, so rich and green that London once called it the Pearl of Africa. Coffee corruption, famously called Magendo, flourishes and Mulji Bhai acquires a new name in town. He is called Mulji Magendo or Mulji the Illicit. Now Minister Bwana Benzi and Mulji Bhai are in extended magendo importation businesses – illicit vehicles and illicit electronic equipment that come in container loads that they supply to several government departments by virtue of Minister Benzi's ethnic tie with the President. "He is blessed," my sister Monghi Bai would say about her husband. There are rise and fall cycles of corrupt dictatorships in the neighbouring countries while Kenya remains what America calls a 'stable country', nurturing the magnificent magendo civilization that pervades every government office, foreign and private business. The United Nations and the World Bank are as active in the magendo business as the Kenyan politician. This I learn about when an occasional corruption scandal breaks out and makes the news. But soon it's forgotten and life goes on.

"There is no place like Kenya on earth. Why do you want to leave this paradise?" asks Mulji Bhai when he comes with Monghi Bai to say goodbye to me. "One can still make good money here. You can stay with us." I know my sister, Monghi Bai, would like me to remain in Kenya for her sake. "We can make Canada here in the Aga Khan Flats like how your neighbours have done. Nanji family has wall to wall carpets, heavy window curtains, washing machine, electric everything in the kitchen, etc, etc."

"But the violence?" I question. "I am afraid of the violence." Do they not understand I am an aging parent and need to be with my children and grandchildren? That is custom. That is where my heart is. I belong there.

All the business licenses of Mulji Bhai are renewed every year without a problem though the Africanization act has not been revoked. "Automatically", as Mulji Bhai puts it. In fact, Mulji Bhai does not have to worry any more about carrying cash for chai money to give to desk clerks. He now operates at a higher level, which means he can send his chai money directly into the officials' wives' accounts overseas. He likes it when the desk clerks show respect to him and not treat him as they would Asians without connections like his. He confides in me with a bit of brag that he is very close to becoming a business partner with one of the President's sons. That would be dealings in stolen vehicles and minerals. That is considered the pinnacle of connections if not achievement among the debauched Asian business community. It will elevate his status in the jamat. He will no doubt be able to contribute more for the welfare of the poor.

I will carry the ginan notebook, hand written by Stepmother Gor Bai, in my handbag and slide Saheb's photo in the inside sleeve. It's a small photo, size of a playing card and in colour. He is wearing a smile and a turban, looking straight. I slip young Haiderali's proposal

600

photograph in the fold of my bandhani. The emankeeki, and the two kangas are in the two other folds. I pack the pregnant bandhani wrapped in a merikani bedsheet, and lay the package into my suitcase. I look at it. My travel companion in a leather jacket that rode with me to my new home in Nairowua with Haiderali's feet on top of it behind the front seat in the Ford. That was when I was sixteen and a bride. Now I am nearly fifty two and a grandmother, and the same suitcase now will travel with me to Canada.

I do not have much to carry to Canada and besides that, Diamond reminds me every time we talk on the phone not to bring junk. Like my tailored clothes that I have preserved are junk, he says. Like the warm military woollen coat from Colpro is garbage, he says. Kenya kitchen pots and spoons, knives, the meat mincing machine in solid iron, and the iron plate for roasting chapattis are all junk, he says. All Kenya things are junk or garbage to my son because in Canada, he says, you get everything new, electric and modern.

"Bring four Akamba woodcarvings for me from Mapara's curio shop. Standing Maasai figures. Also four batiks of animals. Two zebras and two giraffes. The shop is next to the European market." I hear Diamond tell Anil over the phone.

Losing the birthland

Ole Lekakeny would have sighed to the wind because God is de-embellished of ornaments and animals of the savannah which are killed for their ivory by the one called the Elephant Queen. Anil tells me how leopard, zebra and lion skin floor rugs and handbags, ivory bangles, pendants, broaches and earrings are wrapped in brown paper, marked fragile and crated overseas in astounding quantities. Primal trees are cut down in their hundreds at God's sacred groves on Mount Kenya and in the Forest of the Lost Child where the Maasai seer, called the Laibon, resides. The sacred wood is threatened by yet one more development project. Every evening sundowner bonfires of heaped nurse logs stolen from nature, rage in the evening fires at the five star safari lodges, sucking out the nourishment that replenish the savannah for their profits. Ravenous logging and warming of the earth compel Kilimanjaro's glaciers to retreat, leaving her bare, like a mother de-adorned, reduced to humiliation, her nakedness exposed. Kilimanjaro's nudity is a curse, her body declothed in people's eyes. In Africa, to declothe a mother is a shame that is also a curse.

I have a habit of telling my tasbih after dinner. On the string of ninety nine wooden beads, I count forty nine names of the descendants of God's storyteller, Nabi Mohamed, and then the names of the Satpanth guru-pirs, the Imam's storytellers. At seven years of age, in Nairobi's tin town, I had memorized the two sets of sacred names in the daily dua-prayers. Later I taught these holy names at the religion school to young girls preparing to recite prayers before the jamat. I implore the prophets collectively, counting the last two beads of my tasbih, while holding together the silver medallion where the thread ends in a knot made in stiffened zari figure of double four as in Gujarati.

The November night air flows up the ridge. It's moist air and I feel cold. With the current, I hear a faint song and humming. It's our Maasai night watchman, ole Kitungat's brother, who is singing the Song of Engoiteeko to the land he has lost to maendeleo, development, modernity. The song reminds me of Ole Lekekany teaching me how to make the pattern engoiteeko at my bead shop in Nairowua. Engoiteeko in Maasai is the zebra, and it can also be cloud patterns in the sky and on the emankeeki the beaded necklace that I have. The night watchman is one of those thousands who haunt Nairobi's valley slums during the day and at night they sing to the pain in their hearts. He sings the loss of land, the Ornament of God beaded in colours of Muain Sidain. He sings how the death of animals of the savannah kills the spirit of the land. The nomad's pasture is fenced, excluded and marked in Swahili and English: HATARI! PRIVATE PROPERTY TRESPASSERS WILL BE PROSECUTED. He sings how Muain Sidain, that is beauty, is captured, and chained like a slave. Like the land, Muain Sidain can no longer be what it is because it cannot celebrate e'sikar which to the Maasai means beauty, happiness and freedom as one.

I stroll into the backyard where I had planted a row of onions with my bare hands like a peasant woman bending her back to the red earth. Another row of potatoes and carrots, and ginger in a box of sand. I stand by the wild olive tree, the sacred tree of aboriginal Africa and pre-European Christianity. For a while, I watch its leaves quake in the beam of light refracted from the three piece mirror of Mrs Damji's dressing table in the bedroom of her apartment on the first floor. I feel the first drops of shower refreshing on my skin washing away the day's tiredness together with stale perspiration. The air smells of mitti attar which is earth's fragrance. In Nairobi, one no longer hears the frogs croak expectant to bathe in fresh water from the night sky. Fear of the unknown grips me but I have to go. I had felt like this one other time. That day, when I was a bride. When my second mother, Gor Bai loosened her arms around me and freed herself of me. She abandoned me and I had to go and cross the threshold into another home. Is my country loosening her embrace and abandoning me today? You have to go when the mother pushes you out. The Asians have to go, politicians tell the nation so.

I clutch my long dress in my left hand above the knee and lift it to make room for legs to bend inside the flares so I may squat at the roots of the sacred tree, and take the red soil in my fist. But the cramp in my leg whines to my head. I straighten up and kick my foot in the air. The feel of the red earth of my birthland reaches my heart. It is the earth where my parents and grandparents are buried in the old Khoja cemetery at Kariokor where there is a well the depth of the height of three men standing one on top of the other. It's near the gate with Om chiselled on the pillar. Here frangipani flowers bloom along rows of graves of our forefathers. Their stories lie with them for who knows and who cares who the Asian Africans were. What stories did they tell? Where did they live? What did they build? Why did they leave?

My fist tightens. I know the earth's smell so well, so deeply indigenous to me. Fear grips me again. Thoughts of loss crowd my head. Will I too lose my story? Will I lose the sense of home that is the land and the sky that imbibes my story? I press the red soil to my left eye and then to the right eye, both moist at the fringe of my lashes. Then I press it between the eyes on the forehead, asking permission to leave the land, and also for forgiveness and blessings on the unknown journey. In that gesture I offer my homage, my shu-khar and my reverence of dast bosi to my birthland. I make a silent oath to the African earth. I will always carry her story in the proverbs of the kanga, and her beauty in the beads of the emankeeki embracing her mountains, the rivers and the savannah mirrored in the sky. In my heart I will carry the zebra's gallop and shadows of the clouds on the savannah. Is beauty not God's ornament? All God's ornaments lie in the folds of the bandhani in my English suitcase packed ready for the long journey over the continent and then over the cold ocean. Haiderali comes to my mind like an apparition. I speak to him in my head.

How I howled back at you like a mad woman because you came home drunk. Dr Joshi told you to stop drinking whisky. I even hid your bottles but you always found ways to hide them again. The plumber found two bottles in the flush cistern high up above the toilet. But it was too late then for you were dead and buried. I did not think of looking there. I should have. I could have saved your life. Sala madderchod! Selfish husband! I gave my life to you! Guilt, anger and regret consume me. I am at a loss.

How we quarrelled and how we loved. How we intimated and how I became him in my feelings. I touch my breast, and feel the tingle on my nipple, his finger moulding around to erect it. He is buried in the warmth of the red soil of Nairowua near the black township. He liked it there where the women he loved live. Yet, without him, I have become incapable of loving myself. Were we not a good match? "A set," they said at our marriage. How can one love oneself without the other when the set is broken?

Tomorrow at this time, I shall be boarding the airplane. The Swahili word for the airplane is ndege, same as for the bird. Tomorrow I will be flying like a bird to my destiny. KILA NDEGE HURUKA NA MBAWA ZAKE, read the words on my kanga, a gift from Nana, Riziki's grandmother, whom they called the Mouth of Mombasa. EVERY BIRD FLIES ON ITS OWN WINGS says my gift.

The night watchman stops to look in my direction and then looks away. He walks into the dark making his rounds, his rungu-club over his shoulder, and singing while he waits the day.

Are we birds that we should live on trees
While they stay below and hurt our land
And make it ugly, the ornament of God
Where our ancestors lived in peace
They weep now

I hear the watchman sing from a distance now. His verses flow like river water into the Song of Emankeeki that Kini and Ntinti sang to me. When the sun rises, the watchman will disappear together with his song, like a dream waking up.

Endnotes

Glossary

aati! (Swahili): as if! (sarcastic).

absakan: unfortunate woman often referred to a widow

attar: perfume.

asal: origin. Asal ma vassal means return or be contained in the origin, meaning death.

asante: thank you.

askari: guard, soldier, policeman.

barabar *chhe*: its fine, it's OK, it's proper.

bh-toh: travel food.

bhai bapa: cajoling, sweet-talk as in persuasion.

bhaaga bhaagi: running about aimlessly.

bhoparo: exposing the secret usually held within a family or a closed group in a way that would be embarrassing or bring shame.

buck buck: irritating often repetitious talk.

buckwaas: nonsensical talk.

bushat: short sleeved loose shirt.

bhoito: From bhoi in Kacchi for servant. Sometimes the word is mistaken for 'boy' as in English.

bhoiti: female servant.

boma: enclosure around homes or animals.

chandraat: evening of the new moon that's also the beginning of the new month in the Islamic calendar. It's the evening when Ismaili Khoja offer confessions and when many prefer to pay the tithe.

chhe: verb or half-verb at the end of the sentence in Gujarati.

chee-chhe-ru: walking round about or puzzling talk.

chini chini: secretly; quietly; illegally.

chotara: bi-racial.

chup chap: quietly.

dal: lentil soup.

Dara Shikoh: Moghul prince of India (1615 –1659). He translated 50 verses of Upanishads from Sanskrit to Persian to interest Moslem scholars in study of Vedic scriptures. He called the translation *The Greatest Mystery* and refers to it as the one stated in the Quran as the *Hidden Book* showing the communion between Islam and Vedic teachings. Dara Shikoh is buried in the recently renovated Humayum's tomb in India.

dhaap: made-up story.

dhorka: white.

dhow: wooden vessel that carry goods and passengers across the Indian Ocean.

darshan: blessed vision. It is the propitious act of seeing an imam, guru, pir or a deity. It can be so potent that a glimpse is believed to bless and even cleanse the believer of his/her misdeeds. Darshan is also used by humbler folk to refer to meeting their superiors like a king or queen, or even their benefactors.

deedar: as in darshan above. Nowadays, Satpanth Ismailis use deedar more often than darshan. However, in their ginans (religious songs), it is the word darshan that is more common. Sometimes, darshan-deedar is combined as one word as is guru-pir showing the Islamic-Vedic duality in their sacred texts.

desh: Indians refer to India as desh or motherland.

dosi: old woman.

dole dole: moving the head from side to side the way Indians do when enjoying music or when talking. The gesture indicating OK or I agree or simply nice.

Draupadi: name of the queen in the Mahabharata who was born of fire and married to five princes.

dudu: insect.

Emperor Akbar: Mughal emperor of India (1542 –1605) who had the Mahabharata translated into Persian and illustrated in Persian style of the time. The translation supported the principle of Din–i-illahi, a belief system derived from core spiritual elements in Islam, Hinduism, Zoroastrianism and Christianity that the emperor promulgated.

engoiteeko: zebra. Also a bead pattern.

en-tomononi: a woman who prayed and received a child.

en-kai: God, sky.

eunoto: Maasai ceremony.

e'sikar: can mean joy, freedom or splendour in Maasai. It can also mean adornment. All meanings imply delight of beauty.

en-turuai: a woman in Maasai who likes to make herself up.

faraak: dress. From English frock.

fagio: broom.

faaraj: obligation to return or pay back.

farman: decree, counsel, dictate.

funga safari: start your journey. Can also mean start packing.

gaando: mad. Crazy, stupid.

gaapa: lies.

gathiya: gram flour flakes eaten as snack.

gheta: sheep.

ginan: Satpanth Ismaili devotional literature in form of lyrics and hymns recited daily in the jamat khana.

gola: derogative word for Africans used by Asians in East Africa. Singular golo.

goma: from ngoma in Swahili meaning dance.

guru-pir (gurpir): Satpanth Ismaili word combing guru and pir. Also used in Sikhism and other religions of India based on Vedic and Islamic teachings.

gupti: hidden; concealed.

guso: anger.

haraakh: inside joy that is not expressed openly. Like being bashful or quietly pleased.

harambee: Kenyan moto used on official government emblems. Praise, shout or saying that means 'In the name of goddess Hare Ambe'.

HATARI!: DANGER.

heimat: total sense of place, belonging, feeling and relationship to home resulting from descent, the environment of growing up, local community, local history and traditions.

ho-ha: commotion.

hivi hivi: not sure.

kaarak: stiff and crispy.

jamat: community.

jamat khana: assembly house. The central area of the jamat khana is the prayer hall. Some jamat khanas have a second prayer hall or chamber that is reserved for meditation. Many jamat khanas have a social hall for communal meals, talks and public events. Often there is a library and an adjacent garden.

ka-rendi: little lady also means a doll.

karo: stone built square in the courtyard where clothes, dishes, buckets and pots are hand washed.

kanga: rectangular piece of waist and chest wrap for women.

kasha: wooden chest. often with carved sides and top used for storage especially clothes.

kasida: Islamic hymn.

kasukoo: parrot.

kati kati: middle.

khulapug faraak: literally open legs frock that can also mean nakedlegs frock.

kiapo: oath.

kichwa potea: lost head or crazy.

kikoi: men's waist wrap.

kiondo: sisal basket.

kipande: used to be an identity card in a metal container attached to a chain. Workers were required to wear it around their necks by law. Nowadays kipande means an ID card.

kisirani: misfortune, evil or mishap. This could be brought about by a thing, time, event or a person.

kula kichwa: literally 'eating head'. Annoying, frustrating.

kunguni: bedbugs.

kumanina: abuse.

kweli: true.

ol-ameyu: drought.

ol-moindi: Indian or Asian in.

ol-nyankusi: 'one-who-captures-for-himself' pl Il-nyankusi. Age group.

ol-opir le nkare: flood or wave of water.

ol-pun-yata: flooded area.

osotua: peace; relationship; umbilical cord.

out-line: not showing behaviour according to community's expectations.

madderchod: mother fucker.

Mahabharata: epic narrative that contains core Vedic teachings in stories and stories within stories. Believed to be the longest poem ever written and the first long narration in the literary genre called Frame Story. Others in this genre like the Canterbury Tales and Arabian Nights appeared a millennium later.

malunga: a single-stringed African musical bow with a gourd resonator.

mandeli: prayer assembly of select members.

manta: a wish that is often prayed for or asked through a sacrifice, talisman or a ritual like feeding little girls or the poor.

masoto: rag used to mop in the kitchen.

matata: trouble, problem.

mee-thai: Indian sweets.

mendo: cockroach.

mgeni: guest.

mhindi: Indian.

Moghul: dynasty that ruled over major part of India from 15th to 19th century.

mothaj: mothaj refers to dependency especially on relatives and the community. Mothaj is a highly emotional word that has connotations of loss of dignity, shame and humiliation. The dependent feels (or is made to feel) obligation in a way that carries public disgrace and embarrassment. All this is combined with personal guilt. Mothaj is a sort of dependency that's unwanted, reprehensible and a burden yet unavoidable because of circumstances such as poverty, illness, old age, disability or being orphaned or dispossessed. The family or the community is obliged to bear the responsibility of supporting the deprived because of custom and social pressure. So painful is mothaj that one would hear Ismaili Khoja say: Death is better than mothaj. At funerals it is not uncommon to hear Ismailis say: He/she has been freed of mothaj or shu-khar for he/she died without being a mothaj on anyone. So dreaded a condition is mothaj that in the daily collective jamat khana prayer, one line pleads God 'not to make us mothaj on anyone.'

mandaleo: development.

mitti: soil.

mirija: straw to drink with.

muain sidai: beautiful or proper combination of colours literally.

mukh mukh: inside smile with little outward expression like stretched lips often masked in shyness.

614

mukhi: head in charge of jamat khana religious functions such as marriages, births and funerals. He also manages all the volunteers, committees and secular functions in the jamat khana.

mukhiani: mukhi's wife.

murid: one who takes an oath of allegiance to the imam. Satpanth Ismailis consider themselves murids of Hazar (Living) Imam known as the Aga Khan in the non-Ismaili world.

mzungu: white man.

naakhra: coyish behaviour.

naandi: collective word for various types of food offerings taken to the jamat khana for daily, monthly and annual thanksgivings and prayers for the departed.

nasto: Indian snacks.

nisasa: painful sighs of the anguished. The hurting expressions may lead to difficulties in the future for those causing the distress. Especially potent when expressed by the elders, poor and disabled. Comes from the belief in the power of emotions felt by the pain in the heart.

noor: light. Figuratively used to mean the divine spirit.

nusu: half.

paatlo: floor stool.

pakit: purse.

palothi: crossed legged.

pambana: struggle.

615

paratha: fatter fried chapatti. Sometimes, ghee or cream is kneaded into the dough.

pir: Sufi master of a specific path. He or she is often a guide to the followers. Satpanth Ismaili ginans (hymns) often end with a pir's name reputed to have written them.

Pir Sadardin: 14th century Persian pir. According to the Ismaili belief he is said to have come to preach Shiite Islam in India on behest of the Imam who resided in Iran. However, what appears to have evolved out of his preaching encountering Vedic religions was the Satpanth faith.

pirshah: Satpanth word of prayer combining two words, pir and shah given equal weight to each as was the belief.

ponga: slang for white people used in 1950s and 1960s.

prayo-pavesa: Ancient practice of Saurashtra that denotes voluntary slow fasting to death of elderly or terminally ill or of those who feel they have lived long enough and have no more responsibilities or reason to live on. Those who commit themselves to prayo-pavesa are often at a stage when they cannot take care of their daily needs such as body hygiene or eating with their own hands due to failing health and old age. They ask to be free of mothaj (see above) that is humiliating dependency on their close relatives. They would begin prayo-pavesa with full knowledge of the community and blessings of the priests. Still a highly esteemed living practice among some Gujaratis in India. Prayo-pavesa is often celebrated with a procession and festivities complete with photographs and videos.

pinjaroo: cage; wooden box pantry with mesh wire sides.

pukka: proper, good, solid.

rangoli: women's floor pattern art. Traditionally done with powder colours.

rass: rass is the essence of temperament, mood or disposition in an aesthetic bliss. It can be in a performance of dance, song, music, a ritual, drama or viewing visual art. Rass is the pitch of artistic mood and pleasure. It is considered to be an emotive internal expression be it love, fear, beauty, melancholy or devotion. Rass is also called the experience of "the mood as a tenor of the heart."

Razmnama: called The Book of War is the translation of the Mahabharata from Sanskrit to Persian. It was commissioned by the Mughal Emperor Akbar (1542 -1605) to the scholars of India and master painters at his atelier. The three-volume Razmnama has 81 miniatures of the Vedic epic in Persian style. The Emperor encouraged Moslem clerics and dons to make copies, and study the book.

roji: important word among the Satpanth Ismailis to show reverence to food that provides not only nourishment but is also medium of offering prayers especially for the dead. Roji vaguely relates to destiny in that one's nourishment, no matter how small, is fated. Thus, Satpanth Ismailis would say, 'One eats what's in one's roji' which suggests one's meals are written in one's kismet that is destiny.

rotlo: black millet bread.

ruh: soul.

rungu: club.

saafai: cleaning.

saala: offensive naming.

saheb: title showing respect and honour.

shaitani: satan.

Satpanth: Satpanth, meaning the True Path, is a subgroup of Nizari Ismaili faith that has two main branches and is practiced by several ethnicities and castes in India. One branch is believed to have been started by Pir Sadardin (1290-1367) and the other by his grandson Pir Imam Shah (1430 -1520). Both branches believe in Naklank avatar as the tenth reincarnation of Lord Vishnu and who is Imam Ali, the cousin and son-in-law of Prophet Mohammad. Satpanth belongs to the greater Guru Pir cluster of ancient Indian religions that were influenced by Islam under Sufi Moghuls. The Moghuls had Vedic texts such as the Mahabharata and the Vedas translated into Persian for use by Moslem scholars of the time. It's probable that they allowed the Sufi pirs to work among the villagers in the Hindu kingdoms under their rule.

sawa sawa: properly, correct, exact.

shenzi: savage, barbarian, stupid, uncouth.

shifta: bandits.

shika: catch, hold.

shosho: grandmother.

shu-khar: among Satpanth Ismailis the word 'shu-khar' (from Arabic 'shukhran' meaning thank you) has come to mean more than thank you. Shu-khar conveys a sense of self-humility as well as gratitude. When shu-khar is said to another person it is often meant to address God not the person spoken to. Shu-khar may also be said to oneself like a one word prayer. Shu-khar may be said to show gratitude for anything like good fortune of having daily meals, health, opportunities or work. The word aligns with divinity in expression of gratitude. It is said as an expression of thankfulness for safe return from a journey, recovery from illness and even for a happy marriage and happiness of children. It is also expressed when an unhappy experience has passed away like an escape from an accident or a bad day. Shu-khar is said as a one-word prayer of thanksgiving after a meal. It could also be a prayer for peace. Or it may be simply for blessings of contentment and gratitude that one often hears Satpanth Ismailis whisper. At funerals Satpanth Ismailis pass on consolations to the bereaved in repetitions of shu-khar expressing gratitude to God for the life of the deceased who has closed the journey on earth as well for the bereaved to bear the loss while thanking God for whatever he wills for us. The reply to shu-khar is also shu-khar.

Sidis: Indians of African descent.

si-ndio **?**: is that right? Is it not so?

siri: nose button.

sufro: special, and often elaborate prayer platter displaying a combination of foods that make wholesome meal for the body and mind as in an Indian menu. Prepared as offering on holy days, or when offered as a prayer for the dead on their anniversaries.

su-khreet: prepared with semolina, sugar and ghee. This fare considered holy, is given at the end of service at the jamat khana.

sweet-pee: diabetes. Called so because the urine showed high sugar level when tested.

thaat maat: elegantly dressed.

thaaso thas: crowded, packed, pushing and pulling.

thorki: white woman (literally).

tik *chhe*: it's fine; OK or proper.

toto: young boy. From Swahili mtoto.

toowal: towel.

taraab: musical genre at the coast of East Africa that blends Indian, Arabic and Swahili tunes.

twanga: hit.

thaso thas: packed tightly often referring to crowded places like in a room or a bus.

yogan: feminine of yogi. Generally referred to women devotees.

utu: humanity.

vedic: adjective of Vedas the Hindu religious text.

vedanta: prominent school of Hindu philosophy.

vrt: self-pride or self-worth as expressed in attitude, could be ego.

wahindi: Indians. Also used for Asians in East Africa.

wajinga (pl): stupid.

wanyonyaji (pl): suckers.

wasi wasi: unsure, hesitant, dithering.

Acknowledgements

The following acknowledgements are in addition to the ones mentioned in *Bead Bai* (2013) the precursor of *Home Between Crossings*.

I am grateful to Sadru (Doori) and Gulzar Madhany for the quotation from the letter from Imam Sultan Mohamed Shah (Aga Khan III) when his father was killed during the Mau Mau uprising.

Najma Dharani for writing about trees of East Africa, especially her book on the Acacias. Mutysia Munuve, curator of Akamba Peace Museum, for his research on the Maweto women. Alwaez Chunara, Kulsum Bai Tejpar, and Taj Bai Abualy Alibhai, for your clarifications.

Salma Ramji, Hanif Patni, Shahira Patni Tejpar, Zul Tejpar, Farouk Verjee, Annar Mangalji, Iqbal Dewji, Salim Ahmed and Mike Molloy for your warm support and spreading the word. Hassan Jaffer who would respond to my research queries without fail.

Ramnik Shah, Rifaat Fay, Jatinder Chana, Sherali Husein, Alex Figueirdo and Iqbal Akthar for your most valuable comments. Christian Steckler, I am lost for words to thank you for your insightful reading and discussion on words and sentences.

Zera and Jasiriat for your thoughts, patience and engagement. Ummat and Ardhiat for your Wows!

I am also indebted to friends and families who lived during the 1950s and 1960s to early 1970s in East Africa. With their stories, they shared their feelings of humiliation and loss of birthland that some find difficult to overcome to this day.

The archives of *Africana Orientalia Forum,* have excellent conversations on the rise of African nationalism, despotism and corruption in East Africa. Their first hand experiences are valuable. africana-orientalia@yahoogroups.com

Similarly of value are postings on memories and discussions on Khoja history and identity today www.khojawiki.org and EAcircle@yahoogroups.com

Writing on the front cover

KILA NDEGE HURUKA NA MBAWA ZAKE
EVERY BIRD FLIES ON ITS OWN WINGS

KILA NDEGE HURUKA NA MBAWA ZAKE is a kanga mithali or proverb that literally translates as EVERY BIRD FLIES ON ITS OWN WINGS in Swahili. It's a mithali that implies a journey. People translate this proverb in many ways depending on the context and situation at the particular time in their life's journey. Birds appear in Quranic verses giving metaphorical meaning in stories about Islam's prophets: Abraham, Solomon, Moses, Jesus, Joseph and David. The Swahili society is rooted in Arabic and African cultures over centuries of mixing and travelling. In fact, the Swahili word mithali comes from Arabic mithal meaning an example or a model that can also be a person's name.

Some would say the kanga proverb about the bird means that one makes one's life according to one's ability or with what one has in terms of material possession. It simply means you accept life with what's yours or what's given to you by God. Others relate the proverb to mean life is a destiny and that's where life's journey will take you like saying: 'You are what you have' or that 'You'll get what's yours'. A teacher or parent would counsel children using this proverb: 'You have potential to overcome (or succeed) with what you have'. Or it can mean the opposite: 'Realize that you have limitations'.

Every bird flies on its own wings also means that what one does in life is within oneself or that actions are one's own responsibility. Then there are other people who think in collective ways. They would say the proverb tells you that one has one's own family, home, country and culture to carry one along life's journey.

Philosophers will tell you KILA NDEGE HURUKA NA MBAWA ZAKE actually means that each human being is an individual. He/she alone makes his/her journey through life like a bird on wings making its own path.

A bird flying on its wings intones imagery of the sky above and the land below. A mortal's walk through life is like the flight of a bird between the earth and the sky.

Sultan Somjee
Autumn, 2016

Useful readings

Akthar, I. 2015. *The Khoja of Tanzania: Discontinuities of a Postcolonial Identity.* Leiden: Brill.

Alam, M. 2004. *The Languages of Political Islam, India 1200 – 1800.* The University of Chicago Press.

Aldrick, J. 2015. *The Sultan's Spymaster Peera Dewjee of Zanzibar.* Old Africa Books, Naivasha, Kenya.

Alphers, E. A. 1997. *The Northwestern Indian Ocean as Cultural Corridor.* The Conference on African Diaspora in the Northwestern India Ocean: Reconsideration of Old Problem, New Direction for Research.

Anderson, D. 2005. *Histories of the Hanged: The Dirty War in Kenya and the End of Empire.* W. W. Norton & Company.

Chua, A. 2003. *World on Fire: How Exporting Free Market Democracy Breeds Ethnic Hatred and Global Instability.* Heinemann.

Ali, A. 2011. *From Satpanthi to Ismaili Muslim: The Articulation of Ismaili Khoja Identity in South Asia.* A Modern History of the Ismailis: Continuity and Change in a Muslim Community, Farahad, D (ed). London: I. B. Tauris in association with The Institute of Ismaili Studies.

Breuilly, J (ed), 2013. *The Oxford Handbook of the History of Nationalism,* Oxford University Press.

Das, A.K. 2006. *Paintings of the Razmnama: The Book of War.* Mapin Publishing Gp Pty Ltd.

D'Souza, Rocha Blanche. 2008. *Harnessing the Trade Winds.* Nairobi: Zand Graphics Ltd.

Fernandes, C. 2016. *1950-1974 Yesterday in Paradise.* Balboa Press, Australia.

Gregory, R. 1993. *Quest for Equality: Asian Politics in East Africa 1900 – 1967.* New Delhi: Orient Longman.

Gregory, R. G. 1992. *The Rise and Fall of Philanthropy in East Africa: The Asian Contribution.* New Jersey: Transaction Publishers.

Hameer, F. 2014. *Crying for Freedom: the Event of Forced Marriages 1970 to 1980 – Zanzibar.* London: Sun Behind the Cloud Publications Ltd.

James, R. B. 2012. *Taifa: Making Nation and Race in Urban Tanzania.* Ohio University Press USA.

Jonathon, G. 2000. _Sorting out the Tribes: The Creation of Racial Identities in Colonial Zanzibar's Newspaper Wars_ in The Journal of African History, no 41 pp. 395-428. Cambridge University Press.

Joanne, N. 2010. 1998._Masculinity and Nationalism: Gender and Sexuality in the making of Nations._ Ethnic and Racial Studies, Volume 21, issue 2.

Khan, M. 2013. _From the Land of Pashtuns to the Land of Maa._ Nairobi: Asian African Trust Heritage Trust.

Khan, D-S. 2004. _Crossing the Threshold: Understanding Religious Identities in South Asia._ London: I. B. Tauris in association with The Institute of Ismaili Studies.

Lahiri, Jhumpa. 2016. _In Other Words._ New York: Alfred A. Knopf.

Mol, F. 1996. _Maasai Language and Culture Dictionary._ Lemek: Maasai Centre, Kenya.

Leopold, A. 1949. _A Sand Country Almanac._ Oford University Press.

Norbert F and D. S, (eds). 1998. _Identity and Intolerance: Nationalism, Racism, and Xenphobia in Germany and the United States._ German Historical Institute, Cambridge University Press.

Sarila, N.S. 2009. _The Shadow of the Great Game: The Untold Story of India's Partition._ Harper Collins.

Shah, R. 2012. _The Nationality Factor in the Migration of Gujaratis to East Africa and Beyond_ in Gujarati Communities Across The Globe: Memory, Identity and Continuity, eds. Mawani and Mukadam. London: A. Trentham Books.

Shah, R. 2011. _The Exodus Revisited - Harvest of a Colonial Fruit._ Nairobi: Awaaz November 2011.

Somjee, S. 2000. Conflicts and Indigenous Knowledge in Kenya. National Consultancy Report (RAF/97/026) Governance for Social Reconciliation in War-Torn Societies in Africa, UNDP.

Sorenson, J. 1996. _Learning to be Oromo : Nationalist Discourse in the Diaspora._ Social Identities Volume 2 October Number 3. UK: Carfax Publishing Company.

Sparks, A. 1990. _The Mind of South Africa._ Knopf.

Wikipedia. Online accessible information with preliminary references to sources that can be further researched and checked out.

Notes on writing

This book, like its predecessor *Bead Bai*, has stories that I heard while curating exhibitions. Stories that I later elaborated by listening to more, and reading for contexts. There are also stories that flowed out of my imagination. When I began writing, the stories appeared like episodes sparked by my feelings that took me back in time to the characters and events. I also fetched stories from my memories through associations with objects, sights and sounds; and from my perceptions of them as a child, youth and then as an adult. Whatever, and however, I could remember, I put them down.

Meanwhile, I continued to research, ask again and again, and to listen differently now as a much older man. Consequently, I began mounting each chapter like a picture frame as if it were an exhibit, and my book an exhibition catalogue. That's how I saw it, that's how I developed the storyline and my writing style.

Thinking back (and that happens often when someone asks me 'how' I write – an impossible question to answer), I feel my writing comes from the life I lived as an ethnographer. In the field, I was a persistent participant observer who lived in a community observing almost everything that went on. Even though Kenya was my birth place, I was not fluent in any of the sixteen or so ethnic languages of the people I worked with, and lived among. I knew only some functional vocabularies like names of colours and items of material culture. I was brought up speaking languages indigenous to me - Kacchi, Gujarati and Swahili. I tried to intuit what was being said from speech tones and expressions. This came to me almost naturally because of the long years when I tried to make sense of English while I tried to make myself better at it primarily to get through the British curriculum at school.

In the field, what I relied on was my sketches, and some photography. I made notes as sketches all the time. Drawing became my language for knowing the people, and for documentation. Later, when I put up exhibitions of material culture that I had collected, my field sketches guided me to construct the dioramas.

In terms of the genre, my creative writing structure follows Frame Story. It's a genre about storytelling in layers or telling stories within stories. In that way, it is close to oral traditions and setting up scenes in an exhibition narrative. The stories may appear disjointed, but the reader knows all the time that there is a storyteller, and that storyteller is the connecting thread. It's the voice that echoes in waves resounding personalities and the situations that the protagonist encounters in life's journey. The storyteller is the curator of the book.

Frame Story complements descriptive ethnography or 'thick descriptions' as the famed ethnographer, Clifford Geertz, called it. Early examples of works written in Frame Story are the Mahabharata, Arabian Nights and Canterbury Tales. Later came more e.g. Wuthering Heights.

About the author

Photo by Jasiriat

Working as an ethnographer in Kenya, Sultan Somjee collected material culture, staged exhibitions and listened to stories that emerged from artefacts. He has published several articles and two guide books, *Material Culture of Kenya* and *Stories from Things*. Somjee is the author of *Bead Bai*. *Home Between Crossings* is his second book of stories. He writes from British Columbia, Canada, where he lives with his wife, Zera, and teaches writing stories from things.

Made in the USA
Charleston, SC
22 December 2016